RESTRICTIVE COVENANTS AND FREEHOLD LAND
A PRACTITIONER'S GUIDE

2nd Edition

RESTRICTIVE COVENANTS AND FREEHOLD LAND
A Practitioner's Guide

2nd Edition

Andrew Francis MA Oxon
Barrister, Serle Court
6 New Square, Lincoln's Inn

JORDANS

2005

Published by
Jordan Publishing Limited
21 St Thomas Street
Bristol BS1 6JS

British Library Cataloguing-in-Publication Data
A catalogue record for this book is available from the British Library.

ISBN 0 85308 936 1

Typeset by Jordan Publishing Ltd
Printed and bound in England by Antony Rowe Ltd, Chippenham, Wiltshire

FOREWORD

Restrictive covenants impinge, sometimes unexpectedly, on the use and development of land. Often a restrictive covenant lies scarcely remembered until some development, or proposal recalls it to active life. When this happens those who may be subject to the burden and those who may be entitled to the benefit of the covenant will require to know where they stand in law and what they can do to protect themselves. This book, now in its second edition, provides a helpful and well-structured guide to the law and gives the practical advice that those affected require. It will be great assistance to the practitioner who needs an understanding of this somewhat inaccessible area of the law and seeks on behalf of his clients practical and expeditious solutions to the problems that arise.

George Bartlett QC
President of the Lands Tribunal
February 2005

FOREWORD

PREFACE TO THE FIRST EDITION

'I am not determining a point of law; I am restoring tranquility.'
(Edmund Burke)

As its title says, this is a practitioner's guide. It has been written with the aim of restoring tranquility (and understanding) to the minds of those seeking guidance in the field of restrictive covenants which affect freehold land.

But, in writing such a guide, on a dry and difficult topic, it is hard to know where to begin both in the literary and the geographical sense.

It is common for authors to visit the places associated with the work they are attempting to pen. This may be done in order to understand the character of the subject of a biography, or an attempt to waken the Muse in something more romantic, or it may even be compulsory, as in the study of battlefields. Where should you start when writing a book on restrictive covenants? This is a difficult question.

Is it logical to start in some well-maintained suburb where the covenants remain intact to preserve the ideas of the aesthetically-minded original owner? Or should it be the Old Hall in Lincoln's Inn, where so much of the equity on which the rules which follow are based has its origin? By design I have settled on Leicester Square, if for no other reason than everyone who has ever touched on this subject will recall the authority of *Tulk v Moxhay*. Although the somewhat worn appearance of the Square is hardly a testament to a strict control of land use (and its preservation owes more to the mid-Victorian efforts of a flamboyant Kidderminster MP, Albert Grant, than the victory of Mr Tulk), it was a good starting point for one other reason. In the Square there are two statues; one of William Shakespeare and the other of Charlie Chaplin. Each of them has been an example to me; the former as a master of written English and the other in achieving mass appeal. So, with their example in mind, I have tried to write a book which is clear and which will tempt those seeking a practical guide to the subject. I hope it meets those aims.

I decided to write it because of a demand which I perceived existed for a simple explanation of a tricky area of land law. The major works on the subject are detailed and contain much learning. I express my indebtedness by references to them in the footnotes in this book. But I feel the busy practitioner is stranded by the absence of a simple explanation of many of the rules and practice in the field of restrictive covenants. I have, therefore, attempted to write such an explanation. It is intended to be used as a first resort, and potentially as a last resort, when clear advice on restrictive covenants is required; these days invariably required urgently and by 'return of fax'. There is a danger of over-simplification and I hope that I have not fallen prey to that danger. Those seeking more detail can consult other works on the subject and where necessary I refer to them – gratefully. I have tried to explain matters in a way which will give those advising clients the ability to find the answer to the problem before them with the minimum of difficulty.

I have to thank Julie Abbott of Royal Sun Alliance for her contribution in the form of Chapter 18 which deals with insurance against risks posed by restrictive covenants. Her practical knowledge and experience is, I believe clearly demonstrated by her chapter, which I know I could not have written. She wishes to acknowledge the help given to her by Joan Hornsby also of Royal Sun Alliance.

I gratefully acknowledge the help which I have received from my colleagues in Chambers, friends in Lincoln's Inn, the many practising solicitors who have given me great insight into many of the day-to-day problems which arise in this field of property law and the publishers.

I am particularly indebted to His Honour Judge Marder QC, who, until the end of July 1998 was the President of the Lands Tribunal, for his invaluable help and for taking the time and trouble to read the draft chapters and for writing the foreword.

Last, but certainly not least, I express my debt of gratitude to my wife and children for the forbearance which they have displayed for more than a year while this book was in the process of gestation.

Despite this assistance I have been given, all errors are my own.

I have endeavoured to state the law at 1 March 1999, although account has been taken so far as possible of new Civil Procedure Rules coming into effect on 26 April 1999.

A J Francis
Lincoln's Inn
Lady Day 1999

PREFACE TO THE SECOND EDITION

A new millennium

The first edition of this book was published in the last year of the twentieth century.

Six years later, this second edition is the first book on the subject of restrictive covenants affecting freehold land to emerge in the new century and millennium. The timing is coincidental, but one date happens to be significant. 2005 marks the 80th anniversary of the Law of Property Act 1925 and its sister legislation passed in that year. It was that Act (and the Land Registration and Land Charges Acts of 1925) which reformed the law of real property. A system of registration of interests ensured that restrictive covenants imposed on or after 1 January 1926 must be registered if they were to be valid against successors in title to the original covenanting party. That was a major change in the law. At this point in the history the pace of legislative change slackens for nearly 80 years. The Land Charges Act 1972 and the Land Registration Act 2002, both repealed their predecessors, but made little change to the law of restrictive covenants. So, after 80 years, the statutory rules governing restrictive covenants affecting freehold land have remained almost static.

Old rules in a modern setting

What is also noteworthy about this area of law is the fact that in the early years of the twenty-first century all of the non-statutory rules which govern restrictive covenants are rather antique. In this category lies the principles governing the running of the burden of restrictive covenants. The principles were finally determined in December 1848 (a year of revolution in Europe) by the Lord Chancellor in *Tulk v Moxhay*; an authority which is now a mere 157 years old. As to the running of the benefit, the rules about annexation and building schemes have their origins in the early nineteenth century, although the main authorities that are cited for the statement of the law are mere striplings at about 100 years old; and might charitably be described as 'quite old'. (*Rogers v Hosegood* (1900) and *Elliston v Reacher* (1908)). Even *Federated Homes v Mill Lodge Properties* decided in November 1979 has now celebrated its quarter century and, as is seen below has recently been subject of reconsideration. But antiquity does not lessen the importance of rules of law. Restrictive covenants continue to benefit and burden land and for that reason they have to be understood. New covenants must be created, for planning laws are no guarantee of protection against unwanted development. What is striking about the present era in which these ancient rules find themselves is that there is an ever-increasing pressure on land use, as government policy requiring increasing numbers of new homes to be built and that in turn favours development of inner-city, or 'brownfield' sites; if green fields are not to be used. This means that old covenants are encountered with greater frequency than in the past. In an age when quality of life and the environment ought to be treated with increasing care, covenants have a vital role to play in protecting and preserving the little patch of green and that unspoilt view which the landowner wants to preserve. Unless covenant problems are resolved, they can be a threat to new development. On the other hand they have a constructive role to play in regulating land use effectively.

Why a new edition?

The foregoing describes the general background to this new edition. The particular backdrop against which it is set consists of three main features. Each of them demonstrates how this book is timely. First, there are the legislative changes which have occurred since publication of the first edition in 1999. These are, specifically, the Land Registration Act 2002 (in force 13 October 2003) and the Commonhold provisions of the Commonhold and Leasehold Reform Act 2002 (in force 27 September 2004). To a lesser extent account must now be taken of the Convention Rights in force since 2 October 2000, under the Human Rights Act 1998. As Chapter 20 shows, there is speculation as to how far these rights will have an impact on the law of restrictive covenants. Whilst it may be thought 'fashionable' to include references to such rights in almost every aspect of law today, the author has tried to make a serious attempt to address the issues arising under the 1998 Act. Of course answers cannot be given to all the questions raised. But in a 'Convention Rights aware' society, within the expected life of this edition, someone will probably have to deal with the issues set out in that chapter in a real claim. If it does nothing more, Chapter 20 provokes thought about possible issues arising in this area of the law. Secondly, there are changes in the common law. The courts never cease to interpret and develop the law in the light of the documents and evidence before them. Since 1999 there have been at least a dozen major decisions in the Court of Appeal which have dealt with the law covered by this book. Added to this there are a similar number of first-instance decisions of significance, and a far greater number of decisions in the Lands Tribunal exercising its jurisdiction under section 84 of the Law of Property Act 1925. There is one major decision of the Court of Appeal which has been incorporated into this new edition. That is *Crest Nicholson v McAllister*, decided on 1 April 2004. This authority has forced a reconsideration of the approach to the question, 'who has the benefit of this restrictive covenant?' In addition there have been a number of decisions in 2003 and 2004 (both at first instance and in the Court of Appeal) dealing with the meaning of words in covenants. In deciding issues of construction, these cases are an important reminder to practitioners to look at the words used in their context before any decision is reached as to their meaning. The effect of these decisions should not be lost on draftsmen who also need to choose their words carefully. The final feature of the landscape which has formed the backdrop to this new edition is the plain one of improvement. After 5 years there have been suggestions from colleagues, thoughts by the author and, to be frank, the perception of errors, which had to be dealt with in the text. It is hoped that all these changes have refreshed the text and removed the flaws in the old work.

Whilst all the factors referred to above have been taken into account, the original aim of the first edition, which was to create a clear guide to a difficult area of law, has not been forgotten.

Acknowledgements

I have to deal here with the general and well as the particular, which is always a hard thing to do in this context.

As in the preface to the first edition I must mention first, and in the 'general' category, all my colleagues, readers and friends, whether at the Bar, or in practice as solicitors, or in other walks of life. They have supplied me with ideas, cases and constructive criticism, and are to be thanked for supplying new ingredients, now safely in this edition. Their number does not diminish my gratitude to each person in this class. I wish I could name them all.

In the 'particular' category, and in alphabetical order, I thank:

Mark Davies, Senior Underwriter, of Stewart Title for revising and bringing up to date Chapter 18 (insurance). (My original thanks to Julie Abbott who contributed that chapter in the first edition are repeated.) I am grateful to Stewart Title for their kind consent to reproduce the specimen policy at Appendix 5.

Malcolm Dowden and Louise Dyke, both of Charles Russell, for their considerable assistance in commenting on the first drafts and supplying helpful notes, as well as assisting with the proofs.

Emma Humphries, also of Charles Russell, for her general and enthusiastic support and for checking the first proofs.

My sincere thanks go to George Bartlett QC, The President of the Lands Tribunal, for writing the foreword.

There are two 'final' categories deserving special mention.

First, the publishers, Jordans, who took on the task of publishing the new edition. At Jordans I thank, in particular, Tony Hawitt, Kirsten Robertson, Deborah Saunders and Leah Woolcock, and their colleagues, who have all done sterling work, in a short time, to produce order out of chaos; my draft manuscript being of the latter sort.

Secondly, my wife and children who have (yet again) endured my absence during writing spells in 2004 with such fortitude as they have been able to muster. My regret from their point of view is that a law book does not give them much reward in any real sense. They have no limelight to enjoy compared with the partners and children of popular novelists. There are no gala dinners, red carpets, prizes, or displays in High Street bookshop windows. I can only offer them faintest pleasure in knowing that in offices, chambers and libraries up and down the kingdom (it is hoped) the product of my labours and the cause of my absence from family life sits on the shelves, and when resorted to, is found to be of some use.

All errors are my own. I have attempted to state the law as at 31 December 2004. However, some decisions of the courts in early 2005 have been incorporated into the text.

Andrew Francis
Serle Court
6 New Square, Lincoln's Inn
January 2005

CONTENTS

TABLE OF CASES

References are to paragraph numbers.

TABLE OF STATUTES

References are to paragraph numbers.

TABLE OF STATUTORY INSTRUMENTS

References are to paragraph numbers.

EU LEGISLATION

GENERAL INTRODUCTION

'Many thousands of words of restrictive covenants clutter the titles of house property and bedevil modern conveyancing. In many cases these covenants are difficult to construe and there is doubt as to whether they are enforceable or whether anyone has power to release them.'[1]

SETTING THE SCENE

The words extracted above summarise the difficulties in one paragraph. Restrictive covenants come in many shapes and forms, both as to their terms and the problems they pose.

A familiar story?

Restrictive covenants have always been the bane of the law student's life, placed in the same untidy corner as perpetuities and the rule against double portions. The law of covenants was never reformed to any great extent in 1925; hence the complexity. The most we recall at college is that the rules which relate to them owe something to a decision in 1848 about Leicester Square. It is at this point that our grasp slackens, until we enter practice.

From there on, if we are conveyancers, we see great tracts of them daily, copied in title documents, or more rarely nowadays, occupying acres of abstracts and eating up pages of epitomes. Unless we are litigators we never really see them work. We try to explain them to clients, but the references to motor houses, fellmongers, catgut spinners, and beaters of flax, bring blank (or black) looks. The odd client may raise a question about the neighbour's garage, or washing line. We look at the title and it seems to be silent on the topic of new garages, or washing lines blocking out the light. Developer clients may hurry into a development without much more than a passing word of caution from us about them. We cross our fingers. We mutter something about the Lands Tribunal and having found that whatever magic wand this body may wave can take some time, and may cost as much as a full trial, we move on, usually none the wiser. We may trouble to insure against them.

But then, one day, thump, and a really large restrictive covenant problem emerges. The client's neighbour is threatening to put up the carbuncle of all time. We look for yellowing land charge searches and blackening photocopies reminiscent of Mr Fox Talbot's 'sun pictures' at Lacock Abbey, and we look at the title and we find that what is called 'the benefit' is not there. We are dismayed to say that we do not really know whether the client can sue, or whether he can get any damages, and if he can, how much. If we act for a Really Big Developer we are uncertain whether it will be injunctions at dawn, or worse. It is at this moment that we study the textbooks and wish we had paid attention in 1975, or 1985, or 2004 in a lecture

---

[1]   Royal Commission on Legal Services, Annex 21, para 3 (1979) Cmnd 7648.

theatre with the sun coming through the windows – just as it sometimes shines in Leicester Square.

It is at this moment that we recall *Tulk v Moxhay*, but little else.

Grim reality?

You are faced with a client who is a developer and who is considering acquiring land for that purpose. The title shows that it is affected by restrictive covenants, potentially preventing the planned development. You do not know how to find out whether anyone could prevent the development. Once you have discovered that there is a risk of prevention, what do you do next? Is insurance an option?

A country client has just been served with a claim form seeking an order that stables (which have been in use for some years – albeit in breach of covenant) be knocked down and that a projected extension is restrained. How far should the client defend the claim?

Another client has an inner-city site where covenants will fetter development. Can these restrictive covenants be removed, and if so, how long will it take? Can the threat of an injunction be avoided by a declaration that those with the benefit of the covenants are not entitled to enforce?

Finally, a client in a leafy suburb has the benefit of a covenant restricting the use of the neighbouring property to occupation by one family. The local health authority plans to use the property as a home for elderly folk. What remedies are available to your client? What if the land next door was compulsorily acquired; what would the remedy be for breach of covenant?

Relief is at hand?

This book is designed to meet the need of the busy practitioner who requires easy access to a topic which often seems difficult to understand and where existing publications may not serve that need. To that end the emphasis is on practical answers rather than academic scholarship. The aim is to give answers to the questions which restrictive covenants raise in practice. The scene set above shows the sorts of problems which can arise. If it does nothing else, the book should give the answers to those, and other, problems.

THE SCHEME OF THE WORK

In keeping with the aim expressed above, this book is divided into chapters which deal with the following topics:

–   Explaining the **words used** in the field of restrictive covenants, and the meaning of 'restrictive covenant' (Chapters 1, 2 and 3).
–   Identifying how the **existence** of covenants can be found, and whether they are **valid** (Chapter 4).
–   How covenants can be made to **work**, both in terms of enforcement by the person entitled to the benefit of them and against the person bound by them (Chapters 5, 6, 8 and 9).
–   What do certain covenants **mean** and how do we construe them?

– Can covenants be **extinguished or modified**? (Chapter 16).
– If there is a breach of covenant (following the rules of construction in Chapter 14) and assuming they are valid and in existence as covenants which can be enforced, how can they be enforced and what **remedies** exist for that purpose? (Chapter 15).
– Is it possible to **insure** against the risk of restrictive covenants being enforced, and in what way can this be done? (Chapter 18).
– What special rules apply where restrictive covenants are encountered in the context of **public and other authorities** where statute defines their powers? (Chapters 10, 11 and 12).
– Questions arising from Commonhold Titles (Chapter 19).
– Human Rights Act 1998 issues in the field of restrictive covenants (Chapter 20).
– Are there any **drafting rules** to be followed? (Chapter 17). There are **precedents** at **Appendix 7**.
– The statutory and other material for reference at **Appendices 1–3**.

HOW TO USE THIS BOOK

Trying to make it simple

The best place to start is the *flowchart* at pages 5–7.

With the aid of the flowchart, use of the checklists at the end of Chapter 2 can assist in identifying the matters which need attention if a problem is to be solved.

In addition, here are some simple rules to follow when looking at restrictive covenant problems in practice.

Rule 1

Whenever you have a problem which requires looking at restrictive covenants ask yourself, *what does the covenant mean?* Always start here.

Is my client (or the other side) doing anything which falls within it?

If the answer is no – end of problem.

(Under this rule we look at problems of construction particularly in the light of *Mannai Investments v Eagle Star Life Assurance Co Ltd* [1997] AC 749, and also at the problems posed by covenants requiring the consent of a specific person or persons.)

Rule 2

If what is proposed to be done, or is being done, falls within the covenant, *is it restrictive?* This means that for the covenant to be restrictive it must be negative in effect.

(Under this rule we look at what is a 'restrictive covenant' as opposed to a positive one).

Rule 3

If the covenant was created after 31 December 1925 and if the person against whom it is to be enforced is not the original party who gave the covenant, that person is not going to be bound *unless* the covenant is registered. If it is not, you cannot be sued on the covenant; so end of story. (There may be an exception in rare cases where the Land Registry have failed to register covenants and the register is rectified against you.) Under this rule we look at the manner in which successors in title to the original covenantor can be bound; in the case of pre-1926 covenants the doctrine of notice still applies; for those covenants created after that date we look at either the D(ii) entry, or the entry on the register according to whether the title is registered or not.

Rule 4

If you are not the original person in whose favour the covenant runs you will have to show that you have the benefit of the covenant. This is often the difficult bit, as not only are the rules tricky, the Land Registry do not help as their policy has historically been not to enter the benefit of the covenants on the register of title to the land which can (arguably) claim such benefit. If you don't have the benefit, you cannot sue; so end of story again.

(Under this rule we look at the effect of section 78 of the Law of Property Act 1925 on post-1925 covenants and, in cases to which that section does not apply, at express annexation, express assignment of the benefit and at building schemes.)

Rule 5

If you are unable to show who has the benefit, you *may* be able to convince an insurance company to take on the risk (at a price) of someone eventually proving you wrong.

(Under this rule we look at the factors which apply to those cases where indemnity policies may be available.)

Rule 6

If you can show that you have the *benefit* and that the neighbour is subject to the *burden* you may be able to sue to prevent the threatened eyesore from ever happening – or at least to get damages for it. But what does it take to get an injunction, and what sums of damages are we talking about?

(Under this rule we look at the vexed question of injunctions, particularly the David and Goliath problems posed by interim applications. We also look at damages and the 'ransom' principle.)

Rule 7

There are special rules which apply to local and public authorities which allow them:

    (a)   to enforce certain types of covenant even though they own no land in the vicinity;

    (b)   to do things in breach of a covenant – or even to override it – on payment of compensation only.

These need to be examined carefully.

Rule 8

It is possible to remove or vary restrictive covenants by application to the Lands Tribunal under section 84(1) of the Law of Property Act 1925. In addition the High Court can declare what covenants mean and who may enforce them under section 84(2) of that Act.

In addition, Chapter 19 examines the effect on restrictive covenants where the title is held commonhold.

WHAT IS NOT COVERED IN THIS BOOK

As the title suggests, positive covenants are not dealt with in detail, but to assist the reader in view of the fact that positive and restrictive covenants may sometimes be intertwined, at Chapter 1 below there is a summary of the rules which affect the enforceability of such covenants.

I have also not dealt with rent charges, covenants for title and, again as the title indicates, covenants in leases.

LAW REFORM PROPOSALS

The Law Commission is currently (November 2004) considering the modernisation and simplification of the law of restrictive covenants as part of a wider review of the law relating to easements and analogous rights and hopes to publish a consultation paper towards the end of 2005 on these subjects.[2] The review will take into account the development of commonhold and the Land Registration Act 2002.

In respect of past recommendations for reform, the position is as follows. Whilst the Government did not accept the recommendations contained in Law Com Number 127 (1984), this was on the basis that the Law Commission reconsider the recommendations in that report in the light of anticipated future developments in property law. It was understood at the time (March 1998) that the Lord Chancellor had the possible introduction of a system of commonhold in mind.[3] Similarly, the recommendations contained in Law Com Number 201 (1991) were not implemented. This was due to concerns about the potential cost to the public of the recommended scheme put forward in that report.[4]

Following the grant of Royal Assent in May 2002 to the Commonhold and Leasehold Reform Bill, the content of Law Com Numbers 127 and 201 (referred to above) is being considered afresh. The Law Commission's aim is to produce a

---

[2] I am greatly indebted to members of the Property and Trust Law Team at the Law Commission, for their kindness in supplying the information as to the reform, both future and past, which I have summarised here. For further information on Law Commission reports and proposed reforms, see the Law Commission's website, which is regularly updated, at www.lawcom.gov.uk.

[3] See Law Commission, 7th Programme of Law Reform, Item 5, p 13 and footnote 62 (available at www.lawcom.gov.uk). See also *Hansard*, HC Deb, vol 587, col 213 (19 March 1998).

[4] See *Hansard*, HC Deb, vol 566, col WA91 (17th October 1995).

coherent scheme of easements, analogous rights and covenants which will be compatible with both commonhold and the Land Registration Act 2002.[5]

It is, therefore, the position (in November 2004) that reform to any substantial extent of the law of restrictive covenants affecting freehold land would appear to be some way in the future.

FURTHER REFERENCE

As this is a practical guide, I have attempted to draw a course through the rocks and shoals of the subject with as much clarity as possible. As in the case of a map or chart, that does not aways give the fullest picture, and where necessary, I refer in the footnotes to the other works on the subject where greater depth of treatment is available.

I have included in the appendices much statutory material. Some of it is crucially important such as the extracts from the Law of Property Act 1925; other extracts are less important, but may be difficult to find (even on websites, without a full set of statutes, or other volumes of government material) and may be useful when agreements, or deeds are seen which refer to the statutory provisions in question, and when drafting where such material has to be considered.

---

[5] Land Registration Act 2002 brought into force 13 October 2003, commonhold brought into force 27 September 2004. See Chapter 19 below for commonhold.

Chapter 1

INTRODUCTION

This chapter examines:

– the words used in the context of restrictive covenants and their meanings;
– the reason why the law of restrictive covenants is difficult;
– the different rules which apply to positive covenants.

THE MEANING OF WORDS

1.1   The law in respect of restrictive covenants which affect freehold land can be difficult and confusing. Much of the difficulty arises from the words used. The starting point is with the two key words, 'restrictive' and 'covenant'.

'Restrictive' means that the obligation is negative in substance, even though the language may be in positive terms. Chapter 3 deals with this aspect of the law in detail.

'Covenant' means a promise contained in a deed or a contract. There are two points of importance here.

(a)   The law of restrictive covenants falls within two areas: that of contract and that of land law. As to the contractual element, a covenant is no more than a contract made by deed. As we will see further on, the difficult part comes when we look at the land law element.

(b)   Section 1 of the Law of Property (Miscellaneous Provisions) Act 1989 governs the formalities which attend the making of a deed. We are not concerned with them here, but to be enforceable as a covenant, it requires consideration being given for it, either by virtue of the execution of the deed, or by virtue of the terms of the contract. A deed is not always required.

'Freehold land' denotes the estate to which the restrictive covenant relates. Covenants in leases are outside the scope of this book.

1.2   The right to enforce the covenant is 'the benefit'. The obligation to observe is 'the burden'. In terms of the parties it is 'the covenantee' who has the right to enforce and it is 'the covenantor' who is under the obligation to observe.

Those terms will be used in that sense in this book.

Where the word 'covenant' is not used, there can be doubt as to whether a covenant (in the strict sense of the word) is being given. The parties may agree to a set of **stipulations**, eg 'to hold unto the purchaser subject to the stipulations (or conditions) set out in the schedule hereto'. In such a case there may be doubt as to whether the parties did intend to create an equitable burden on the land so as to bind successors. In such cases the stipulations may bind the original parties only. It is the policy of the Land Registry to enter stipulations in such a way as to make it clear that no words of covenant have been given.[1] In practice you should avoid using words which are ambiguous in this sense, unless you want to create stipulations only.

WHY ARE RESTRICTIVE COVENANTS DIFFICULT?

1.3   The operation of restrictive covenants affecting freehold land is governed by the special rules which allow these covenants to be enforced not only by and against the original parties, but also by and against successors to those parties who are the owners of freehold land to which the covenant relates.

If the law of restrictive covenants was simply governed by the law of **contract**, the rules of privity would only allow enforcement by the original parties to the contract. Unless the non-parties were the personal representatives of the original parties, or unless there was evidence of the assignment of the benefit of the contract (but not the burden), the covenant would not be enforceable by or against non-parties. Because of this contractual liability, the original covenantor remains liable on the covenants into which he has entered, in theory, until the covenants are released or in some other way brought to an end. The original covenantee may also sue even after he has parted with the land for which the covenant was taken, but would only get nominal damages.

In practice, the liability of the original covenantor will be limited by words in the instrument creating the covenants which terminate such liability once he ceases to have an interest in the property burdened by the covenants. In addition he (and his successors) will obtain a covenant of indemnity from the transferee of the land against any liability which may attach under the covenants for future breaches.[2]

It is to overcome this limitation that special rules have been developed which allow restrictive covenants to be enforced by and against successors to the original covenanting parties. These rules have developed for two reasons.

1.4   First, because of the limits on enforceability which the common law imposed on such covenants. The Courts of Equity devised rules in the first half of the nineteenth century to overcome those limitations, but it is those rules which are themselves complex. Since 1875 when law and equity were fused we should not really need to worry about the historic difference, but there are some circumstances when we need to remember the distinction, such as in the context of damages, dealt

---

[1]   See *Re Rutherford's Conveyance* [1938] Ch 396; *Kingsbury v Anderson* (1979) 40 P&CR 136. The absence of the verb 'to covenant' was not a bar to the Lands Tribunal treating the application before it as one involving covenants, within the jurisdiction under s 84 of the Law of Property Act 1925: see *Re Crest Homes' Application* (1983) 48 P&CR 309. See Chapter 16 below for the extent of this jurisdiction.

[2]   See *Emmet on Title* (Sweet & Maxwell, looseleaf), para 19–021, and s 189 (2) of the Law of Property Act 1925, annexing the benefit of an indemnity covenant to the land in which the indemnity is intended to relate. It is debatable whether an indemnity covenant can be used to enforce a covenant which is not registered: see Chapter 4. But if the original covenantee was the original covenantor, the latter can recover any losses he may incur from his successor under the indemnity covenant. Indemnity covenants are considered further at **4.24** below.

with in Chapter 15. As this is a practical guide the emphasis will be more on the rules which have to be satisfied rather than their origin, but an understanding of the background shows why the rules are complex.

Secondly, if restrictive covenants are to be effective and to satisfy the needs of the landowner who retained land and who wanted protection, it is essential that the covenants are fully enforceable both by and against the parties' successors. The first half of the nineteenth century was a period of economic expansion, and without any other means of control over building and development, the restrictive covenant had to be effective in securing control.

This is where rules which have more to do with land law come in, and which lead to the result that a restrictive covenant is, as to its burden an equitable interest in land (if fully enforceable) and as to its benefit, a right which is enforceable by successors who can show that the benefit is vested in them. It is the rules which deal with the manner in which the burden and the benefit run which cause the difficulty. As will be seen below, the running of the burden is often easier to prove than the running of the benefit. That is one reason why the former will be taken first.

POSITIVE COVENANTS

1.5 Although this is a book about restrictive covenants, some understanding of the law of positive covenants is required. The appreciation of this distinction is required in view of the different rules which apply to the enforcement of positive covenants as between successors in title to the original parties.

The principal and most important rule regarding the enforcements of positive covenants against successors to the original covenantor is that the burden does not run against such successors. Thus, a covenant to pay a sum of money on a defined event (eg to pay the uplift in value of land on the grant of planning permission) will not be enforceable against a successor of the original covenantor, even if he has notice of the covenant. As will be seen below, the rule regarding the running of the burden of a restrictive covenant is different – and in most cases the covenant is enforceable against a successor.

1.6 There is only one exception to the rule which prevents enforcement of positive covenants against successors, but it is limited and requires the person seeking to enforce the positive burden to show that for the successor in title to the covenantor to enjoy certain benefits which are conditional on the performance of certain burdens, he must discharge the latter. It is also necessary to show that the benefit and the burden must be relevant to each other and it is not enough simply to attach a right (eg to use services) to a condition for payment to make the positive condition enforceable against a successor.[3]

---

[3]   See *Rhone v Stephens* [1994] 2 AC 310, affirmed in *Thamesmead Town Ltd v Allotey* (1998) (76) P&CR D20. See also *Halsall v Brizell* [1957] Ch 169 (covenant requiring contribution to services enforceable as linked to easement granted to use roads and drains). See also *Allied London Industrial Properties v Castleguard Properties* [1997] EWCA Civ 2180, for an application of the principles in that code.

In order to circumvent the strict limitation on enforcement of the burden of positive covenants it is common to employ devices such as the use of legal or equitable charges to secure payment obligations, estate rent charges, rights of re-entry, ransom strips, the enlargement of long leases into freeholds and restrictions on the register of title. Chapter 17 and the precedents at Appendix 7 below deal with this subject further.

COMMONHOLD COVENANTS

1.7   The relationship between restrictive covenants and obligations as to use etc in commonhold units is set out in summary in Chapter 19.

Chapter 2

FLOWCHART AND CHECKLISTS

2.1   In this chapter a flowchart shows how it is possible to answer the question 'Is a restrictive covenant enforceable?'

The questions asked are those which a practitioner might ask when acting for either a potential claimant (seeking to enforce a covenant) or a potential defendant (seeking to resist enforcement).

The flowchart identifies the areas as they are covered in the following chapters.

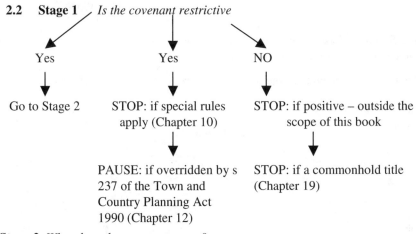

2.2   Stage 1   *Is the covenant restrictive*

| Yes | Yes | NO |

Go to Stage 2

STOP: if special rules apply (Chapter 10)

STOP: if positive – outside the scope of this book

PAUSE: if overridden by s 237 of the Town and Country Planning Act 1990 (Chapter 12)

STOP: if a commonhold title (Chapter 19)

Stage 2   *What does the covenant mean?*

(STOP: unenforceable on grounds of public policy or by EC Treaty, Article 81) (Chapter 14)

(VOID: if in breach of Chapter 1 of the Competition Act 1998 and outside the exclusion of the Land and Vertical Agreements Order 2000)

– Is it personal? If so, STOP if enforcement is not between original parties

– Check for evidence of variation or discharge, whether by agreement, deed or Order under the Law of Property Act 1925, s 84(1)

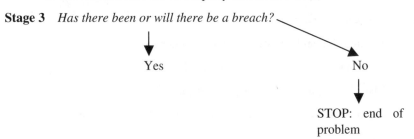

Stage 3   *Has there been or will there be a breach?*

Yes

No

STOP: end of problem

Stage 4   *If there is a potential or actual breach:*

- Who is in breach?
- Original covenantor?

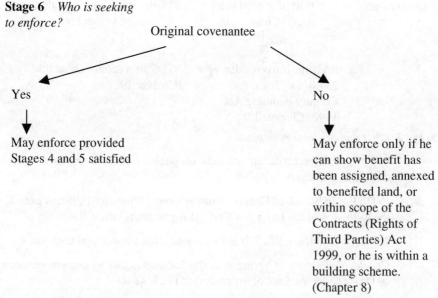

Yes

No

Enforceable (provided Stage 6 is satisfied)

Is it registered (if created after 31 December 1925, *or* if prior to 1 January 1926, does the owner of the burdened land have notice?) (Chapter 4)

Stage 5   *Only if the registration or notice test is satisfied can the covenant be enforced against the successor to the original covenantor.*

If the answer is yes, go to **Stage 6**. If no, the covenant cannot be enforced.

Stage 6   *Who is seeking to enforce?*

Original covenantee

Yes

No

May enforce provided Stages 4 and 5 satisfied

May enforce only if he can show benefit has been assigned, annexed to benefited land, or within scope of the Contracts (Rights of Third Parties) Act 1999, or he is within a building scheme. (Chapter 8)

Stage 7   *Consider if in doubt:*

- Extinguishment by unity of seisin (Chapter 13)
- Do you need to insure? (Chapter 18)
- The effect of indemnity covenants (Chapter 4)
- Do you need an order for discharge or modification or a declaration as to enforceability? (Chapter 16)

–   Human Rights Act 1998 (Chapter 20)

Stage 8 If proceeding to enforce, what is the remedy?

–   Declaration as to enforceability?

–   Injunction?

–   Damages

(all in Chapter 15)

CHECKLIST OF QUESTIONS

When acting for the potential claimant

2.3   (1)   What covenant is the claimant seeking to enforce?
- Is it restrictive? (Chapter 3)
- Does the claimant have the benefit of it? (Chapter 8)
- Is it personal to the original parties?

      (2)   Is the potential defendant liable?
- Which rules as to validity apply? Is it valid? (Chapter 4)
- Is it potentially enforceable against him as a burden on his land? (Chapter 5)
- Is it personal to the original parties?

      (3)   Is what is proposed or occurring a breach?
- Consider the questions of construction in Chapter 14.

2.4

      (4)   Is this a case where a declaration of right, or a declaration under section 84(2) of the Law of Property Act 1925 (Chapter 15) is necessary, or desirable?

      (5)   Is this a case where an application under section 84(1) of the Law of Property Act 1925 to discharge or modify the covenant has ever been made, and with what result? Is the defendant likely to make such an application in this case? (Chapter 16) Has there been a variation or release by agreement or deed?

      (6)   What is the remedy for any breach? (Chapter 15)
- Will the defendant want to negotiate a release and what will the claimant's price be? (Chapter 15)
- Is this a case where an injunction will be granted, or is this a case where damages will be the appropriate remedy? (Chapter 15)

When acting for the potential defendant

2.5   (1)   What covenant is the claimant seeking to enforce?
- Is it restrictive? (Chapter 3)
- Which rules as to validity apply, is it valid? (Chapter 4)
- Does the claimant have the benefit of it? (Chapter 8)
- Is the covenant a burden on the defendant's land? (Chapter 5)

     –   Is the covenant personal to the original parties?

(2)   Is what is proposed incurring a breach?
- Consider the questions of construction in Chapter 14.
- Consider negotiating a release; what will the price be? (Chapter 15)

(3)   What is the claimant's remedy and what defences does the defendant have? (Chapter 15)

(4)   Should the defendant apply to discharge or modify the covenant under section 84(1) of the Law of Property Act 1925? Has there been any Order made under this jurisdiction in the past? Has there been a variation or release by agreement or deed? (Chapter 16)

(5)   Should the defendant consider making an application for a declaration of right, or a declaration under section 84(2) of the Law of Property Act 1925 (Chapter 15), or insuring (Chapter 18)?

2.6 Special situations

(1)   When acting for a client where the covenants were imposed, or granted under statutory authority, consider the effect of the statute on the ability of any party to benefit or be bound by the covenant (Chapters 10, 11 and 12).

(2)   If a breach of covenant is threatened, or committed under statutory authority, consider the limits on the remedies for breach. If acting for the authority seeking to act in breach, consider the ways in which covenants can be overridden (Chapter 12).

(3)   What is the effect of indemnity covenants? (Chapter 4).

(4)   If public authorities are involved, are there any Human Rights Act 1998 issues? (Chapter 20).

Chapter 3

IDENTIFICATION OF COVENANTS WHICH ARE TRULY RESTRICTIVE

3.1   This chapter considers how a covenant can be defined as truly 'restrictive'.

As every law student knows, the leading case on the identification of whether a covenant is restrictive or not is *Tulk v Moxhay*,[1] concerning the obligation to keep what is now Leicester Square open. The text of the covenant runs as follows:

> 'that [the covenantor] his heirs and assignees should, and would from time to time, and at all times thereafter at his and their own costs and charges, keep and maintain the said piece of ground and square garden, and the iron railing round the same in its then form, and in sufficient and proper repair as a square garden and pleasure ground, in an open state, uncovered with any buildings, in neat and ornamental order.'

3.2   What is interesting in the text of the covenant is that it is expressed in positive terms, but amounts in substance to a negative obligation, ie not to build. Statutory definitions of a 'restrictive covenant', which have been interpreted broadly, are to be found in:

(1)   Land Charges Act 1972, section 2(5)(ii): 'a covenant or agreement ... restrictive of the user of land ...';
(2)   Leasehold Reform Act 1967, section 10(4): 'a covenant or agreement restrictive of the use or of any land or premises ...'.

The textbook writers differ in terms of how they define the test,[2] but in practical terms and for the purposes of the practitioner, the test is relatively easy to perform.

You ask yourself this question:

Does this covenant require the expenditure of money for its performance and does it restrict the use and enjoyment of the land affected?

If it does not require such expenditure and if it affects the use and enjoyment of land in a restrictive sense, it is negative in substance.[3]

---

[1]   (1848) 2 Ph 774; 41 ER 1143. This was not the first case which defined the circumstances in which the burden of a restrictive covenant would run in equity, but is the one which is regarded as decisive. The covenants imposed in that case were considered more recently when a proposal was made to construct an electricity sub-section in the Square. See *R v Westminster City Council, ex parte Leicester Square Coventry Street Association* (1989) 59 P&CR 51. See below at **8.11** and **11.9.**

[2]   *Preston & Newsom's Restrictive Covenants Affecting Freehold Land* (Sweet & Maxwell, 9th edn, 1998) para 3–07; Megarry & Wade, *The Law of Real Property* (Sweet & Maxwell, 6th edn, 1999), pp 1012–1013; Scammell, *Land Covenants* (Butterworths, 1996), p 11; *Halsbury's Laws*, vol 16(2), para 788.

[3]   For a modern example of a *Tulk v Moxhay* type of restrictive covenant, see *Abbey Homesteads Developments Ltd v Northamptonshire County Council* (1986) 53 P&CR 1. In addition, the authority of *Langevad v Chiswick Quay Freeholds* (2000) 80 P&CR 26, CA, provides a modern

Positive covenants (eg to repair) are, therefore, excluded from this definition.

3.3 In practice there are certain 'hybrid' forms of covenant which may be less easy to identify. These may be classified as:

(1)   Those which appear to be positive covenants but are in reality negative. The commonest example is the covenant not to build without first submitting plans.[4] The payment of the fee for approval does not alter this conclusion, for compliance with the covenant against building requires no action or payment. Compare, also, modern user covenants in leases, such as to use for specified retail purposes.[5]

(2)   Those which appear to be restrictive but which are in reality positive. One example is an obligation not to sell without offering the land to a specified person first.[6]

3.4

(3)   Those where positive and restrictive obligations are mixed up. *Tulk v Moxhay* was an example of this, in that the obligation encompassed the maintenance of the Square. The court's approach here will be to separate (so far as possible) the positive from the negative. If that is not possible it may be that the covenant will not satisfy the test of negativity.[7]

(4)   Certain covenants are imposed under statutory authority. They may contain both positive and negative elements, but because of the special rules which apply to them, they do not fall within the general classification of 'restrictive covenants'.[8]

Indemnity covenants (ie those used by way of indemnity to secure the obligation between the covenantor and his successors) are considered at **4.29** below.

---

definition of what is a restrictive covenant in the context of s 10 of the Leasehold Reform Act 1967, in which the court rejected any distinction between covenants against user of land and covenants against development of land or buildings on it. This authority applies the principle of the words 'restrictive covenant' applying to a whole range of covenants and not just those which are narrowly 'user' restrictions. See also *Re Blumenthal's Application* LP/34/2002 (decision 14 January 2004); affirmed by Court of Appeal [2004] EWCA Civ 1688. See **16.6** below.

4   See *Ridley v Taylor* [1965] 1 WLR 611.

5   *Montross Associated Properties v Moussaieff* [1990] 2 EGLR 61 and see *Re Blumenthal's Application*, at n 3 above.

6   *Manchester Ship Canal Co v Manchester Racecourse Co* [1901] 2 Ch 37.

7   See *Shepherd Homes Ltd v Sandham (No 2)* [1971] 1 WLR 1062. Much obviously depends on the style of drafting. Using a modern form where covenants are listed *seriatim* in a schedule the court ought to be able to sever the positive from the negative. See Chapter 17 *et seq* on drafting covenants and precedents at Appendix 7.

8   See Chapter 10 *et seq* for the manner in which such covenants arise.

Chapter 4

IDENTIFYING THE EXISTENCE OF RESTRICTIVE COVENANTS WHICH ARE VALID AND BINDING

4.1   This chapter looks at two questions.

First, how does the existence of restrictive covenants manifest itself?

Until you can establish whether covenants exist to operate as a potential burden or as a potential benefit over your clients' land, everything else which follows is academic. This also requires an answer to the question whether a covenant operates purely personally between the original parties.[1]

Secondly, what rules apply to determine the *validity* of restrictive covenants against persons *other than* the original covenantor. The word 'validity' is used in the sense that the covenant has in some way to bind such persons, as opposed to the use of that word denoting the legality, or illegality, of the covenant and its enforceability as a matter of law or public policy. In the latter sense of the word such an inability to sue or be sued on the covenant will affect not just successors but also original parties. Covenants which are an unreasonable restraint of trade are an example of the latter.

The answer to the two questions posed above is not always easy and a summary of the answers is placed at the beginning of the chapter.

SUMMARY

Existence

4.2   The existence of covenants will be determined by the type of title to which the burdened and the benefited land belongs.

(a)   Finding the burden

Finding whether the land is burdened by covenants should be easy. There are two historic divisions. Covenants created after 31 December 1925 have to be registered to be valid against successors who have acquired the burdened land for value, and, therefore, their existence must be disclosed by evidence of registration. In the case of covenants created on or before 31 December 1925, their validity will depend on notice which must be apparent from the title disclosed.

---

[1]   *Morrells of Oxford v Oxford UFC* [2001] Ch 459.

(b)   Finding the benefit

Finding whether land has the benefit of a covenant is more difficult, particularly where the title is registered. The reasons for this are set out below and there may be no substitute for detective work amongst a number of neighbouring titles – and not just your client's.

Validity

4.3   The rules governing the *validity* of covenants in order to bind a successor in title to the original covenantor are as follows:

–   Covenants created on or before 31 December 1925: the equitable doctrine of *notice* applies.
–   Covenants created after 31 December 1925:
    (a)   *unregistered titles:* void against a purchaser for money or money's worth of the legal estate unless registered against the name of the estate owner of the burdened land when created as a D(ii) Land Charge.[2]
    (b)   *registered titles:*
        (i) before 13 October 2003, void against a purchaser of the burdened land if not entered on the Charges Register to that title, or given limited protection by the entry of a caution;
        (ii) on or after 13 October 2003, void if not the subject of an entry on the register of the title when there is a registrable disposition for valuable consideration of that title, or any part of it.

Problems can arise as a result of errors in registered entries and searches. The key is to ensure accuracy both in the original registration and in subsequent searches.

VALIDITY DISTINGUISHED FROM ENFORCEABILITY

4.4   Putting the question of the existence of covenants to one side for the present, and turning to the question of validity, it is vital at this stage to appreciate the distinction between the validity of a restrictive covenant and its enforceability.

The word 'validity' is used in this chapter to mean the manner in which a covenant is protected by notice, or registration so as to bind a successor in title of the original covenantor. The use of that word in the sense of 'illegality' (such as covenants which infringe legislation, or which may be unenforceable on the grounds of public policy) is a separate subject and it is assumed that the covenants referred to in this chapter are valid and enforceable in that sense.[3]

---

2   For recent authority on what is a 'purchaser for money or money's worth', see *Merer v Fisher* [2003] EWCA Civ 747.
3   See Chapter 14 below where certain types of covenant (eg those to protect certain trades) pose problems in the context of restraint of trade and infringement of Art 81 of the EC Treaty or which may be caught by Chapter 1 of the Competition Act 1998 which avoids competitive agreements, including those which include trading conditions which have as their object or effect 'the prevention, restriction or distortion of competition within the United Kingdom', unless exempt from that Chapter.

Validity is a question which arises when a covenant is to be enforced against a person other than the original covenantor (or his personal representative). It requires an answer to the question whether (in the case of covenants created prior to 1 January 1926) the potential defendant is or is not a *bona fide* purchaser of the burdened land without notice, and in the case of covenants created on or after that date, whether the registration requirements have been met. In essence the enquiry is whether, for the covenant to *bind* that successor, it is protected by complying with those rules. (See the flowchart at pages 5–7 above.)

It is only *after* the question of validity of the covenant has been determined that it becomes necessary to consider enforceability. The answer to the latter depends upon an application of the rules of law and equity which specify how the burden and benefit of a (valid) covenant can run.

It is, therefore, premature to consider enforceability prior to validity

If the answer on enquiry is that the covenant is not valid (eg because it has not been registered) that is an end to the matter if enforcement is sought against a successor in title of the covenantor. Look at the flowchart to see at what point the question as to validity cuts in (at pages 5–7 above).

Even though a covenant may not be valid (because it is not registered) it is still open, in theory, for the original covenantee (or his successor) to sue the *original* covenantor for breach of covenant. (This is provided there is no limitation on liability limited to the ownership of the land by that covenantor.) If such an action is brought it is open to question what damages, or other remedy can be recovered against the original covenantor, who is usually, quite ignorant of the breach. That covenantor may be able to claim against his successor on the indemnity covenant into which his successor will in all likelihood have entered. It is also open to question whether on strict principles of causation (the 'but for' test) the original covenantor can be eligible for loss suffered by the original covenantee (or his successor) as the true cause of the loss (and the inability to pursue the covenantor's successor) is the failure of the original covenantee to protect the covenant by registration.[4]

DISCOVERING THE EXISTENCE OF A COVENANT: REGISTERED AND UNREGISTERED TITLES

4.5 Discovery of the existence of a covenant, particularly the benefit of one, is not always so simple.

The existence of any restrictive covenants will be revealed by:

(a)   the documents of title themselves;
(b)   abstracts, or epitomes of title;
(c)   Land Charges Registry searches;
(d)   official copies of registered titles.

---

[4]   See **4.24** below. See *Galoo v Bright Grahame Murray* [1994] 1 WLR 1360, for a clear discussion of the principles relating to causation in the context of breach of duty in contract – and tort.

Classes (a), (b) and (c) are relevant in unregistered land only. In cases of such land it is assumed that any practitioner will have investigated title for the statutory period of at least 15 years.[5] As regards undisclosed land charges not disclosed by such investigation, compensation for them is provided for them under section 25 of the Law of Property Act 1969.[6]

(Note that contracting purchasers of unregistered land are not deemed to have notice under section 198 of the Law of Property Act 1925 of registered land charges at the time of entry into the contract, unless they or their agents have actual notice of them.[7] This protects purchasers of such land and requires disclosure from the vendor. The position is the same as regards purchasers of registered land.)

4.6   What follows is the detail of how the existence of restrictive covenants will reveal themselves and what will govern validity by registration.

The first question to ask is whether the freehold title(s) under consideration is or are registered at the Land Registry, and if so, with which class of title. The question usually needs to be asked twice because the answer will require knowledge of the status of both the burdened and the benefited land. There are four permutations, which are discussed below.

4.7   (1) *A restrictive covenant is taken for the benefit of plot A over plot B. Both titles are freehold. Neither title is registered at the Land Registry.* In this case the rules relating to the protection of the validity by notice, or registration of covenants in unregistered land will apply. In terms of discovery of the existence of the covenants it will be the documents of title which will give the answer, coupled with any Land Charges Registry certificates.

(2)   *As in (1) save that plot A is registered with title absolute at the Land Registry and plot B is not.* In this case, for the reasons given below at **4.19** the existence of the benefit of the covenant may not appear from A's title at the Land Registry. To be valid, the covenant which burdens plot B must satisfy the rules relating to the protection of the validity of covenants in unregistered land; as in Example (1) above. Discovery of the benefit may, therefore, be a problem, but discovery of the burden will not be if the covenant is to be valid and bind a successor of the original covenantor.

(3)   *As in (1) save that plot A not registered at the Land Registry but plot B is, with absolute title.* In this case the existence of the benefit should appear from plot A's title deeds. To be valid and bind a successor of the original covenantor the burden must be entered on the charges register of B's title at the Land Registry and if so, will appear there. Discovery of both benefit and burden should be relatively easy.

(4)   *As in (1) save that both plots are registered at the Land Registry with title absolute.*[8] In this case the benefit will not appear on A's title. The burden, for the covenant to be valid and bind a successor of the original covenantor, must

---

[5]   Law of Property Act 1969, s 23.

[6]   See *Ruoff & Roper on the Law and Practice of Registered Conveyancing* (Sweet & Maxwell, looseleaf), para 9.019.

[7]   Law of Property Act 1969, s 24(1) and see *Emmet on Title* (Sweet and Maxwell, looseleaf), para 1.016.

[8]   In the event that the titles are registered with a class of title less than absolute (qualified or possessory) see *Ruoff & Roper*, paras 6.005–6.006, and below.

appear on the charges register to be B's title; as in (3) above. In this case (which represents an increasing number of situations concerning two titles) the discovery of the benefit of the covenant will be difficult, but the burden easy.

4.8   What if the registered title is possessory only?[9]

(1)   In such a case the task may be more difficult, although the covenant may still be valid against the owner of the burdened land for the reasons which appear below.

(2)   If the class of title registered is possessory (as opposed to absolute) the *burden* of the covenant will not appear on the register for the simple reason that no deeds will have been produced on first registration. In such a case, the covenant will still be valid and binding on the first registered proprietor and his successors provided the covenant was valid at the time of first registration.[10] In other words, the rules which determine the validity in unregistered land (against successors in title of the original covenantor) of pre-and post-1925 covenants set out at **4.11** below must be satisfied. This means that while there may be nothing on the register of the burdened land, there may be a valid covenant binding it, and the pre-registration deeds and Land Charges Registry searches will reveal the existence of a covenant and (according to the rules set out below) its validity. That is the danger in possessory titles.

(3)   In so far as the *benefited* land is registered with possessory title, there will, for the same reason, be nothing on the register and the same searches will have to be made to see if the benefit of any covenant can be claimed.

(4)   In some cases the Registry will put an entry on the register of the burdened land to the effect that the title is subject to such covenants as may have been imposed thereon prior to first registration so far as they are legally enforceable. This is because the squatter (with the possessory title) cannot defeat the right of the covenantee and his successors to enforce any valid covenants against the former.[11]

4.9   What if the registered title is qualified?[12]

(1)   Such titles are rarely encountered. They are usually granted where, for example, title is defective up to a certain date. There will usually be a provision in the register excepting from the effect of registration any interest arising before a certain date or under a document described in the register. Thus the title is, in effect, absolute, but is qualified in a certain way.

(2)   Discovery of the existence of covenants in such titles may, therefore, be complicated by the fact that there are two periods to be looked at. The first is the period covered by the exception where the title is defective and is not shown. The second is that period where the title is shown fully on the register.

(3)   Any covenant which falls within the terms of the exception (the first period) will be valid (as to the *burden*) according to the same principles as are set out

---

9   See Land Registration Act 2002, ss 9 and 10(7).

10   Where a possessory title is registered as a result of adverse possession, restrictive covenants entered into by the 'paper owner' will bind that land: *Re Nisbet and Potts Contract* [1905] 1 Ch 391.

11   See *Ruoff & Roper*, see n 6 above, para 6.006 and 9.030, and see n 8 above.

12   See Land Registration Act 2002, ss 9 and 10(6); *Ruoff & Roper*, see n 6 above, para 9.018.

in **4.8** above for possessory titles. The existence of covenants burdening the land within the title will have to be found in the same way from pre-registration deeds and Land Charges Act searches. Discovery of covenants created during that period which *benefit* the land with a qualified title can only be found in the deeds and searches lying off the register, as in possessory titles; see **4.8(3)** above.

(4)   Covenants which fall within the second period where the title is shown and which burden the land within the title must conform with the requirements of registration on the title to the burdened land in absolute titles. The discovery of the existence of the burden will also be as in unqualified absolute titles. The treatment of the benefit of covenants created within the second period will also follow the same rules as in unqualified absolute title; for which see **4.19** below.[13] In practice the benefit will not appear and may be hard to find; see situation (2) and (4) at **4.8** above.

Having been able to discover the existence of the restrictive covenant the next stage is to look in detail at whether the covenant is 'valid' in accordance with the meaning of the word at **4.4** above, in order to discover whether successors in title to the original covenantor will be bound.

THE RULES AS TO THE VALIDITY OF RESTRICTIVE COVENANTS

4.10   It is these rules which indicate whether, having discovered the existence of a restrictive covenant which appears to affect land, such a covenant is valid and binding against successors in title of the original covenantor.

4.11   The validity of restrictive covenants against non-parties is governed by the following principles:

(1)   Restrictive covenants created before 1 January 1926 and disclosed in the documents of title will only affect and be enforceable against a *bona fide* purchaser[14] for value of the legal estate with notice, or against a person holding an interest less than a legal estate, such as lessees, squatters, licensees and occupiers at will.

'Notice' in practice means disclosure in the documents of title referred to at **4.5** above. Because the minimum period for examination of title has, since 1970, been 15 years and because of the increasing passage of time since 1926, and with the growth in registered titles, cases where the purchaser for value is without notice may arise infrequently.[15] However, problems can still arise in respect of pre-1 January 1926 covenants. This is because in some instances research has revealed that, on first registration, the abstracts or epitomes supplied gave notice of pre-1 January 1926 covenants, but for some reason they were not entered. See **4.13** below.

---

[13]   See *Ruoff & Roper*, n 6 above, para 6.005.
[14]   A 'donee' will not be a purchaser, but a lessee may be a 'purchaser'. So a lessee may be liable under covenants on the reversion of which he has notice.
[15]   On first registration the policy of the Land Registry in such cases is as set out in *Ruoff & Roper*, see n 6 above, para 12.20.

(2)   Restrictive covenants created on or after 1 January 1926 require:
   –   in unregistered land, registration as a Class D(ii) Land Charge, against the name of the estate owner of the land burdened by the covenant;[16]
   –   in registered land, a notice of the covenant on the Charges Register.[17]

NB: Two points to remember in practice.

(1)   Registration of the burden of such a covenant which relates to a registered title at the Land Charges Registry is of *no effect*; Land Charges Act 1972, section 14(1). (The Land Charges Registry is not obliged to see whether the covenant affects a registered title; ibid section 14(2).) So, a Land Charges Registry search showing the entry of a covenant against the owner of a registered title is (literally) not worth the paper it is written on. (There is a warning on the back of the standard search certificate!)

(2)   The application for a notice of the restrictive covenant on the title of the burdened land is the only way to ensure validity of such a covenant.[18]

THE EFFECT OF A FAILURE TO OBSERVE THE RULES

4.12   *In unregistered titles*, if the covenants are not registered as a Class D(ii) Land Charge, they will not bind successors to the original covenantor and are void against a purchaser of a legal estate for money or money's worth, unless registered before the completion of the purchase.[19]

In registered titles, if the covenants are not entered on the Charges Register of the title of the burdened land to which they relate at the time of completion of the registerable disposition, a purchaser of that land (being a person who acquires that land under a registerable disposition for valuable consideration) is not bound

---

[16]   Land Charges Act 1972, ss 2(5)(ii) and 3(i). If so registered, that constitutes notice to all the world under Law of Property Act 1925, s 199(l). Note that by the Land Charges Act 1972, s 14(3) (as amended) a vendor of unregistered land need not register covenants imposed on that disposition (if it induces compulsory registration of the title to that land) under the Land Charges Act 1972, but must instead ensure registration of that title, with a notice of the covenants, under the Land Charges Act 1972, s 6. See *Ruoff and Roper*, n 6 above, para 9.020.

[17]   Land Registration Act 2002, ss 11 and 32. Prior to 13 October 2003, the benefit of restrictive covenants was rarely entered and then only in qualified terms. See **4.19** for detail.

[18]   Before 13 October 2003 attempts were sometimes made to protect the burden of a covenant by way of a caution. That cannot be used after that date, although there may still be rare cases, no doubt diminishing as time passes, where a caution was used for this purpose. *Clark v Chief Land Registrar* [1994] Ch 37 indicates the limited protection a caution could give under the old law.

[19]   Land Charges Act 1972, s 4(6). Note the use of the priority notice under s 11. It may be possible to defeat the unregistered covenant by selling on before any one wakes up to the fact of non-registration. It may be negligent for a solicitor acting for a client who has an interest in avoiding the covenant not to do that and it will certainly be negligent of him to make the position worse (for his client) by drawing the other party's attention to a failure to register; see *Hartle v Laceys* [1997] EWCA Civ 1130, [1999] Lloyds Rep PN 315. (The covenants in that case was limited to the seisin of Mr Hartle.) For authority on the meaning of 'purchaser' under s 4(6) of the Land Charges Act 1972, see *Merer v Fisher* [2003] EWCA Civ 747. (Party not a 'purchaser'; as consideration for the acquistion of the legal estate not provided by that party. Therefore, that party did not take free from unregistered right of pre-emption.)

by them.[20] Unregistered covenants which fall outside any priority period will also fail to bind a purchaser.

PROBLEMS WHICH CAN EMERGE IN PRACTICE

4.13   A number of problems present themselves in practice when applying these rules. These problems are partly caused by the manner in which the registration system works and partly by the policy of the Land Registry of not entering the *benefit* of restrictive covenants on registered titles.

The principal problems which emerge are:

(a)   Defective entries and searches at the Land Charges Registry.
(b)   Covenants which have been overlooked on first registration, or which appear, erroneously, on the register of title.
(c)   The general policy of the Land Registry of not entering the benefit of covenants on the title of the benefited land.
(d)   The effect of 'general' references to covenants on the register where no deeds were supplied on registration.
(e)   Questions arsing from the modification of covenants.

(a)   Defective entries and searches at the Land Charges Registry

4.14   There are two reasons why defective entries and searches at the Land Charges Registry occur. First, where the original registration was incorrect in some vital particular, such as the name of the estate owner, or of the land burdened by the covenant registered. Secondly, where the search itself is incorrectly framed. To some extent the problem is less acute under the computerised system which has been in operation since 1974. Prior to that date the old manual system operated by the Land Charges Registry at Kidbrooke relied, to some extent, on the 'lateral thinking' of the searchers thereby allowing entries to be found even where the search was not 100 per cent correct. Equally that system was known to produce clear searches where the computer would now give an entry. In many cases the old system produced a clear search against the same (correctly named) estate owner because the manner of description of the land affected differed between the registration particulars and those on the application to search. A computerised search may well reveal the entry if the estate owner's name and the county accord with the registration particulars even though some other details may be at variance. In particular, parish and place names can be notoriously difficult to get right.

4.15   The following principles appear to be applicable:

–   To ensure that the burden of the covenant runs and the covenant does not lose the advantage of enforceability against successors to the original covenantor, it is clear that care must be taken to identify and describe correctly the name

---

[20]   Land Registration Act 2002, ss 11(4), 29 and 32; Land Registration Rules 2003, r 35. See s 132(1) of that Act for the definition of 'valuable consideration' which does not include 'marriage consideration or a minimal consideration in money'. Compare the definition of 'purchaser' in ss 4(6) and 17(1) of the Land Charges Act 1972.

of the estate owner, the land and county when registration is effected.[21] In cases where local government reorganisation has led to county changes (both as to names and changes of boundaries) the county identity requires special care, both at registration and when searching. Notorious areas of change are the West Midlands and the Dorset/Hampshire boundary changes in 1973.

– The same degree of care must be exercised when searching and with online searches.[22]

4.16 The reason why these principles are important is because of the effect of the following statutory provisions:

– Land Charges Act 1972, section 10(4) which provides:

> 'In favour of a purchaser or an intending purchaser, as against persons interested under or in respect of matters or document entries of which are required or allowed as aforesaid, the certificate (sc. of search) according to its tenor, shall be conclusive, affirmatively or negatively, as the case may be.'

– Law of Property Act 1925, section 198(1) which provides:

> 'The registration of any instrument or matter in any register kept under the Land Charges Act 1972 or any local land charges register shall be deemed to constitute actual notice of such instrument or matter, and of the fact of such registration, to all persons and for all purposes connected with the land affected, as from the date or registration or other prescribed date and so long as the registration continues in force.'

4.17 When taken together these two provisions mean the registration of a covenant as a Class D(ii) Land Charge operates as actual notice to all the world (section 198(1), *but* that is subject to the effect of section 10(4)).

Thus, where a search is made the result as stated on the certificate is conclusive of the state of the register. If the result is clear, the purchaser takes without notice, and section 10(4) prevails over section 198(1).[23]

But what if the *search* is carried out in error? If the search is one which gives reasonable scope for misunderstanding, the result will not be conclusive

---

[21] The name of the estate owner should be that given in the conveyancing documents; what other name would a purchaser (or a vendor in the case of purchaser's covenants) know? In respect of estate owners who have died after 1 July 1995, registration against that person's name and not his personal representative will suffice; Law of Property (Miscellaneous Provisions) Act 1994, s 15. It is usually thought that registration will be too late after the estate owner subject to the covenant has disposed of his legal estate – unless registration is coupled with the use on a priority notice under Land Charges Act 1972, s 11. For authority on the problems posed by names on registration see *Standard Property Investment Plc v British Plastics Federation* (1985) 53 P&CR 25; *Diligent Finance v Alleyne* (1972) 23 P&CR 346. For problems posed by place names, see *Horrill v Cooper* (2000) 80 P&CR D16, CA, affirming, on other grounds (1999) 78 P&CR 336.

[22] References to searching in this respect means making an official search; the same protection is not given by personal searches or by the result of a telephone search alone, unsupported by the certificate which follows.

[23] See *Ministry of Housing v Sharp* [1970] 2 QB 223, where the Court of Appeal held that the clear certificate was conclusive, albeit in error, overruling Fisher J on this point, thereby allowing the purchasers of the land affected to take free from a claim for repayment of compensation for lost development value under Town and Country Planning Act 1947 and related legislation.

under section 10(4).[24] In such a case section 198(1) will operate so as to treat the person whose search is made in error as having notice and he will be bound by the covenant, assuming of course the benefit is enforceable under the general principles relating to enforceability.[25]

For the practitioner the following *key points* should be borne in mind when dealing with the registration of covenants and the searches for them in unregistered titles:

(1)   If you wish to ensure that a covenant binds third parties it must be registered as a Class D(ii) Land Charge with the care referred to above. Registration is not retrospective. Plans rather than a description may be preferable in some cases.

(2)   A clear search may not mean what it says. It may be that the person claiming the benefit of a covenant will, by checking old search certificates, copies of applications for registration and even descriptions in abstracted documents, show that a clear search has been given in error. Thereby he may be able to show that the burden of the covenant is, prima facie, enforceable.

(3)   As appears from **10.9** below, where covenants were entered into with local authorities before 1 August 1977, it will be necessary to carry out a Local Land Charges search, to check the validity of such covenants.

(b)   Problems with covenants and registered titles

4.18   Problems can arise in practice when covenants fail to get noted on first registration, or where covenants (which are plainly unenforceable) are erroneously noted on the register.

The first problem (failing to note the covenant) is usually fatal to any prospect of enforcing the covenant against a successor to the original covenantor who is the registered proprietor, and a purchaser under Land Registration Act 2002, section 29, for he will take free from any covenant not entered on the register.[26] Even if it is a case where it is possible to alter the register of title to the land burdened by the covenant, under Land Registration Act 2002, section 65 and Schedule 4, such alteration will not be retrospective so as to adversely affect the interest of a person who has taken free.[27] There remains the open question of whether the covenantee would be entitled to an indemnity under section 103 and Schedule 8 to that Act for any loss suffered during the period prior to alteration. The terms of section 103 and Schedule 8 and *Freer v Unwins* suggest there is no right to an indemnity. Even if an indemnity is payable in a case where the register is not rectified, the value of the

---

[24]   *Du Sautoy v Symes* [1967] Ch 1146 (description of land faulty); *Oak Co-Operative Building Society v Blackburn* [1968] Ch 730 (description of estate owner's name faulty); *Horrill v Cooper* (2000) 80 P&CR D16, CA, affirming on other grounds, (1999) 78 P&CR 336 (problems of place names).

[25]   Chapter 8 below.

[26]   Land Registration Act 1925, s 29.

[27]   *Freer v Unwins* [1976] Ch 288; *Kitney v MEPC* [1977] 1 WLR 981; *Malory Enterprises v Cheshire Homes (UK) Ltd* [2002] Ch 216. In respect of any error prior to 13 October 2003 it is hard to see how the right to rectify in such a case could be an overriding interest within Land Registration Act 1925, s 70(1)(g) and thereby binding on a successor as in *Blacklocks v JB Developments (Godalming) Ltd* [1982] Ch 183. After 13 October 2003 it is suggested that the same right may rank as an interest which overrides within the Land Registration Act 2002, Scheds 1 and 3, if protected by actual occupation. See *Ruoff & Roper*, n 6 above, paras 10.016, 15.031 and 17.011. See **15.42** below for alteration of the register generally.

claim will be limited to the loss suffered at the time of the error, which could have occurred years ago. Indeed that may be a reason for arguing that there should be alteration, and that against a proprietor in possession it would be unjust not to alter the register against him. Where it is clear that the owner of the burdened land has bought with notice of a registered covenant (even though it has not been revealed on a search which is made not containing any error) and that by reason of the clear search, the Land Registry has not registered the burden of the covenant, the court may alter the register against that purchaser.[28]

The second problem (noting invalid covenants) arises where on first registration the policy of the Land Registry is to enter covenants disclosed on the title unless it is plain that they are void for non-registration.[29] In this instance such entry does not give the covenant any validity it would not otherwise have. If it has not been registered as a Class D(ii) Land Charge and there has been a disposition of the burdened land which renders the covenant void against a *successor* of the original covenantor as a purchaser for money or money's worth of the legal estate, the registered proprietor of that estate takes free, and may seek rectification of the register to remove the entry.[30] The original covenantor may remain liable on the basis of privity of contract.

(c) The practice of not entering the benefit of covenants on the title to the benefited land

4.19   A major difficulty which lies in the way of discovering whether a covenant may be enforced arises because of the policy of the Land Registry of not normally entering the benefit of covenants on the register of title to the land benefited by the covenant. There are now two periods which have to be considered.

The position before 13 October 2003

4.20   In view of the terms in which the policy was expressed, it was *possible* to secure the entry of the benefit in two cases. First, where there was a defined building scheme (as to which see Chapter 8 below). Secondly, where application was made with a certified copy of the deed imposing the covenant and a clear definition of the land benefited. Even so the entry was in terms which did not guarantee the ability to enforce, for the standard form of entry stated that the covenants were only 'expressed to be for the benefit' of the land in the title.

The position on and after 13 October 2003

4.21   It is now harder, to secure the entry of the benefit of a restrictive covenant on the benefited land. The Land Registry has the power to enter the benefit of an apportionment right on the register (on first registration) if the Registrar is satisfied that the right subsists as a *legal estate* and benefits the registered estate.[31] This is a

---

[28] *Horrill v Cooper*, see n 24 above. Fortunately, this task is now much easier with online searches through Land Registry Direct, or one of the NLIS channels (www.nlis.org.uk).

[29] See *Ruoff & Roper*, n 6 above, para 9.020.

[30] *Kitney v MEPC*, see n 27 above, at 994, per Buckley LJ.

[31] Land Registration Rules 2003, SI 2003/1417, r 33.

discretionary obligation only. The benefit of a restrictive covenant is not a 'legal estate', but is rather an equitable interest. So to enter the benefit of the covenant, there appears to be no rule which allows applications, and furthermore the difficulty of proving what land has the benefit may be insuperable.[32]

One other task (which may be necessary in many cases) is to ascertain whether one has the benefit of a covenant at all. If adjacent land is registered, searches of the registers of title to such land may reveal the existence of covenants burdening that land, the benefit of which may be enforceable, in accordance with the principles set out in Chapter 8. If the land is unregistered the task will be impossible, unless you are within a defined building scheme, or where local knowledge establishes that there are covenants over a defined area, which might allow you to claim the benefit of them.

(d)   Cases where covenants are not identified specifically on the register

4.22   A registered title may be expressed to be subject to covenants but their precise identity is not known because either the land is registered with possessory, or qualified title (as to which see **4.8** and **4.9** above), or because no evidence, or particulars of the covenants were produced on first registration, or subsequently. The model forms of entry on the charges register will refer to the fact that the land may be affected by covenants but no particulars can be given for the reasons stated. This is a problem in practice in that whether any restriction can be enforced may be uncertain for both the party with the potential benefit and the party potentially subject to these unspecified covenants.

From the point of view of the owner of the burdened land the course to take in such cases (apart from digging out the evidence of the covenants and their terms) is to insure. (See Chapter 18 for insurance.)

(e)   Modification of covenants

4.23   Problems sometimes emerge when covenants are modified.

If a covenant is modifed (whether by agreement, or by order of the Lands Tribunal under section 84 of the Law of Property Act 1925), the parties sometimes forget to record the modification by re-registering the D(ii) entry (unregistered titles) or by applying for variation of the Charges Register entry in the register of title to the burdened land. It is more unusual to 'forget' in the case of a Lands Tribunal order. (In the rare instance where the benefit is noted the same process should be observed.[33])

The burden of covenants can sometimes not be registered in the manner appropriate to the title burdened, ie whether registered or unregistered title. Entering into an agreement to vary would appear to be an acceptance of the burden by a successor in title of the covenantor even though the covenants (in their initial

---

[32]   As to the latter see **8.18** below and *Crest Nicholson v McAllister* [2004] EWCA Civ 410.
[33]   See Chapter 16 for the discharge and modification of restrictive covenants, and **16.112** thereof for the manner in which orders should be dealt with.

form) would have been initially void against him for non-registration. He may be estopped from denying the validity of the covenant.[34] An earlier failure to register may, therefore, be 'cured' by subsequent variation. For the practitioner the important point to bear in mind is the need to protect such a variation, once made, by registration. **6.15** below deals with estoppel in more detail.

OTHER MATTERS

Indemnity covenants

4.24 Whilst the Land Registry may enter indemnity covenants on the register,[35] these will not give validity to covenants which are not themselves the subject of a notice under section 32 of the Land Registration Act 2002, or rule 35 of the Land Registration Rules 2003. (The same observation may be made about the power to enter notice of positive covenants under rule 64 of those rules.) It is also clear from *Kitney v MEPC*[36] that the mere reference on the title to covenants which become void for non-registration prior to first registration will not give those covenants validity.

An indemnity covenant may allow recourse to the indemnifier by the indemnified where the latter has suffered loss, even though the covenant may not be enforceable between those other than the original parties. This point has been referred to at **4.4** above. But the fact that one party (the indemnified) may have a remedy on the indemnity covenant should not affect the principle that a successor in title to the original covenant will not be bound by unregistered covenants created after 31 December 1925. (The same is true, in theory at least, as regards pre-1 January 1926 covenants, to which the doctrine of notice applies; although in such cases the indemnity covenant itself will invariably provide the necessary notice.[37])

---

[34] See *Taylors Fashions v Liverpool Victoria Trustees Co Ltd* [1982] 1 QB 133.
[35] Land Registration Rules 2003, SI 2003/1417, r 65.
[36] See n 27 above.
[37] See **1.3** above. See also s 189(2) of the Law of Property Act 1925.

Chapter 5

MAKING COVENANTS WORK: IS THIS COVENANT ENFORCEABLE?

5.1 This chapter looks at the general question of *enforceability*. By this stage the covenant (which has been ascertained to exist) has been established as valid in the sense that it binds successors in title of the original covenantor.

We now have to look at whether a restrictive covenant can be enforced *by* and *against* those affected.

SETTING THE SCENE

5.2 Once you have discovered the existence and validity of covenants the next stage is to consider how they may be made to work.

As covenants are designed to operate as restrictions on the use and/or enjoyment of land, their function would be incapable of performance if they did not work. It is, therefore, obvious that the real question which arises is whether the covenant is capable of enforcement. This is a separate question from validity. As explained in the previous chapter, a covenant's validity is independent from its enforceability.

It is in the context of *enforceability* that the real difficulties as regards restrictive covenants are encountered by practitioners. This is partly because validity is confused with enforceability and partly because of the rules which apply to ascertain whether a covenant is enforceable or not.[1] It is remarkable in how many instances a prolonged inquiry as to enforceability can be shortcircuited by the discovery that the covenant is void for want of registration.[2]

WHO IS SEEKING TO ENFORCE THE COVENANT AGAINST WHOM?

5.3 To answer the question 'is this covenant enforceable?' the answer has to be given from the standpoint of both the potential plaintiff (seeking to enforce) and the potential defendant (resisting enforcement). Clearly the interests of each will

---

[1] This and subsequent chapters on the question of enforceability proceed on the assumption that any covenant under consideration is valid in the sense that it is properly registered according to the status of the title of the land burdened by it and is not unenforceable as a covenant which illegal, or created by a body acting in excess of its powers, or unenforceable as being contrary to public policy, or contrary, for example, to Arts 81 and 82 of the EC Treaty. See Chapter 14 below, for certain types of covenant which pose problems of enforceability in the alternative sense in which that word is used.

[2] See the flowchart at pp 5–7 above, for a reminder.

differ; the former being concerned to prove enforceability and the latter the contrary.

There are four situations in which the question posed above arises. In each case whether the covenant works or not depends upon the application of a different set of rules.

5.4   The four situations are as follows.

–   *Situation 1:* the original covenantee wishes to enforce against the original covenantor.
–   *Situation 2:* the original covenantee wishes to enforce against a successor of the original covenantor.
–   *Situation 3:* a successor of the original covenantee wishes to enforce against the original covenantor.
–   *Situation 4:* a successor of the original covenantee wishes to enforce against a successor of the original covenantor.

Each situation is examined in the following four chapters.

Chapter 6

ENFORCEMENT OF COVENANTS BETWEEN THE ORIGINAL COVENANTING PARTIES

6.1 This chapter looks at the rules which determine enforceability of covenants between the original parties.

SUMMARY

6.2

(1) As a general rule a covenant may be enforced by and against the original parties without exception.

(2) In respect of non-executing parties they will both be bound and be entitled to enforce.

(3) In respect of non-parties, only those within the ambit of a deed poll or section 56(1) can enforce, and non-parties cannot be bound.

(4) In very rare cases the Contracts (Rights of Third Parties) Act 1999 ('the 1999 Act') may apply to allow a covenant to be enforceable by a person who can claim the benefit of that Act. The 1999 Act is only applicable to contracts entered into after 11 May 2000 unless between 11 November 1999 and 11 May 2000 the contract expressly provided for the Act to apply.[1] The 1999 Act only applies if the contract expressly provides that a person not a party to it may enforce or if it confers a benefit on him by a term of the contract, unless in the latter case the parties did not intend the term to be enforceable by him.[2] He must be identified by name, or as a member of a class, or as answering a particular description. He need not be in existence when the contract is made.[3]

(5) Special rules apply where local authorities have been dissolved and their rights and liabilities are passed to new authorities (see **6.10** below).

(6) Estoppel may provide an exception to the general rule at (3).

---

[1]   Contracts (Rights of Third Parties) Act 1999, s 10.
[2]   Ibid, s 1.
[3]   Ibid, s 1(3).

THE SITUATION

6.3   The original covenantee wishes to enforce against the original covenantor.

The general rule

The covenant is enforceable by the covenantee and the covenantor is bound by virtue of the usual principles of privity of contract and by virtue of consideration having been given for the covenant.

Are there any problems with the general rule?

6.4   There ought to be no problem in practice with the general rule. But, as with all rules, they can contain exceptions.

Potentially tricky points can arise where the general rule may not be applicable. These are:

–   whether a person *named* in the deed but who is *not a party* can claim the benefit of it;
–   whether a party *named* in the deed but *who has not executed it* can enforce it, or be bound by it.

In practice, examples of these points may arise in the following manner.

Consider a deed made between A and B whereby A covenants with B that he will not do certain things on his (A's) land. B can enforce against A.

But what if:

(a)   the deed is a Land Registry transfer and B has not signed it;
(b)   the covenant is for the benefit of C and he has not signed the deed;
(c)   the covenant is not with B or C, but with the owners for the time being of the remainder of the X Estate, which B is selling off;
(d)   A is not a party to the transfer, or if a party, he has not executed it?

For reasons which are explained below, dealing with each example in turn, the answers are as follows:

(a)   B can enforce against A even though B has not executed it;
(b)   C can enforce against A by virtue of the transfer being a deed poll;
(c)   the owners for the time being of the remainder X estate if then in existence at the date of the deed can enforce by virtue of section 56(1) of the Law of Property Act 1925;
(d)   as A is not a party to the transfer he cannot be bound by it. If he is a party but has not executed it he will be bound if he is in possession of the land burdened by the covenant.

Unless the reader needs to know the detailed background to and the reasons for these answers, he need not read further. In the vast majority of cases the covenant will be enforceable by an application of the general rule, and in the circumstances set out above. However, there are some technical points which may cause problems in certain situations.

The technical points which cause problems in the application of the general rule

6.5   Before we can discover the reasons behind the answer to the two problems described at **6.4** above, we have to identify the type of deed which creates the covenant. We also have to understand the effect of the Law of Property Act 1925, section 56(1).

These two problems may be summarised as:

(1)   the distinction between an indenture and a deed poll;
(2)   the effect of the Law of Property Act 1925, section 56(1).

(1)   Indenture v deed poll

6.6   An indenture is a deed made *inter partes*. The classic instance being the usual form of conveyance of unregistered land, or a deed of covenant expressed to be made between A and B.

A deed poll is a deed made by one party only, as a unilateral act.[4] By virtue of section 56(2) of the Law of Property Act 1925 a deed *inter partes* has the effect of an indenture even though it is not indented, nor expressed to be an indenture. What this means is that a deed between two parties will operate as an *inter partes* deed however it is formally expressed.

(2)   Section 56(1) of the Law of Property Act 1925

6.7   This provides:

'A person may take an immediate or other interest in land or other property or the benefit of any condition, right of entry, covenant or agreement over or respecting land or other property, although he may not be named as a party to the conveyance or other instrument'

It is this section which allows a third party to enforce a covenant where he is within the ambit of the covenant, ie the covenant must be made with him and it is not enough that the covenant may be for that person's benefit.[5] In the context of restrictive covenants, the formula often adopted, in order to take advantage of section 56(1), is to express the covenant to be with the owner or owners for the time being of defined property, so that there are, in effect, words of covenant with those persons.[6]

---

4   We are not concerned here with the old 'physical' distinction between an indenture and a deed poll in that the former was made in two identical parts and 'indented', ie cut with a wavy line at the top or down the middle, whereas the latter was made in one part only. For the history see *Halsbury's Laws*, vol 12, para 1303. These distinctions, curiously, survive the formal changes as regards execution by s 1 of the Law of Property (Miscellaneous Provisions) Act 1989.
5   See *Amsprop Trading Ltd v Harris Distribution Ltd* [1997] 1 WLR 1025.
6   See Chapter 17 for drafting points and precedents at Appendix 7. This form of words allows adjoining owners who may have purchased adjoining plots *prior* to the conveyance containing the covenant to claim the benefit of the covenants if the covenant is expressed to be with them. See also *Re Shaw's Application* (1994) 68 P&CR 591 where adjoining owners had the benefit under section 56(l) of a covenant to approve plans. That authority was, however, criticised by the court in *Amsprop Trading* (above) and the stricter view that the covenant must be expressed to be with the

The operation of section 56 is limited by the additional rule that the person claiming the benefit must have been in existence at the date of the deed creating the covenant.

The detailed answer to the problems in paragraph 6.4

6.8 With these distinctions in mind how does a covenant work in the circumstances posed in **6.4** above?

First, who can claim the **benefit** *of the covenant?*

By way of background, at common law, a person who was not a party to an indenture could not sue on it. That rule has been qualified by section 56(1), as explained above. But at common law a person who was within the ambit of a *deed poll* and entitled to the *benefit* of any covenant in it could enforce the covenant. The circumstances in which a person can claim to be within the ambit of a deed poll are the same as those which arise when considering whether a covenant is purportedly made with someone for the purposes of enforcement under section 56(1). That rule still applies, so in cases where covenants are imposed by a deed poll, the assistance of section 56(1) is not required. The only other factor to bear in mind is the 1999 Act which may be applicable, if at all, to covenants created in agreements made after 11 November 1999 or 11 May 2000, as stated at **6.2**.

The commonest example of a deed poll is the standard Land Registry transfer form. As that operates as a deed poll, any covenants in it can be enforced by the covenantee, even though not a party to the transfer, or, if a party to it, in the absence of execution by that party.[7]

The answer to the problem, in summary, is therefore:

–   where the deed is *inter partes* and is, in effect, an indenture, section 56(1) will apply to allow the benefit to be claimed by persons who are not parties to an indenture, provided the covenant is purported to be made with them, eg the owners for the time being of the adjacent land;

–   where a *deed poll* is used (eg a Land Registry transfer) a person within its ambit (eg defined as the covenantee(s) in the example just given) can claim the benefit of the covenant either at common law, or under section 56(1); although a claim under the section is strictly unnecessary;

–   those who are named as parties but who have simply failed to execute can take the benefit and enforce the covenants;

–   *but* a claim to the benefit of a covenant by a person who is not a party to the deed will not be possible where an indenture is used and where section 56(1) does not assist, eg where the covenant does not purport to be made with the person attempting to enforce it;

---

person claiming the benefit of it prevailed. See also *Beswick v Beswick* [1968] AC 58. See **8.30** for the problem posed if this form is not used.

[7]   *Chelsea & Walham Green BS v Armstrong* [1951] Ch 853; Megarry & Wade, *The Law of Real Property* (Sweet & Maxwell, 6th edn, 1999), pp 986–997; *Emmet on Title* (Sweet & Maxwell, looseleaf), para 11.001–2. See Land Registry form TR1 for example.

–   in very rare cases the 1999 Act may allow a third party to enforce.

Secondly, who can be bound *by the covenant?*

6.9   Fortunately, the rules here are simple.

–   A non-party cannot be bound, and section 56(1) has no application as it concerns the benefit of the covenant only. Likewise, the 1999 Act has no application.

–   In the case of a deed of either variety (ie whether an *indenture* or a *deed poll*) which has not been executed by a party to it (the covenantor) the burden is enforceable against him.[8]

SPECIAL SITUATIONS WHERE PUBLIC AUTHORITIES HAVE CEASED TO EXIST LEAVING STATUTORY SUCCESSORS

6.10   On the dissolution of public bodies and the transfer of their undertakings to new bodies by Act of Parliament (whether a Public or Private Act), it will usually be clear, from the relevant statutory and other material which may record the transfer of functions, that the new body is to be regarded as the direct successor of the old. This means that there should be no difficulty in enforcing restrictive covenants by the new body, or against that new body, to which the old body was a party.

6.11   Greater difficulties can be encountered, however, in the instance of covenants entered into by *local authorities*. This difficulty arises in the context of reorganisation of local government during the past 30 years. This reorganisation can affect the enforceability of restrictive covenants entered into by local authorities which have ceased to exist. In each case, where the question of enforceability arises, it is necessary to examine the title and the instrument which imposed the covenant. This will identify the relevant local authority and any powers under which it will be acting. In the light of legislation brought into force after the date of the instrument imposing the covenant, the changes which may have occurred to that local authority have to be considered. That will reveal what is the statutory successor to that authority. Once that has been done, it is then necessary to ask whether the rights and liabilities under the covenant passed to the successor Authority. In this context, the principal question is generally whether a successor Authority has *the benefit* of any particular covenant and is, therefore, entitled to sue upon it. The question is not so much whether the burden runs, because that will normally be plain from the face of the register of title, or from any Land Charges Act D(ii) entry against the burdened land. The rest of this paragraph, therefore, looks at the matter principally from the point of view of establishing whether or not a successor authority has the *benefit* of the restrictive covenant. That question itself arises not only when the successor authority has to consider enforcement action, but also from the point of view of a potential, or

---

[8]   In the sense that the burden of the covenant will be enforceable in equity against the non-executing party who has accepted the benefit of the deed (eg by going into possession of the land conveyed): *Formby v Barker* [1903] 2 Ch 539.

actual, defendant who will have to be advised as to his position in terms of liability if made the subject of a claim to enforce by the successor authority. He will need to satisfy himself that that body has the benefit of the material covenant which entitles it to do that.[9]

6.12   Location and dates

There are three principal areas where this question arises in terms of both geography and location.

(1)   Where the covenant was imposed by, or secured against, a Local Authority before 1 April 1974 (other than in London).

(2)   Where the covenant was imposed by, or secured against, a Metropolitan Authority prior to the changes which affected such an Authority following the Local Government Act 1985. This caused the abolition of Metropolitan County Councils with effect from 1 April 1986.[10] The changes which affected other local authorities following reviews under the Local Government Act 1992 with consequent abolition of certain authorities under that Act also arise for examination.

(3)   Where the covenant was imposed by, or secured against, an authority having jurisdiction in London and the former London County Council (LCC) and Greater London Council (GLC) areas.

Dealing with each in turn.

6.13   (1) Covenants imposed by local authorities before 1 April 1974

(a)   In cases where the Local Government Act 1972 abolished the former local authorities with effect from the 1 April 1974, all property and liabilities were transferred by Order, or by mutual agreement specified in such an Order, to the appropriate new local authority.[11] This means that the covenants entered into by the old pre-1 April 1974 county councils, urban district councils, rural district councils

---

[9]   For recent authority raising this issue see *University of East London v London Borough of Barking and Dagenham* [2004] EWHC 2710 (Ch).

[10]   The Metropolitan Counties were defined by Sch 1, Pt II, of the Local Government Act 1972: see s 1(1) thereof. These were Greater Manchester, Merseyside, South Yorkshire, Tyne and Wear, West Midlands and West Yorkshire. On the abolition of the function of the Metropolitan County Councils, their functions were exercised by the Metropolitan District Councils in the districts covered by the former Metropolitan County Councils: see ss 1 and 16(2) of the Local Government Act 1985.

[11]   See Local Government Act 1972, ss 254(1) and 254(2)(a). The relevant order for the purposes of transfer of rights and liabilities (which seemingly includes those arising under restrictive covenants) is, as to England, the Local Authorities (England) (Property etc) Order 1973, SI 1973/1861, as subsequently amended. As to Wales, see SI 1973/1863, as also subsequently amended. *Halsbury's Laws of England* and *Halsbury's Statutes* will have the full details of the relevant legislation and the statutory instruments.

In *Walters v Babergh District Council* (1983) 82 LGR 235, it was held that 'liabilities' under the principal Order (namely that referred to above under SI 1973/186, Art 16(3)(a)) included contingent liabilities. It is, therefore, suggested that the burden of a restrictive covenant would pass as a contingent liability. 'Rights' would include the benefit of a restrictive covenant. See *University of East London v London Borough of Barking and Dagenham*, at n 9 above, at paras 44–49.

and (old style) borough councils will be enforceable by and against the new county, borough and district councils replacing them.

6.14 (2) *Metropolitan and other councils* other than in London – *where covenants were imposed on or after 14th April 1974*

Changes caused by the abolition of the Metropolitan County Councils on 1st April 1986

So far as the rights and liabilities of the abolished Authorities were not specifically transferred by the Local Government Act 1985[12] and Orders made thereunder,[13] those rights and liabilities vested in the Residuary Body for each Metropolitan County Council; see sections 57 and 62 of the Local Government Act 1985. Each Residuary Body was constituted by Order on various dates in August and September 1985.[14] The benefit, or burden of restrictive covenants passed to each of the Residuary Bodies for the old Metropolitan County Councils in question. During the life of each Residuary Body that Body transferred property by Order (following approval by the Secretary of State of proposals for the transfer under section 67(2) of the Local Government Act 1985) to local authorities within its district. The benefit of covenants may, therefore, be in the transferee authority as a result of such an Order. This is certainly the case in most instances where the benefit of covenants was not dealt with by a transfer Order made under section 100 prior to the vesting of rights in the relevant Residuary Body. The terms of any Order made under section 67(2) will have to be examined to see precisely what was transferred in any individual case. Each Residuary Body was abolished following winding up under section 67 of the Local Government Act 1985. Following schemes made by the Secretary of State, those rights and liabilities (including those arising under restrictive covenants) already vested in the Residuary Body (so far as not already transferred out in each case) became vested in the authority designated in the Order following the approval of the schemes by the Secretary of State. The Orders provided generally that, unless there was an agreement for the disposal of immovable property to a designated authority, all other property (whether immovable or movable) and rights and liabilities of the Residuary Body were to vest in the Council of the District in which the property was situated. Therefore, it would appear that, in the case of an abolished Metropolitan County Council, under the Local Government Act 1985, the likelihood is that the benefit of any covenant entered into by such a body will be vested in the Council of the District in which the property is situated.[15] This means that, unless there is evidence that the Residuary Body transferred property or rights and liabilities *during its existence*, the benefit of a restrictive covenant imposed by the old Metropolitan County Council will be in the council of the district in which the property is situated.

---

[12]   See Local Government Reorganisation (Property etc) Order 1986, SI 1986/148, Arts 4, 5, 6 and 7.
[13]   Section 100 of the Local Government Act 1985.
[14]   See *Halsbury's Statutes*, vol 25, under the notes to s 57, for the precise dates.
[15]   See, for example, Tyne & Wear Residuary Body Winding Up Order 1988, SI 1988/1590. The 'transfer date' when all rights and liabilities passed under Art 2 of that Order was 11 October 1988.

*Changes caused by Local Government reorganisation pursuant to the Local
Government Act 1992*

Under this Act the Local Government Commission (established by Part II of the
Local Government Act 1992) was empowered to report to the Secretary of State on
a review of local government with recommendations for changes to, *inter alia*,
structural and/or boundary changes. (See section 17 of the Local Government Act
1992.[16]) In practice, the changes have caused some authorities to be abolished
(eg Avon County Council), and that, in turn, means that the rights and liabilities of
an abolished authority will have vested in a successor authority. In some cases,
where there is only one successor authority, the rights and liabilities of the
abolished authority vest in that successor authority.[17] Where there is more than one
successor authority, the position and the task of discerning in whom rights and
liabilities vest can be more complex. In broad terms, there are two possible
alternative outcomes. *First*, the abolished authority and the successors (*note the
plural*) will have agreed how the rights and liabilities are to be allocated, or
transferred to them. Usually the agreement will contain a schedule (or an
abstracted copy of the relevant parts will be provided) showing the transfer by
reference to the land in question and any references to the title. The agreement will
also usually contain a provision whereby any rights and liabilities vested in the
previous authority will become vested in the authority in respect of which the land
is now situated. That will invariably be the district council.[18] This means that
detective work in tracing the agreement (if any) will be needed and the current
Local Authorities may have to be approached to see what agreements exist. Parties
may, of course, be reluctant to alert such authorities to the existence of restrictive
covenants and the fact that they may have the benefit. However, there seems little
escape from this task, particularly if a release is to be obtained, or if satisfactory
insurance cover is to be obtained. *The second alternative outcome* is that, where
there was no agreement made, rights and liabilities in the abolished authority will
have vested in the Local Government Residuary Body established by section 22 of
the Local Government Act 1992. On the assumption that that Body itself did not
transfer the property to which the covenant relates, or the assigned benefit of it by
some agreement while it existed, on the abolition of that Residuary Body on
15 November 1999 any residual functions and rights passed to the Secretary of
State for the Environment, Transport and the Regions, which is now the Office of
the Deputy Prime Minister. Therefore, in such cases, the benefit of a covenant not
expressly provided for will, in theory, have vested in the Office of the Deputy
Prime Minister, and that will, of course, require consultation with that particular
Government Department.[19]

---

[16] See *Halsbury's Laws of England*, vol 29(1), para 62, for the details.
[17] Local Government Act 1992, s 17, SI 1995/402, Art 6(2)).
[18] *For example*, land with the benefit of a covenant was originally vested in the Mayor Aldermen and
      Burgesses of Borough *X* in 1968. By SI 1973/1861, that land was vested in the new Council of the
      Borough *X* (see para 1 above under the Local Government Act 1972) with effect from 1 April 1974.
      By virtue of Art 6(4) 1995/402 and an agreement dated [ ], on the abolition of the Council of the
      Borough *X* under the Local Government Act 1992, the land became vested in the Council of the
      Borough *Y* on 1st April 1996, *or as the case may be*.
[19] See Local Government Residuary Body (England) (Winding up) Regulations 1999, SI 1999/2890.

Changes in Wales under the Local Government (Wales) Act 1994

On the 1st April 1996 all of the counties and district councils in Wales established by the Local Government Act 1972 were abolished and replaced by the bodies created by the Local Government (Wales) Act 1994. As regards the transfers of rights and liabilities in the context of restrictive covenants, the Act provided for the establishment of Principal Councils and, by virtue of the relevant Statutory Instrument,[20] rights and liabilities of the 'old' Welsh authorities have transferred to the successor authority, in the case of a single successor. Where the change under the 1994 Act leads to more than one authority becoming the successor authority, then, by virtue of Article 6 of the same statutory instrument, rights and liabilities will vest in the successor body in which the land, or the property is vested; see Articles 6 and 8 thereof.[21]

6.15   (3) London

The position as regards the enforceability of covenants in London – and particularly as to the benefit of such covenants – is complex because of the many changes which have occurred in the government of London over the past 120 years or so. In summary, the principal 'milestones' which will be relevant for determining the proper party to enforce covenants, or to claim the benefit of them, will be as follows.

(a)   From 1889 until 1 April 1965 the LCC was the authority which administered the old County of London, which, in broad terms, comprised what we would now know as the Inner London Boroughs (excluding the City of London). The rights and liabilities of the LCC were passed to the GLC on 1 April 1965.[22]

(b)   From 1 April 1965 until 1 April 1986 the authority which administered the government of London was the GLC. Its administration spread over a wider area than the old LCC by virtue of the London Government Act 1963. At the same time, the boroughs within the Greater London Area (GLA) (established by the London Government Act 1963) had greater powers. In the context of restrictive covenants, as those boroughs continue to exist, there is usually no difficulty in ascertaining the right to enforce, as the same borough will have had a continuous existence since 14 April 1965.[23] Covenants entered into by the LCC (abolished by the London Government Act 1963), following the transfer of authority over the wider area to the GLC with effect from 1 April 1965, were enforceable by and against the GLC until its abolition on 1 April 1986 by the Local Government Act 1985. Thereafter, the rights and liabilities of the GLC were transferred out to the London Boroughs and to the Common Council of the City of London. In some cases, functions were

---

[20]   SI 1996/532, Art 4.

[21]   The Schedule to the Order provided for specific vesting of certain holdings of land in successor authorities, set out in Sch 3 to the Order, but, for present purposes, this is not material.

[22]   See The London Authorities (Property, etc) Order 1964, SI 1964/1464. The City of London has its own exclusive jurisdiction over the City and, in the case of restrictive covenants, there is normally no difficulty encountered where the Corporation of London is a party, as that body has had a continuous existence for centuries. See *University of East London v London Borough of Barking and Dagenham*, at n 9 above.

[23]   See London Government Act, Sch 1, for the definition of the 'old' and the 'new' boroughs.

transferred to Central Government and new bodies created by the Local Government Act 1985.[24] For the purposes of discovering the transmission of rights and liabilities under restrictive covenants, Orders were made under section 100 of the Local Government Act 1985.[25] In each case it will be necessary to check which London Borough may now have the benefit of (or be subject to the burden) of the material covenant(s).

After 1st April 1986 (non-Inner London Education Authority (ILEA) cases)

The position as regards the rights and liabilities entered into by the GLC after its abolition on 1 April 1986 can be complex. The following summary may assist in determining in whom the benefit, or the burden of the covenant entered into by the GLC now vests.

(a)   As to the burden, assuming that the burden of the restrictive covenant is registered against the land in question, it would be enforceable against the owner of that land in the usual way. (See Chapter 4 above). It will be assumed that the covenant was not personal to the GLC (unlikely). If the covenant was made under the Greater London Council (General Powers) Act 1974, section 16 (see Appendix 2), it will bind the owner of the land under that Act in any event.

(b)   As to the benefit of covenants entered into by the GLC, as in the case of the Metropolitan Councils referred to above at **6.13**, many of the rights and liabilities of the GLC were transferred under Articles 5, 6 and 7 of the 1986 Local Government Reorganisation (Property) Order[26] and vested in the appropriate new Authority. This is the London Borough in which the land to which the benefit of the covenant was annexed was situated.[27]

(c)   Insofar as the benefit of such covenants may *not* have passed to the appropriate London Borough under Part II, Local Government Act 1985, there is scope for argument that the benefit passed to the London Residuary Body. On the winding up of that body on 30 March 1990, the benefit passed to the London Borough Council, or District Council (if outside the GLC area) in which the land to which the benefit of the covenant was annexed was situated.[28]

(d)   ILEA cases

In the case of land owned by the Inner London Education Authority, or where covenants were imposed by the Inner London Education Authority, that body was abolished by the Education Reform Act 1988 on 1 April 1990.[29] Between the abolition of the GLC on 1 April 1986 and the abolition of ILEA on

---

[24]   The abolition of the Inner London Education Authority (ILEA) was dealt with differently; see below.

[25]   The principal Order is SI 1986/148, as amended.

[26]   SI 1986/148.

[27]   See Part II, Local Government Act 1985.

[28]   Local Government Act 1985, s 67; London Residuary Body (Transfer of Property, etc) Order 1990; SI 1990/419, Art 4(1)(f) and (g). Where the benefited land is in the City of London, the benefit passes to the Common Council of the Corporation of London. Reference is made below to the 'statutory quirk' of the existence of the ILEA, and the different way in which the rights and liabilities of that body pass.

[29]   ILEA was in fact not a separate body from the GLC during its existence, but was in fact the name which the GLC gave to a Special Education Committee acting as Local Education Authority (LEA) for the Inner London Area.

1 April 1990, ILEA became a corporate body. Where covenants were imposed by, or against ILEA, those covenants are now enforceable by or against the Borough in which the land is situated. The benefit of covenants entered into by the GLC, acting for ILEA before 14 April 1986, or by ILEA as a corporate body before 1 April 1990 are enforceable by the London Borough in which the land to which the benefit of the covenant is annexed is situated.[30] In some cases, after 1 April 1990 (the date of the abolition of ILEA), covenants were entered into on behalf of ILEA by the London Residuary Body acting under section 164 of the Education Reform Act 1988, which was winding up the affairs of ILEA. On the winding up of the London Residuary Body (for the purposes of its functions under the Education Reform Act 1988, and in particular in respect of its functions winding up ILEA), under section 187 of the Education Reform Act 1988, on 29 March 1996, the rights and liabilities passed to the London Borough of Bromley, so far as they still remained with the London Residuary Body at that date. In practical terms, therefore, it is conceivable that the benefit of some covenants may be enforced by the London Borough of Bromley to the extent that they had not been assigned by the London Residuary Body after 1 April 1990 and before 29 March 1996, to a specific authority.[31]

6.16   ESTOPPEL CASES

Although the analysis above as regards the enforceability of restrictive covenants has concentrated on the law of contract as between the parties and the rules which govern the passing of the benefit and burden, it is clearly possible that, by virtue of the doctrines of promissory (if not proprietary) estoppel, a covenant may be held to be binding between parties where they have satisfied the principles which govern the doctrine of estoppel. As this is not a text book on the law of estoppel, the reader is referred to those dealing with that subject.[32] If the conditions for the application of the principles of estoppel apply, why should not the burden of a restrictive covenant be enforceable in respect of the burden?[33] Additionally, the benefit of a covenant may be enforceable by virtue of estoppel in view of the unconscionability which would otherwise result if the party did not have the benefit of that covenant. Thus, if the requirements for estoppel are met (assurances given which were intended to be relied on, and are in fact relied on, complied with detrimental reliance on those assurances), it is conceivable that restrictive covenants may be enforceable, both as to the benefit and the burden.[34]

---

[30]   See Education (ILEA) (Property Transfer) Order 1990, SI 1990/124, as amended. See Art 3(1) thereof. See the Order made under s 168 of the Education Reform Act 1988.

[31]   See SI 1996/557 which determined the date of the abolition of the London Residuary Body for the purposes of s 187 of the Education Reform Act 1988.

[32]   For example, *Snell's Principles of Equity* (Sweet & Maxwell, 31st edn, 2004) and Spencer-Bower, *Estoppel by Representation* (Butterworths, 4th edn, 2003).

[33]   See *Taylor's Fashions Ltd v Liverpool Victoria Trustee Co* [1982] 1 QB 133, where, withstanding the non-registration of an option, which but for the estoppel would have made it void against the defendants for want of registration, the defendants were estopped by their conduct from relying upon the invalidity of that option by virtue of the non-registration.

[34]   See *Gillett v Holt* [2001] Ch 210; *Jennings v Rice* [2002] WTLR 367.

But it is an open question as to whether or not the strict rules relating to the registration of interests can easily be overcome by the application of principles of estoppel.[35] As was stated by the Court of Appeal in *Horrill v Cooper* (see above at **4.15**), the doctrine of registration and the absence of any requirement of notice is paramount in the context of enforceability of restrictive covenants. Such a principle casts doubt on how far estoppel may go to negative the principle that unless a covenant is registered (or, if imposed before 1926 is one to which the doctrine of notice applies) it cannot bind successors. But there may be cases where it would be inequitable to prevent enforcement of the burden of a covenant (despite non-registration, or a lack of notice) and equally there may be cases where, notwithstanding the want of compliance with strict rules (Chapter 8) as to the passing of the *benefit* of covenants to successors, a party may be estopped from denying that the other can enforce.[36]

As between original parties, where promises and conduct may affect the enforcement of covenants between them, and where the doctrine of estoppel can apply freely, there is no conflict between any statutory rules and the effect of an estoppel, so the same difficulty does not arise. On balance it is suggested that it may not always be wrong to allow an estoppel to negative the operation of the principles which allow covenants to bind successors in title, particularly the statutory rules applicable to covenants imposed after 31 December 1925. The same ought also to be true of the ability to claim the benefit.[37] There is clearly room for the development of the law here.

---

[35] Unless the estoppel is between the parties who are seeking to rely on it, the estoppel should not be able to bind successors: *Ashburn Anstalt v Arnold* [1989] Ch 1.

[36] See *Rhone v Stephen* [1994] 2 AC 310, casting doubt on principles set out in *Tito v Wadell* [1977] Ch 106, at p 290 in the context of positive covenants. See Chapter 1 above, where positive covenants are referred to.

[37] Such a conclusion is not consistent with the general rule that estoppel, whether promissory, or proprietary, cannot negative the operation of a statute. But in *Taylor's Fashions* (see n 33 above) the landlord was estopped from relying on the unenforceability of an option to review a lease as an unregistered Class C (iv) Land Charge. See Spencer-Bower at VII, 5.1–5.5 for a detailed analysis of these principles.

Chapter 7

ENFORCEMENT OF COVENANTS BY THE ORIGINAL COVENANTEE AGAINST A SUCCESSOR OF THE ORIGINAL COVENANTOR: MAKING THE BURDEN OF THE COVENANT RUN

7.1 This chapter considers how the *burden* of a restrictive covenant can be made to run with the land and against successors of the original party who gave the covenant.

SUMMARY

7.2 For the burden of a restrictive covenant to be enforceable against successors in title of the original covenantor it must be shown that:

–   the covenant is restrictive
–   it protects adjacent land
–   it is not a personal covenant
–   it was validly granted
–   it satisfies the notice or registration requirements so as to bind that successor.

THE SITUATION

7.3 The original covenantee wishes to enforce against a successor of the original covenantor.

THE GENERAL RULE

7.4 A covenant will only be enforceable against a successor of the original covenantor if it is:

(1)   restrictive (according to the rules defining such a covenant)[1] and
(2)   if:
    (a)   the covenant has been taken to protect the covenantee's retained land which is so retained at the time of the conveyance and at the time of enforcement;
    (b)   the covenant benefits that land as a matter of evidence;

---

[1]   See Chapter 3 above for what is a 'restrictive' covenant.

(c)   the covenant is not a purely personal one between the original parties;[2]
(d)   the covenantor who gave the covenant was competent to give it;
(e)   the covenant satisfies the requirement of validity set out in Chapter 4 above.

The conditions under (2) are referred to as 'the five conditions'.[3]

By way of an historical note, as these conditions for enforcement are the product of the Court of Equity (the common law refusing to allow the burden of a covenant to run with the land) only equitable remedies are available in respect of any breach.[4]

ENCOUNTERING THE FIVE CONDITIONS IN PRACTICE AND SATISFYING THEM

7.5   Taking each in turn.

Condition No 1: The covenantee must retain land at the date when the covenant is given or entered into and has retained land which is capable of benefiting at the time he seeks to enforce[5]

The condition analysed

In most cases of freehold conveyancing where covenants are taken for the benefit of defined land of the vendor, the purchaser's successor will be bound and it will be easy for the vendor to show the land for the benefit of which the covenant was taken.

But there are three problems that can arise in practice:

(1)   The first requires a knowledge of the order of conveyances by the covenantee if he was selling off plots one at a time.
(2)   The second concerns covenants taken for the benefit of the covenantee's leasehold estate.
(3)   Finally, there are the statutory exceptions to the rule.

The three problems examined

(1) Last man out escapes liability (See Appendix 6).

7.6   A problem of enforcement arises where the covenant is imposed in the context of an estate-type development and the enforceability of the covenant is

---

[2]   See *Morrells of Oxford Ltd v Oxford UFC* [2001] Ch 459 for an example where there were restrictive covenants imposed in the same deed, but where one set was held to be personal to the original parties and the other set was not. Only the latter could be enforced by a successor to the original covenantor.
[3]   It is these conditions which are the product of the decision in *Tulk v Moxhay*; see Chapter 3 above.
[4]   See Chapter 15 for remedies. In view of the ability of a modern court to award not only injunctive relief, but also damages in lieu, the inability to obtain common law damages for breach in such a situation seems rather academic.
[5]   *Millbourn v Lyons* [1914] 2 Ch 231; *LCC v Allen* [1914] 3 KB 642.

being tested against the owner of the last plot to be sold off. That owner is a successor to the original covenantor.

Unless there is a scheme of development, or building scheme,[6] the common vendor who is the covenantee will not be able to enforce the covenant. This is because the common vendor retained no land when the last plot was conveyed.

This is not a common problem, although it can often arise unexpectedly, and may be overlooked, particularly when the full sequence of conveyances may not be known until litigation is commenced and at the stage of disclosure of documents under Part 31 of the CPR.[7] The wise defendant in this situation should check at an early stage whether or not his predecessor was 'the last man out'. It is possible to detect the order of conveyances made by the former common vendor by using the right to obtain official copies of the registered titles in order to detect which plot was the last to be conveyed. This method will only work where the titles are few in number and easily identified. But in most cases armed with a plan of all the neighbouring houses, and a set of office copies, it is possible to work out in what order the sales off were made. Online searches facilitate this task.

There is one snag which can arise (and nowadays rather more frequently) in estates where the covenants were imposed in the 1930s or 1950s and the land was first registered at that stage. Unless each title has a reference to the common form of covenants imposed by the common vendor, so that the order of sales can thereby be deduced, the modern computer-generated certificates will omit historic entries. In theory those covenants should be there on the register (and if they are not they will not bind successors) but it is sometimes harder to get a complete picture with the modern form of register than the old manually compiled ones with entries crossed out in red. (Looking at Plan 1 it will be seen that D cannot be sued *by* A, B or C but may *sue* any of them.)

(2)   When the lease ends, so does the liability

A landowner grants a lease of part of his land and covenants with the lessee to restrict the use, by the lessor, of his adjoining freehold land for the protection of the land demised.

The liability of the lessor's successors will only endure for the term of the lease.[8] It is, however, worth noting that in respect of covenants between landlord and tenant (and others with derivative interests in the reversion) the landlord's interest in that reversion removes the need to retain other land for the covenant to be enforceable. The same principle may also apply to mortgagees of the benefited land.[9]

(3)   Can statutes create exceptions to the rule?

Numerous statutory exceptions exist in respect of the rule which requires the retention of land by the covenantee. These allow covenants to be enforced by certain bodies 'in gross'and are dealt with at Chapter 10 below.

---

[6]   See **8.28** below.
[7]   See **15.1** below. As pointed out there, it ought to be possible to check the order of relevant dispositions before any claim is brought in view of the need to comply with the General Protocol and the use of pre-claim letters.
[8]   *Golden Lion Hotel (Hunstanton) Ltd v Carter* [1965] 1 WLR 1189. Questions may, of course, arise in such cases as to whether the lease in question has been extinguished, by merger, for example.
[9]   See Megarry & Wade, *The Law of Real Property* (Sweet & Maxwell, 6th edn, 1999), p 1019.

Condition No 2: The covenant must benefit the covenantee's land as a matter of evidence when he comes to enforce

The condition analysed:

7.7   The condition raises three questions:

(1)   Is the land for the benefit of which the covenant was taken sufficiently defined or ascertainable?
(2)   Is that land capable of being benefited by the covenant?
(3)   What does 'benefit' mean?

Taking each question in turn, the answers are:

(1) Defining the land

There are two broad distinctions here.

–   First, those cases where the words of the covenant specifically define the land for which the benefit runs.[10]
–   Secondly, where the terms of the covenant confine the benefit to the land remaining unsold.[11]

In either case, extrinsic evidence should be capable of showing the extent of the land which is within the scope of the benefit on the face of the words used to identify the defined land. There is, sadly, a 'hybrid' line of authority where it was unclear, as a matter of construction, as to what was comprised within the scope of the benefited land. Therefore, in some cases the drafting of the covenant may cause doubt to arise on its face, quite apart from the evidential requirement to identify the benefited land.[12]

(2)   Is that land capable of being benefited by the covenant?

The general rule was stated by Wilberforce J in *Marten v Flight Refuelling*.[13]

> 'If an owner of land, on selling part of it, thinks fit to impose a restriction on the user, and the restriction was imposed for the purpose of benefiting the land retained, the court would normally assume that it is capable of doing so. There might, of course, be exceptional cases where the covenant was on the face of it taken capriciously or not bona fide, but a covenant taken by the owner of an agricultural estate not to use a sold-

---

10   See *Lord Northbourne v Johnston & Son* [1922] 2 Ch 309 (the Shipcote Estate, Gateshead); *Re Ballard's Conveyance* [1937] Ch 473 (the Childwickbury Estate, Herts); *Marten v Flight Refuelling* [1962] Ch 115 (the Crichel Estate, Dorset); *Earl of Leicester v Wells-next-the-Sea UDC* [1973] Ch 110 (the Holkham Estate, Norfolk); *Wrotham Park Estate Co Ltd v Parkside Homes Ltd* [1974] 1 WLR 798 (the Wrotham Park Estate, Herts).

11   *Marquess of Zetland v Driver* [1939] Ch 1; *Cryer v Scott Bros (Sunbury) Ltd* (1986) 55 P&CR 183. *Crest Nicholson v McAllister* [2004] EWHC Civ 410; see Chapter 8 below. This problem is more acute where the claimant is *not* the original covenantee. As Chapter 8 points out, that claimant must prove not only that this condition 2 is satisfied, but also that he has the benefit of the covenant by annexation, assignment, or under a building scheme.

12   See *Re Jeff's Transfer (No 2)* [1966] 1 WLR 841; *Eagling v Gardner* [1970] 2 All ER 838; *Allen v Veranne Builders Ltd* [1988] NPC 11. But see *Dano Ltd v Earl Cadogan* [2004] 1 P&CR 13, for an example of where there was no longer any land within the scope of the definition, as a matter of construction, which was benefited.

13   [1962] Ch 115 at 136.

off portion for other than agricultural purposes could hardly fall within either of these categories'.[14]

What does this mean in practice?

7.8 First, if it can be shown that the covenant relates to specified land of the covenantee, there is a (rebuttable) presumption that the covenant is capable of benefiting the land specified. It will be for the covenantor's successor to adduce evidence to show that this presumption no longer applies.[15] Invariably this will require expert evidence from land agents and valuers.

Secondly, where there is an issue as to what land was within the scope of the benefit of the covenant and whether it is capable of being benefited by it, there are no presumptions and the covenantee will have to produce evidence on both questions.[16]

The meaning of 'benefit'

7.9 In the archaic language of lawyers the concept of the benefit conferred by a covenant may be reduced to the phrase 'touch and concern'. In modern parlance this is neither helpful or desirable.[17]

Benefit, in modern terms, means 'preserve value' or 'amenity'.

Thus, unless the covenant preserves the value of the covenantee's land, it is not restrictive and is not enforceable against a successor of the covenantor.

Modern cases show that 'value' may be preserved in a number of ways, ie:

– by protection from competing trades.[18] But note that personal covenants restricting types of trades or sales of branded goods, may not be enforceable against successors as a restrictive covenant, and they may be held to be unenforceable as an unreasonable restraint of trade, or infringing Art 81 of the EC Treaty.[19]

---

[14] See also Brightman J, in *Wrotham Park Estate Co Ltd v Parkside Homes Ltd* [1974] 1 WLR 798 at 808, where he emphasised that it will be the reasonably held view of the estate owner (covenantee) which will prevail in the absence of the contrary being proved. See the detailed examination of the evidence on this point in *Dano Ltd v Earl Cadogan* [2003] 2 P&CR 10 (affirmed by the Court of Appeal [2004] 1 P&CR 13 on a ground not raising this issue) where the extent of the benefit to the Cadogan Estate in Chelsea of a covenant to use land for 'housing of the working classes' was considered. See 'Issue 3' in *Cryer v Scott Bros (Sunbury) Ltd*, at n 11 above.

[15] Evidence for both sides was before the court in *Marten v Flight Refuelling*, above, but no evidence was placed before the court in *Earl of Leicester v Wells-next-the-Sea UDC*, above, to contradict the evidence that the covenant in question was of benefit to the Holkham Estate.

[16] As occurred in *Newton Abbot Co-operative Society Ltd v Williamson & Treadgold Ltd* [1952] Ch 286. See *Dano v Earl Cadogan* [2003] 2 P&CR 10, at para 49, for a discussion of the need to identify the lands to be benefited.

[17] For a modern authority on the question in the context of landlord and tenant and petrol station ties see *Caerns Motor Services Ltd v Texaco Ltd* [1994] 1 WLR 1249.

[18] See the *Newton Abbot Co-operative Society* case, see n 16 above.

[19] See Chapter 14 below. See *Crehan v Inntrepreneur Pub Co* [2004] EWCA Civ 637, applying Art 81 in the light of *Delimitis v Henniger Bräu AG* [1991] ECR 1-935 in the context of beer supply agreements, and the Block Exemption for such agreements. For Art 81 see the following website: www.europa.eu.int/comm/competition/legislation/treaties/ec/art81_en.html.

–   by protection from certain forms of development – to include protection of a
    view.[20] Modern authority stresses the distinction between covenants imposed
    to protect or preserve amenity and those imposed to protect, or allow recovery
    of an increase in value. This latter purpose, often described as 'overage' or
    'clawback' may be regarded as one lying outside the scope of the benefit of a
    restrictive covenant. The right to a payment of money on account of an
    increase in the value of the covanantor's land is not related to the preservation
    of the value, or the amenity of the covenantee's land. Such a right is more in
    the nature of a privilege which is designed to enhance the value of the
    covenantee's pocket rather than his land. However, the fact that a covenant
    requires the payment of a sum of money will not prevent it from 'touching
    and concerning' the land as long as it is connected with something to be done
    on or in relation to the land.[21]

Condition No 3: The covenant is not a purely personal one between the original parties

7.10   Whether a covenant is so regarded depends upon its terms and the date of
the instrument creating it.

The relevant periods are as follows, taking them in reverse historical order, on the
footing that the more recent the covenant, the more likely it is going to be
encountered.

(1)   Covenants entered into after 31 December 1925

Subject to the contrary being expressed, Law of Property Act 1925, section 79 will
treat the covenant as having been entered into with the covenantor, his successors
in title, and the persons deriving title under him. This section has been described as
a mere 'word saving' section.[22] However, this section does not have the effect of
making a personal covenant one which is 'non-personal'; ie binding on successors
to the original covenantor.[23]

(2)   Covenants entered into on or before 31 December 1925

The answer depends on the words of the covenant and whether there are words
which indicate that the covenantor's successors are to be bound. Thus not only will
words such as 'the covenantor for himself, his heirs, executors, administrators and
assigns' allow the court to find that the covenant binds successors, but also the

---

20   *Wrotham Park Estate Co v Parkside Homes* [1974] 1 WLR 798; *Gilbert v Spoor* [1983] Ch 27.
21   *P&A Swift Investments v Combined English Stores Group* [1989] AC 632. See also *Harbour Estates v HSBC Bank plc* [2004] EWHC 1714. See *Re Withinlee* (2003) Lands Tribunal (NJ Rose), 11 February 2003.
22   *Sefton v Tophams* [1967] 1 AC 50 at 73. In *Morrells of Oxford Ltd v Oxford UFC*, see n 2 above, it was held by the Court of Appeal that s 79 did not make *all* covenants binding on successors in title to the original covenantor. The section only had that effect if the covenant was not intended to be personal. See also *Allied London Industrial Properties Ltd v Castleguard Properties Ltd* [1997] EWCA Civ 2180, for an example of a personal obligation on the 'purchaser' to carry out certain work to a roadway.
23   *Morrells of Oxford v Oxford UFC*, see n 2 above.

nature of the obligation placed on the covenantor will also indicate whether successors are to be bound. An example of the latter may be the obligation to 'procure' that something be done or not done.[24] The same question as to whether the covenant was intended to be personal one also arises as under (1) above.

Condition No 4: The covenantor who gave the covenant was competent to give it

7.11 The question whether the covenantor had the power to give the covenant arises infrequently. In most cases whether the power existed will be answered in the affirmative, and particular in the following cases where the question of *vires* may be raised.

(a)   Trustees for sale of land, personal representatives and tenants for life

(1)   Covenants entered into on or after 1 January 1997

7.12 Save for pre-existing strict settlements, trustees or the personal representatives will be fully empowered to impose or accept restrictive covenants; Trusts of Land and Appointment of Trustees Act 1996, sections 6(1) and 18. The breadth of this power is only qualified by the overriding fiduciary duties owed by such persons and any express restrictions in the instrument from which the trustee or personal representative derives his power. Section 8(3) of the Trustee Act 2000 gives trustees all the powers of an absolute owner in relation to land they have acquired under section 8 of that Act.

For pre-existing strict settlements the position is as before that date, as to which see below.

For charity trustees the power under the 1996 Act extends to them in like manner as to trustees of private trusts.

(2)   Covenants entered into before 1 January 1997

Unless the instrument from which the trustee or personal representative derives his power confers a wider power, the rules as to *vires* are as follows:

– trustees for sale;
– personal representatives;
– tenants for life and statutory owners.

All have the power to grant or accept a covenant on the occasion of the sale of land vested in them; section 49(1) of the Settled Land Act 1925.[25]

If the covenant is taken or imposed without a sale, or without an order of the Court under Trustee Act 1925, section 57 or Settled Land Act 1925, section 64, the covenant may be voidable only at the suit of a beneficiary, save that where a tenant for life takes or imposes a covenant other than within the power conferred by

---

[24]   See *Re Fawcett and Holmes' Contract* (1889) 42 Ch D 150, for an example of the former and *Re Royal Victoria Pavilion Ramsgate* [1961] Ch 581, for an example of the latter.

[25]   Applicable to trustees for sale by Law of Property Act 1925, s 28(1) and to personal representatives by Administration of Estates Act 1925, s 39(1)(ii).

section 49(1), it will be void under section 18(1)(a) of that Act and will not bind the legal estate.

As to charity trustees, they have the same powers as the class described above by virtue of Settled Land Act 1925, section 29, and to the extent that they do not, the scheme jurisdiction may supply it.[26]

(b)   Limited companies

7.13   Since the abolition of the ultra vires doctrine by Companies Act 1985, section 35, a company entering into a covenant will be taken to have full power to do so.

(c)   Bodies created by statute

7.14   The existence of the power will depend upon the authority given to the body by the Act which constitutes that body. Most such bodies are empowered to enter into covenants. If in doubt ask for the statutory authority.

The most commonly encountered instance is that of local authorities, who have the wide powers conferred under Local Government Act 1972, section 123.

As to the question whether the covenant interferes with the statutory purposes for which the land is held see Chapter 10 below.

(d)   Trustees in bankruptcy, liquidators and receivers

Trustees in bankruptcy

7.15   The bankrupt's property will vest in him under section 306 of the Insolvency Act 1986, so he will be bound by the covenant. In exercise of his powers under Schedule 5, Part 2, paragraph 9 to that Act he can impose or accept covenants over the land being sold. He can also enforce (with Court's sanction) under Part 1 of that Schedule.

Liquidators

Although the assets of the company do not rest in the liquidators of a company in a winding-up, the powers conferred by Schedule 4, Pt III, paragraph 6 to the Insolvency Act 1986 allow the liquidator to sell and, if necessary, impose or accept covenants on a transfer of the Company's property without the need to obtain the Court's sanction. Court sanction may be required to bring or defend proceedings (in the context of this book they will no doubt be relating to restrictive covenants) depending upon whether the winding up was voluntary (no sanction needed) or ordered by the Court (sanction needed); Insolvency Act 1986, Schedule 4, paragraph 4 (Part II).

Administrators, Administrative Receivers and Receivers

Care should be taken to identify the precise nature of the person in the context of corporate insolvency who has the right to enforce or impose covenants. Reference

---

[26]   Charities Act 1993, ss 26 and 36.

should be made to the relevant documents in order to ascertain under which regime that person is operating.

In the case of administrators and administrative receivers appointed by the Court or by floating charge holders (so far as permitted) or by the company or its directors under Parts II and III of the Insolvency Act 1986 the powers in sections 14 and 42 of and Schedule I to the Insolvency Act 1986 (as amended by the Enterprise Act 2002) with prospective effect from 15 September 2003 allow administrators and administrative receivers to impose, or accept covenants on sale of any land in the name of the company.[27] As to proceedings by them, or brought against them Schedule 1, paragraph 5 to the Insolvency Act 1986 allows these persons to bring and defend proceedings in the name of and behalf of the company, without any Court sanction needed.

Receivers appointed by debenture holders, or banks under mortgages under section 109 of the Law of Property Act 1925 will invariably have the powers of the freehold owner (as agent of the mortgagor – section 109(2), ibid) and, therefore, will have full power under the terms of their appointment to impose, or accept covenants on sale and to sue, or be sued on them.

(e)   *Persons without the freehold legal estate*

(1)   *Lessees*

7.16   The covenant is valid and binding for the duration of the term.[28]

(2)   *Parties with a contractual right only*

The covenant will be valid and will invariably bind the legal estate on completion.[29]

(3)   *Mortgagors*

Subject to any restrictions in the mortgage deed, they have the legal estate and can enter into covenants.[30]

(4)   *Mortgagees in possession*

Subject to wider powers in the mortgage deed, the power to impose restrictions under Law of Property Act 1925, section 101(2)(1) on sale.

---

[27]   See also the powers contained in Sch B1 to the Insolvency Act 1986 as inserted by Sch 16 to the Enterprise Act 2002, with effect from 15 September 2003.

[28]   *Golden Lion Hotel (Hunstanton) Ltd v Carter* [1965] 1 WLR 1189.

[29]   See *Re Rutherford's Conveyance* [1938] Ch 396.

[30]   But 'tie' covenants may not survive the terms of the mortgage. See Chapter 14 below for the problems which commercial 'tie' and related covenants can create as regards restraint of trade and infringement of Art 81 of the EC Treaty. See n 19 above.

Condition No 5: The covenant satisfies the requirements of notice, or registration

7.17   Chapter 4 above deals with this rule.

It is stressed that in the case of a successor in title to the original covenantor, unless the requirements of registration (or of notice in the case of the 1926 covenants) are met, there can be no enforcement against such successors in title.

CONCLUDING SUMMARY

7.18   Before a successor in title of the original covenantor can be made liable on a restrictive covenant, the claimant who is the original covenantee must show that:

–   he has retained land which is capable of benefiting from the covenant;
–   the benefit to his land is not just something which is of monetary value to his pocket, eg under a clawback or overage arrangement;
–   the covenant is not a purely personal one;
–   the original covenantor had power to give it;
–   the covenant is not invalidated by the rules relating to notice (pre-1926 covenants) and registration (post-31 December 1925 covenants).

Chapter 8

ENFORCEMENT OF COVENANTS AGAINST THE ORIGINAL COVENANTOR BY A SUCCESSOR OF THE ORIGINAL COVENANTEE: MAKING THE BENEFIT OF THE COVENANT RUN

8.1 This chapter considers how the benefit of a restrictive covenant can be made to run with the land in favour of the successors of the original covenantee who imposed the covenant.

SUMMARY

8.2 For the benefit of a covenant to be enforceable by a successor of the original covenantee it must be shown that:

(1) The covenant was taken for the advantage of some land which it benefits as a matter of evidence; in the sense that any breach of the covenant would affect its value or amenity.[1]
(2) The claimant is the owner of such land, or has a sufficient interest in it.
(3) The benefit of the covenant has passed to the claimant by one of three means, ie:
  –   annexation
  –   assignment
  –   the imposition of a scheme of development.

THE SITUATION

8.3 A successor[2] of the original covenantee wishes to enforce against the original covenantor.

THE REQUIREMENTS WHICH HAVE TO BE MET BY THE CLAIMANT OR INTENDING CLAIMANT

8.4 A covenant will only be enforceable by a successor of the original covenantee against the original covenantor if the following requirements are met.

---

[1] See **7.9** above: see also *Dano v Earl Cadogan* [2003] 2 P&CR 10, at **7.7** above.
[2] Or person deriving title under, eg lessee. In the following paragraphs, 'successor' includes such persons. See *University of East London v London Borough of Barking and Dagenham* [2004] EWHC 2710 (Ch), at para 30.

(1) *The covenant is not a purely personal one.*

This means that the covenant must not be personal to the original covenantee.[3]

(2) *The covenant touches and concerns the claimant's land.*

The covenant must satisfy the requirement that the covenant was taken for the benefit of the land in which the claimant has an interest and that it does in fact do so (in the sense of 'touching and concerning' it[4]).

(3) *The claimant has the standing to claim.*

The claimant is either the freehold owner of the benefited land or is a true successor in title, or has an interest recognised as one which gives him standing in which to claim. Examples of the latter are:

(a) A person deriving title from the original covenantee, eg a tenant.[5]

(b) a contracting purchaser of the legal estate;[6]

(c) a beneficiary under a trust who is entitled to call for an assignment of the covenant, if not of the land which is benefited by it;[7]

(d) licensees who are 'occupiers' within the Law of Property Act 1925, section 78;[8]

(e) a trustee in bankruptcy where the bankrupt's estate has vested in him pursuant to Insolvency Act 1986, section 306;

(f) a person to whom the benefit will have passed by operation of law, such as a personal representative, under Administration of Estates Act 1925, section 1;[9]

(g) a person without title (eg a squatter) would not appear to have standing.

(4) *The claimant can satisfy a court that he has acquired the benefit of the covenant in one of three ways.*

The claimant has acquired the benefit of the covenant by one of three methods, namely:

(a)   annexation either by virtue of the terms of the instrument creating the covenant, or by Law of Property Act 1925, section 78 if the covenant was created after 31 December 1925;

(b)   assignment;

(c)   the imposition of a building scheme, or scheme of development.

(5) *The defendant is bound by the covenant.*

The covenantor as a potential defendant satisfies the requirements set out in Chapters 6 and 7 above, and is liable to be sued as an original covenantor.[10]

---

[3]   See **7.10** above. It is clear that if the benefit of the covenant is not intended to pass to a successor in title of the original covenantee none of the subsequent requirements can be met.

[4]   See **7.9** above.

[5]   See *Smith and Snipes Hall Farm v River Douglas Catchment Board* [1949] 2 KB 500, at 509, and 516–517. See *University of East London v London Borough of Barking and Dagenham*, at n 2 above.

[6]   See *Re Rutherford's Conveyance* [1938] Ch 396.

[7]   *Newton Abbot Co-operative Society Ltd v Williamson & Treadgold Ltd* [1952] Ch 286 at 291.

[8]   This is by no means established: see *Re Da Costa* (1986) 52 P&CR 99, where a licensee of land to which the benefit of a covenant had been annexed under the Law of Property Act 1925, s 78, had no standing to object to an application under s 84(1) of that Act.

[9]   *Newton Abbot Co-operative Society Ltd v Williamson & Treadgold Ltd* (above); *Earl of Leicester v Wells-next-the-Sea UDC* [1973] Ch 110.

[10] See Chapter 9 below where the claim is made against a successor to the original covenantor.

8.5 The requirements set out above reflect the way in which Courts of Equity have defined how the benefit is to pass. Even though the benefit of a restrictive covenant can pass at common law under somewhat simpler rules,[11] the rules of equity (as summarised above) are now regarded as applicable in all claims and it is, therefore, these rules which have to be satisfied. It is the complexity of these rules which can cause difficulty in deciding who has the benefit of restrictive covenants. Although the Law of Property Act 1925, section 78, as interpreted in *Federated Homes Ltd v Mill Lodge Properties*[12] has made the task of determining whether the benefit runs much easier in cases to which it applies (in practice the majority of covenants created after 1925) there are still areas where that section has no application and it is here that the rules are complex. The decision in *Crest Nicholson v McAllister* has emphasised the need to be able to identify the land which is intended to be benefited by the covenant, even where the covenant was created after 31 December 1925.[13]

PRACTICAL PROBLEMS IN DECIDING WHETHER THE BENEFIT OF A COVENANT IS POTENTIALLY ENFORCEABLE

8.6 Before analysing the rules which determine how the benefit can pass, as summarised under **8.2** above, we have to consider how the potential to enforce a restrictive covenant will manifest itself. In essence, what does the title of the potential claimant show?

Registered titles throw up the problem of knowing whether you have the benefit. Because of the policy of the Land Registry of not entering the benefit of covenants on the land which is (potentially) benefited, there may be an initial difficulty in ascertaining whether the potential claimant has any cause of action at all on any covenant.[14] There is also a difference in approach depending on whether the title is registered, or unregistered.

Registered titles

8.7 The remedy where titles are registered lies in a degree of detective work which requires consideration of the following matters.

(1) Look at what is registered on the Charges Register to see whether the covenants which bind the title give some clue as to the benefited land. Often the covenants are expressed to be for the benefit of the X estate or the Y land, and that may well include the land comprised in the title.

---

[11] To the effect that the covenant was enforceable if (a) it touched and concerned the benefited land and (b) the covenantee and his successor had a legal estate in that land. Since 1926 that does not have to be the same legal estate; see the Law of Property Act 1925, s 78 and *Smith and Snipes Hall Farm v River Douglas Catchment Board*, see n 5 above. *Regent Oil Co Ltd v Gregory* [1966] Ch 402. See **8.4** above.
[12] [1980] 1 WLR 594; see para 8.16 below.
[13] [2004] EWCA Civ 410.
[14] See **4.19** above.

(2)   If the manner in which the Land Registry have entered the covenants has been the 'filed and sewn up' method (ie by referring directly to the instrument imposing the covenants) sight of a copy of that instrument will confirm the extent of the covenants and their format, thereby giving an indication of the location of the benefit. (The instrument should be with the certificate of title, or at least obtainable from the Registry by reference to the title number given.)

(3)   You may be in a situation where the vendor has given covenants in favour of the purchaser, and these may be shown on the title in the property register.

(4)   If there is a building scheme, the policy of the Registry is to make an entry on the title referring to the existence of such a scheme, and its extent by reference to a plan.

(5)   Local knowledge may count for a lot where defined estates were developed by a common vendor and either a scheme or a set of like covenants is known to be enforceable.

(6)   Searching the neighbour's title (being the neighbour threatening to infringe) and obtaining a copy of his title, if registered, may well solve the problem as the burden should appear on his title.[15]

(7)   Retention of pre-registration deeds may, for practical reasons, be unwelcome, but may shed light on the extent to which the land has the benefit of covenants.[16]

(8)   Preparation of a 'master plan' to show the dates of sales off by the common vendor. (See Appendix 6 for an example.)

Unregistered titles

8.8   In unregistered titles the documents of title ought to show the extent to which covenants have been taken for the benefit of the land. Although these are now becoming a rarity, it is important to bear in mind that on first registration the Land Registry will not enter the benefit on the title on first registration.[17] (See **4.19**.)

---

[15]   It is assumed, of course, that this will not throw up the problem of a failure by the Land Registry (or any other person concerned) to enter the burden of the covenants on the neighbour's title. See **4.18** for the difficulty of enforcement this poses. The potential claimant may be left with an indemnity claim under Land Registration Act 2002, s 103 and Sch 8. See **4.21** as to the practice after 13 October 2003 in respect of the entry of the benefit of restrictive covenants.

[16]   From the point of view of the owner of the burdened land (who might consider whether there are persons who know of the covenant's existence). It would appear that he would (more likely than not) lie low and say nothing. But in the context of potential development land something may have to be said, if only to the insurers when an indemnity policy is required. See Chapter 18 below on insurance in this context. See *Hartle v Laceys* [1997] EWCA Civ 1130, where the developer's solicitor negligently drew the attention of the covenantee to unregistered restrictive covenants; see **4.12** above.

[17]   In view of the decision of the Court of Appeal in *Crest Nicholson v McAllister* [2004] EWHC Civ 410, pre-registration deeds and documents may well be of crucial importance in identifying the land intended to be benefited by the covenant. See **8.18**.

DO I HAVE THE BENEFIT? THE IMPORTANCE OF THE DATE OF THE COVENANT

8.9   Having located the instrument containing the covenant which is to be enforced, whether the covenant was taken on or before 31 December 1925, or after that date, will be of critical importance in determining the rules which apply in deciding the manner in which the benefit of the covenant will run.

Covenants imposed on or before 31 December 1925

In the case of covenants imposed on or before 31 December 1925, the instrument imposing it and the title deduced must be examined for signs of *one* of the following:

– express, or implied annexation of the benefit of the covenant;
– the creation of a building scheme;
– a chain of assignments of the benefit of the covenant.

Covenants imposed after 31 December 1925

In the case of covenants imposed after 31 December 1925 it is possible to enforce covenants of that age by satisfying one of the three conditions set out in **8.4(4)**.

But it may well be unnecessary to do so.

This is because of the effect of the Law of Property Act 1925, section 78. This section achieves annexation of the benefit of the covenant without the need for special words of annexation, provided the land intended to be benefited can be identified from either the instrument imposing the covenant, or from other evidence, and can easily be so ascertained, or unless that section is excluded by words in the instrument imposing the covenant.[18]

Thus, armed with (a) the instrument creating the covenant (b) evidence of devolution of the title since creation (including evidence of the assignment of the benefit of the covenant) and (c) knowing whether the covenant is pre- or post-1 January 1926, the next stage is to examine in detail the means by which the benefit of the covenant can be transmitted in each case.

DO I HAVE THE BENEFIT? SEPARATING THE EASY FROM THE HARD PARTS

8.10   It is usually easy to decide whether or not four out of the five requirements as set out at **8.4** have been satisfied. In practice, therefore, the potential claimant can usually show that:

(1)   the covenant touches and concerns his land;
(2)   he has sufficient interest to enforce;

---

[18]   *Crest Nicholson v McAllister*, see n 13 above, at para 32, citing *Marquess of Zetland v Driver* [1939] Ch 1.

(3)   the grantor can be bound;

(4)   the covenant is not personal to the original covenantee.

The hard part lies in satisfying the fifth requirement; namely that the benefit is vested in the successor by one of the three established methods:

–   annexation;

–   assignment;

–   the imposition of a building scheme, or scheme of development.

The rest of this chapter will be directed at looking at how the fifth requirement can be met, dealing with each method in turn.

ANNEXATION

8.11   There are two ways in which annexation can be achieved:

–   by express words of annexation;

–   by the application of the Law of Property Act 1925, section 78 (post-31 December 1925 covenants only).

If there are express words of annexation present (or words from which an intention to annex can be implied) whatever the date of the covenant it is not necessary to consider whether section 78 applies. If there are no express words of annexation, or if the implication cannot be made, then if the covenant was imposed after 31 December 1925, section 78 *may* apply so as to annex the benefit of the covenant.

In those cases where it is clear that *Federated Homes* and section 78 do effect annexation, it is not necessary to consider the technical rules of annexation, although, as **8.18** points out, it is still necessary to consider what land is within the scope of the benefit as annexed and whether it is in fact benefited. To that extent some of the dry and technical rules set out in **8.13** have to be satisfied even when section 78(1) may apply.

Express annexation

8.12   What does 'annexation' mean and how do you recognise it?

(1)   In its simplest form, annexation denotes words 'attaching' the covenant to the property which it is to benefit. The effect is similar to that of an easement being annexed to the land which is to be benefited by that easement. Once annexed, it is there forever, subject only to the Lands Tribunal's jurisdiction to discharge, or modify under the Law of Property Act 1925, section 84.[19] Unlike an easement, the benefit so annexed may be something of which the (potentially) proud owner may be unaware; hence the poetic description of such a benefit as 'a hidden treasure which may be discovered in the hour of need'.[20]

---

[19]   See Chapter 16 below.

[20]   Per Simonds J, in *Lawrence v South County Freeholds Ltd* [1939] Ch 656 at 680. Whether a covenantor's successor, who finds that the treasure has been found and is threatened with

(2)   The *essential thing* is that the words of annexation (if they are to be construed as such) must (a) identify the land to be benefited and (b) show that the land so identified is intended to be benefited by the covenant. A covenant merely with 'heirs, executors, administrators and assigns' is not enough to achieve annexation, as there is no reference to any land.[21]

The importance of effective words of annexation is now of a high order in the light of *Crest Nicholson v McAllister*, discussed at **8.18** below.

(3)   Examples:
(After the words of covenant)

'to the intent that the benefit may be annexed to and run with [the land of the Vendor shown on the plan annexed hereto edged green] [the X Estate] [and each and every part thereof]'

'[for the benefit of] [each and every part] [of the land adjoining or near to] [the land being sold with the benefit of the covenant]'[22]

'[for the benefit of] the Vendor's [adjoining and neighbouring] land',[23]

'to benefit and protect [each and every] [such] part[s] of the Vendor's land at X as shall for the time being remain unsold'[24]

a covenant with 'QB his heirs and assigns owners for the time being of freehold properties in [Leicester Square]'[25]

---

enforcement of a supposed 'extinct' covenant would regard this description as helpful, may be open to doubt. See n 16 at **8.7** in this context.

[21]   See *Marquess of Zetland v Driver*, see n 18 above; *Shropshire County Council v Edwards* (1982) 46 P&CR 270, at pp 277–278, and see **8.18** below.

[22]   Held a valid form of words of annexation in *Rogers v Hosegood* [1900] 2 Ch 388. See *Crest Nicholson v McAllister* (at n 13 above), at para 31.

[23]   Words of annexation approved in *Russell v Archdale* [1964] Ch 38. See also *Re Selwyn's Conveyance* [1967] Ch 674 for a variation on these words.

[24]   Words of annexation approved in *Marquess of Zetland v Driver*, see n 18 above. In *Howard Pryor Ltd v Christopher Wren Ltd* (unreported) 24 October 1995, per Knox J, it was held that 'for the time being' meant 'from time to time' in the context of the development then being construed. In *Crest Nicholson v McAllister* (n 13 above) it was held (at para 48) that the words of annexation ('for the benefit of the property at Claygate aforesaid belonging to [the company] or the part thereof for the time being remaining unsold') meant that land sold thereafter by the company (the original covenantee) was excluded from the land intended to be benefited as 'for the time being' meant 'from time to time' and that would exclude land later sold off by the company. Thus the intention was to limit the annexation of the benefit to the land retained, and not sold off. The justification (at para 48 of the judgment of Chadwick LJ) was that, unless this construction was adopted, the benefit of (for example) consent covenants would be vested in every subsequent purchaser, and that person's ability to enforce would depend on the order of sales off: see **8.18**. *Howard Pryor* appears not to have been cited in *Crest Nicholson*. In *Howard Pryor*, Knox J came to the same conclusion as regards the need to limit the scope of the consent covenants to the original vendors in order to avoid a large number of persons (as successors to the vendors in respect of sold-off plots) whose consent might have to be obtained.

[25]   Held sufficient words of annexation in *R v Westminster City Council, ex parte Leicester Square Coventry Street Association Ltd* (1989) 59 P&CR 51. In that case the covenants which had been before the Court in *Tulk v Moxhay* in 1848 were under review, as that case also concerned Leicester Square. See also *Re Ballard's Conveyance* [1937] Ch 473, where the covenant was with the vendor and 'her heirs and assigns and successors in title owners from time to time of the Childwickbury Estate.'

'for the benefit of the company's estate at Croydon' [held sufficient words of annexation in *Whitgift Homes v Stocks* [2001] EWCA Civ 1732]

'with intent that the covenant may enure to the benefit of the vendors their successors and assigns and others claiming under them to all or any of their lands adjoining'[26]

'with the vendors and his assigns owner or owners for the time being of the Vendor's X estate using that term in the broad and popular sense'[27]

'the covenants are to run with the lands of the Vendor'[28]

'adjoining property of the vendor' (*Stilwell v Blackman* [1968] Ch 508.)

Where there are no express words of annexation

Other rules for annexation to be effective.

This is a dry and technical area of law and it is easy to get lost in the welter of authority which exists on the subject. But for those who need some relatively simple guidance on the annexation of pre-1926 covenants, or in cases of post-1925 covenants where there may be an issue over whether section 78 applies, here are some rules which may assist.

Rule 1

8.13 *The land intended to be benefited must be easily ascertainable.* If the benefited land is identified and if (*but only if*) the instrument containing the covenant (or from admissible external evidence) shows clearly that the land so identified is *intended* to be benefited by the covenant, annexation will be achieved.[29] There must be no evidence of the reservation of the benefit of the covenant to the vendor on subsequent sales off by him.

This rule excludes from annexation, cases where the land intended to be benefited cannot be identified under the test above and cases of personal covenants. It also excludes covenants which merely affect the covenanting parties in a personal capacity, such as certain 'tie' covenants, so far as they may be enforceable. Another example where such an intention to benefit in accordance with the principles set out at **8.4** above may not be present, is in the case of covenants taken by the owner of a highway when, after adoption, the restrictions do not touch and concern the interest retained by the owner who remains owner of the sub soil of the highway.[30]

---

[26] The 'classic formula' expressed in Megarry & Wade, *The Law of Real Property* (Sweet & Maxwell, 6th edn, 1999), at p 1026.

[27] As in *Wrotham Park Estate Co Ltd v Parkside Homes Ltd* [1974] 1 WLR 798.

[28] As in *Shropshire County Council v Edwards* (1982) 46 P&CR 270.

[29] *Crest Nicholson v McAllister*, see n 13 above (post-1925 covenants); *Re MCA East Ltd* [2003] 1 P&CR 9 (pre-1926 covenants).

[30] *Kelly v Barrett* [1924] 2 Ch 379. Also excluded will be cases where there are words showing that unless certain conditions are met (eg express assignment) the benefit will not pass; see *Marquess of Zetland v Driver* [1939] Ch 1; *Roake v Chadha* [1984] 1 WLR 40. The words used identifying the

Rule 2

The form of words used to annex the benefit of a covenant is not the only material which can be used (and see the various forms at (3) above) but it must be possible to find either express words, or surrounding circumstances which allow (by the admission of extrinsic evidence) the instrument containing the covenant to be construed as one which manifests an intention that the benefit should be annexed to the land retained by the covenantee.[31]

Rule 3

8.14 A covenant which is imposed to allow the vendor to exploit the benefit of it by assigning the benefit of it at a future date to individual purchasers, or by exacting further payments as the price of a release, will not be found to be annexed.[32]

Rule 4

In the case of covenants entered into between 31 December 1881 and 31 December 1925, section 58 of the Conveyancing and Law of Property Act 1881 does not effect annexation where there is no express, or implied intention to annex the benefit of the covenant in accordance with rule 2 above.[33] That section is in different terms from section 78.

Rule 5

If rules 1 and 2 are satisfied, it is still necessary to identify the land to which the covenant is annexed.

Where plans are not used, and where words such as 'adjoining' or 'neighbouring' or 'near to' or 'adjacent' are found, this may prompt an inquiry as to what land was within the scope of those words at the time the covenant was taken.[34]

---

benefited land may themselves be inflexible and at a later date it may be possible to argue that the land as described no longer exists and the covenant is 'spent'. For a recent example, see *Dano Ltd v Earl Cadogan* [2004] 1 P&CR 131 'the Cadogan Settled Estate in Chelsea'.

[31] Authority for rules 1 and 2 is also found in modern form in *J Sainsbury Plc v Enfield Borough Council* [1989] 1 WLR 590, at 595–597; *Robins v Berkeley Homes* [1996] EGCS 75; and in *Re MCA East Ltd* [2003] 1 P&CR 9. See *Crest Nicholson v McAllister*, see n 13 above, and at **8.18** below.

[32] As was found to be the case in *J Sainsbury v Enfield LBC*, above and in the earlier authority of *Chambers v Randall* [1923] 1 Ch 149.

[33] Section 58 is printed at Appendix 1. See *J Sainsbury Plc v Enfield LBC*, above, at 601, per Morritt J.

[34] See **7.5** above. See *Wrotham Park Estate Co Ltd v Parkside Homes Ltd* [1974] 1 WLR 798 at 806. See *Dano v Earl Cadogan* [2003] 2 P&CR 10 (at para 49, per Etherton J) where it was agreed that 'neighbouring' meant property capable of being benefited by the covenant. See also *Cobstone Investments v Maxim* [1985] 1 QB 140 (cited in that paragraph) on the meaning of the word 'adjoining'.

Rule 6

8.15 There is a rebuttable presumption that the covenant will allow the land (identified under rule 5 as the benefited land) to derive value from the existence of the covenant. (In lawyers' words the land will be presumed in the absence of evidence to the contrary to be 'touched and concerned' by the covenant).[35]

Evidence may, therefore, have to be adduced as to the extent to which the benefit can be shown to be of value to the land so identified.[36]

Rule 7

If the benefit of the covenant can be shown only to benefit a portion of the land identified (as the land to which the covenant is annexed) it may be difficult to sever the covenant and treat it as annexed to that part of the land which derives value from it, but not to that part of the land which does not derive value.

This rule shows the danger of describing the benefited land in terms which are too wide; eg in terms of 'the X estate'.[37]

The rule will not apply where it can be said that the benefit of the covenant is annexed to each and every part of the benefited land. For in such a case the court is entitled to find that the benefit of the covenant can be shown to run for the benefit of a particular part and there is no need to sever the good from the bad.[38]

In view of rule 8 below, since the decision in *Federated Homes*, it is open to question whether, if (as a matter of implication) the covenant is annexed to each and every part of the benefited land, there will nowadays be the need to 'sever' the benefit of the covenant for the purposes of annexation of the benefit to part of the land but not another part. There may yet be an instance where rule 8 does not apply and, therefore, as a matter of construction, the covenant is annexed to the whole and the problem of severance will be present. The decision in *Crest Nicholson v McAllister* (above) whilst not dealing with the 'each and every part' issue, does raise the question, when considering the identity of the land intended to be benefited, whether each and every part was in fact *intended* to be so benefited. To this extent this aspect of the decision in *Federated Homes* may have to be reconsidered by a court in the light of *Crest Nicholson*.

---

[35]　See **7.9** above for the main authorities, and see *Cryer v Scott Brothers (Sunbury) Ltd* (1986) 55 P&CR 183, where the presumption was upheld.

[36]　As it was in the *Wrotham Park* case, at n 34 above.

[37]　This was the result in *Re Ballard* [1937] Ch 473, where the court refused to sever a covenant annexed to the Childwickbury Estate amounting to 1700 acres, where the benefit of the covenant was shown (on uncontradicted evidence) not to extend over the whole of the area. The same problem is encountered in restraint covenant cases, where the court will not sever where the effect would be to alter the nature of the covenant. See Treitel, *The Law of Contract*, (Sweet & Maxwell, 11th ed, 2003), pp 504–512, for the court's approach in that area. In *Hallam Land v UK Coal* [2002] 2 EGLR 89 (in the context of the exercise of an option) the words 'development of the property' meant the entirety of the property, and not just part thereof.

[38]　As in *Marquess of Zetland v Driver*, see n 18 above.

Rule 8

8.16 It will generally be presumed that the benefit of a covenant will be annexed to each and every part of the land for which it is expressed and intended to be taken. However, in the light of the observation at the end of paragraph 7 it is suggested that care should be taken when applying this 'rule'.

Quite apart from potentially solving problems of severance referred to under rule 7, the rule will avoid the need for argument on the question whether, in cases where the retained land has been subdivided since the covenant was taken, the potential claimant has the benefit vested in him as the owner of such a part. The general rule will be that he does.[39] The rule will be displaced if there is clear evidence to show, as a matter of construction of the instrument containing the covenant, that the covenant is taken for the benefit of the land expressed as a whole only.[40]

Implied annexation

8.17 As will be seen from the text above, annexation will be implied where in the light of the surrounding circumstances as they existed at the time the instrument was entered into, an intention can be found to annex the benefit of the covenant to identifiable land of the covenantee.[41]

There are certain specific 'telltale signs' from which the implication of annexation can be accepted or, if absent, rejected.

(1) Were the covenants made with the covenantees as owners of any neighbouring retained land? If not, annexation will not be implied. The mere use of the words 'heirs' and 'assigns' is not enough.

(2) Were the covenantees resident on the retained land, or did they intend to reside there? If not, annexation will not be implied. (This may be difficult evidence to find in the case of old covenants.)

(3) An intention that the covenants should be with vendors personally so that they can exploit them, by way either of express assignment of the benefit to particular purchasers, or by obtaining payment for release or modification will usually be an indication of an absence of an intention to annexe the benefit of the covenants.

(4) The mere fact that the neighbouring estate of the vendor might be more valuable if the benefit of the covenant was annexed to it is not in itself evidence of an intention to annex the benefit of a covenant.[42]

---

[39] This rule is derived from *Federated Homes Ltd v Mill Lodge Properties Ltd* [1980] 1 WLR 594, at 606, per Brightman LJ, his dictum being supported by the other members of the Court of Appeal at 607–608.

[40] *Crest Nicholson v McAllister*, see n 13 above, reinforces this point in view of the need to identify the land intended to be benefited; was it the whole or each and every part of it? In *Whitgift Homes v Stocks* [2001] EWCA Civ 1732, it was conceded (by covenant for the appellant's developers) that if the benefit of the covenants was annexed to the whole of the land potentially having that benefit, it was also annexed to a particular part of it. See **8.32** where this authority is discussed in the context of schemes of development.

[41] *Re MCA East* [2003] 1 P&CR 9, at paras 20–28, per Blackburne J, applying *Reid v Bicherstaffe* [1909] 2 Ch 305, *Drake v Gray* [1936] Ch 451, and *J Sainsbury v Enfield LBC* [1989] 1 WLR 590.

[42] See *Re MCA East Ltd* above.

Annexation under Law of Property Act 1925, section 78(1): the effect of *Federated Homes* and *Crest Nicholson v McAllister*

8.18   *Pre-and post-31 December 1925 restrictive covenants: annexation*

In respect of covenants imposed before 1 January 1926 in the absence of a chain of assignments, or the imposition of a scheme of development, it is necessary to show that the benefit of the covenant was *annexed* to land. That requires the instrument creating the covenant to be construed so as to show what land is intended to be benefited together with an intention to benefit that land, as opposed to an intention to benefit the covenantee personally. In respect of covenants imposed after 31 December 1925, section 78 of the Law of Property Act 1925 will apply so as to effect annexation of the benefit of the covenant, *provided* that the covenant is enforceable at the suit of a successor in title of the covenantee (ie it is not personal) or a person deriving title under the covenantee (ditto). In such a case the owner or occupier of the land intended to be benefited by the covenant can enforce. The significant condition for section 78 to apply is that there will *only* be annexation by that section to the land *intended to be benefited* by the covenant. It will be seen below, if that land cannot be easily identified there will be no annexation under section 78.[43]

8.19   (1) Section 78(1) states:

'A covenant relating to any land of the covenantee shall be deemed to be made with the covenantee and his successors in title and the persons deriving title under him or them, and shall have effect as if such successors and other persons were expressed.

For the purposes of this subsection in connexion with covenants restrictive of the user of land "successors in title" shall be deemed to include the owners and occupiers for the time being of the land of the covenantee intended to be benefited.'

8.20

(2) Section 78(1) will only apply so as to permit a claimant relying on it to enforce a covenant if the following requirements are met:

(a)   The covenant must have been made after 31 December 1925.

(b)   The covenant must be one which was entered into at a time when the covenantee had land and the covenant must be one which 'touches and concerns' that land; see **7.9**.

(c)   The covenant must 'relate to' the land of the covenantee, or at least to part of it. Note the use of those words in section 78(1). Following a dictum of Brightman LJ in Federated Homes, 'relate to' has the same meaning as 'touch and concern'.[44]

(d)   The potential claimant, seeking to enforce its reliance upon section 78 must have an interest in that land, either as a freehold owner, or as a

---

[43]   *Federated Homes v Mill Lodge Properties* [1980] 1 WLR 594; *Staffordshire County Council v Edwards* (1982) 46 P&CR 270; *Crest Nicholson Residential (South) Ltd v McAllister* [2004] EWHC Civ 410.

[44]   *Federated Homes v Mill Lodge Properties*, at 605B–C.

person with the right to call for the legal estate, or as an occupier; see **8.5** above.[45]

(e)   The land intended to be benefited by the covenant must be clearly and easily ascertainable from either the instrument imposing the covenant or from other admissible evidence. In practice this may be the difficult part. Evidence of the land intended to be benefited may be hard to find, especially in registered titles, where pre-registration deeds have been destroyed or lost. See **8.13** above.

(f)   Section 78(1) must not be expressly, or impliedly, excluded.

8.21   Section 78 may be excluded by words which make it plain that there is to be no annexation, or that it is to be limited. One example would be where the benefit is not to pass unless expressly assigned.[46]

It is possible to satisfy section 78 and the requirement that the covenant must relate to land of the covenantee which is intended to be benefited where there are no actual words in the instrument which expressly, or by implication identify that land. *Crest Nicholson* establishes (on the basis of earlier authority such as *Marquess of Zetland v Driver*) that it is possible to adduce evidence from outside the instrument to allow such identification. Whether that evidence comes from the instrument, or is extrinsic to it, should not matter; there must be something in the extrinsic evidence which will allow the court, on the balance of probabilities, to find that the *covenant relates to certain land intended to be benefited by it.* But the effect of *Crest Nicholson* often places a heavy burden on a claimant who has to prove with evidence that may be hard or impossible to find, that he has the benefit.

8.22   Two final points under this paragraph.

(1)   It seems reasonably clear from such authority as there may be that annexation cannot be achieved by contending that Law of Property Act 1925, section 62(l) effects annexation by the general words which apply on a conveyance of land.[47]

---

[45]   A licensee may not be within the scope of s 78(1). He did not have standing to object to an application under s 84(1) where he was the licensee of land to which annexation had been effected under s 78 in *Re Da Costa's Application* (1986) 52 P&CR 99.

[46]   At para 43 of the judgment of the court in *Crest Nicholson*, Chadwick LJ, explains the difference between s 78(1) and 79 and the reason why the words 'unless a contrary intention is expressed' are found in the latter, but not in the former provision. This is because that qualification (namely the ability to exclude section 78(1) by and expression of contrary intention) is implicit in the words which define 'successors in title' as including the owners and occupiers for the time being of the land of the covenantee *intended to be benefited.* Thus s 78(1) will not apply where, for example, an express assignment of the benefit of the covenant is required; as in *Marquess of Zetland v Driver,* at n 18 above, or *Roake v Chadha* [1984] 1 WLR 40. In such a case the owners and occupiers of the land sold off are not 'successors in title' and they are not owners and occupiers of the land 'intended to be benefited'. In *Roake v Chadha* (above), the court refused to accept that s 78 had a mandatory operation, even though the express words in s 79 ('unless a contrary intention is expressed') are not found in s 78(1). The express words of the covenant were against automatic annexation under s 78(1). (An argument based on implied annexation under the Law of Property Act 1925, s 62 also failed; see the report at p 47.) See also *Robins v Berkeley Homes* [1996] EGCS 75, for an important analysis of the manner in which s 78 will apply so as to annex the benefit of a covenant. In *Crest Nicholson v McAllister,* at n 13 above; *Roake v Chadha* (above) was applied (and approved). *Robins* appears not to have been cited.

[47]   *Roake v Chadha,* above; *Kumar v Dunning* [1989] QB 193. For recent authority (in the context of a break clause in a lease) on the scope of ss 62 and 63 of the Law of Property Act 1925, see *Harbour Estates Ltd v HSBC Bank plc* [2004] EWHC 1714 Ch (15 July 2004, Lindsay J).

(2)   It is unclear whether unilateral action by the covenantee (who has the
       benefit by assignment) to 'annex' the benefit of the covenant, without
       the consent of the covenantor can be effective.[48] It is suggested that
       there is no reason why a benefit cannot be so annexed. Nor is there any
       reason why a benefit should not be conferred on a third party without,
       even, his knowledge, or approval.

(3)   As is pointed out by Chadwick LJ, at paras 45–52 of his judgment in
       Crest-Nicholson the land 'for the time being remaining unsold' of the
       vendor limits annexation to land 'from time to time' remaining unsold.
       This limits annexation to land retained by the company and does not
       annex the benefit to land sold off at a later date. See **8.29** below.

ASSIGNMENT

What is assignment?

8.23

(1)   This is the process whereby the benefit of a covenant (being in essence the
       right to sue which is a form of chose in action) can be passed by an express
       form of words which show that A (the assignor) intends to and does assign
       the benefit of the covenant to B (the assignee).

(2)   The need to prove assignment of the benefit of a covenant is generally limited
       to cases where covenants were entered into before 1926, or in the case of
       post-1925 covenants, where section 78 is not applicable.

How will assignment be revealed?

8.24

(1)   The title should show that in each instrument by which the freehold land
       benefited has passed, there has been an express reference to the benefit of the
       covenant and that it is to pass to the assignee. If there is no such reference,
       and unless annexation is found, the benefit of the covenant will not pass.

(2)   In unregistered titles the deeds forming the evidence of title back to the root,
       or beyond if the covenant is earlier, will indicate, one way or another, whether
       there is evidence of assignment of the benefit.

(3)   In registered titles, it may be more difficult to detect whether there has been
       such assignment. As explained at **4.19** and **8.7** above, because the general
       policy of the Land Registry is and has been not to enter the benefit of
       covenants on the benefited land, detection of any assignment will require an
       examination of the transfers whilst the land has been registered (copies should
       have been filed with the register by the Land Registry) and an examination of
       the deed inducing registration (a copy of which should be kept by the Land

---

[48]   This concept was referred to in *Federated Homes*, above, by the first instance court and the Court
       of Appeal as 'delayed annexation by assignment' but no approval to this concept was given by
       either court; see [1980] 1 WLR at 603H.

Registry) and any pre-registration deeds of earlier vintage coming into existence subsequently to the imposition of the covenant.

What other technicalities are there for an assignment to be valid?

8.25

(1) Whether assignment of the benefit has been achieved ought to be a simple affair. But a number of highly technical rules have developed in this area of law, and the following rules have to be observed before it can be said that the benefit of the covenant has passed by assignment.

(2) These rules are normally only applicable when it is an assignee of the covenantee who is suing a successor of the covenantor. The latter is only liable if the covenant satisfies the *Tulk v Moxhay* requirement that it is a restrictive covenant which 'touches and concerns' the covenantee's land. (See Chapter 7 above.)

(3) In cases where the original covenantor is being sued by an assign of the covenantee, the latter need only prove the fact of the assignment to him.

(4) The rules on the assignment of the benefit of a covenant where successors in title are suing and being sued, are, therefore as follows:

8.26

(a) *Rule 1: The covenant must have been taken for the benefit of ascertainable land of the covenantee which is capable of being benefited by the covenant.*
     This rule follows the requirement in annexation (as to which see **8.11** above). However, in view of the fact that in the instrument creating the covenant there will be no words of the type found where there has been annexation to identify the land benefited, other evidence must be adduced of the circumstances surrounding the taking of the covenant. Sometimes this evidence may be difficult to establish, particularly where the covenants are old, but that may be seen as the penalty for not annexing the benefit.[49]

(b) *Rule 2:* The assignment must be made at, or substantially at, the same time as the conveyance of the benefited land. If made at a later date, it will be effective to satisfy the outstanding equitable right in the assignee to have the assignment perfected.[50]

(c) *Rule 3:* An assignment may be made in respect of part of the benefited land.[51]

---

[49] See *Miles v Easter* [1933] Ch 611. See *Newton Abbot Co-operative Society Ltd v Williamson & Treadgold* [1952] Ch 286, for the approach to the question of an intention to benefit as shown from the circumstances and see also *Marten v Flight Refuelling* [1962] Ch 115 for the 'broad and reasonable view' to be taken as to the identity of the land to be benefited. See the *Crest Nicholson* decision refered to at **8.18** above, which it is suggested, applies in this context so far as it emphasises the need to identify the land intended to be benefited, even though that was a decision on annexation.

[50] *Miles v Easter*, above, at 632 per Romer LJ.

[51] *Russell v Archdale* [1964] Ch 38.

8.27

    (d)   *Rule 4:*   There must be a complete chain of assignments.[52] A separation of the title to the land from the benefit of the covenant is fatal.

    (e)   *Rule 5:*   The assignment must comply with the Law of Property Act 1925, section 53(1)(a). It must, therefore, be in writing and signed by the assignor, or his agent, in order to be valid.

(5)   The extent to which an assignment has to comply with the Law of Property Act 1925, section 136(1) seems debatable. Although that section requires notice to be given to the owner of the burdened land, it seems that this is not frequently done. In practice, a failure to comply should not affect the right of the assignee to enforce, provided he gives notice under section 136 prior to bringing any claim on the covenant; for example to enforce it.[53]

SCHEMES OF DEVELOPMENT

What's in a name?

8.28   An original developer of land may decide to set up a comprehensive scheme of covenants which are designed to be enforceable by and against all the owners from time to time of land on the estate governed by the scheme. The schemes are variously called 'schemes of development' and 'building schemes'. In this chapter the former name will be used.

Why are schemes of development used?

8.29

(1)   A person seeking to enforce a covenant must show that he has the benefit of the covenant. The earlier chapters have shown that unless he is the original covenantee, or unless he has the benefit of an assignment, or the annexation of the covenant to his land (expressly, or by statute), he will be unable to enforce the covenant which might seem to be in his favour.

(2)   This is because of the 'before and after' problem. This manifests itself in two ways, depending on the order and form of the conveyance from the common vendor who took and imposed the covenants. Invariably, an estate is developed by sales of individual plots and the vendor takes a covenant from the purchaser of each plot (for the benefit of the vendor's unsold land) to the effect that the purchaser will comply with a set of covenants designed to preserve the appearance and amenity of the estate. (See Appendix 6.)

---

[52]   *Re Pinewood Estate Farnborough* [1958] Ch 280. For a detailed analysis of how there may be assignment by implication, see Scamell, *Land Covenants* (Butterworths, 1986), at pp 102–106. While the latter point is open to doubt, practitioners can only safely rely on the complete chain of assignments.

[53]   See Treitel, n 37 above, pp 676–704, for the formal rules governing assignments under s 136. In the rare cases where a chain of express assignments have to be relied upon, the important point for the practitioner is to give written notice of the assignment before action is brought; notice to the covenantor in some other way (eg by disclosure in the claim) has been held not to be good enough; see Treitel, at p 676.

This produces a series of conveyances, or transfers, each diminishing the land of the covenantee vendor, until by the last disposition there is none left. This situation produces the two problems referred to below.

8.30

    (a) *Problem No 1:* The intending claimant's title is derived from a conveyance by the common vendor which is earlier than the potential defendant's title derived from the same vendor.

        Example (See Appendix 6.)

        The common vendor (V) sells the Chesney Wold estate imposing covenants on each transfer for the remainder of that estate belonging to the vendor. A's predecessor acquires title from V on 1 January 1990. B's predecessor acquires title from V on 1 March 1990. A wishes to sue B for breach of covenant by B on his land. C also wishes to sue B, having acquired title on 1 November 1989.

        The problem A's covenant is with V made on 1 January 1990 and the benefit is annexed to V's land at that date. But on 1 March 1990 V did not own A's land and B covenanted only with V for the benefit of the remainder of the estate.

        Unless the covenant is expressed to have been made with and for the benefit of those who have already bought, and not just V, B can say that the covenant was not with anyone other than V, and was not made with A.[54]

        The irony in this situation (described as 'Gilbertian' by Stamp J in *Re Jeff's Transfer*) is that B can sue A for breaches of covenant on A's land. This is because B has the benefit of the covenant A gave V which was annexed to the remainder of the Chesney Wold estate on 1 January 1990, and part of which was bought by B on 1 March 1990. C, who took title from V on 1 November 1989, cannot sue A or B, but may be sued by either of A or B.[55]

8.31

    (b) *Problem No 2:* This problem is less often encountered than problem No 1, and is caused by the failure of the common vendor to annex the benefit of the covenants being imposed when the estate is being sold off, or to have express assignments of the benefit, or to identify the land intended to be benefited. In view of the decision in *Crest Nicholson v McAllister* [2004] EWCA Civ 410 (at **8.18** above) it is possible that this problem may emerge in the case of post-1925 covenants where there is a failure to annex the benefit of the covenants to the land retained to *each and every part* of the vendor's estate by the Law of Property Act 1925, section 78(1).[56]

        Example (See Appendix 6.)

---

[54] Law of Property Act 1925, s 56, may be thought to be a way round this problem in the sense that the section extends the scope of the benefit of the covenant to the earlier purchaser. But A is not within the ambit of any covenant given by B to V; see **6.7** above. It is also assumed that the Contracts (Rights of Third Parties) Act 1999 has no application.

[55] See *Crest Nicholson v McAllister*, at n 13 above and see **8.21** above.

[56] See *Allen v Veranne Builders* [1988] NPC 11. See **8.16** above.

The dates of sales off have been altered as below. As in problem No 1 above, V is selling off the Chesney Wold Estate, but the forms of conveyance of each plot do not annex the benefit of the covenant to the remainder of the unsold estate, or there is a failure to identify the land intended to be benefited. There are no express assignments. A's predecessor acquired his title from V on 1 March 1990. B's predecessor acquired his title from V on 1 January 1990. A wishes to sue B for breach of covenant on B's land.

The problem

A cannot sue B because B's covenant was given to V for the benefit of the whole of the Chesney Wold estate unsold on 1 January 1990, and not just the part A acquired on 1 March. Alternatively, as in *Crest Nicholson*, there is a failure to identify the land intended to be benefited. The benefit of B's covenant is not, therefore, annexed to A's land. In the absence of a chain of assignments of the benefit of the covenant from V to A, A cannot enforce against B. By a twist of the same irony which arises in problem No 1, B cannot sue A for the reasons stated under that heading. See **8.21** above.

(3)   The two problems show that dates in the order of conveyances and their form[57] are going to be of critical significance in many cases. Without the 'right' order of sales off, or words of annexation, or claims of assignments, it may be possible to enforce the covenant.

(4)   The difficulty can be at its most acute where the potential defendant's title is, historically, the *last* sale off by the common vendor. All the potential claimants will, therefore, be prior in time and there can have been no land retained by the common vendor to which the covenant could have been annexed. The covenants given by the owner of the last plot cannot be enforced by the prior plot owners.[58]

(5)   It should be apparent at this stage that the order of sales off by the original common vendor is very important. If the claimant is to enforce without knowing that order, he takes the risk that until service of the defence, he may be ignorant of the order. It should be possible to discover at an early stage whether the potential defendant's title is derived from an earlier, or later sale off, by examining the defendant's register of title at the Land Registry. Online search facilities must, therefore, be used to assist this task. The detective work and the use of a 'master plan' referred to at **8.7(8)** above will be required. This should refer to the covenant imposed by the common vendor. The date of the conveyance imposing it will tell the claimant whether it is before (bad news) or after (good news) the defendant's title. If the title is unregistered it is a wise precaution to seek early disclosure of the potential defendant's title;

---

[57]   That means identifying the land intended to be benefited.

[58]   See the 'last man out' scenario at **7.6** above. The position whereby (on the footing that there has been effective annexation of the benefit) in a 'non-scheme world' the first purchaser cannot enforce any of the covenants of the later purchasers from the common vendor, and where the last purchaser can enforce all of them, was described as 'a building scheme in Alice in Wonderland' by Ungoed-Thomas J. In *Eagling v Gardner* [1970] 2 All ER 838, cited in *Crest Nicholson* at para 48, see **8.21** above. It will also be recalled from Alice in Wonderland that in the game of croquet (using flamingos) there were no winners, or losers, but 'all shall have prizes'. This is not quite the same when considering who can enforce restrictive covenants.

the latter can hardly object in view of the fact that, if the title deduced shows an earlier sale off, that will be an end of the claim. If later, such title would have had to be deduced as part of the disclosure in the claim in any case. The same point is also true to the extent that the form of words in the conveyance imposing the covenants, or the presence (or absence) of assignments will indicate whether there is an additional problem is establishing that the potential claimant has the benefit of the covenants at all. In present day litigation, as is pointed out in Chapter 15, the 'rules of engagement' now require early disclosure. Compliance with early disclosure under the General Protocol is very significant in this context. As is pointed out in that chapter, non-compliance with the General Protocol may have a bearing on the outcome in terms of the cost of any claim.

The scheme of development

8.32 The scheme of development is designed to avoid these problems and difficulties of enforcement. Where a scheme exists, all owners of plots within the scheme can enforce and be enforced against, irrespective of the order in which the common vendor sold those plots and irrespective of the formalities regarding annexation and assignment of the benefit of covenants.

A word of caution: schemes of development are rare

It is tempting to see schemes of development around every corner when examining titles of building estates. In fact they are quite rare and are far less encountered than might be supposed. [59]

What is required for a valid scheme of development?

8.33   The requirements are:

(1)   Both the claimant and defendant derive title from a *common vendor*.
(2)   Prior to selling the land to which the claimant and defendant are entitled, the common vendor laid out the estate (or a defined portion of it) for sale in *lots*, subject to *restrictions intended to be imposed on all the lots*. Those *restrictions*, although they may vary in details as to particular lots, are consistent and consistent only with some general scheme of development.
(3)   The restrictions are intended by the common vendor to be and are *for the benefit of all the lots intended to be sold*, whether or not they are also intended to be and are for the benefit of other land retained by the common vendor.
(4)   Both the claimant and defendant (or their predecessors in title) purchased their lots from the common vendor on the footing that the restrictions subject to which the purchases were made were to *enure for the benefit of the other*

---

[59]   For a recent example of a scheme of development (or letting scheme) applying in the context of landlord and tenant covenants, as between business tenants of a common landlord in a parade of shops, see *Williams v Kiley* [2002] EWCA Civ 1645; [2004] EWCA Civ 870.

lots included in the general scheme, whether or not they were to enure for the benefit of other lands retained by the vendor.[60]

In many cases the existence of a scheme will be obvious, at least where it is well established that such a scheme affects properties within a given area. In addition, the registered title of a plot owner may contain an entry (usually in standard form) referring to the fact that the land in the title falls within the area covered by a building scheme constituted by a conveyance of given date. The policy of the Land Registry would still appear to enter notice of such schemes on the titles affected where they are established. The Land Registry records and titles are kept in such a way that on first registration of a plot within the area of a scheme, that event will 'trigger' the making of the appropriate entry.

8.34   Whether a scheme of development exists or not, is a question of fact to be determined from the terms of the titles and the relevant circumstances surrounding the sales by the common vendor to the various purchasers. Thus, where there is a question as to the existence of a scheme the burden lies on the party seeking to establish it as a matter of fact within the principles set out at **8.33** above.[61]

Where the existence of a scheme is not clearly established, the following points should be considered when examining whether the four main elements set out at **8.33** are satisfied.

(1)   Is there any doubt as to the common vendor test being satisfied?
  –   It may not matter if during the course of the sales under the scheme, the identity of the 'common' vendor changes.[62]
  –   The identity of the common vendor may be a matter of inference from the title.[63]
(2)   Is the area of the scheme defined, and how is it defined?
  –   Consider the use of maps; clear evidence of the land to which the scheme relates is essential.[64]
  –   Local knowledge may assist in explaining plans.[65]
  –   Are there solicitors with knowledge of the extent of the area?[66]

---

[60]   These four sub-headings are taken from the words of Parker J in *Elliston v Reacher* [1908] 2 Ch 374 at 384 and applied in *Reid v Bicherstaffe* [1909] 2 Ch 305. His classification was described by Browne-Wilkinson V-C as the '*locus classicus*' in *Allen v Veranne Builders* (1988) NPC 11 (judgment delivered 5 February 1988). The modern approach has been to discern the existence of a scheme from the 'wider rule' which forms the basis of such schemes, which is itself founded on the intention of the parties that the various purchasers are to have rights *inter se*; see *Baxter v Four Oaks Properties Ltd* [1965] Ch 816 and *Re Dolphin's Conveyance* [1970] Ch 654, at 663, per Stamp J. In *Whitgift Homes Ltd v Stocks* [2001] EWCA Civ 1732, the Court of Appeal applied the statements of principle set out in *Reid v Bicherstaffe* (above) and summarised under paras (i) to (iv) above, and held that a scheme did not operate over the whole of the site.

[61]   *Jamaica Mutual Life Assurance Society v Hillsborough Ltd* [1989] 1 WLR 1101.

[62]   As it did in *Re Dolphin's Conveyance*, at n 60 above.

[63]   As it was in *Re Elm Avenue* [1984] 1 WLR 1398 at 1406.

[64]   *Jamaica Mutual Life Assurance Society v Hillsborough Ltd*, at n 58 above. *Whitgift Homes Ltd v Stocks*, at n 69 above. This is a pure question of fact.

[65]   As did the solicitor's clerk in *Page v King's Parade Properties Ltd* (1967) 20 P&CR 710, when dealing with the Marine Park Estate at Bognor Regis. If the area of land to which the scheme is said to apply is not clear, or which may only apply to certain properties, the argument in favour of a scheme will fail: *Whitgift Homes Ltd v Stocks* [2001] EWCA Civ 1732, at para 100, per Jonathan Parker LJ. See also ibid at para 111, per Judge LJ.

[66]   As were the solicitors acting for the plaintiffs in *Allen v Veranne Builders Ltd* who had extensive knowledge of the conveyancing history of the Winderness Estate near Sevenoaks in Kent.

(3)   What evidence is there of prior lotting?
   –   Recent authority suggest that this is not essential.[67]
(4)   There must be evidence that it was intended that the purchasers of the lots are to have mutual rights and obligations. *'Reciprocity of obligations between purchasers of different plots is essential'.*[68]
   –   Lack of uniformity in the covenants is fatal to a scheme; some variation may be acceptable within a scheme (eg in a mixed scheme user covenants may vary) but unless there is *substantial* uniformity the essential ingredient of uniformity will be missing.[69]

Problem areas in schemes of development

8.35   Within the rules which apply to schemes of development there are areas where problems arise in practice. These are:

(1)   Sub-schemes.
(2)   The sub-division of lots after the original sale.
(3)   The effect on the scheme of the unity of ownership of plots.
(4)   The existence of the power to waive and vary the covenants.
(5)   Problems of non-registration of covenants within a scheme.
(6)   Changes in the neighbourhood and the effect of acquiescence in breaches.

Dealing with each in turn:

(1)   Sub-schemes

8.36   These arise where, for example, A and B as two plot owners agree a set of covenants between themselves to replace the scheme covenants. These covenants will not affect the ability of the other plot owners to enforce the scheme against A and B, and vice versa. But A and B cannot enforce the head scheme between themselves.[70] Sub-schemes are sometimes found to have arisen where the common vendor sells more than one plot to a purchaser (A) who then sells off each plot separately to B, C and D, imposing covenants on each of B, C and D. The head scheme covenants into which A entered with the common vendor cannot be enforced by B, C or D between themselves. But B, C and D can enforce the covenants each entered into with A, assuming that the benefit can be shown to be enforceable on the usual principles; eg section 78. The head scheme may still be enforceable by persons neighbouring B, C and D's land against any of them in view of A's covenants with the common vendor.

---

[67]   See *Baxter v Four Oaks; Re Dolphin*, at n 60 above. But see the need to define the area of the scheme as emphasised in *Whitgift Homes Ltd v Stocks*, at n 60 above). See also *Re MCA East Ltd* [2003] 1 P&CR 9, at para 32, per Blackburne J where the lack of any clear evidence identifying the scheme area and the absence of an estate plan led to the conclusion that there was no scheme (Springfield Park Estate, Acton, West London).

[68]   *Jamaica Mutual Life v Hillsborough Ltd*, at n 61 above, at 1106, per Lord Jauncey.

[69]   See *Kingsbury v Anderson* (1979) 40 P&CR 136; *Emile Elias & Co Ltd v Pine Groves Ltd* (1993) 66 P&CR 1, for examples of where the uniformity was lacking.

[70]   *Knight v Simmonds* [1896] 1 Ch 653, explained by Megarry J in *Brunner v Greenslade* [1971] Ch 993, at 1001.

(2) Sub-division of plots

8.37 In many estates which were developed in the spacious days prior to the Second, if not the First World War, and particularly at the turn of the nineteenth century, the acreage devoted to each house plot was, by modern standards, generous. There is often a later sub-division of the lot. Alternatively, A may acquire two or more lots from the common vendor, and then sell them on as individual lots: see above. In both instances the authorities suggest that, in the absence of an intention expressed at the time of division (eg by the creation of a sub-scheme) the scheme will operate so as to bind and allow the enforcement of it by and against all the sub-purchasers.[71]

(3) Unity of ownership of plots and subsequent severance

8.38 While there is unity of ownership (sometimes referred to a 'unity of seisin') the covenants are unenforceable by virtue of the fact that the owner of the united plots cannot sue himself in respect of his activity on one of the plots he owns. When the ownership is divided again the covenants become enforceable again.[72]

(4) The power to waive and vary the covenants

8.39 There is a conflict in the authorities as to whether the insertion of such a power is consistent with the existence of a scheme, or whether the existence of such a power is such as to negative the concept of mutuality. The modern view seems to be that the existence of such a power will not prevent a scheme from existing.[73] There is a subsidiary point which is whether the power to waive, or vary (or give consent in certain cases) must be exercised by the named vendor, or may be exercised by his successors and assigns.[74] But what if the vendor, is a company and is defunct? In that case it may be necessary to consider applying to the Bona Vacantia department of the Treasury Solicitor for consent, assuming it is not possible to restore the vendor company under Chapter VI of the Companies Act 1985.[75]

---

[71] See *Brunner v Greenslade*, above, approved by the Privy Council in *Texaco Antilles Ltd v Kernochan* [1973] AC 609, at 626, per Lord Cross. See also *Briggs v McCluster* [1996] 2 EGLR 197 (Camden Park Estate, Chislehurst).

[72] See *Texaco Antilles Ltd v Kernochan*, above. The position is different where no scheme of development exists; see, *Re Tiltwood* [1978] Ch 269, referred to at Chapter 13 below.

[73] See *Re Wembley Park Estate Co Ltd's Transfer* [1968] Ch 491, for a collection of older authorities on the subject. See *Re Elm Avenue* [1984] 1 WLR 1398, *Allen v Veranne Builders Ltd* (1988) NPC 11 (5 February 1998), and *Re Bromor's Application* (1995) 70 P&CR 569, for more modern authority in support of the view that such a power does not negate a scheme. In practice the existence of such a power is just one matter to be looked at in the context of the whole in deciding whether a scheme exists. *Allen v Veranne* was considered and applied in *Whitgift Homes Ltd v Stocks* (above at **8.33** and **8.34**). The conclusion in that case was that the ability of the vendor to lay out the land belonging to the vendor without restriction, coupled with the fact that there was no identification of the beneficiary of the covenants, meant that no scheme was intended. Such a clause took 'its flavour from the surrounding circumstances', para 101; per Jonathan Parker LJ.

[74] If there are no words in the relevant deed to include successors and assigns, the power would appear to be personal to the vendor; *Bell v Norman C Ashton Ltd* (1956) 7 P&CR 359. See **14.10** below.

[75] In *Crest Nicholson v McAllister*, at n 13 above, it was held by Neuberger J, that a 'consent' restriction was spent on the dissolution of the company which had power to give that consent.

(5)   Problems of non-registration of covenants in schemes

8.40   As explained in Chapter 4 above, in the case of registered and unregistered land, for a restrictive covenant created after 1925 to be enforceable against the defined classes of successors in title to the original covenantor, it must be registered in accordance with the rules set out in that chapter.

Covenants taken and imposed in the context of a scheme of development are required to be registered in exactly the same way. But unlike covenants taken to protect one piece of land, or in a no-scheme world, the failure to register post-1925 covenants in a scheme can lead to rather more damaging consequences. In essence, the failure to ensure registration will cause gaps to arise as between plot owners, leading to fewer plot owners able to enforce, thereby weakening the overall effect of the scheme; the term 'haphazard islands of immunity' comes to mind.[76]

(6)   Changes in the neighbourhood and the effect of acquiescence in breaches

8.41   It is suggested that there will have to be a radical failure to observe the scheme if covenants in it are to be unenforceable. Whilst acquiescence may affect the remedy, it does not follow that such conduct would automatically lead a court to find the covenants unenforceable as such.[77]

At an early stage in considering the 'unity' of the scheme, evidence should be prepared to test how far the scheme is, or is not, intact. Quite apart from planning records and photographic evidence and Ordnance plans, the use of transparent or computer graphic overlays will show, one way or the other, how far the original scheme has been observed. Evidence presented in this way can be a dramatic demonstration in many cases of how piecemeal departures over a large area of the original scheme has destroyed the unity of it. It is always going to be a matter of fact and degree how far departures from the scheme will affect the Court's willingness to grant injunctive relief. It is suggested that in cases where there is clear evidence of a departure from the scheme, declarations as to non-enforceability may be an option under the Law of Property Act 1925, section 84(2) and the Lands Tribunal may be more willing to modify, or discharge under section 84(1) than in cases where the scheme is still tightly enforced and intact.[78]

That authority suggests that in cases where it is not possible to restore the company to the register, there will be no 'vendor' whose consent is required. See **14.10** below.

[76]   The words used by Megarry J in *Brunner v Greenslade*, above. For an example of the effect of a failure to register see *Freer v Unwins* [1976] Ch 288. See **4.19** above for the practice of the Land Registry when entering the benefit of restrictive covenants.

[77]   See *Knight v Simmonds*, at n 70 above; *Bell v Norman C Ashton Ltd*, at n 74 above; *Chatsworth Estates v Fewell* [1931] 1 Ch 224; *Robins Ltd v Berkeley Homes* [1996] EGCS 75. See **13.3** below.

[78]   See Chapters 15 and 16 below.

Chapter 9

ENFORCEMENT OF COVENANTS BY A SUCCESSOR OF THE ORIGINAL COVENANTEE AGAINST A SUCCESSOR OF THE ORIGINAL COVENANTOR: MAKING BOTH THE BENEFIT AND THE BURDEN OF THE COVENANT RUN

9.1 This chapter looks at the enforceability of covenants between successors to the original parties, not only as regards the benefit of the covenant, but also as regards the burden.

SUMMARY

9.2 In cases where enforcement of restrictive covenants is by and against successors in title to the original parties, the rules which apply to the passing of the benefit and of the burden of the covenant have to be complied with. In essence this chapter pulls together the rules contained in the last two chapters.

THE SITUATION

9.3 A successor of the original covenantee wishes to enforce against a successor of the original covenantor.

THE GENERAL RULE

(1) The claimant must show that he has *the benefit* of the covenant in accordance with the rules set out in Chapter 8 above.
(2) He must also show that the potential defendant is *liable* in that the covenant is:
  (a) valid and binding in accordance with the rules in Chapter 4; and
  (b) enforceable against him in accordance with the rules in Chapter 7.

As this situation is often the most commonly encountered when covenants are being enforced the checklist below, which also summarises the rules for validity and enforcement, can be used. The flowchart at pages 5–7 will also assist.

CHECKLIST

9.4

(1)   Is the covenant binding on the potential defendant as a properly registered covenant (or one to which the doctrine of notice applies)? (Chapter 4)

(2)   Is the covenant restrictive, not being purely personal, and was it taken to protect the covenantee's retained land? (Chapters 3 and 7)

(3)   Does the covenant satisfy the presumption that it benefits land owned by the potential claimant? (Chapter 7)

(4)   Can the potential claimant show that he has the benefit of the covenant by any of the methods set out in Chapter 8? In particular can he show that he has the benefit under the Law of Property Act 1925, section 78(1)?

(5)   If the parties' properties are not within a scheme of development, are there problems with the order in which the parties' predecessors' titles were conveyed by the common vendor? If the claimaint's title is derived from a conveyance from that vendor which is earlier than the defendant's title, the claimant may be unable to enforce, unless the words of the covenant extend to prior purchasers from the common vendor. Is the potential defendant 'the last man out'? If he is and in the absence of a scheme, was no land retained by the common vendor when the defendant's predecessor purchased and gave covenants? (Chapters 7 and 8)

(6)   Is this a case where special statutory rules apply which allow the benefit to be enforced even though no land is retained? (Chapter 10 below.) (Refer also to the checklist at pages 5–7 if necessary.)

Chapter 10

RESTRICTIVE COVENANTS AND PUBLIC AUTHORITIES

10.1   This chapter considers the special rules which apply to restrictive covenants which are created by public authorities acting under statutory powers.

INTRODUCTION

10.2   Special rules govern the enforceability of covenants and other agreements of a similar nature entered into by local and other public authorities, and other bodies with powers derived from statute.

The aim of these special rules is to avoid the problems inherent in enforcing restrictive covenants which private law poses. The principal problem being the inability of a successor of the covenantee to enforce if it possesses no interest in land capable of benefiting from the covenant.[1] The other difficulty, but lying outside the field of restrictive covenants, is that of the general inability of successors in title to enforce positive covenants. Although the subject of positive covenants is outside the scope of this book, it is mentioned if only to demonstrate how Parliament can legislate to overcome the shortcomings of common law and equity, albeit in a limited context.

It should be relatively easy to spot where these special rules apply. The deeds, or agreements in which the covenants are contained will invariably be made expressly under the statutory authority conferring the power to make them. The purpose of this chapter is to identify the statutory provisions which specify the manner in which covenants entered into under them are enforceable.

THE SCHEME OF THE LEGISLATION

10.3   In view of the need to allow enforcement where the covenantee (ie the public authority) has retained no land capable of benefiting from the covenant and a successor to that authority is the enforcing party, Parliament has adopted two methods to allow such enforcement. Each is based on a 'fiction'.

The first is to assume that the authority/covenantee has adjacent land and that the covenant is taken for the benefit of it.

The second is to deem successors to be the original covenantor for the purposes of enforcement.

---

[1]   See **7.5** above.

In some instances the statute incorporates both fictions, or adopts a further variant which treats the ability to enforce positive covenants as if they were negative.

See **6.10** above in respect of the transfer of undertakings and rights and liabilities between public authorities.

THE LEGISLATION

10.4   This divides itself into three broad categories:

(1)   Agreements made with local planning authorities under the Town & Country Planning Act 1990 and its predecessors.

(2)   Agreements made with local and other public authorities for the purpose of enabling those authorities to carry out their statutory functions; eg in respect of roads or housing.

(3)   Agreements made with other bodies where specific statutory provisions allowing enforcement apply.

It will be a matter of construction of the statute as to whether the general law is applicable (so that the covenant may be unenforceable for the reasons summarised at **10.2** above), or whether the statute creates a statutory scheme which may be enforced without the restrictions of the general law.[2]

The legislation is set out at **10.6 below**. But before coming to it, there is one area which can affect the ability to enforce and that is the question whether the covenant taken is within the powers of the body imposing it. Is the covenant *ultra vires*?

A NOTE ON *ULTRA VIRES*

10.5   One of the spectres which occasionally appears in the context of bodies upon which limited powers are conferred is that of the limit of those powers. In the particular context of restrictive covenants, this means that the body may not impose restrictions which conflict with the purpose for which the acquisition is made or with the limit of the statute under which the authority was acting when it imposed the covenant.[3]

---

[2]   See *Peabody Donation Fund v London Residuary Body* (1987) 55 P&CR 355 for an example of how a statute may be construed so as to give effect to conditions entered into under the Act as part of a statutory scheme.

[3]   See *Ayr Harbour Trustees v Oswald* (1883) 8 App Cas 623; *Re South Eastern Railway Co & Wiffin's Contract* [1907] 2 Ch 366; *Stourcliffe Estates Co Ltd v Bournemouth Corp* [1910] 2 Ch 12; *Re Heywood's Conveyance* [1938] 2 All ER 230; *Earl of Leicester v Wells-next-the-Sea UDC* [1973] Ch 110. See *R v Braintree DC ex parte Halls* [2000] 80 P&CR 266, CA, for an example of a covenant being found to be outside the policy and objects of the Housing Act 1985: the 'right to buy' legislation. So far as the covenant (restricting user of the plot to a single dwellinghouse only) was imposed to realise any future development value of the land, that was outside the policy and objects of that Act. The demand by the council for 90 per cent of the open market value of the building plot was, therefore, unlawful. An appeal to the local authority's fiduciary duty to the local taxpayers did not assist the authority in the Court of Appeal.

But the effect of the rule may be less draconian by virtue of:

(a) The principle (expressed in the authorities) that the covenant will not be *ultra vires* and, therefore, will be binding, even if that covenant prevents the covenantor from exercising other statutory powers in respect of the same land.[4]

(b) The wide power conferred by Local Government Act 1972, section 123 giving principal councils power to dispose of land held by them in any manner they wish (subject to the restrictions set out in that section).[5] In practice the width of this power will prevent an *ultra vires* argument being available where covenants are being imposed on disposal.

Finally, the existence of a covenant to use land acquired by a public authority for certain statutory purposes will not prevent that authority from using the land for other statutory purposes at a future date. It may then be open to the authority to consider exercising its powers to pay compensation in respect of any breach under the Town and Country Planning Act 1990, section 237, or to apply to release, or modify under the Law of Property Act 1925, section 84.[6]

THE LEGISLATION

Section 106 of the Town and Country Planning Act 1990[7]

10.6   For the full treatment of this section reference should be made to Volume 2 of the *Encyclopedia of Planning, Law and Practice*, and Volume 5 for the text of DOE Circular 1/97.

In the context of the enforceability of covenants entered into under this section, the following points should be noted:

(1) As a generic class, 'section 106 agreements' will be readily identifiable by virtue of the fact that they will declare on their face the authority under which they are made.

(2) The current terms of section 106 have been in force since 25 October 1991 and, therefore, only agreements entered into after that date are caught by its terms. By subsection 3 any person deriving title from the original covenantor will be bound.[8]

---

4   See *Stourcliffe Estates v Bournemouth Corp*, above, where the covenant against the erection of certain structures validly prevented the construction of public lavatories under statutory authority, whilst not interfering with the main purpose of the acquisition of land as a public park. See also *Cadogan v Royal Brompton Hospital National Health Trust* [1996] 2 EGLR 115, where the covenant restricted the use of the site to one type of hospital and *Thames Water Utilities v Oxford City Council* [1998] EGCS 133 where the use of a football stadium in breach of covenant was not authorised by s 237 of the Town and Country Planning Act 1990.

5   This power extends to those 'principal councils' defined by s 270(1) of the 1972 Act, being county, borough, district and London borough councils and is also extended to include joint authorities in London and elsewhere and police authorities; see s 146A of the 1972 Act.

6   See *Marten v Flight Refuelling* [1962] Ch 115, at 151–3; *Earl of Leicester v Wells-next-the-Sea UDC*, at n 3 above, at 127; see Chapter 12, below, as to the exercise of powers under s 237 and related legislation.

7   Printed at Appendix 2.

8   For the definition of a person deriving title, see s 336(8) of the 1990 Act. This would not appear to include a squatter in view of the fact that his title arises in spite of the title of the dispossessed

(3)   The immediate predecessor of the present version of section 106, which will
      apply to agreements entered into after 14 August 1990 but before 25 October
      1991 was different in that subsection 3 included the 'fiction' of the notionally
      adjacent land, which the agreement benefited. In view of the terms of the
      subsection there appears to be an irrebuttable presumption that the 'notional'
      adjacent land is capable of being benefited by the agreement.[9]

(4)   The statutory predecessors of section 106 of the 1990 Act were:

      Town and Country Planning Act 1971, section 52 in force from 1 April 1972
      Town and Country Planning Act 1962, section 37 in force from 1 April 1963
      Town and Country Planning Act 1947, section 25 in force from 1 July 1948
      Town and Country Planning Act 1932, section 34 in force from 1 April 1933

Agreements made under these statutes during the period for which they were in
force will still be encountered and as regards enforcement, the principles are the
same as under the original terms of section 106. Each incorporates the 'fiction' of
adjacent and benefited land. There is power in the Secretary of State (DEFRA) to
modify or discharge planning agreements under section 106A of the 1990 Act. For
a recent example see *Caton's Application.*[10]

By virtue of the Planning and Compulsory Purchase Act 2004, sections 46–48, the
current regime under sections 106 and 106A of the Town and Country Planning
Act will come to an end when those sections are brought into force. (Schedule 9 of
the Planning and Compulsory Purchase Act 2004 repeals sections 106–106B from
a future date when the provisions of sections 46–48 are brought into force.) At the
time of writing, it is anticipated that, owing to Government policy, and in particular
Treasury policy on a proposed Planning Gain Supplement (in respect of which the
Government will report at the end of 2005), it is unlikely that the terms of
sections 46–48 will be brought into force until early 2007. It is also noteworthy
that the terms of sections 46–48 of the Planning and Compulsory Purchase Act
2004 are very much in skeletal form and the precise terms of the new forms of
agreement to replace those entitled under the current regime will depend on
regulations which, at present, are not even in draft form.

(paper) owner. There appears to be no authority where a squatter as 'successor' to a covenantor has
been the subject of proceedings to enforce a s 106 Agreement. Would a local planning authority in
those circumstances have to show the existence of land capable of being benefited by the terms of
the covenant in the agreement according to private law principles? *Re Nisbet & Pott's Contract*
[1906] 1 Ch 386, decided that a squatter can be made liable upon covenants affecting the land in
respect of which he is in possession.

[9]   See *Gee v National Trust* [1966] 1 WLR 170. That case concerned s 8 of the National Trust Act
      1937. Lord Denning MR favoured this approach, but the other members of the Court of Appeal
      reserved their opinions on it.

[10] [1999] 38 EG 193. For full treatment of this jurisdiction, see the *Encyclopedia of Planning, Law
      and Practice*, vol 2. It also possible to agree a modification or discharge with the authority having
      the benefit of the s 106 Agreement, see s 106A (1) (a)

Other legislation[11]

10.7 Of general application:

- Highways Act 1980, section 35
- Wildlife and Countryside Act 1981, section 39
- Local Government (Miscellaneous Provisions) Act 1982, section 33[12]
- Pastoral Measure 1983, section 62

Of more specific application:

- National Trust Act 1937, section 8 and the restriction imposed on applications under the Law of Property Act 1925, section 84 by the National Trust Act 1971, section 27
- Green Belt (London and Home Counties) Act 1938, section 22
- City of London (Various Powers) Act 1960, section 33
- Leasehold Reform Act 1967, section 19 and the Leasehold Reform, Housing and Urban Development Act 1993, Chapter IV, sections 69–75
- National Parks and Access to the Countryside Act 1949, section 16
- Countryside Act 1968, section 15
- Greater London Council (General Powers) Act 1974, section 16
- Ancient Monuments and Archaeological Areas Act 1979, section 17
- Housing Act 1985, section 609
- Other local Acts: eg Oxfordshire Act 1985, section 4; West Glamorgan Act 1986, section 52.

REGISTRATION OF AGREEMENTS WITH LOCAL AUTHORITIES

10.8 Section 1 of the Local Land Charges Act 1975 makes provision for the registration of prohibitions or restrictions on the use of land binding on successive owners of the land affected.

Section 1 applies to those covenants imposed by local authorities, Ministers of the Crown, or Government departments. It also applies to those covenants which are expressly made local land charges by the legislation conferring power on the body

---

[11] Printed at Appendix 2.

[12] This section has its antecedents in earlier legislation which was designed to overcome the problem described at **7.5**, namely that where no land is owned by the covenantee (or his successors) enforcement of the covenant is impossible. This was the finding in *LCC v Allen* [1914] 3 KB 642, although it was not until 1 July 1925 and the Housing Act 1925 that the problem was addressed in favour of local and other public authorities. The history of what is currently section 33 of the Local Government (Miscellaneous Provisions) Act 1982, as amended, is as follows, by reference to the predecessor Acts and their dates of operation:

2 December 1974–13 July 1982:	Housing Act 1974, section 176
1 September 1957–2 December 1974:	Housing Act 1957, section 151
1 January 1937–1 September 1957:	Housing Act 1936, section 148
1 July 1925–1 January 1937:	Housing Act 1925, section 110

Each of these provisions were in a form which allowed a statutory authority, in whose favour a restrictive covenant could run, to enforce that covenant, notwithstanding that they were not in possession of, or interested in, any land for the benefit of which the covenant was entered into. The fiction was created as if the Local Authority had been possessed of, or interested in, such land.

concerned to enter into them. (For example, Town and Country Planning Act 1990, section 106(11).)

Excluded from the class of local land charges are those covenants entered into by a public body which are taken for the benefit of land owned by it: section 2 thereof. These have to be protected by registration in the usual way.[13]

10.9 Failure to register a local land charge which is properly registrable has the following consequences:

(1) *Covenants entered into before 1 August 1977*. If unregistered, void against a purchaser for money or money's worth of a legal estate in the land affected.[14]

(2) *Covenants entered into on or after 1 August 1977*. If unregistered, the covenant is still enforceable, but a purchaser for valuable consideration who has made a search of the local land charges register and has a 'clear' certificate, has a compensation claim against the registering authority.[15]

There are, however, some covenants which must be registrable to be enforceable, in which case the statutory provision to that effect overrides section 10.[16]

10.10 In respect of post-1 August 1977 covenants which are not registered as local land charges, does it matter whether the title to the land affected is either registered, or unregistered?

It should not in practice matter for the following reasons.

(1) *Unregistered land:* enforceability will depend upon whether a bona fide purchaser for value has notice, or not.

(2) *Registered land:* the same principle should apply. Before 13 October 2003, even though the class of overriding interests included 'rights under local land charges unless and until registered or protected on the register in the prescribed manner' (Land Registration Act 1925, section 80(1)(i)), the mere status as an overriding interest did not affect the inherent quality of a covenant as an equitable interest, and enforceability still depended on notice.

(3) As regards the position after 13 October 2003, local land charges take effect as interests which override under Schedules 1 and 3 to the Land Registration Act 2002. By section 55 of that Act a local land charge which creates a charge over registered land may only be realised if the title to the charge is registered (on the title to which it is subject). It is suggested, therefore, that whilst entry of a notice of the interest on the register of title is not required, it would be prudent to do so in order to ensure that there is 'double protection' by virtue of the entry in the Local Land Charges Register as well as at the Land Registry on the title affected. This point may be of significance if the local land charge secures positive obligations (eg an obligation to pay money)

---

[13] See Chapter 4 above.

[14] Land Charges Act 1925, s 15(1). See *MHLG v Sharp* [1970] 2 QB 223, for an instance of the effect of an erroneous clear search under that Act.

[15] Local Land Charges Act 1975, s 10(1). Note the definition of 'purchaser' in ss 10 (1), 3(a) and the definition of the time by which the search has to be made by subs 3(b). Note also s 11 of that Act as regards claims made by mortgagees and other limited owners. The commencement date of the Act was 1 August 1977. See *Emmet on Title* (Sweet & Maxwell, looseleaf), para 10.0581 for the compensation provisions.

[16] See, for example, Leasehold Reform Act 1967, s 19, printed at Appendix 2.

for section 55 of the Land Registration Act 2002 requires registration under that Act if the charge is to be enforced.[17]

SUMMARY

10.11 Provided the body imposing the covenant under statutory authority is within its powers, a covenant so imposed will have its own special force.

Therefore the problems of enforcement of private covenants which are present where either no land has been retained by the covenantee, or as between successors in title to both the orginal covenantor and covenantee (ie the running of the burden and the benefit), are avoided.

In any case where covenants are imposed by statute, regard must be had to the statute, not only for the manner in which the covenant is to be regarded as enforceable, but also as to whether such a covenant is to be protected as a local land charge, or in some other way.

In most cases the covenants imposed by statute will be registrable as local land charges. Even if they are unregistered, they will be enforceable against a bona fide purchaser for valuable consideration with notice if created after 1 August 1977.

---

[17] See *Ruoff & Roper on the Law and Practice of Registered Conveyancing* (Sweet & Maxwell, looseleaf), para 27.023.

Chapter 11

ACQUISITION OF LAND FOR PUBLIC PURPOSES AND THE EFFECT ON RESTRICTIVE COVENANTS

11.1   This chapter looks at the relationship between the acquisition of land by public authorities and restrictive covenants on that land, or neighbouring land.

INTRODUCTION

11.2   There are two issues which arise where land, which is subject to restrictive covenants, has been acquired under compulsory powers, either when the powers have been exercised, or when the proposed exercise of these powers has led to acquistion by voluntary agreement.[1]

These issues are:

(1)   What is the effect of the acquisition upon the covenant?
(2)   What, if any, relief can the covenantee obtain in respect of a breach of the covenant? What is the effect of any claim for relief on the covenant?

In addition there are two further questions which arise in this context, namely:

(1)   When there is a sale onwards by the acquiring authority of land compulsorily acquired, what effect will that sale have on restrictive covenants which burden such land?
(2)   What powers do local authorities have to override covenants in respect of land acquired, or appropriated by them for planning purposes?[2]

THE EFFECT OF THE ACQUISITION OF THE BURDENED LAND ON THE COVENANT

11.3   The rule is that the covenant continues in existence as a burden on the land acquired. It is not discharged, or overridden.[3]

---

[1]   Note the important point that the principles will apply whether the acquisition is by exercise of the statutory powers, or by voluntary agreement: *Kirby v School Board for Harrogate* [1896] 1 Ch 437. See the Local Government Act 1972, s 120 for powers of local authorities to acquire land by agreement under compulsory powers. Care should also be taken to examine the Act under which the power to acquire is being exercised to ascertain on what basis compensation is payable and whether the Compulsory Purchase Act 1965, s 10 applies, even where the acquisition is by agreement. (For example, see the Telecommunications Act 1984, s 40.)

[2]   See Chapter 12 below.

[3]   See *Re 6, 8, 10 and 12 Elm Avenue New Milton, ex parte New Forest DC* [1984] 1 WLR 1398, at 1405, per Scott J, and the earlier authorities cited therein.

WHAT RELIEF CAN THE COVENANTEE OBTAIN?

11.4 The rule is that the covenantee cannot obtain relief which would prevent the statutory purpose being carried out for which the acquisition took place. Nor can the covenantee obtain damages. The only remedy for the covenantee is to claim compensation under Compulsory Purchase Act 1965, section 10 for 'injurious affection'.[4]

An injunction will not lie to restrain a breach if that would interfere with the purpose for which the land is being used under the statute for which it was acquired. However, if compliance with the covenant will not interfere with the discharge of the statutory body's functions, an injunction may lie to enforce. For example an obligation to submit plans for consent prior to building may be enforceable by injunction.[5]

The covenantee may need to establish (by means of a declaration under Law of Property Act, section 84(2)) whether or not he has the title to enforce the covenant and by what means, if there is doubt as to whether the benefit of the covenant is vested in him.[6]

IN WHAT CIRCUMSTANCES WILL A CLAIM LIE FOR INJURIOUS AFFECTION WHERE THE CARRYING OUT OF THE STATUTORY PURPOSE HAS BROKEN THE COVENANT?

11.5 The covenantee must show:

(1) that what is being done would be a breach of covenant (but for the protection of the statutory acquisition);
(2) that he has the benefit of the covenant, ie the ability to make a claim;
(3) that damage has already occurred; prospective loss would appear not to be within the scope of 'injurious affection'. Damage means diminution in the value of the land and does not allow a 'ransom' element.[7]

FOR WHAT LOSS IS COMPENSATION GIVEN?

11.6 The compensation payable under section 10 will extend to injurious affection resulting from the *execution of the works* carried out by the acquiring authority. This means compensation will be awarded for the effect of the carrying out of the building works on the adjacent (burdened) land, but *not* for loss arising

---

[4]   *Brown v Heathlands Mental Health NHS Trust* [1996] 1 All ER 133, at 136, per Chadwick J. This authority conveniently collects the earlier authorities on this question. See also *Cadogan v Royal Brompton Hospital NHS Trust* [1996] 2 EGLR 115 and *Thames Water Utilities Ltd v Oxford City Council* [1999] 1 EGLR 167. See also n 1 above. For the nature of a claim for 'injurious affection' and its scope see *Halsbury's Laws of England* (4th ed), vol 8(1), paras 353–358.

[5]   *Cadogan v Royal Brompton Hospital NHS Trust*, above.

[6]   See Chapter 15, below, for applications under s 84(2).

[7]   *Wrotham Park Settled Estates v Hertsmere BC* [1993] 2 EGLR 15.

from the *use* of the land, or for the use of the works for the purposes for which the land was acquired.[8]

WHAT IS THE EFFECT OF A CLAIM UNDER SECTION 10 UPON THE COVENANT?

11.7   There appears to be no decided authority on this question.

One view is that a claim under section 10 will extinguish the covenant.[9]

Another view makes the distinction between those cases where compensation has been awarded under section 10 on a 'permanent' non-compliance basis and those where the non-compliance is temporary.[10]

It is hard to see where the distinction between these two forms of compensation lies.

If compensation is awarded for the breach, that would seem to put an end to the enforceability of the covenant; at least while the statutory purpose for which compensation is made is being carried out. In most cases that would be regarded as putting an end to the right to enforce the covenant. But the covenant does not cease to exist merely because it is unenforceable.[11]

In view of the uncertain nature of this area of the law, in an attempt to give some guidance to the practitioner encountering it, the following points may assist:

(1)   If the covenantee has already received compensation under section 10 for the effect of the injurious affection and the statutory purpose is *still* being carried

---

[8]   In *Thames Water Utilities Ltd v Oxford City Council* [1999] 1 EGLR 167, HH Judge Rich QC (sitting as a Judge of the High Court) declined to follow the reasoning of Chadwick J in *Brown*, see n 4 above, and held that compensation under s 10 could not be recovered for the effect on the covenantee of the use of land. See also *Wildtree Hotels v Harrow LBC* [2001] 2 AC 1, HL. *Wildtree Hotels* restores the law to the position it was in before the decision of Chadwick J in *Brown*, at n 4 above, when it was suggested that injurious affection compensation was available under s 10 of the Compulsory Purchase Act 1965 for the effect of the use of the land on its neighbouring properties. See also *Wrotham Park v Hertsmere BC* [1993] 2 EGLR 15 on the scope of compensation for injurious affection. It is important to note that if the *use* of the works is not the subject of compensation, then that use will not be within the scope of the exercise of the power to override under s 237 of the Town and Country Planning Act 1990 considered in Chapter 12. This means that the *user*, if in breach of covenant, will not be authorised: see *Thames Water Utilities v Oxford City Council* [1999] 1 EGLR 167 for such a finding where the operation of a football stadium, once constructed, could not be identified as the execution of works, and its use involved a breach of covenant.

[9]   See *Ellis v Rogers* (1885) 29 Ch 661. That was a case where the land compulsorily acquired by a railway company was burdened by covenants and the claimant in the action had the benefit of an agreement that the railway company would grant leases over the land to the claimant. The claimant agreed to assign the benefit of the agreement to the defendant. The claimant and the defendant both (erroneously) thought that the effect of the compulsory acquisition was to free the land from the covenants. The *obiter* dictum of Kay J, at 666, is the nearest one gets to a statement that the effect of (what is now) a payment under s 10 is to free the land from the burden of those covenants. The Court of Appeal held that as a matter of title, the existence of the covenants prevented the claimant from enforcing the agreement with the defendant.

[10]   Scamell, *Land Covenants* (Butterworths, 1996), at p 200.

[11]   The covenant may be regarded as suspended in such a case; see *Bird v Eggleton* (1885) 29 ChD 1012.

out by the acquiring authority, in practical terms it cannot be possible for the covenantee to claim 'second time round' for the same injury.[12]

(2)   The same principle expressed under (1) should apply if the acquiring authority transfers the land to a third party.

(3)   If the acquiring authority carries out a different activity which amounts to a breach of covenant, it may be possible to argue that the covenant is still effective to allow a section 10 claim.

(4)   If the different activity is carried out by a successor to the acquiring authority it would seem that the covenant is fully enforceable in the sense that all civil law remedies will be available.[13]

SALES ONWARDS AND OTHER TRANSFERS BY THE ACQUIRING AUTHORITY

11.8   It may well be that the acquiring authority has decided that the land acquired is surplus to requirements. One of two things will usually happen.

(1)   There will be a sale to a third party (invariably after the land has been offered back to the original owner from whom it was acquired).[14] Sales by a local authority may be under Local Government Act 1972, section 123, or under Town and Country Planning Act 1990, section 233 where land has been held for planning purposes.

(2)   There will be an exercise of the power to appropriate the land for any purpose for which the land may be acquired, if the land is vested in a local authority, under Local Government Act 1972, section 122, or if held for planning purposes, under Town and Country Planning Act 1990, section 232.

11.9   If (1) occurs there seems no reason why the covenant should not continue to be fully enforceable with all the usual civil law remedies at the covenantee's disposal.

However, by virtue of Local Government Act 1972, section 131(1)(a), sales under section 123 cannot be made in breach of a covenant against alienation, although a sale which required the purchaser to carry out works in breach of covenant would be permitted under that section, albeit without prejudice to the covenantor's remedies.[15] Sales under Town and Country Planning Act, section 233 are without restriction and, in any event, in respect of land held by local authorities for planning purposes, they have the power to override any covenant under section 237 of that Act. As to the scope of that power, see Chapter 12 below.

---

[12]   The objection might be put on the footing of 'issue estoppel', or simply on the basis that there would be double recovery for the same loss. See *Johnson v Gore Wood & Co (No 1)* [2002] 2 AC 1 for recent authority on the scope of this principle.

[13]   *Marten v Flight Refuelling* [1962] Ch 115, at 152. See also nn 4 and 8 above. If the activity is not the subject of compensation for injurious affection then it seems that civil remedies, such as an injunction, are available. See Chapter 20 below on the Human Rights Act 1998 implications when rights are being acquired by public, or quasi public, bodies.

[14]   See DOE Circular 6/93, paras 19 and 29, and circular letter of 30 October 1992, reproduced in Vol 2 of the *Encyclopedia of the Law of Planning, Compulsory Purchase and Compensation* (Sweet and Maxwell, looseleaf), paras 4–912/l; 'the Crichel Down' rules.

[15]   See *R v Westminster City Council, ex parte Leicester Square Coventry Street Association* (1989) 59 P&CR 51. (Proposal to erect electricity substation under Leicester Square.)

If (2) occurs section 122(4) of the 1972 Act will treat any work done on the land after the appropriation as if it had been done under the original authority to acquire and any claim by the covenantee will be limited to the remedy under Compulsory Purchase Act 1965, section 10; ie injurious affection.[16]

THE EFFECT OF COMPULSORY ACQUISITION OF THE BENEFITED LAND

11.10 Finally, what is the effect of compulsory powers on a covenant which is annexed to the land (ie where a covenant is there to benefit that land)?

(1) The general rule is that where powers are given to acquire land compulsorily, the whole of the land and the interests in it must be taken. This means that the acquiring authority will have the same right to enforce as any other owner. The rights of the original owner will be extinguished as part of the price paid for the land.[17]

(2) Some statutes confer specific power to take an interest in land without acquiring the freehold, but restrictive covenants do not appear to fall within the class of interests to be acquired.[18]

(3) There are some statutory provisions which confer power on the acquiring authority to acquire certain adverse rights over land only, including restrictive covenants. In such cases it is clear that the acquisition of the right (for which compensation is given) causes it to be extinguished.[19]

(4) Note that if land is compulsorily purchased which is subject to the burden of a covenant, that acquisition will not affect those whose land is not so acquired and who have the benefit of the same covenant. In such circumstances it will be for the local authority to exercise its powers under the Local Government Act 1972, s 122 and the Town and Country Planning Act 1990, s 237, to appropriate the relevant burdened land and thereby those with the benefit of the covenant can claim compensation under the Compulsory Purchase Act 1965, s 10. See Chapter 12.

SUMMARY

11.11 Acquisition of land which is subject to restrictive covenants does not extinguish them, but alters the way in which the person with the right to enforce that covenant can exercise that right.

The normal civil remedies of an injunction or damages may not be available. Instead statutory compensation is awarded for injurious affection. In some cases an

---

[16] This appears to be the case from the *obiter* dictum of Scott J in *Re Elm Avenue*, at n 3 above, at 1404. Chadwick J declined to express a view on this point in *Brown*, above.

[17] See Compulsory Purchase Act 1965, s 23(6). This principle must not be confused with the effect on the adjoining land of the covenantee (not being acquired) of a payment of compensation under s 10 of that Act; see **11.6** above.

[18] See *Halsbury's Laws*, vol 8(1) and see, for example, Highways Act 1980, s 250 giving power to acquire rights over land, but this does not appear to include a right in the nature of the benefit of a restrictive covenant.

[19] For example, Requisitioned Land and War Works Act 1945, ss 33 and 39.

injunction may still lie if its grant will not hinder the carrying out of the purpose for which the land was acquired.

The effect of an award of compensation may or may not affect the future right to enforce the same covenant in respect of which that compensation was granted. The amount of compensation will reflect the effect of the carrying out of the work (in breach) on the land acquired but not the effect of the use (in breach) of the land acquired upon the land with the benefit of the covenant.

Where land is sold on by the acquiring authority the same principles will in most cases apply in respect of any activity carried out by the purchaser which is in breach of covenant.

Where land which has the benefit of a covenant is compulsorily acquired, the right to enforce will usually pass to the acquiring authority.

Chapter 12

THE POWER OF LOCAL AND OTHER AUTHORITIES TO OVERRIDE RESTRICTIVE COVENANTS

12.1 This chapter considers the powers given to local authorities (and other bodies so empowered) to override restrictive covenants which would otherwise prevent the use of land vested in them.

INTRODUCTION

12.2 Whereas Chapter 11 has been concerned with the effect of the acquisition of land under compulsory purchase powers upon covenants which burden or benefit that land, or upon neighbouring land, in this chapter consideration is given to the ways in which local authorities (and other bodies) can avoid the effect of restrictive covenants which might otherwise act as a fetter on their plans for the use of the land vested in them. The effect of Town and Country Planning Act 1990, section 237 should not be overlooked. It is particularly important in the context of redevelopment by local authorities of land which they have acquired or appropriated for planning purposes, and may benefit those who derive title from such authorities.

THE STATUTORY PROVISIONS

12.3 These are:

- Town and Country Planning Act 1990, section 237.[1] (This power is quite frequently encountered.)
- Requisitioned Land and War Works Act 1945, sections 33–38. (This power is much less frequently encountered.)

---

[1] Printed at Appendix 2. Applicable to the wide class of 'local authorities' defined by s 336(1) and (10) of the 1990 Act. The origins of s 237 go back to the Town and Country Planning Act 1944, s 22; Town and Country Planning Act 1947, s 44(1); Town and Country Planning Act 1962, s 81; Town and Country Planning Act 1971, s 127.

SECTION 237 OF THE 1990 ACT

12.4

(1) This allows local authorities which own land acquired, or appropriated by them for planning purposes to override restrictions (and other rights) where development is carried out in accordance with planning permission.[2] *It is important that if there is to be an appropriation, it is valid, and for planning purposes.* An appropriation to sell land purely for the purpose of development would not be a valid appropriation and section 237 cannot, therefore, be invoked.[3] It is important to note that this power should only be exercised where it is necessary to interfere with rights of third parties which are known to exist; in other words some care should be given to a consideration of the necessity in each case of exercising the power, in view of the effect on third party rights. If care is not taken, the exercise of the power will be judicially reviewable, with all the delay that will mean for the authority concerned and, no doubt, to the developer waiting to pay a hefty price to the hard pressed authority.[4] The proposed development (in respect of which the power under section 237 is invoked) must be related to the planning purposes for which the land was acquired or appropriated.[5]

(2) Compensation is payable under subsection (4) on an 'injurious affection' basis.[6]

(3) Significantly, the development which allows the covenant to be overridden may be a second or subsequent redevelopment.[7] To attract the immunity it would seem that the work done (whether by the local authority or the person deriving title under it) must be related in some way to the planning purposes for which the land was acquired, or appropriated.[8]

(4) The power to override extends to 'a person deriving title under' the local authority, if the work for which the planning permission exists is done by that person. That is important in the context of sale by local authorities of land

---

[2] For the wide scope of 'planning purposes' see ss 226 and 246 of the 1990 Act. Section 122 of the Local Government Act 1972 gives the power to appropriate land. See Appendix 2 for that section. The Planning and Compensation Act 2004, s 99 amends s 226 from a date to be appointed (not yet in force at January 2005).

[3] As occurred in *Sutton LBC v Bolton* [1993] 2 EGLR 181. See also *R v Bromsgrove DC, ex parte Morton and Anor* [1998] JPL 664, for an example of the need to exercise the power to appropriate under s 122 of the Local Government Act 1972, having regard to good and proper reasons, and not ignoring matters (eg objections) which ought to be taken into account. For judicial review, see CPR, Pt 54.

[4] See *R v Leeds City Council, ex parte Leeds Industrial Co-operative Society* (1996) 73 P&CR 70, for authority on the need for care in the exercise of the power and for an example of the problems created by judicial review applications which can hold up development plans. For judicial review, see CPR, Pt 54.

[5] See *Midtown v City of London Real Property Co* [2005] EWHC 33 (Ch), at paras 33–48.

[6] See Chapter 11 above. See *Ward v Wychavon DC* (1986) 279 EG 77, for a claim under the predecessor to this section (1971 Act, s 127) for loss arising from interference to an easement, which, on the facts, failed. But note that the acts of the authority causing the compensation to be payable must be ones which fall within s 237. If they do not, no compensation will be payable; *Thames Water Utilities Ltd v Oxford City Council* [1999] 1 EGLR 167 and see **11.6** above.

[7] *R v City of London Corporation, ex parte Barbers' Company* (1996) 95 LGR 459. This may include a lessee as a person 'deriving title' under the local authority (see item (4) below). This authority was considered in *Midtown v City of London Real Property Co*, see n 5 above.

[8] *R v City of London Corporation, ex parte Barbers' Company*, at p 466, per Dyson J

which they have acquired, or appropriated for planning purposes, to third parties, who then have the benefit of the section, albeit subject to the obligation to pay compensation. (Section 237(5) places the liability to pay on the local authority in those circumstances; no doubt a local authority will secure its position *vis-à-vis* the purchaser by means of an indemnity or bond.) It appears from the *Barbers* case[9] that where the section is being used by a person deriving title from the local authority, the work done by it must be related in some way to the planning purpose for which the land was acquired or appropriated. So, for example, if land was acquired or appropriated for housing purposes, the person deriving title could not claim the benefit of section 237 if the redevelopment was for offices.

(5) Because compensation is based on an 'injurious affection' measure, a 'ransom' element will not be recoverable.[10]

(6) Compensation will only be awarded where the covenant which is overridden is one which is capable of enforcement (ie not obsolete). The relevant date for valuing loss is when the works in breach of covenant are carried out; generally that will be the start of the works.[11]

(7) Loss caused by the breach of contract is limited to the work carried out by the authority (or a person deriving title under it) on the land which is the subject of the appropriation, or occupation. The effect of work on other land which is not within that definition (eg highway works carried out under the orders of the local highway authority) will not be material in the claim for injurious affection under the Compulsory Purchase Act 1965, section 10.[12]

(8) For limitation purposes, section 9(1) of the Limitation Act 1980 limits claims to a period of six years from the time when the cause of action accrued should have been notified.[13]

---

[9]   See n 7 above. This is an important case in that a local authority, acting within the terms of planning permission, can use s 237 to acquire adverse rights on any number of developments, on the same site and the benefit of that section can be used by developers who have acquired the site from such an authority, within the limit expressed in the text. This is based on the provisional view of Dyson J expressed at p 466 of the Report.

[10] See *Wrotham Park Settled Estates v Hertsmere BC* [1993] 2 EGLR 15. See also *Thames Water Utilities Ltd v Oxford City Council*, above, for authority on the limit to the amount recoverable and the heads of damage within an injurious affection claim. In that case the effect on the plaintiff's land of the subsequent use of the buildings and development authorised under s 237 was not something which could be within a compensation claim under that section. See **11.6** above. See also *Wildtree Hotels v Harrow LBC* [2001] 2 AC 1, cited at **11.6** for the limits on compensation for injurious affection.

[11] This is considered to be the effect of s 237(4).

[12] See *Puttock v LB Bexley* (ACQ 101/2003) (decision 19 April 2004). (Lands Tribunal.)

[13] Where a claim for compensation arises under s 237(4) (by reference to s 10 of the Land Compensation Act 1965) the precise date on which the 'cause of action' accrues is not entirely clear. One view is that it arises when the right is acquired, or appropriated under section 237(1). (Compare with the finding that the date of entry by the acquiring authority starts time running, see *Hillingdon LBC v ARC Ltd* [1998] RVR 754.) The other view is that time does not start running until the 'interference or breach' (refered to in s 237(4)) occurs. (For example, the breach of the covenant acquired or appropriated.) It is suggested that the only safe course to take is to assume that time will start running from the acquistion, or appropriation. The person with the benefit of the covenant will know about that, or should become aware of it early on in the development. Estoppel *may* defer the period; see *Hillingdon LBC v ARC Ltd (No 2)* [2002] RVR 145. For a full discussion see the *Encyclopedia of the Law of Planning, Compulsory Purchase and Compensation* (Sweet & Maxwell, looseleaf), vol 1, paras B–0291.1 and B–0477.

SECTIONS 33–38 OF THE 1945 ACT

12.5

(1) Whilst not often encountered in practice, these provisions allow the Ministry of Defence the right to acquire a restrictive covenant which might otherwise hinder the use of land for MOD purposes.

(2) Compensation is payable in accordance with the Land Compensation Act 1961; section 39 of the Requisitioned Land and War Works Act 1945.

Chapter 13

EXTINGUISHING RESTRICTIVE COVENANTS

13.1 This chapter examines the circumstances in which restrictive covenants will cease to be enforceable by virtue of their discharge, or extinguishment.

INTRODUCTION

13.2 In some cases it will be obvious that a covenant has ceased to bind land; for example where there is an order of the Lands Tribunal for the discharge of a covenant. In other cases it will be less obvious; for example where a breach of covenant has been acquiesced in for many years so that the covenant is, in effect, abandoned.

The following events will cause restrictive covenants to be regarded as discharged or extinguished.

(1) By the absence of a competent claimant, or defendant.
(2) By express release.
(3) By operation of law.
(4) By an order of the court under Law of Property Act 1925, section 84(2).
(5) By an order of the Lands Tribunal under Law of Property Act 1925, section 84(1).
(6) By virtue of Town and Country Planning Act 1990, section 237.

Taking each in turn, the principles are as follows.

THE ABSENCE OF A COMPETENT CLAIMANT OR DEFENDANT

13.3 It is clear that when using the flowchart at pages 5–7 above, there will be circumstances where a restrictive covenant ceases to be enforceable as result of either the inability of the claimant to show that he has the benefit of the covenant, or the defendant's ability to show that he is free from its burden.

In the case of pre-1926 covenants it is conceivable that where the benefit of covenants has not been expressly annexed, and where there is no chain of assignments, or scheme of development the benefit will be lost. No-one can sue on the covenants. In view of the effect of the *Federated Homes* decision on post-1925 covenants, that situation will be rarer in the case of such covenants because of the application of the Law of Property Act 1925, section 78; although in the light of *Crest Nicholson v McAllister*[1] there may now be a greater number of cases where

---

[1]   [2004] EWCA Civ 410. See **8.18** above.

no-one can claim the benefit of covenants in view of the lack of any evidence of the identity of the land intended to be benefited.

There are also cases where the covenants can be regarded as discharged because of the failure over many years to enforce the covenants. Thus where breaches have gone unchallenged, the covenants can be regarded as lost by, what is, in effect, abandonment.[2]

13.4   If a court refuses an injunction to enforce a restrictive covenant the covenant is *de facto* unenforceable – at least between the parties to the claim. It is open to the victor to apply under Land Registration Act 2002, section 65 and Schedule 4, or under Land Registration Rules 2003, rule 87 and rules 126–129, if the title to the burdened land is registered, for the entry of the covenant to be cancelled (or for the order of refusal to be noted on the title). In practice the Land Registry is reluctant to cancel the entry in view of the problem of satisfying itself that all those with the benefit are bound; see paragraph 13.6 below. It seems that the Land Charges Registry is likely to be as reluctant, and there is no equivalent provision in the Land Charges Act 1972, although Land Charges Rules 1974, rule 10 allows vacation where the charge can be shown to be 'discharged ... or of no effect'. The problem with satisfying the Land Charges Registry is the same as that referred to above in cases of registered titles and at **13.6** below.[3]

BY EXPRESS RELEASE

13.5   It is open to the person having the benefit of a covenant to release it, expressly, in writing and ideally (to avoid any claim that there is a want of consideration) by deed.[4]

---

[2]   See *Hepworth v Pickles* [1900] 1 Ch 108, applied in *Att-Gen of Hong Kong v Fairfax Ltd* [1997] 1 WLR 149. Both authorities were considered in *Dano Ltd v Earl Cadogan* [2003] 2 P&CR 10. See also *Knight v Simmonds* [1896] 2 Ch 294 and *Robins v Berkeley Homes* [1996] EGCS 75. In the former case the question arose in the context of covenants in a scheme of development. In the latter it was argued, unsuccessfully, that the Camden Park Estate at Chislehurst, had changed in such a way that the covenants between two plots were no longer enforceable. Much will depend on what is regarded as 'the neighbourhood' for the purpose of deciding what changes have occurred within that area (eg infilling in breach of covenant) which might allow a court to find that the covenants are no longer enforceable. This area of law rests partly on the question how far a court will grant specific relief (eg by way of injunction) where the original object of covenants (eg the preservation of value or amenity) can no longer be carried out. (See Chapter 15 for remedies against breaches of covenant.) It is important to keep these principles of law separate from the question the Lands Tribunal has to decide on an application under the Lands Tribunal Act 1925, s 84(1)(a) based on a covenant which is 'obsolete': see Chapter 16 for that jurisdiction. Much will depend on the nature of any breaches and their extent. Acquiesence in one type of breach will not support an argument of 'change in the neighbourhood' if the threatened breach is of a different sort: *Osborne v Bradley* [1903] 2 Ch 446.

[3]   Land Charges Act 1972, s 1(6) permits vacation pursuant to an order of the court, but that requires the court to be satisfied that all those potentially able to enforce the covenant are before the court in a claim where an injunction is refused, or where the court has made an order under s 84(2).

[4]   As to writing which is required for 'interests in land' see Law of Property Act 1925, s 53(1)(a). The benefit of a restrictive covenant is such an interest: *LSWR v Gomm* (1882) 20 ChD 562, at 581. As to the formalities governing deeds see Law of Property (Miscellaneous Provisions) Act 1989, s 1. Because tenants may enforce under the Law of Property Act 1925, s 78, those with the benefit of any covenant being released should be joined as parties.

Whether or not a release is coupled with a variation it is important to remember to apply to alter the registration of the original covenant. If the title to the burdened land is registered – the entry in the Charges Register has to be modified. If title to the burdened land is unregistered, there needs to be a new registration of a Class D(ii) land charge against the estate owner of the burdened land (where there is a modification), coupled with an application to vacate the old Land Charge. See the next paragraph for the difficulty in securing a cancellation of the old registration.

13.6 Where the title to the burdened land is registered the policy of the Land Registry is normally to note the deed of release on the register and not to cancel the original entry.

This is because the Registry takes the view that it is difficult in the vast majority of cases to show that all those with the benefit of the original covenant have been party to the release or modification.[5] The same view is taken by the Land Charge Registry at Plymouth when dealing with applications to cancel the old land charge registration.

It is obvious that any release or modification will only be effective if all those who are known to have the benefit of the covenants which are the subject of it are parties. This will include tenants as well as freeholders in view of the ability of the former to enforce under the Law of Property Act 1925, section 78.[6]

A deed will not be required where all those entitled to the benefit of the covenant have (expressly or impliedly) by their acts or omissions agreed to the discharge or modification of the covenant and the Lands Tribunal so orders under the Law of Property Act 1925, section 84(1)(b).[7]

BY IMPLIED RELEASE

13.7 A restrictive covenant will not usually be regarded as extinguished merely because a condition (eg the grant of planning consent) has lapsed. Unless there is some limit of time on the covenant (or the obligation under it) it will continue without limit of time.[8] However, a restriction may become spent if, for example, a party whose consent is required for the approval of building plans has died, or if a company which has the power to give consent to plans etc, has been dissolved.[9] A covenant can also be spent if there is no longer any named estate in existence in any recognisable form to which that covenant relates.[10]

---

[5] For the Registry's practice on removing and cancelling an agreed notice, see *Ruoff & Roper on the Law and Practice of Conveyancing* (Sweet & Maxwell, looseleaf), para 42.009. See **4.23** for further analysis of the effect of the variation of unregistered covenants.

[6] See *Smith and Snipes Hall Farm v River Douglas Catchment Board* [1949] 2 KB 500 and **8.5** above.

[7] See Chapter 16 below.

[8] *Federated Homes v Mill Lodge Properties* [1980] 1 WLR 594 at p 603; *Re Abbey Homesteads Application* (1986) 53 P&CR 1.

[9] See *Crest Nicholson v McAllister* [2004] EWHC Civ 410 and **14.9** below.

[10] *Dano Ltd v Earl Cadogan* [2004] 1 P&CR 13.

BY OPERATION OF LAW

13.8 Where the whole of the burdened and the whole of the benefited land become vested in one person who then owns the freehold of the two parcels (free from any leasehold or other interest which might be entitled to enforce covenants which ran for the benefit of one of the parcels and bound the other) the covenant which benefited and burdened the respective parcels comes to an end. It will not be revived on a subsequent severance of the unified title, unless recreated by the common owner.[11] The unification of the freehold ownership in the two parcels of land is sometimes referred to as 'unity of seisin'. The land must be held by that party in the same interest; eg not in capacity 'A' in respect of the burdened land and capacity 'B' in respect of the benefited land. If that difference is present, there will be no extinguishment of the covenant.[12]

Where only part of the freehold of the burdened land becomes vested in the freehold owner of the whole of the benefited land (free from any third party right to enforce) the extinguishment of the covenant is confined to the part of the burdened land which is vested in the common owner. He can still enforce against that part of the burdened land not vested in him.[13] Unless recreated on a division, the covenants are, therefore, extinguished as to those parts in common ownerships.[14] There is (as above) no automatic revival on severance.

Where part of the benefited land and the whole or part of the burdened land come into common freehold ownership (free from any third party right to enforce), the same result occurs as under the previous paragraph. In other words, as to those parts where burden and benefit are united, there is extinguishment without automatic revival on severance. As to those parts where there is no unity the covenants remain in force.[15]

13.9 Where a scheme of development applies there is extinguishment on unity of ownership (in accordance with the rules stated above), but there is an automatic revival on severance, unless:

(1) The entirety of the land subject to the scheme comes into common ownership. This is an unlikely event.
(2) Where the parties to the severance agree that the scheme covenants are no longer to apply and agree to enter into new covenants, thereby creating a sub-scheme.[16]
(3) There is some other reason to conclude that the original covenants are not to be regarded as having revived, even if there is nothing stated in the conveyance or transfer severing the formerly united properties. One example is where during the unity of seisin a breach of the scheme covenant is

---

[11] *Texaco Antilles v Kernochan* [1973] AC 609. Applied in *Re MCA East Ltd* [2003] 1 P&CR 9, para 40. See **13.9** below for revival.
[12] *University of East London v London Borough of Barking and Dagenham* [2004] EWCA Civ 2710, at paras 52–60.
[13] *Cryer v Scott Bros (Sunbury) Ltd* (1986) 55 P&CR 183 at 188.
[14] *Re Tiltwood* [1978] Ch 269. See also, for an interesting academic discussion, (1977) *The Conveyancer*, vol 41, 107. *Re Tiltwood* was followed in *Re Victoria Recreation Ground's Application* [1979] 41 P&CR 119.
[15] *Re Tiltwood*, above.
[16] See **8.35** above and *Knight v Simmonds* [1896] 1 Ch 653.

committed by A on one of the plots. The plot is then sold by A and the breach continued by the new owner. The person who retains the other plot (A) cannot, it seems, sue the new owner for breach even though the owners of other plots (not affected by the unity of seisin) could sue to enforce the scheme covenants. The rationale for this example of the exception to the usual rule in scheme covenants appears to be based on the ground that it would be a derogation from the grant of the vendor (A) to sue his purchaser for breach of a covenant of which the vendor had himself been in breach. Whether or not this is the correct rationale, or whether some other ground could be used to justify the rule (eg estoppel), it is probably true\ that where there are circumstances which indicate that the scheme covenants are not to apply, they will not be revived where there is a severance of the formerly united properties.[17]

WHAT IS RE-CREATION?

13.10 In cases of unity of seisin followed by severance, other than where schemes of development are involved, what is required to re-create the covenant?

An express affirmation, or confirmation of the covenants should be used to ensure revival. In the conveyance, or transfer reference should be made (i) to the original covenants, (ii) to the fact of unity of seisin and (iii) the fact that it is intended that the covenants (formerly extinguished) are to be revived.

A suggested form of words in the operative part of any conveyance or transfer to avoid any doubt is:

> 'The parties intend that the covenants referred to at clause [   ] are hereby expressly confirmed to be binding between the parties as if they had never been extinguished and to the intent that the benefit and burden thereof shall run with and bind the land so expressed to be benefited and burdened in accordance with the terms of [the instrument originally imposing the covenants]'[18]

It is debatable whether, either a mere assignment of the benefit (where the common owner is disposing of the benefited land), or a mere expression that the burdened land is conveyed 'subject to' the original covenants (when the burdened land is being disposed of by the common owner) will be sufficient to effect re-creation. Such expressions may not be an adequate indication of an intention to re-create. The same observation may also be made as regards the presence of an indemnity covenant, as between vendor and purchaser.[19]

---

[17] See *Texaco Antilles Ltd v Kernochan*, above, at 625, per Lord Cross, and at 626, affirming *Brunner v Greenslade* [1971] Ch 993, on the general rule applicable to revival of scheme covenants on severance. See *Johnstone & Sons v Holland* [1988] 1 EGLR 264 and *Petra Investments v Jeffrey Rogers* [2001] 81 P&CR 267, for discussion of the doctrine of derogation from grant.

[18] See **A7.2**, below, for further drafting suggestions.

[19] See **4.24** above.

OTHER MEANS BY WHICH COVENANTS ARE EXTINGUISHED

By an order of the court under Law of Property Act 1925, section 84(2)

13.11   See Chapter 15 below for the manner in which land may be freed from restrictive covenants under this provision.

By an order of the Lands Tribunal under Law of Property Act 1925, section 84(1)

See Chapter 16 below for the manner in which this jurisdiction is exercised.

By the exercise of powers under Town and Country Planning Act 1990, section 237

See Chapter 12 above for the operation of this section.

Where a court has refused an injunction and all parties capable of enforcing the covenant are before the court

13.12   As explained at **13.4** above, it is possible to ask for the notice of the entry of the covenant on the register of title or the land charge entry to be cancelled or vacated, following the court's refusal to enforce a covenant, but as explained there and at **13.6** above, there may be difficulties in proving that all persons with the benefit are bound. If it is so possible, there is no reason why the covenant should not be regarded as at an end.

Where statutory provisions or orders under statutory powers override the covenant

13.13   For example:

(1)   Orders of the County Court under the Housing Act 1985, section 610, allowing subdivision of houses, even if contrary to covenant.
(2)   The terms of the Allotments Act 1950, section 12 allowing the keeping of hens or rabbits on any land (ie not just allotments) and structures to house them, even if contrary to a covenant, other than by way of trade or business and provided no nuisance is committed.[20]

Note that there is no extinguishment where covenants are acquired as part of the acquisition of land under statutory powers; see **11.3** and **11.7** above for the effect of a payment under the Compulsory Purchase Act 1965, section 10 which does not, it is thought, extinguish the covenant.

---

[20]   Statutory provisions are at Appendix 2. The terms of s 12 are a legacy of the Second World War and the campaign during it to encourage self-sufficiency in the provision of food; rabbits then being a cheap and easy way of providing part of the diet when meat was strictly rationed!

RESTRICTIVE COVENANTS AND PERPETUITIES

13.14 In essence, the law of perpetuities is designed to ensure that interests arise or vest within the period allowed by either the common law or (whose covenants are imposed after 15 July 1964) the Perpetuities and Accumulations Act 1964. If a restrictive covenant is regarded as creating an *immediate* interest in land, it is not subject to the rule against perpetuities. This is because, if there is a breach of that covenant at a future date, so there cannot be any argument that the vesting of such an interest could take place outside the perpetuity period, no interest in land is created at that date.[21]

In *Dano Ltd v Earl Cadogan* [2003] 2 P&CR 10, at para 45, per Etherton J, it was held that the covenants in question applied from the outset (in 1928) so that a breach in the future would not bring about the vesting of any interest in the land.

However, there may be instances where restrictive covenants are to come into existence at a future date (eg on phased plot sales, or on a given future event) and if those covenants are to give rise to rights and obligations between persons other than the original contracting parties, the law relating to perpetuities may apply. This is because the interest created may come into effect at a future date, and, unless that date is within the perpetuity period allowed by law, the interest will be void, save as between the original contracting parties.[22] The question will then be whether the interest under the covenant arises at the future date, or whether it took immediate effect from the date of the instrument creating the covenant. This will be a matter of construction.

The overall message is that the law of perpetuities *may* have an impact on the law of restrictive covenants, so this technical aspect of the relationship between the two fields of law cannot be ignored.

---

[21] See Megarry & Wade, *The Law of Real Property* (Sweet & Maxwell, 6th edn, 1999), Chapter 7, para 7–130 for this view and ibid, for the law of perpetuities in detail.

[22] See *Dunn v Blackdown Properties* [1961] Ch 433 (an easement to arise at a future date); *Marten v Flight Refuelling* [1962] Ch 115 at p 136; *Adams v Rushmon Homes* (2001) (unreported) 5 April 2001, Blackburne J.

Chapter 14

THE CONSTRUCTION OF RESTRICTIVE COVENANTS

14.1 This chapter looks at the principles of construction which apply to restrictive covenants and the way in which certain covenants are construed. The purpose of this chapter is not to provide a textbook on interpretation, but rather to highlight the main principles and some of the problems which the more commonly encountered covenants present.

GENERAL PRINCIPLES OF CONSTRUCTION

14.2 The construction of restrictive covenants is carried out by a court in the same way as with any other words which are intended to have a specific meaning in a document. As a general rule, the aim of the court is to ascertain the intention of the parties from the words used, considering those words in the light of the factual circumstances in which they appear; the last factor is sometimes referred to as the 'factual matrix'.

Recent authority suggests that the process of construction may require a wider search for the meaning of words and thus it may be permissible, within limits, to look at any evidence which would have affected the way in which the language of the document would have been understood by a reasonable man. The limits to such a process exclude previous negotiations and expressions of subjective intent; such evidence may only be admissible in an action to rectify.

14.3 If the words are clear their meaning should be plain by application of the principles set out above. Equally if the wrong words, or grammar are used the court is not obliged to attribute to the parties an intention they could not have had.[1]

In the specific context of restrictive covenants the words used should make it plain that the purpose is to govern the use of land by means of a restriction. It may sometimes be less than obvious how that is to be achieved (eg in the context of

---

[1]   For a very useful guide to interpretation, see Lewison, *The Interpretation of Contracts* (Sweet and Maxwell, 3rd edn, 2004). For the 'modern' approach see the House of Lords' decisions in *Mannai Investment Co Ltd v Eagle Star Life Assurance Co Ltd* [1997] AC 749; *Investors Compensation Scheme Ltd v West Bromwich Building Society* [1998] 1 WLR 896 and *BCCI v Ali* [2002] 1 AC 251 at p 259F, per Lord Bingham, p 267B-D, per Lord Nicholls, p 269E–G and p 276H, per Lord Hoffmann and at p 281G–282G, per Lord Clyde. For recent authority on the interpretation of words in a conveyance which takes not just those words into account but also the practical result of any construction, see *Hotchkin v McDonald* [2004] EWCA Civ 519. (Grant of easement of way for all purposes in connection with use of property on dominant land held to include, not just the use within the scope of the covenant imposed at that date (1965) but also any use of that property authorised by any order of the Lands Tribunal modifying the covenant under the Law of Property Act 1925, s 84(1).)

consents to plans etc) but in most cases the problems of construction should be more easily resolved than in some other areas, such as commercial contracts.

There is a rebuttable presumption in the case of contracts and deeds that they are to be interpreted with the meaning and the understanding current when they were made. (This is the converse of the presumption which applies to the construction of statutes, which are to be interpreted according to their meaning from time to time.) But as in the case of all rebuttable presumptions, meanings may change and in the case of restrictive covenants, which are intended to last (in theory at least) in perpetuity, it is not usually the case that words should only bear the meaning they would have had when the covenant was imposed.[2]

SPECIFIC QUESTIONS OF CONSTRUCTION WHICH ARISE IN THE CONTEXT OF RESTRICTIVE COVENANTS

The following questions frequently arise.

Are the words of the covenant aimed at protecting the land of the covenantee?

14.4   Do the words of covenant used affect the value of the land to be benefited, or amenity in the sense of 'touching and concerning it', or are they aimed at protecting some other interest, such as trading interests only and protection from competition?[3]

–   If of the former type, the covenant will have all the qualities of an equity binding the covenantor's land, the benefit of which is capable of running with the covenantee's land. If of the latter type, it may be binding only between the original parties.[4]

–   Certain types of covenant, such as tie covenants, or those directed at restrictions on the brand identity, or manufacturer of goods to be sold from land may be affected by the rules which make such covenants unenforceable, or void, either as an unreasonable restraint of trade, or as infringing

---

[2]   See, for an example of this principle, *Dano Ltd v Earl Cadogan* [2003] P&CR 13, on the meaning of 'working classes'.

[3]   Restraint covenants of the type considered in *Esso Petroleum Co v Harper's Garage* [1968] AC 269, may be an example of the latter. See *Young v Evan-Jones* [2002] 1 P&CR 14 for the application of the law relating to restraint of trade in the context of a pharmacy in a medical centre. The restraint on relocation was held to be reasonable. See Art 82 of the the the EC Treaty; abuse of dominant position.
     See www.europa.eu.int/comm/competition/legislation/treaties/ec/art82_en.html.

[4]   For trading interests etc, see Chapters 1 and 2 of the Competition Act 1998 and the Land and Vertical Agreements Exclusion Order 2000 (SI 2000/310). The Order excludes a 'land agreement' from the ambit of Chapter 1 of the 1998 Act. This is provided for by s 50 of the Competition Act 1998. A 'land agreement' is defined (in essence) as one between undertakings which creates, alters, transfers or terminates an 'interest in land'. If a restrictive covenant is seen as an 'interest in land' (which it ought to be, if it is not purely a personal agreement) and contains terms which are anti-competitive (eg to buy goods at certain prices from a certain source) and which is not in an agreement which falls within the Order, it will be caught by Chapter 1 of the 1998 Act. It is recommended that where restrictive covenants are potentially within the scope of competition law, specialist advice must be sought. Section 106 Agreements and other planning agreements and obligations are exempt from Chapter 1 of the Act by virtue of Sch 3, paragraph 1 thereof.

Articles 81 and 82 of the EC Treaty. This is a complex and developing area of law where space does not permit a full analysis. However, the practitioner should be aware that such covenants may not be enforceable, or valid, between the original parties and successors. The present law appears to be that if land is already encumbered with such covenants and the purchaser acquires the land subject to them, the restraint of doctrine will not apply.[5] However, if the land is acquired and only later is the covenant imposed, the restraint of trade doctrine may apply and the reasonableness test will apply to that material covenant.[6] The distinctions are fine ones and may not be entirely logical. Moreover, in any case it is open to raise invalidity under Articles 81 of the EC Treaty, but in order to succeed on that ground it has to be proved that the covenant in question has a particular economic effect (ie the prevention, etc of competition within the terms of Article 81) at the time when its validity is being considered. There is no automatic invalidity and in many cases a successful challenge to a 'tie' covenant will require a mass of economic data concerning the trading methods of the covenantee (eg the brewery, or tyre manufacturer) and the effect of the covenant on the covenantor (eg the tenant of the pub, or the owner of the tyre-fitting bay).[7] It has yet to arise, but there is no reason in theory why a 'tie' covenant could not be the subject of an application under Law of Property Act 1925, section 84(1).

Are the words of the covenant truly restrictive?

See Chapter 3 above.

Are the words sufficiently certain so as to be enforceable?

14.5

– Covenants which affect 'amenity' may be attacked for being too broad, although in general the court will try to give effect to the words used.[8]
– The 'blue pencil' test may be used to remove those parts which are too uncertain.
– Where the uncertainty is clearly an error of drafting, the court may enforce the true intention of the covenant and ignore words in accordance with the 'modern' approach to construction referred to at **14.2** above.

---

[5]   See the *Esso Petroleum* case, at n 3 above.
[6]   See *Alec Lobb (Garages) Ltd v Total Oil (GB) Ltd* [1985] 1 WLR 173.
[7]   See *Delimitis v Henniger Bräu AG* [1991] ECR 1-935 and *Crehan v Inntrepreneur Pub Co* [2004] EWCA Civ 637, for the way in which infringement of Art 81 is treated. In this context block exemption under Art 81 (eg Reg 1984/83 as to beer tie agreements) may be relevant. See Treitel, *Contact* (11th ed), pp 475–477, see n 3 above, for full treatment of the restraint of trade doctrine. See *Europa* website (see n 3 above) for Arts 81 and 82 of the EC Treaty.
[8]   See *National Trust v Midlands Electricity Board* [1952] Ch 380, for an example of the court's refusal to enforce covenants which were directed at preserving the amenities of the Malvern Hills. Whether the same decision would be reached today is open to doubt.

Are there any limits on the scope of the persons who can sue, or be sued on the covenants?

14.6

– Are there words limiting the effect of Law of Property Act 1925, sections 78 and 79 which would otherwise permit full enforcement of post-1925 covenants?
– Whether or not the covenant was made before or after 1926, are there any indications that the covenant was purely personal, or in some other way limited to the original parties?[9]

Is the original covenantor liable for the acts and omissions of subsequent owners and occupiers?

14.7

(1) The starting point is that the original covenantor (A) remains liable (by virtue of privity of contract) on the covenants into which he has entered. This liability will be remain even though A may have disposed of the land over which the covenant runs, and even though the original covenantee may no longer retain any land benefited by the covenant.[10]

(2) As to liability for the acts, or omission of successors, unless there is an express exclusion of the liability, the original covenantor (A) is deemed to covenant on behalf of himself, his successors in title, and those deriving title under him: Law of Property Act 1925, section 79(1). 'Successors in title' include owners and occupiers for the time being of the land: section 79(2), which applies that definition to covenants restrictive of the user of land.

(3) It is by no means clear whether the words implied by section 79(1) (and in the case of pre-1926 instruments invariably expressed) are merely there to show that the covenant is intended to run with the land and not to impose liability on A for the acts or omissions of his successors.[11] The alternative view is that the words extending the covenant to successors etc are such as to extend the original covenantor's 'original' liability to those successors, even when he has disposed of the burdened land.

(4) This area of law may be of significance where an original covenantor is sought to be made liable for breaches of covenant which bind him, but which for non-registration, do not bind his successors.[12] Because of the invariable practice of taking an indemnity covenant on a disposition of the burdened land, the 'original' liability of A will, if it exists, be passed to his successors by the effect of the indemnity covenant. But see **4.24** above for a potential limit on the liability of the indemnifier.

---

[9]   See **7.10** and **8.20** above.
[10] Compare the position before 1 January 1996 where the principle of the original tenant's liability to the landlord applied even after an assignment of the lease. That principle no longer applies to leases granted on or after 1 January 1996: Landlord and Tenant (Covenants) Act 1995.
[11] This is the view taken in *Powell v Hemsley* [1909] 1 Ch 680 at first instance. The point did not arise on appeal: [1909] 2 Ch 252.
[12] See Chapter 4 above.

(5) But in some cases A may covenant in such a way as to effectively warrant performance of the covenant by his successors, eg by the use of the word 'permit' considered at **14.19** below.

(6) Irrespective of the words of the covenant, A may be liable in tort where he transfers land to B in circumstances where he knows that B will use the land transferred in breach. This consequence may also follow such a transfer where a covenant is directed against a certain use of the land being permitted. A may be liable for permitting it even though it is B who has caused it.[13]

(7) Where the covenant contains an express provision excluding the liability of the covenantor after parting with all interest in or possession of the burdened land, that should put an end to the covenantor's liability. This type of clause is often refered to as one which limits the covenantor's liability to his seisin. The scope of such a clause may, however, depend upon the terms of the covenants and what has been disposed of by the covenantor. If there is a disposal of the freehold and the covenants do not contain any warranty of performance by the covenantor, the clause may be regarded as unnecessary. If there is a warranty of performance in the covenants and the covenantor has merely given up possession of the land he may be liable for the acts of licensees. Further, if the covenants are in terms that a certain use is not to be permitted he may be liable for the acts of others if he has not disposed of all interest in the land. The solution to the problem of whether a clause excluding liability after disposal is effective is to look at (a) the provision limiting liability to determine its scope; (b) the covenants themselves to see whether any warranty of performance is given (eg by the use of the words 'permit' or 'suffer'); and (c) whether the covenantor has given up his freehold or merely possession.[14] Clearly a tightly worded clause will avoid liability on the disposal of any interest on the burdened land and on the giving up of possession of it.

Liability for the acts or omissions of earlier owners or occupiers

14.8

– Unless the present owner has acquired the burdened land with notice of a registered[15] pending action, or a claim form or order affecting that land, he will not be liable for the acts, or omissions of his predecessors. This rule appears to apply only to single breaches; eg a past breach as to user which has ceased.

– However, in some cases the breach may be in the nature of a continuing one which may render the present owner liable for the sins of his predecessor, eg the use of a building in breach of covenant which continues.

– It may be that the covenant is directed at a particular act: eg directing that only a particular class of building be erected. There is some authority for

---

[13] *Sefton v Tophams* [1965] Ch 1140, and see **14.18** below on the effect of the word 'permit'.

[14] See *Ives v Brown*, unreported, 6 March 1997, CA for a case where the question of construction arose on the issue of whether merely giving up possession (as opposed to disposing of the freehold) was enough to avoid liability.

[15] That is to say in unregistered titles registered under Land Charges Act 1972, ss 5 or 6, and in registered titles, registered under Land Registration Act 2002, ss 34 and 42 and Land Registration Rules 2003, SI 2003/1417, r 172.

saying that in such circumstances the person who acquires the land on which
a building has been erected in breach is not liable by virtue of his mere
acquisition. However, he may be liable if he uses it in breach, or if he
participates in the breach by acquiring the property (which is the source of the
breach) in the course of the construction of the building which is in breach.[16]

– The last distinction seems a fine one; it may be that a modern court would
look at the question of whether the present owner was in breach more
broadly, both as a matter of construction and as a matter of determining the
nature of the breach. In many cases no modern purchaser will unwittingly
acquire land where it is plain that some breach of covenant has occurred
without the protection of an indemnity from the vendor, or insurance. In the
latter case the construction of the covenant alleged to have been broken will
be crucial in determining the risk.

The problems of consents

14.9   Three problems emerge:

(1)   Who is to give consent?
(2)   Is there to be an implication (in the absence of express words) that consent is
not to be unreasonably withheld?
(3)   Can terms, such as the payment of money, be imposed?[17]

14.10   The following text deals with each question in turn:

(1)   Who is to give consent?

In the absence of words indicating that the consent may be given by successors in
title, the granting of consent has been regarded as personal to the original party.[18]
This principle is one which can cause much difficulty. On the one hand, a wide

---

[16]   *Powell v Hemsley*, above at n 11. *Wrotham Park Estate Co Ltd v Parkside Homes Ltd* [1974]
1 WLR 798.

[17]   See the warning given by Jacob LJ, in *Mortimer v Bailey* [2004] EWCA Civ 1514, as to the
potential risk of being stopped by an injunction, or forced to pull down work, if a chance is taken to
build in breach of a consent covenant which is enforceable. And see also *Re Beechwood Homes
Ltd's Application* [1994] 2 EGLR 178, and *Briggs v McCusker* [1996] 2 EGLR 197, both
considered in *Crest Nicholson v McAllister* [2002] EWHC Ch 2443, at paras 32–39, of the
judgment of Neuberger J.

[18]   See *Mayner v Payne* [1914] 2 Ch 555; *Bell v Norman C Ashton Ltd* (1956) 7 P&CR 359; which are
both examples of a narrow construction. In *Wrotham Park*, above, the parties conceded that the
word 'the vendor' meant his successors. In the context of *Mannai Investments* (see n 1 above) it is
frankly hard to believe that such a narrow view would now prevail. In *Hale v Bellway Homes*
[1998] EGCS 83, an opportunity arose to decide the point, but sadly the parties agreed to defer
consideration of it, so the point remained undecided. See also *Howard Pryor v Christopher Wren
Ltd* (1995) (unreported) 24 October 1995, Knox J where 'the vendor' was construed as meaning
only one vendor, or in the case of trustees, one set of vendors. Otherwise there would be a
multiplicity of persons involved, as successors in title of the vendor (as owners of land sold by the
vendors) from whom consent to plans etc would have to be obtained and that 'would lead both to
contradiction and disorder'. In *Crest Nicholson v McAllister*, at n 17 above, it was held by
Neuberger J at first instance, that the restriction as to building without the prior consent of the
vendors, or a company was spent on the dissolution of the company and on the death of the
survivors of the two vendors. The Court of Appeal, whilst allowing the appeal on grounds not
argued at first instance, saw no reason to differ from the conclusions reached by Neuberger J
on that issue.

construction of 'the vendor' will admit successors as persons whose consent should be obtained. On the other hand, if the words are so limited in scope, why should a wider meaning be given? A modern court might well apply the principles set out at **14.2** above, in view of the commercial purpose behind such consent provisions. But on such authority as there is, a narrow construction may prevail.

Problems can arise in particular in the context of schemes of development where consents are required for the modification of scheme covenants, or for consents to works. The scheme may become unworkable if there is no-one whose consent can in practice be obtained, or if there is lengthy argument over whose consent is required.

It will usually be sufficient to identify the owner for the time being of the unsold part of the original covenantee's land rather than have to approach his successors, as owners of the plots on the whole estate.[19] But even this point is not free from doubt. Where the persons whose consent is required are numerous (as successors in title to the common vendor) there may be good reason why, as a matter of construction, their consents are *not* to be obtained.[20]

Restrictions on the titles to registered land can sometimes be used to reinforce covenants, particularly where consents of third parties are required. They are more commonly used where positive obligations are imposed. But in any case care must be taken to ensure that there is going to be some means of obtaining a consent (thereby lifting the restriction) in the event that the named party is dead, or no longer in existence. In the latter class limited companies can be particularly dangerous in that once they are in liquidation, or wound up, or struck off the register it can be a complex task to take steps (which may include restoring it to the register of companies) to require the company to grant the consent.[21]

If consent is to be granted by the 'estate surveyor' or the 'vendor's surveyor' (or agent) and if there is no longer any such person or body, it is an open question whether a surveyor or agent can be appointed *ad hoc*, assuming the appointor can be identified. If the 'agent' is a named company or firm, and that entity no longer exists, the consent restriction is spent, and it is doubtful whether another new body can be appointed.[22]

Even if the consent proviso is spent, other restrictions, eg as to user or identity, may still be effective and enforceable (*Crest Nicholson v McAllister*, above).

The only solution to many of these problems may be declaration under the Law of Property Act 1925, section 84(2), or under the inherent jurisdiction of the court; see Chapter 15 below.

---

[19] See *Everett v Remington* [1892] 3 Ch 148; *Cryer v Scott Bros (Sunbury) Ltd* (1986) 55 P&CR 183.
[20] In *Hale v Bellway Homes*, above, over 100 successors to the original vendor were, arguably, in a position to grant or withhold consent. See *Howard Pryor v Christopher Wren Ltd* (above) for an example where a multitude of persons whose consents were to be obtained was avoided.
[21] See the precedents at Appendix 7 below and **8.39** above. See *Crest Nicholson v McAllister*, at n 17 above, for an example where the company entrusted with granting consent to plans for building was dissolved in 1968.
[22] See *Crest Nicholson v McAllister*, at n 17 above.

(2)   Is there to be an implication of reasonableness in the giving of consent?

14.11 Unless those who are required to consider whether, or not to give consent have an existing duty to act in good faith, there will be an implied obligation not to withhold consent unreasonably.

Where the consent required relates to a 'general' matter (eg to a particular trade) there may be no implication as to reasonableness.

However, where the consent is required for a specific matter (eg plans for a building) reasonableness will be required. Otherwise business efficacy could not be given to such a condition if it was open to the covenantee to refuse consent to plans 'which are free from any tenable objection.'[23]

It is obvious that where the terms of the instrument show that the implication is meant to be excluded (eg where some covenants in the same instrument are expressly qualified and others are not) the implication will not be made – unless there is clearly an error of drafting.[24]

If it is not present the Lands Tribunal has no jurisdiction to add the implication as to reasonableness, as that would amount to a rewriting of the original covenant.[25]

It is open to question as to whether any liability can attach to the grantor of consent for the consequences of any wrongful delay or refusal of consent. Unlike the position under section 1 of the Landlord and Tenant Act 1988, there is no statutory duty on the grantor to conduct himself in any particular way. It is suggested that the position here is the same as under the law of landlord and tenant prior to the commencement of that Act, where no liability for the consequences of delay or refusal lay on the landlord.[26]

(3)   Can terms, such as the payment of money, be imposed?

14.12 If the price of consent is stated expressly, even in amounts which nowadays might be considered nominal (eg one guinea – £1.05) that is the end of the matter and that is the price payable, unless the parties agree a greater sum. In the absence of any specific reason to the contrary (eg that it would be *ultra vires*, as it was in *R v Braintree DC ex parte Halls* (2000) 80 P&CR 266, see **10.5** above) there is no reason why the party giving approval or consent should not be able to require a reasonable payment, or other reasonable terms in the price of his consent. It may well be that there is no express obligation to pay a fee, but unless a fee is unreasonable it would be difficult to challenge a condition on which approval

[23]   Per Megarry V-C. in *Clerical Medical and General Life Assurance Society v Fanfare Properties*, unreported, 1981, cited in *Cryer v Scott Bros (Sunbury) Ltd*, at n 19 above. See also *Gan Insurance v Tai Ping Insurance (No 2)* [2001] 2 All ER (Comm) 299.

[24]   See *Hale v Bellway Homes* [1998] EGCS 83. For other authority on the question of the implication of reasonableness see *Price v Bouch* (1986) 53 P&CR 257, *King v Bittlestone*, unreported, 22 October 1997, Blackburne J, and *Re Jilla's Application* [2000] 23 EG 147.

[25]   *Re North's Application* (1997) 75 P&CR 117.

[26]   *Norwich Union v Shopmoor* [1997] 1 WLR 531 and *Footwear Corp v Amplight Properties* [1999] 1 WLR 551 for the landlord and tenant position.

was to be granted which included payment of a fee, unless such a fee was without any rational basis.[27]

In some cases there may be a Private Act of Parliament governing the regulation of private estates and the covenants over them; for example the Wentworth Estate near Sunningdale, Berkshire and the St George's Hill Estate near Weybridge, Surrey. In such cases the relevant Act should be considered carefully to see whether the proposed charges are within the terms of the Act or any regulations made under it.[28]

QUESTIONS OF CONSTRUCTION WHICH ARISE FROM CERTAIN TYPES OF RESTRICTIVE COVENANT AND THE WORDS USED IN THEM

14.13   In this part of the chapter there is a selection of the words and phrases which appear to be the most frequently encountered in practice and which raise problems. It should be noted that following the application of the general principles set out at **14.2**, the meaning of words must be dependant on their context and the circumstances in which they are found. To this extent, whilst it is tempting to use statutory definitions in some instances, such definitions can only be regarded as a starting point, if that.[29]

(1)   Covenants directed against buildings and the like

14.14 'building'	denotes something enclosing an air space, and that is the true meaning in many cases. It can also mean hoardings and depending on the context, walls.[30] The definition has included a substantial brick barbecue,[31] a bay or bow window in advance of a house and a glazed lean-to. An underground structure may be a building.[32]
'house'	denotes a permanent building for habitation. The word can include a building containing residential flats if no qualification is given to the word; as to which see 'single' or

---

[27]   See *Reading Industrial Co-operative Society Ltd v Palmer* [1912] 2 Ch 42 (no liability to pay a fee, but no case for reasonableness argued); *Cryer v Scott Bros (Sunbury) Ltd*, at n 19 above; *McCarthy & Stone (Developments) Ltd v Richmond upon Thames LBC* [1992] 2 AC 48 (fees for pre-planning consultations unlawful).

[28]   See for example, *St George's Hill Residents Association Ltd v Cadogan Ltd* (2003) (HHJ Bishop, Kingston-upon-Thames County Court, 7 March 2003, where the St George's Hill Weybridge Estate Act 1990 was considered in the context of charges for the approval of new house building.)

[29]   For example, the definition in the Leasehold Reform Act 1967, s 2(1) of 'house' is designed to exclude flats, which by that Act were outside the enfranchisement legislation. For a collection of definitions against many of the words which appear below reference should be made to Stroud's judicial Dictionary; although a note of caution in applying specific statutory definitions to such words in the context of restrictive covenants should be borne in mind when using Stroud.

[30]   In *Urban Housing Co v Oxford City Council* [1940] Ch 70 a wall was held not to be a building in the context of the covenants in that case.

[31]   *Windsor Hotel (Newquay) v Allan* (1980) *The Times*, 2 July 1980; it can include a block of flats – *Kimber v Admans* [1900] 1 Ch 412.

[32]   *R v Westminster City Council* (1989) 59 P&CR 51.

'single private' dwelling house below.[33]

'dwelling house'

this may be more restrictive than 'house', requiring personal habitation and excludes non-residential use. There may, however, be multiple occupation.[34] It has been held that a private dwelling house may not be used for holiday letting.[35] Use of land subject to a covenant limiting user to 'a private residence only' as a roadway leading to other land is a breach of that covenant.[36] But in *Roberts v Howlett* [2002] 1 P&CR 19, letting a house to students at the University of Durham was not a breach of covenant not to use the property 'other than as a single private dwelling house'. That was a case of permanent residence by four students, as a social unit in quite a substantial house for a year, compared with transitory weekly or fortnightly holiday lettings. *C&G Homes v Secretary of State for Health* [1991] Ch 365, was considered and applied by the judge. Compare the provision of service accommodation to licensees in *Falgor Commercial SA v Alsahabia Iwac*.[37]

14.15 'a single dwelling house'

this is even more restrictive than 'dwelling house' used alone, for it prevents sub-division and multiple occupation.[38]

'a private dwelling house'

as in the last example, multiple occupation will be in breach.[39]

'a' may, or may not, connote singularity. It will depend on the context in which the word is used. At first instance in *Crest Nicholson v McAllister*[40] it was held that 'a private dwelling house' meant only one such dwelling house, a conclusion which the Court of Appeal expressed agreement had it been necessary to decide the case on that point: see **8.18** for the issue raised in the Court of Appeal. However, in *Martin v David Wilson Homes*,[41] the Court of Appeal held that a covenant restricting the use of the land to that of a 'private dwelling house' on each plot was descriptive of the

---

33 See n 31 above.
34 See *C&G Homes v Secretary of State for Health* [1991] Ch 365 for an example of where use of this word alone would have allowed multiple occupation of a house by persons in care. However, if stress is placed on the article 'a' that may restrict the covenant and exclude multiple occupation: *Berton v Alliance Economic Investment Co* [1922] 1 KB 742.
35 *Caradon DC v Paton* [2000] 35 EG 12.
36 *Jarvis Homes Ltd v Marshall* [2004] EWCA Civ 839. See also *Cala Homes (South) Ltd v Carver* [2003] EWHC 1995 (Ch); block of flats held not to be a 'detached house'.
37 [1986] 1 EGLR 41.
38 *Barton v Keeble* [1928] Ch 517.
39 *Barton v Keeble*, above. In *C&G Homes v Secretary of State for Health* [1991] Ch 365, it was held that the use of a house for persons in care was a breach of such a covenant, although it might not have been a breach if the covenant had been merely to use the property as a dwellinghouse.
40 [2004] EWCA Civ 410, CA, on appeal from [2002] EWHC 443.
41 [2004] EWCA Civ 1029; 39 EG 134.

user of the buildings and did not carry the meaning of constructed and did not carry any necessary implication of singularity. The contrary view expressed by Neuberger J in *Crest Nicholson* was described as 'erroneous' and it would seem to be the case that this authority determines the meaning of 'a private dwelling house', in the absence of factors suggesting a different construction. What is clear is that not only the restriction on building has to be considered, but also (if any) a restriction on user. See also to the same effect as *Martin, Briggs v McCluster*[42] where the word 'a' was descriptive of user and not of the number of residences.

'a single private dwelling house'

the word 'single' may define the use which may be made of the dwelling house (eg 'to use any building erected on the land as a single private dwelling house') or it may define the number of dwelling houses which may be built on the land, eg not to use the property conveyed or any part of it for any purpose other than that of a single private dwelling house.[43] This latter type of covenant will prevent the erection of further dwelling houses where one is already built on the burdened land. There appears to be no authority on the question whether, if one house is built straddling two plots (each subject to a restriction limiting each plot to one house), a subdivision of one plot would allow the building of one house on the plot so sub-divided. The diagram below shows what is meant in practice. The answer (depending no doubt on the construction of the precise covenant in question) is that the erection of the additional house on that part of plot B which is sold off is a breach, in that the entirety of plot B has two houses on it even though it might be said in pure mathematical terms that there are one-and-a half houses on it; that would still be a breach, being more than one. The diagram shows how this problem arises in practice.

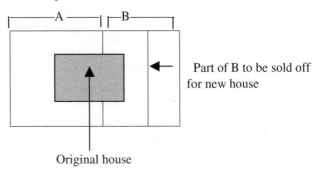

Part of B to be sold off
for new house

Original house

---

[42]   [1996] 2 EGLR 197.

'residential'	Means use as a residence, ie with a degree of permanence. It does not exlude multiple occupation.
'structure' or 'erection'	potentially wide in scope; wider than 'building'; can include poles, fences and walls. Potentially this can include diving-board, grab-handles and other superstructures associated with outdoor swimming pools.[44] A roadway may not be an 'erection' but lamp-posts will be.[45]
'bungalow'	means a building where the walls, save the gables, are no higher than the ground floor and where the roof starts at a point not substantially higher than those walls.[46]
'height'	when used by reference to existing buildings can include the height of chimneys and not just the 'roofline', but there may be real scope for dispute about the meaning unless clearly defined.[47]
'curtilage'	A small area around a building.[48]

(2)   Land use generally

14.16

'agricultural' purposes	statutory definitions are wide in their scope, eg Town and Country Planning Act 1990, section 336(1); a similar definition in Agricultural Tenancies Act 1995, section 38(1). Greenhouses used for trading purposes have been non-agricultural for rating purposes. It is possible for the words 'agricultural land' to exclude a farmhouse with its garden in the context of Inheritance Tax.[49] The main point to watch when using covenants aimed at preserving an agricultural use is that the land or buildings which are being used for such a purpose are not themselves productive of nuisances or annoyances; see below for those words. In this context it is often useful to consider specific agricultural activities such as intensive pig rearing,

---

[43] *Re Enderick's Conveyance* [1973] 1 All ER 843. The proposed erection of two blocks of flats was held to be a breach of covenant limiting development to 'detached houses' and user to 'a private dwelling house only': *Cala Homes v Carver* [2003] EWHC 1995 (Ch).

[44] For poles see *National Trust v Midlands Electricity Board* [1952] Ch 380; for walls and fences see *Urban Housing Co v Oxford City Council* [1940] Ch 70, at 82. For 'structure', see *Hobday v Nicol* [1944] 1 All ER 302 (artificially created, but permanent, water tanks filled with rubble and hard core). See also *Watson v Smythe* (1991) 64 P&CR where a ha-ha wall was a 'structure' and see the OED definition. For 'erection' see *Long Eaton Recreation Grounds Co Ltd v Midland Railway* [1902] 2 KB 574; railway embankment, and *Jarvis Homes v Marshall* [2004] EWCA Civ 839. See also *Halsbury's Laws of England*, vol 46, para 3, for the meaning of such words in the context of planning law. Care must be taken in the context of construing deeds in their context, as opposed to applying 'pure' planning definitions: *Hallam Land v UK Coal* [2002] EWCA Civ 982.

[45] *Jarvis Homes Ltd v Marshall*, above.

[46] *Ward v Paterson* [1929] 2 Ch 396.

[47] *Queen Elizabeth's School Blackburn v Banks Wilson* [2001] EWCA Civ 1360.

[48] See the authorities collected in *Dyer v Dorset CC* [1989] 1 QB 346.

[49] See *Starke v IRC* [1994] 1 WLR 888.

or battery hen-houses, which may themselves be capable of creating a nuisance, and if they are to be proscribed, the covenant should be drawn to say so.[50]

'annoyance' or 'nuisance'

words which include within their meaning a wide category of conduct. 'Annoyance' may be wider than 'nuisance'.[51] Mere economic loss caused by reduced marketability of property will not amount to a 'nuisance, annoyance, danger or detriment'.[52] Under this head may also be brought the notion of an 'offensive' use of the land; whether as part of a trade or business or some other use. It will be a question of fact whether what is being done is offensive in all the circumstances. How far the authorities in the nineteenth century are of much assistance is open to doubt. The modern test will invariably be one based on the nature of the locality and the environment generally in which the conduct occurs. A fried fish shop or takeaway in some parts of a town may not be offensive, whereas it may be in other parts of it. It is sometimes the case that the covenant is expressed so that it is for a third party to say whether in his opinion an annoyance, etc has been caused. In such cases, whilst the third party is not acting in a judicial capacity, he must act bona fide in forming a view as to whether the act complained of has occurred.[53]

'the working class' and other social groups

recent authority has held that if the words used to have a recognised and certain meaning at the time the covenant was imposed, the words of the covenant will be found to be capable of application, and, if necessary, enforcement, if they have a sufficiently certain meaning when the time for enforcement, or the determination of that meaning arises. Thus 'working classes' means today those on low incomes and 'housing' for them means housing for those on low incomes who might find it difficult to purchase, or rent suitable and appropriate accommodation in the private sector.[54]

---

50 See *Jobson v Record* (1998) 09 EG 148 for authority (in the context of the construction of an easement) that storage of cut timber (not grown on the land served by the easement) was not an agricultural purpose.

51 *Ives v Brown* [1919] 2 Ch 314 at 321. In the case of nuisance covenants one has to prove private nuisance, being an unlawful interference with a person's use or enjoyment of land. That may be difficult to prove; see *Hunter v Canary Wharf* [1997] AC 655 for an instance where no cause of action lay for interference with television reception.

52 *C&G Homes v Secretary of State for Health* [1991] Ch 365.

53 *Zetland v Driver* [1939] Ch 1. It is unlikely that a decision in such a case would be judicially reviewable, but it would be open to the person alleging breach to sue for an injunction restraining it and, if necessary for a declaration that the decision of the third party is ineffective; see *R v Disciplinary Committee of the Jockey Club, ex parte Aga Khan* [1993] 1 WLR 909.

54 See *Dano Ltd v Earl Cadogan* [2003] 2 P&CR 10, at paras 69–104 per Etherton J. See also *Westminster City Council v Duke of Westminster* [1991] 4 All ER 136, per Harman J, and [1992] 24 HLR 572, CA.

14.17 'trade or business' — there is a distinction between these two words. Trade is a wider word than business. In practice and ignoring some of the 'Victorian' distinctions, it will be a question of fact and degree whether what is being done falls within either of those words. It is often the case that the words are found in conjunction with the obligation to use the property only as a private dwelling house. In such cases what may be done may well not amount to a trade, or even a business (eg using property as a charitable boarding institution) but will be a breach of the dwelling house covenant. Likewise payment may not be an essential ingredient of carrying on a business. But payment will be for a trade to be carried on.[55]

'not to let the property for a [particular] trade' or 'other than for [a particular trade]' — there must be a substantial degree of identity where a prohibited trade is threatened. Where a covenant is restricted to a certain trade by way of user it will be a question of fact whether the user falls within the permitted description.[56] Note the constraints of the law referred to at **14.4** above in the context of restraints of trade and the EC Treaty and the Competition Act 1998.[57]

(3)   Covenants requiring the submission of plans

14.18 'to submit plans of any proposed building or alteration' — this will be treated as a negative covenant and as an obligation not to build, etc until plans, etc are approved.[58] 'Alteration' admits of a wide variety of meaning.

'with the consent of the vendor and his successors' — see **14.9** above for the problems associated with consent provisions.

---

[55] For consideration of this type of covenant, see *C&G Homes v Secretary of State for Health*, at n 52 above, at pp 380–384, per Nourse LJ.

[56] *Rother v Colchester Corporation* [1969] 1 WLR 720. On the remedy for breach of a covenant to use for a certain trade see *Co-operative Insurance Society Ltd v Argyle Stores (Holdings) Ltd* [1998] AC 1, and see **15.26** below.

[57] See *Young v Evans-Jones* [2002] 1 P&CR 14 for a covenant in a lease held to be a reasonable restraint of trade over the use of premises within a medical centre as a pharmacy.

[58] *Powell v Hemsley* [1909] 1 Ch 680. But note from that case the fact that, if a breach of such a covenant occurs, a successor in title of the covenantor in breach will not be liable. See **14.7** above.

(4) 'permit' and 'suffer'

14.19 'permit'   means the giving of leave for an act to be done (or
                         prevented) which the person permitting has power to
                         cause to be done or prevent. 'Permit' should only be
                         used in covenants where the original covenantor has the
                         power to control his successor. In ordinary sales of
                         freeholds from A to B, A will have no control over B
                         once A has sold up. But where used, the covenantor can
                         be made liable for his successor's breach.[59] An answer to
                         such a claim might be (as between successors to the
                         original covenantor and covenantee) that a restrictive
                         covenant cannot require the expenditure of money, so A
                         can hardly be required to take action preventing the
                         occurrence of a breach by B which A has allegedly
                         permitted.

'suffer'   this may have a wider meaning than permit.[60] This may
                         require the taking of legal proceedings to prevent the
                         breach by the successor, notwithstanding the argument
                         (at least as between successors to the original covenantor
                         and covenantee) that the covenant should not require
                         expenditure.[61]

(5) Breach 'by association'

14.20 Where, for example, a covenant is directed against the use of land for a
business, or where a specific use is proscribed, it may be possible to be in breach
where use of the land is closely associated with the activity prohibited by the
covenant, if what is being done could be said to fall within the words of the
covenant. However, there must be something being done which, on any reasonable
view amounts to a breach. Thus, use of land for access to a business will not
amount to use of that land as a business, and use of land as a landscaped area for a
superstore will not amount to breach of a covenant against food retailing.[62]

---

[59] See *Sefton v Tophams* [1967] 1 AC 50.
[60] *Barton v Reed* [1932] 1 Ch 362 at 375.
[61] See *Barton v Reed*, above, and *Berton v Alliance Economic Investment Co* [1922] 1 KB 742. For a
      longer analysis of the effect of the words 'permit' and 'suffer' see *Preston & Newsom's Restrictive
      Covenants Affecting Freehold Land* (Sweet & Maxwell, 9th edn, 1998), paras 6-61–6-76.
[62] See *Elliott v Safeway Stores* [1995] 1 WLR 1396; *Co-operative Retail Services Ltd v Tesco Stores
      Ltd* (1998) 76 P&CR 328, for examples of each occurrence. But see *Jarvis Homes v Marshall*
      [2004] EWCA Civ 839, where land subject to a covenant for use only as a private residence, was
      not to be used (as to part) as a roadway to gain access to the land. See also *GLN (Copenhagen)
      Southern Ltd v Tunbridge Wells BC* [2004] EWCA Civ 1279 for consideration of the two
      authorities above and further analysis of what is 'ancillary'.

(6)   Covenants relating to rights of light

14.21   These covenants are sometimes encountered when consideration is being given to development in conurbations. They pose particular problems in view of the complexity of the law of light. In the context of their existence as restrictive covenants the following short observations may assist in understanding their effect.

(1)   Covenants may be imposed so as to prevent the acquisition of light by or against neighbouring properties. Depending upon the words used, if effective, they will prevent acquisition of a right to light by the principal means of implied acquisition, these being prescription under the Prescription Act 1832, or (outside the City of London) by the application of the doctrine of Lost Modern Grant. Some covenants allow development by the owner of the land with the benefit of the covenant without regard to interference with any light received by his neighbour, and subject to the covenant. Other covenants restricting building will also determine whether and if so, to what extent building is permitted within defined limits. Such covenants may be designed to protect rights of light so that any future building must conform to the restrictions in the covenant.

(2)   Covenants against building may be either restrictive or permissive. If restrictive, that operates as a restrictive covenant and any breach is actionable. (eg a covenant that A is not to build more than 50 feet above a datum line; or that A is only to build within the terms of certain plans). A permissive deed is one where the covenant gives liberty to build to a certain height or within a certain envelope. In such a case any building which exceeds the permission will not be actionable as such. It will only be actionable if it can be shown that the excess is an actionable interference with the light enjoyed by the dominant owner.

(3)   A covenant may restrict the covenantor's right to build, and may also allow the covenantee a right to build to any height (or only to a defined height), whether or not that interferes with the covenantor's enjoyment of light. Such a covenant is not only restrictive, but also prevents any acquisition of light by prescription under the Act (or by lost modern grant) by the covenantor's property.[63]

---

[63]   *Haynes v King* [1893] 3 Ch 439. See further Bickford-Smith & Francis, *Rights of Light: The Modern Law* (Jordan Publishing Ltd, 2000), Chapter 9, for discussion and analysis of these covenants. See *Midtown v City of London Real Property Co* [2005] EWHC 33 (Ch), at paras 27–31, for a recent review of rights of light agreements and covenants, and the earlier authorities on such terms.

Chapter 15

LITIGATION AND RESTRICTIVE COVENANTS

15.1   The previous chapters of this book have been concerned with setting the scene for this chapter, which deals with the claims which relate to restrictive covenants. Claims may be brought to determine the meaning of covenants, whether and how they can be enforced and what remedies lies for breach of them. As this book is not one which deals in detail with general civil procedure, the chapter assumes that the reader is either familiar with, or has access to, up-to-date material on civil procedure. The emphasis is, therefore, on those features of claims which present themselves in litigation affecting restrictive covenants.

What is *not* covered in any detail is:

– the general approach to claims under the Civil Procedure Rules (CPR) and avoiding them, if possible, by mediation;
– the need to follow the general protocol;[1]
– the general rules of procedure as to the issue of claims (whether under Part 7 or Part 8) and the management of such claims until hearing;
– the rules of procedure at hearings of claims: whether interim, or final, and the enforcement of judgments;
– costs rules and in particular the rules under Part 44.3.[2]

What must, however, be stressed at the outset of this chapter is that in *any* litigation over covenants, particularly where it is between neighbours, the court will be concerned to ensure that, where possible, the dispute can be settled by mediation. Where this is not possible, the overriding objective will be followed to ensure a just dismissal of the claim. In addition, that objective, and the way in which the courts deal with costs issues under Part 44, means that it is now bad practice to waste the court's time and parties' costs with irrelevant or hopeless points. In most claims over restrictive covenants the issues can and should be reduced to what is relevant for the determination of the dispute. What follows, therefore, focuses on the *specific* issues which arise in the context of litigation and restrictive covenants.

The chapter is divided into four parts.

> Part I: Applications for a declaration under Law of Property Act 1925, s 84(2) or for a declaration of right under the inherent jurisdiction of the court.
> Part II: Claims for an injunction.
> Part III: Claims for damages, either at common law, or in lieu of an injunction.
> Part IV: Rectification claims.

---

[1]   Civil Procedure Rules (CPR), Practice Direction – Protocols, para 4.
[2]   As it is so important Part 44.3 of the CPR is reproduced at Appendix 7.

PART I: APPLICATIONS FOR A DECLARATION UNDER LAW OF PROPERTY ACT 1925, SECTION 84(2)

15.2   The Law of Property Act 1925, section 84(2) states:

'The court shall have power on the application of any person interested –

(a) to declare whether or not in any particular case any freehold land is, or would in any given event be, affected by a restriction imposed by any instrument; or

(b) to declare what, upon the true construction of any instrument purporting to impose a restriction, is the nature and extent of the restriction thereby imposed and whether the same is, or would in any given event be, enforceable and if so by whom.'

There are certain features as to the scope of section 84(2) which should be noted:

15.3

–   The terms of section 84(2) are broad and provide a potentially useful means by which the validity, or enforceability, of covenants can be tested. In particular the jurisdiction allows covenants which are plainly unenforceable to be 'cleared off'. However, as will be seen below the difficulty in finding all those entitled to enforce may prove an expensive and time-consuming business. Because the section operates *in rem* (ie directly upon the property benefited by the covenant) the court will require evidence that all those potentially affected have been notified of the intention to apply under section 84(2). The procedural steps required before a final hearing are off-putting in cases where the benefit of a covenant may be annexed to a wide, or an uncertain area. It is often the case that, rather than use section 84(2), insurance (see Chapter 18) will be considered a cheaper option, particularly where the time taken to complete an application under section 84(2) would be unacceptable to a developer. It may also be the case that in view of the decision in *Greenwich Healthcare NHS Trust v London & Quadrant Housing Trust,*[3] a declaration under CPR, Part 40, rule 20 could be obtained as an alternative to proceedings under section 84(2); this remedy is dealt with at **15.19** below.

–   The section applies to leases granted for a term of over 40 years of which 25 years are expired: section 84(12).

–   Covenants over land given for charitable and public purposes are within the scope of section 84(2).

–   Covenants over Royal and other land within section 84(11) are within the scope of section 84(2). Likewise, this jurisdiction can be exercised in respect of covenants imposed on the occasion of a disposition made gratuitously or for a nominal consideration for public purposes (section 84(2), excluding sections 84(7) and 84(11)).

–   Covenants entered into under statutory authority are within the scope of section 84(2), even though they may not be within the scope of the Lands Tribunal's jurisdiction under section 84(1).[4]

---

[3]   [1998] 1 WLR 1749.
[4]   For example, National Trust Act 1971, s 27, in Appendix 2, below.

– As stated above an Order under section 84(2) operates *in rem* by virtue of section 84(5); in effect it binds the land benefited by the restriction and all persons capable of being entitled to the benefit whether they are parties, or whether they have been informed of the proceedings or not. It is this provision which demonstrates why such care has to be taken to identify all those with the benefit of the covenant.

When can section 84(2) be used?

15.4

(1) Where it is necessary to 'clear off' restrictions which, on their face are unenforceable because:
   (a) the benefit of the covenants (which are not annexed to the benefited land) has not been assigned;
   (b) where the annexation of the benefit is to the whole of the benefited land rather than to each and every part of it;[5]
   (c) where the benefited land cannot be ascertained;[6]
   (d) where a scheme of development has been invalidly created, or where the existence of such a scheme is in doubt;
   (e) where some other point of construction of the covenant makes it doubtful that the covenant can be enforced;
   (f) where notwithstanding the apparent unenforceability of the covenant (or the difficulties therein), insurance is not an option.

(2) Where it is necessary to resolve some question of construction.
For example:
   (a) whether the giving of consent should be qualified by an implied term as to reasonableness, and if so, by whom it should be given;
   (b) whether particular development, or other activity would be in breach of covenant.

15.5

(3) Where it is necessary to resolve some question as to enforceability or construction even though the question is only likely (if at all) to arise at a future date, or on future events which have yet to happen. This is an exception to the general rule that the courts will not grant declarations on 'hypothetical' questions. It is in the nature of the jurisdiction under section 84(2) that future questions may arise. For developers wanting an answer to the effect of covenants if certain events happen in the future, the jurisdiction

---

5 This is unlikely to arise often since the dictum is *Federated Homes v Mill Lodge Properties* [1980] 1 WLR 594, to the effect that the benefit runs with each and every part of the benefited land; see **8.15** above.

6 In the light of the decision of the Court of Appeal in *Crest Nicholson v McAllister* [2004] EWCA Civ 410, which emphasises the need for easy ascertainment of the land intended to be benefited as a condition of annexation under the Law of Property Act 1925, s 78, it is anticipated that there may now be more applications under s 84(2) than before that decision, when it was often assumed that the effect of *Federated Homes v Mill Lodge Properties* [1980] 1 WLR 594, had achieved such annexation. See **8.18** above. The point will also arise in respect of pre-1926 covenants, as it did in *J Sainsbury v Enfield LBC* [1989] 1 WLR 590, which was an application under s 84(2) in view of the non-application of s 78. See also *Whitgift Homes v Stocks* [2001] EWCA Civ 1732, for a declaration as to the non-existence of a building scheme; see **8.32** above.

is, therefore, potentially useful.[7] This jurisdiction is also useful to residents having the benefit of certain restrictions where it is necessary to obtain an Order in terms declaring that certain covenants are enforceable and that at the date of the Order, the claimants are not barred from seeking to enforce, if necessary, by injunction. This provides a firm basis on which to enforce, if necessary, at a later date and can act as a 'warning' to developers who might be tempted to ignore, or treat lightly, covenants about which, but for the Order, there might be doubt over enforceability.[8]

Who can apply?

15.6   Section 84(2) states that 'any person interested' can apply. That comprises a wide class of persons and will include:

– the owner of the freehold (or leasehold) burdened land;
– the owner of the freehold (or leasehold) benefited land;
– a mortgagee of any of the above;
– a person contractually entitled to the burdened or benefited land.[9]

How is the application to be made?

15.7

– By application in the Chancery Division of the High Court, either in London, or in the most convenient Chancery Registry outside London.[10]
– The relief sought will need to be tailored to the precise ground on which the application is being made. There may also need to be relief by way of an Order that the entries of the covenants at the Land Charges Registry, or on the titles of the affected properties, if registered, be vacated, or in some other way dealt with so as to reflect any Order made in the application.
– By counterclaim in a claim to enforce by injunction; see **15.20** below.

Who should be the respondent?

15.8

This should be:

– Anyone who has an arguable claim to the right to enforce the covenant, eg the original covenantee. It may be that such a person may take the view that he is not entitled to enforce – but initially at least such a person should be joined.[11]
– Anyone who is an objector under the procedure set out below – even if, at the stage of joining them, it is unclear whether they have the right to enforce.[12]

---

[7]   See **15.19** below as to the jurisdiction to grant declarations which may be an alternative to an application under s 84(2) in appropriate cases.
[8]   An Order was made in such terms in *Johnson v Whipp* (unreported) 19 November 2001.
[9]   As in *J Sainsbury v Enfield LBC*, at n 6 above.
[10]   Under CPR, Part 8. It is unlikely to be the case that the facts will be in dispute in many claims under s 84(2). So use of a Part 7 Claim Form will be rare.
[11]   *Re Sunnyfield* [1932] 1 Ch 79. That was an example of a case where the original covenantee took the view that it was not entitled to enforce the covenants.
[12]   Consideration should be given to the use of CPR, Pt 19, rr 6 and 7 (representative parties where a number are in the same interest or where some parties in that interest cannot be ascertained) and

Defining at the pre-claim stage who might be a respondent

15.9 As indicated at **15.3** above, one of the features of an application under section 84(2) is the need to ascertain who is entitled to enforce the covenant, and to ensure that if opposing, they can be heard at any hearing. In some cases the scope of such a class and the identity of its members may be limited and easy to define; in others it may be hard to define the class for a number of reasons. Not the least of which may be the difficulty of identifying the land benefited by the covenant.[13]

To this end, the practice has developed of sending a 'circular' to all those potentially entitled to enforce with the aim of weeding out those who are not so entitled and those who do not oppose the application, leaving a 'rump' of objectors who will be respondents to the summons.

As will be seen the task of preparing for the despatch of the circular, and its terms and the follow-up to it is not always an easy one. In many cases either the alternative of insurance, or even a declaration under the inherent jurisdiction may be far more attractive. But in other cases there may be no alternative to seeking relief under section 84(2) with all the preparation that it entails. Bear in mind that using a 'circular' may preclude insurance in respect of the covenant that it advertises.

The 'circular' and its preparation and use

15.10 The following steps should be taken to identify who should be respondents to the claim form (in addition to the original covenantee, if applicable).

Step I

15.11 Ascertain the full extent of the land which may have been capable of benefiting from the covenant. In effect this is the whole of the covenantee's land at the date of the instrument creating the covenant which is the subject of the application under section 84(2). If the application relates to a scheme of development, the benefited land will include the whole of the estate subject to the scheme. If the covenant is annexed by reference to a plan that will make the task much easier. It is at this stage that the text of the original instrument does need to be examined in order to see how the benefit of the covenant has been annexed, or if not, by what means the benefit of the covenant is expressed to pass. In the latter case the area may be undefined, and it may be very difficult to see what land is capable of benefiting.

Step II

Try (as best one can) to ascertain who owns each and every part of the land identified at Step I. (Use, for example, Land Registry on-line searches, including searches of the index maps, under the Land Registration Rules 2003, SI 2003/1417,

---

whilst these claims are not strictly within Pt 19, r 8A, in managing the claim the court may want to notify parties of the claim and give them an opportunity to become a party.

[13] See *Crest Nicholson v McAllister* [2004] EWCA Civ 410, see **8.18** above.

rule 145 (using form SIM) or under rule 155 (using form OS3) (individual titles) (all of which may be made electronically) or the electoral roll where the title is still unregistered).

Step III

15.12   Send to each of the persons identified at Step II a form of letter ('the circular') which should state:

(1)   The identity of the client's property and the covenants which are the subject of the application.

(2)   What is proposed by way of development (for example) which would potentially be a breach of covenant. (If planning consent has been obtained, refer to that).

(3)   That the client has been advised that the covenant is no longer enforceable (or has a certain meaning) which has led the client to consider making an application under Law of Property Act 1925, section 84(2), for a declaration that the covenant is no longer enforceable (or has a certain meaning to the effect that the proposed development would not be a breach of it, as the case may be).

(4)   That the addressee is asked to say whether he wishes to consent to an Order being made in form requested in the proposed application, or if he wishes to object and thereby be a respondent to it. If the course of objection is proposed the addressee should be informed that he will in due course have to say on what basis he claims the right to enforce the covenant. That may have to be done by his solicitor and production of his title will be required. It is sometimes the practice to send a second letter to any objector (once the form expressing a lack of consent is received) asking for particulars of the manner in which the benefit is vested in the objector and disclosing the evidence of title on which that assertion is based.

(5)   There should be enclosed with the letter:

   (a)   a copy of the draft application[14] and such other evidence as is relevant in support to enable the addressee to decide how he is to respond;

   (b)   a form of consent or objection with spare copies for co-owners.

(6)   The addressee should be asked to identify any other person having an interest in the land at the address given; eg a tenant or a mortgagee.

(7)   A time within which a response should be given and an invitation to take legal advice on the letter should be included; an sae is a tactful enclosure.

(A draft form is at **A7.5**).

Step IV

15.13   Having allowed for the response time to the initial letter, chasers and other letters to mortgagees, etc, it will be possible to say how the application should proceed and against whom. One of four situations will, probably, emerge.

---

[14]   Part 8 Claim Form would be the usual way of starting this type of claim.

(1) It is impossible to identify those who may be entitled to enforce from initial research and/or from the response to the circular.
(2) All consent to the application.
(3) None consent to the application.
(4) Some do and some do not consent to the application, or at least some are silent.

Step V

15.14 Those who are to be respondents will be all those under (3) and those objecting under (4). If they are numerous and appear to have an identity of interest, a representation Order may be advisable under CPR, Part 19, rules 6 or 7. It is possible to issue a Part 8 Claim Form without naming defendants: Part 8, rule 2A.

Making the application

15.15

(1) The witness statement under Part 8, rule 5, in support of the application, should be put into final form. No witness statement can ever be the same as another, but some pointers as to contents are as follows.

   (a) Exhibit the best evidence of the instrument imposing the covenant which is the subject of the application. In registered titles the pre-registration deeds may still be located, and the District Registry at which the register of title is maintained should have filed a copy of the instrument. It is sometimes unsafe to rely on what is on the register itself in view of the (unnoticed) errors that can occur in copying at first registration.

   (b) A large scale plan to identify the burdened and (potentially) benefited land at the date the covenant was imposed; if a scheme covenant show the extent of the area covered by the scheme. The better the plan the clearer your case will be. Bad small-scale photocopies with smudges and thick lines are no use!

   (c) Show the devolution of title to the respondents, so far as revealed, at this stage. It is this point which makes it desirable as early as possible to get the potential objectors to show their title in order to show how they claim the benefit of the covenant. The circular can make this request, but invariably such a request is only likely to produce results once solicitors are instructed on behalf of respondents. In many cases the production of title will show the absence of annexation, or a scheme and the absence of a chain of assignment, thereby leading the respondent to concede that he is not entitled to object. Unless there has been progress on this aspect of the application at an early stage, the person making the witness statement may be unable to state on what basis the respondents seek to assert the right to enforce.

   (d) Exhibit the circular, and all responses, if necessary explaining the research which went into the compilation of the list of addressees.

   (e) Where no responses have been received identify those cases, showing that the special delivery service has been used. Where inconclusive replies have been received, exhibit those. In each case it may be that

> further enquiries are being made to clarify whether there will or will not be objections, in which case say so.
>
> (f) Explain what is being proposed by way of development, etc, which causes the application to be made. If there is to be a declaration defining the nature and extent of the covenant say what is relied upon in support of the declaration sought.

(2) Draw the claim form in its final form, issue and serve on the respondents.

(3) If there are no objections, or if there is no evidence as to who has the benefit of the covenant, you can make the application ex parte.

(4) It may be necessary once the application is made and there are doubts over the right to enforce by any of the respondents to seek specific orders for the disclosure of title documents, eg where chains of assignment are being relied upon, where are the assignments?

(5) In the unlikely event of contention over the basic facts use a Part 7 Claim Form with Particulars of Claim and a Statement of Case under CPR, Part 16.

Important points to remember about applications under section 84(2)

15.16 It is easy to under-estimate the difficulties which this type of application can present. In applications based on the inability of anyone to enforce, the burden on the claimant is a heavy one. He must show that either there was no annexation of the benefit of the covenant, or no chain of assignment of the benefit (a fact which may not be plain until titles are disclosed after the application is brought), or no effective scheme of development, or the fact that there is no land capable of being benefited by the covenant, or that by virtue of a failure to register, the covenant is not binding. The guiding rule is:

'The Court ought to be clear that the property is not burdened by restrictions.'[15]

This is the practical consequence of an Order made under the section operating *in rem*; see paragraph 15.3 above.[16] Hence the need for clear evidence in support of the application.

Even where all that is being sought is a declaration as to construction, the claimant still has to satisfy the court that all parties who have an interest in one or other of the forms of construction which could be put forward, are there to do so. In some cases it may be necessary for the representative of the 'active' opponents to address the court at the hearing on behalf of the non-appearing (but not consenting) opponents to ensure that all views are known.[17]

The circular and subsequent steps taken in response to it should be aimed at eliciting proof of entitlement, or lack of entitlement, to the benefit of the covenant which is the subject of the application. There is a danger in drafting a circular which merely asks for approval, or disapproval of a particular development. An expression of approval in such a case will not be evidence of a lack of entitlement

---

[15] Per Scott J in *Re Nos 6,8,10 and 12 Elm Avenue New Milton* [1984] 1 WLR 1398 at 1407. In that case the claimant had to show that there was no scheme of development affecting the land, which it failed to do on the evidence.

[16] For an example of the evidential difficulties see *Re Wembley Park Estate* [1968] Ch 491.

[17] As occurred in *Re Tiltwood* [1978] Ch 269.

to the benefit and the applicant will, therefore, fail to obtain a declaration that certain covenants are not enforceable.[18]

Orders made under section 84(2)

15.17 Apart from the obvious form of the declaration which will be sought as to the enforceability or effect of the covenant, the Order may have to deal with the manner in which the burden of the covenant is protected by registration. The practice appears to be as follows:

– If the Order simply declares the construction of the covenant, it seems unlikely that any change must be made to its registration, although it will be kept with the deeds (unregistered titles) and in registered titles it might be prudent to lodge a copy at the District Land Registry where the title to the burdened land is maintained and the Order may be noted against that title. The latter course should be taken in the rare case where the benefit of the covenant is entered.

– If the Order is to the effect that the land is no longer affected by the covenant (eg because of unity of seisin) or if the Order is to the effect that there is noone entitled to enforce the covenant, the ability to change the registration will depend upon whether all the burdened land was within the application, or was not.

– If all the burdened land is within the application and if the Court is satisfied that the land is no longer affected by the covenant, or noone is entitled to enforce the covenant which is the subject of the application, or if all persons with the benefit consent, if the title is unregistered the Court can order vacation of the land charge protecting that covenant under Land Charges Act 1972, section 1(6). Where the title to the burdened land is registered, modification of the register under Land Registration Act 2002, section 65 and Schedule 4, paragraph 2(1)(b), to bring the register up to date, can be made part of the Order, or follow from it, and the Order should be lodged for this to be done. (See also the Land Registry Rules 2003, SI 2003/1417, rule 87 providing for the cancellation of a notice, by use of form CN1, which would have to be accompanied by a copy of the Order to support the application.) As the Order operates *in rem*, all titles which would (but for the Order) have the benefit of the covenant are affected, so the Land Charges Registry and the Land Registry will only vacate an entry where the Order is made in the circumstances set out at the start of this paragraph.

– If other land is potentially bound, the owner of that land can still be bound and, therefore, vacation of the Land Charge protecting the burden of the covenant over that land will not be ordered. In registered titles there seems no reason why as *regards the title before the court* an Order should not direct modification under either section 50(3) or under section 65 of the Land Registration Act 2002 as is suggested above.

---

[18] This is what seems to have gone wrong with the circular in *Re Elm Avenue*, see n 15 above, although from the report it is not clear precisely why; see per Scott J, at 1407. The burden is on the applicant to 'clear off' opponents by showing they do not have the benefit, and not that they are merely happy with the development proposed. See *Re MCA East* [2003] 1 P&CR 9 for a recent example of a properly made application which was not opposed and which succeeded.

Costs of applications under section 84(2)

15.18   Although the usual judicial discretion in matters of costs will apply in applications under section 84(2),[19] because the aim of the applicant in bringing an application under section 84(2) is to 'clean up' his title as regards the covenants upon it, which is for his benefit, a practice as to costs in such applications has developed which in simple terms means that the discretion will usually be exercised in the manner described below. No doubt there will be cases where circumstances will require the exercise of the discretion differently, but the practice appears to be as follows:

–   The claimant will usually be expected to pay his own costs of the application.
–   The claimant will usually have to pay the respondents' costs down to the time when they are able (on a full appreciation of the matter) to decide whether or not to oppose. If they oppose thereafter, unsuccessfully, they will bear their own costs thereafter – but will not be ordered to pay the claimant's costs. If they are successful in opposing, the claimant will pay the respondents' costs.[20]
–   If the application succeeds on a novel point of law the claimant may be ordered to pay the respondents' costs of the application in its entirety.[21]
–   There is sometimes a distinction drawn between the scale of costs to which the respondent may be entitled. The indemnity basis is usually chosen down to the time when the respondent had the opportunity to make a final assessment of merits; thereafter the standard basis is chosen. (See CPR, Part 44, rule 44.4.)[22]

A claim for a declaration under CPR, Part 40, rule 20

15.19

(1)   For various reasons a developer client may want to know whether a covenant is enforceable or not. In particular, he may want to know whether an injunction will lie at the suit of any person potentially entitled to that remedy. The major difficulty in many cases lies in having the right information which will enable advice to be given as to whether a covenant is enforceable or not. This means asking the question, who has the benefit of the covenant and who has the right to enforce? Furthermore, as has been pointed out above, the nature of an application under section 84(2) hardly endears itself to those (usually developer clients) where time is of the essence and development decisions depend upon the availability of borrowed money. This observation is made notwithstanding the relatively short time these days between the issue of a Part 8 Claim Form and the hearing; particularly when the duration of that hearing is estimated at one day, or less. In many cases the time for disposal

---

[19]   As to which see CPR, Pt 44.
[20]   *Re Jeffkins' Indentures* [1965] 1 WLR 375. Considered and applied in *University of East London v London Borough of Barking and Dagenham (No 2)* [2004] EWHC 2908 (Ch).
[21]   *Re Tiltwood* [1978] Ch 269; but this is by no means automatic and there have been cases where this has not occurred.
[22]   See CPR, Part 44, r 3 and generally as to the court's discretion over costs. See n 20 above and *University of East London v London Borough of Barking and Dagenham* (No 2), for a modern ruling on costs in these claims.

from the start of the claim to final hearing is under 6 months. In very urgent cases the court will give directions for an early hearing date. But this may still be too long a period for certain clients.

(2) There will be cases where it is possible to ascertain with relative case who has the benefit of the covenant. To avoid a period of damaging uncertainty (or a period which might put paid to the plans of a developer, or an unwarranted ransom demand) a declaration should be sought that specified persons are not entitled to enforce a covenant by means of an injunction, or damages.

(3) Such cases will be rare, but there is no reason why the option of seeking a declaration should not be considered. In cases set out in (2) above, particularly where neither agreement nor objection is received from those entitled to the benefit, such a course may well be appropriate. However, the need to ascertain those who have the benefit of the covenant must be stressed. For unless all those so entitled are caught by any declaration the Order will be useless; others not bound could still enforce, and the Order does not operate *in rem* unlike an Order under section 84(2).[23]

PART II: CLAIMS FOR AN INJUNCTION

Introduction and preliminary steps

15.20 This is not a litigation handbook, and, therefore, some knowledge will be assumed as to civil litigation and the remedies of an injunction. The up-to-date edition of *Civil Procedure* and other guides can be used to fill the gaps where extra assistance is required. What is emphasised in Part II (and in Part III where damages are discussed) is the aspect of these remedies particularly at the interim stage which have a particular bearing in the context of restrictive covenants.

15.21 Before contemplating bringing a claim for an injunction the following questions should be asked; it is all too easy to forget them in the hurly-burly of threatened litigation, and they are better asked at an early stage rather than later on when the costs penalties of changing course may be severe.

– If you are acting for the potential claimant, is he entitled to *the benefit* of the covenant by the means set out in Chapter 8? (Look at the summary of Rules at page 10 and the flowchart on pages 5–7.)
– Whether you act for the potential claimant, or defendant (and this question may be more important if you act for the latter) is the defendant *bound* by the covenant? Is the covenant protected by registration if he is not the original covenantor? Is it a covenant where the burden runs? Eg check that it is not a purely personal or trading covenant. Look at the summary to Chapter 4 at page 12.

---

[23] See *Greenwich Healthcare NHS Trust v London and Quadrant Housing Trust* [1998] 1 WLR 1749, where an application for a declaration that (*inter alia*) certain covenants were not enforceable by injunction, or by a claim for damages was granted in accordance with the principles set out above. The case is a useful one in respect of troublesome easements, for there is no jurisdiction to discharge or vary them, unlike restrictive covenants, and declaratory relief may be the only way of protecting against latent objections to varying their terms.

– Has there been a *breach*, or is what is threatened going to be a breach, and if so to what extent? A one inch incursion (even if measurable) into a 'buildings free' zone may not be a very strong basis on which to launch expensive injunction proceedings. Look at Chapter 14 on construction of the words of the covenant. Is there any sense in seeking a declaration under section 84(2) or under the inherent jurisdiction, considered in Part I above?

– *How far has the potential defendant gone?* If he has gone too far in building in breach and your client has stood idly by, you will probably not get an injunction.

– Has the claimant indicated (openly) that all he wants is money. If so, that will usually be fatal to a claim by him for an injunction.[24]

– *Can you afford to claim or defend?* This is not just a question of costs, but the question touches upon the undertaking in damages a claimant will have to give if he is to get an interim injunction (see **15.29** below) and the likely damages a defendant may have to pay if he is found liable in a case where damages are the remedy ordered by the court.

– *Can your client avoid litigation by other means?* Self help may be out, but what about arbitration, mediation, ADR and all the other modern alternatives to litigation?[25]

– Have you complied with the General Pre-Action Protocol?[26]

General principles as to the grant of injunctions when enforcing restrictive covenants

15.22

(1) An injunction will be granted (almost) as a matter of course to restrain a breach of a restrictive covenant. In the older authorities the court said that speaking generally, it had 'no discretion' but to grant such relief, but the modern approach is for the court to recognise that it has a discretion in the award of the remedy, whilst regarding such relief as the 'natural' remedy for breach of a restrictive covenant. The discretion extends to the terms on which an injunction will be granted.[27]

---

[24] *Gafford v Graham* (1998) 77 P&CR 73.

[25] For the modern approach to mediation, see the guidance given by the Court of Appeal in *Halsey v Milton Keynes General NHS Trust* [2004] EWCA Civ 576, and in *Reed Executive Plc v Reed Business Information Ltd* [2004] EWCA Civ 887.

[26] Reproduced at Appendix 7. No advice should be given in any claim, including those relating to restrictive covenants, without having considered the alternatives to litigation. The costs risks in not doing so may be significant. See *Halsey v Milton Keynes General NHS Trust*, n 25 above.

[27] For an example of the old approach, which must now be regarded with caution, see *Osborne v Bradley* [1903] 2 Ch 446, and for the modern approach to the exercise of the discretion, *Gafford v AH Graham* (1998) 77 P&CR 73. See also *Mortimer v Bailey* [2004] EWCA Civ 1514, in which *Gafford v AH Graham* was distinguished in view of the relative promptness of the claimants and their warnings to the defendants who were building in breach of covenant. But note that in *Mortimer v Bailey*, interim relief was refused on the basis that the claimants had delayed too long. That did not stop them from getting a final order at the trial, affirmed by the Court of Appeal. See *Midtown v City of London Real Property Co* [2005] EWHC 33 (Ch), at paras 65–80, for a recent examination of the principles on which an injunction will be granted. (Prohibitory injunction refused as oppressive to defendants to be prevented from pursuing a large scale and 'worthwhile and beneficial' development east of New Fetter Lane, London, EC4.) See **15.39** below for the principles applicable to damages in lieu.

(2) For an injunction to be granted it is not *necessary* for the claimant to prove pecuniary loss as a result of the actual or threatened breach, but it may be *desirable* to do so. *Prima facie* he is entitled to the remedy on proof of breach alone. However, in terms of whether damages in lieu of an injunction will be awarded, the question of loss will be relevant, and the modern approach to the exercise of the discretion will inevitably involve a consideration of the loss caused by breach.[28]

(3) Where there is doubt whether a restrictive covenant applies or whether consent under a restrictive covenant is being unreasonably withheld, the prudent party will get the matter sorted out before starting building. If he takes a chance then it will require very strong circumstances where, if the chance having been taken and lost, an injunction will be withheld.[29]

Specific factors which will hinder or prevent the grant of an injunction

These principles apply to both interim *and* final applications for injunctions.

15.23

(a) *Delay or acquiescence.* Time is 'of the essence' if not in legal, then in factual terms when seeking injunctive relief. Varying degrees of delay and acquiescence will inevitably exist. At one end of the scale is permission openly granted to break the covenant, or allowing a breach in full knowledge of it, or years of delay in seeking to enforce the covenant. At the other end of the scale there is conduct which is equivocal, or trivial in terms of time. Failing to object to planning applications for development potentially in breach may fall more into the latter than the former camp; although generalisations can hardly be drawn too far, even from this example. Modern authorities show that the court will look at all aspects of the parties' conduct before deciding whether such conduct disentitles the claimant from obtaining injunctive relief. The test of whether the claimant should, or should not, be barred by his conduct from obtaining an injunction has been described as one which requires the question to be asked 'would it be dishonest or unconscionable' for the claimant to enforce by means of an injunction?[30] Under this head may also be placed the various categories of estoppel which would prevent enforcement. Thus conduct which would allow the covenantor to believe that there will be no objection to the proposed work may amount to an estoppel. One example in specific terms can be the entry into an agreement to consent to works to which the Party Wall etc Act 1996 applies, or the acceptance of an Award under that Act. Although that Act specifically excludes private law rights under the law of easements, nuisance etc, from its ambit, what the parties have done in the context of party wall matters will be

---

[28] See **15.36** below.

[29] Per Jacob LJ, in *Mortimer v Bailey*, see n 27 above, at para 41.

[30] See *Shaw v Applegate* [1977] 1 WLR 970 at 980; *Gafford v AH Graham*, at n 27 above. The latter authority decided that the defence of acquiescence is to be given equal weight in cases whether the claimant is suing to enforce the covenant at law as an original covenantee, or in equity as a successor in title; for the distinction see **8.4** above, and **15.34** and **15.37** below. See also CPR, Pt 25, r 1. See *Mortimer v Bailey*, at n 27 above, where the claimants' conduct was not unconscionable. A mandatory injunction was awarded to remove the offending extension.

highly significant when the court has to consider conduct in respect of a claim for injunctive relief. But merely negotiating should not deprive the potential claimant of the right to seek an injunction, if the negotiations fail.[31]

(b) *Past history.* Past failures to enforce which have led to a change in the neighbourhood may have deprived covenants of their purpose and thereby lessened the prospect of injunctive relief being granted. The court will not restrain a breach where little purpose would be served by specific enforcement.[32]

(c) *The claimant openly indicating that he will take money.* That is usually fatal to a claimant who persists in seeking an injunction. Unless there is good reason why a claimant should not be held to an openly declared position, he will get damages in lieu of an injunction.[33]

Applications by the defendant to stay the proceedings for an injunction

15.24

(1) If a defendant considers that a defendant has a fair chance of applying to the Lands Tribunal for the discharge or modification of the covenant which is sought to be enforced, he may apply for a stay of the injunction proceedings under Law of Property Act 1925, section 84(9) and for leave to apply to the Lands Tribunal under section 84(1) of that Act.[34]

(A classic instance of this is where a radical change in the neighbourhood has occurred.)[35]

But a defendant who wishes to take this course must undertake to proceed with his application to the Lands Tribunal forthwith and with due diligence, if not under a defined timetable, and the claimant will be given liberty to apply to discharge such a stay if the defendant proves sluggish, or if for any other

---

[31]   See *Gafford v AH Graham*, at n 27 above, at pp 80–81, per Nourse LJ, where the principles of unconscionability as expressed in *Taylors Fashion v Liverpool Victoria Trustees* [1982] QB 133 (at p 155) were applied.

[32]   See *Robins v Berkeley Homes* [1996] EGCS 75 for a modern example of where this argument failed in respect of the Camden Park Estate, Chislehurst, Kent. See also, *Knight v Simmonds* [1896] 2 Ch 294; *Bell v Norman C Ashton Ltd* (1956) 7 P&CR 359. Note the power to cancel entries of covenants where injunctions are refused referred to in **13.4** above.

[33]   *Gafford v AH Graham*, at n 27 above, at p 84, per Nourse LJ.

[34]   See *Luckies v Simons* [2003] 2 P&CR 30 where the defendant developer applied for a stay under s 84(9) on 20 November 2001 (proceedings issued June 2001, defence served August 2001) and on 21 November 2001 made an application to the Lands Tribunal, before the hearing of the application for the stay in April 2002. It was held by HHJ Rich QC that whether the making of the application to the Tribunal precedes the making of the application for a stay, or it being heard, did not affect the jurisdiction granted by s 84(9). An application for a stay under s 84(9) should be made 'with promptitude': ibid, para 20. It is for the claimant (ie the respondent to the application for the stay made by the defendant under s 84(9)) to persuade the court that the stay should not be ordered, for that is the 'normal order': ibid para 27. A stay might not be ordered if, for example, it is clear that the application to the Tribunal had no real chance of success. Likewise, it may be unjust to order a stay if the defendant has conducted himself (either prior to, or during the claim) in such a way as to indicate to the claimant that he has 'elected' not to go to the Lands Tribunal, under s 84(1): ibid at paras 30–31, and see *Chatsworth Estates v Fewell* [1931] 1 Ch 224.

[35]   For the precise grounds on which such an application to the Lands Tribunal would be made, see Chapter 16 below.

reason he needs to press on with the injunction. Each party will have to give an undertaking as to damages as a term of such a stay.[36]

Bearing in mind the timescale of a fully contested application in the Lands Tribunal, and the potential exposure on the undertaking in damages, few defendants will want to stay the injunction proceedings by this route. Most will want to fight the injunction proceedings at the interlocutory stage, or settle on terms. This is particularly the case where the defendant is a developer.

(2) A defendant may wish to seek a declaration (by way of counterclaim in the injunction proceedings) under section 84(2) or under the inherent jurisdiction (see Part I above) as part of his defence if there is a live prior question on the effect, or enforceability of the covenant which the claimant seeks to enforce. In such a case determination of the issue raised under section 84(2) will require a stay of the injunction proceedings, or an order for that question to be heard first. In many cases the question of the effect, or enforceability, of the covenant can be raised without the need for such a formal step to be taken, as such questions can be determined (at least as between the parties) by the court in reaching a decision as to whether any remedy should be granted. Clearly if the covenant is unenforceable, or if the construction of it leads to the conclusion that there has been no breach, the claimant will fail in his action for an injunction, if not damages in lieu.[37]

What sort of injunction is needed?

15.25 There are two types of injunction which can be granted:

– *prohibitory:* an injunction which restrains a breach which is either anticipated or threatened[38] (such as a building which is about to go up) or continuing and which is required to stop (eg trading in breach);
– *mandatory:* an injunction which requires a positive act to be done by the defendant, such as the pulling down of a building.

The problems posed by breaches of covenant and the need to seek mandatory relief whether on an interim or permanent basis

15.26 It should be clear that anyone who delays beyond a point where prohibitory relief will serve no purpose (as in cases of a building in breach of covenant) will have to consider the prospect of seeking *mandatory* relief. That is not an attractive prospect in many cases, as the court may be reluctant to grant such relief.[39] This point reinforces that made at **15.23** above regarding the importance of a quick response to breaches of covenant.

---

[36] See *Hanning v Gable-Jeffreys Properties* [1965] 1 WLR 1390; *Shepherd Homes Ltd v Sandham* [1971] Ch 340 at 353. See *Luckies v Simons*, at n 34 above.
[37] See *Adams v Rushmon Homes*, at **13.14** above, for an example of this result.
[38] Those who have the Latin used to refer to this as a '*quia timet*' (that which is feared) injunction; at least until 26 April 1999, when the CPR came into force.
[39] See *Morris v Redland Bricks* [1970] AC 652 for the general principles on which the court will act when applications are made for mandatory relief. In *Gafford v AH Graham*, see n 27 above, the Court of Appeal refused to grant mandatory relief seeking the removal of a riding school where the claimant had stood by and failed to prevent its erection by seeking interlocutory relief at an

In many restrictive covenant cases the court will refuse mandatory relief because of the extreme effect of such an order; to order demolition of erected houses might well be 'an unpardonable waste of much needed houses'[40] and even a fence may not be ordered to be removed, at least at the interlocutory stage.[41] In some cases however, a mandatory order will be made ordering the demolition of a house where special factors apply; such as the preservation of a sea view protected by the covenant.[42] It is also relevant to note that in rights of light cases the court will be prepared to order demolition, or partial demolition, of buildings causing an interference with light, at least in cases of bad interference.[43] The same practice should apply where the effect of breach of covenant is extreme.[44] Recent authority, *Mortimer v Bailey* [2004] EWCA Civ 1514,[45] indicates that a failure to seek interim prohibitory relief is not fatal to obtaining a final mandatory at trial.

At what stage should an injunction be sought?

15.27 The answer is always given: 'as early as possible'. But the tactical decision to seek early relief requires consideration of two matters:

(1) Will simply issuing a claim form with a claim for an injunction be enough, or do I need to seek interim relief under CPR Part 25?

15.28 To answer this question, consider the following examples.

(a) The defendant (alleged to be in breach of covenant) may be engaged in speculative development with borrowed money and he may be on a tight contract with builders. The mere issue of a claim form may force him to stop acting in breach and sue for peace. If the claim form is registered as a pending land action[46] that will have to be explained to purchasers and the defendant's bank, for anything which threatens the speed at which the development can be completed will be bad news for the defendant and his bank.

---

early stage. By the trial date the building had been up for over seven years. For the recent state of authority on interim applications for mandatory relief (which is a bold course) see *Nottingham BS Eurodynamics Systems* [1993] FSR 468 and CPR, Pt 25, r 1. See **15.28** below.

[40] Per Brightman J in *Wrotham Park Estate Co Ltd v Parkside Homes Ltd* [1974] 1 WLR 798 at 811.

[41] See *Shepherd Homes Ltd v Sandham* [1971] Ch 340, where a five month delay in seeking removal of the fence was also a factor in refusing a mandatory injunction. For 'interim' injunctions see **15.30** below.

[42] *Wakeham v Wood* (1981) 43 P&CR 40.

[43] See *Deakins v Hookings* [1994] 1 EGLR 190, where an upper floor extension was ordered to be cut back; anyone standing at the bus station in Wimbledon who sees a building where the upper storey looks like a slice of cheese will be looking at the location of that case! See also *Mortimer v Bailey*, n 27 above (loss of light and view).

[44] As to the practice of the court in granting mandatory injunctions in the context of covenants to carry on a trade or business, and the general policy of refusing such relief where it would require such a trade etc, to be carried on, see *Co-operative Insurance Society Ltd v Argyle Stores (Holdings) Ltd* [1998] AC 1.

[45] See n 27 above.

[46] In registered titles use an unilateral notice under Land Registration Act 2002, ss 34(2)(b), 35 and 87(1) or, in unregistered titles, register a pending land action under Land Charges Act 1972, s 5; see *Ruoff & Roper on the Law and Practice of Registered Conveyancing* (Sweet & Maxwell), Chapter 42.

(b) The defendant is trading in breach of covenant and will continue to do so notwithstanding the issue of the claim form.

In both cases the claimant runs a risk if he does not seek interim relief. In the first case it is tempting to think that the claimant can simply wait until trial, but in the meanwhile, the defendant can seek to strike out the claimant's action as an abuse of the process where it is plain that either the claimant is only after damages, or where the prospects of obtaining injunctive relief are remote. The claimant may be forced to elect whether to move for interim relief, or suffer a striking out. In the second case the conduct of the defendant will clearly require an application for interim relief, but in that case, if not in the first, the claimant has to consider the problem of the undertaking in damages.[47]

(2) *The problem of the undertaking in damages*

15.29 The usual practice when seeking interim relief is that the court may require the claimant to undertake to pay the defendant the loss which it has suffered should it turn out at the trial that the injunction obtained on an interim basis is not to be made final.[48] This may be a heavy burden for a claimant to bear and although there are exceptions, any claimant contemplating enforcement of covenants by injunction must be prepared to give such an undertaking. The counterpart to this predicament lies in the fact that a defendant who is faced with a claim for an injunction without any interim application being made, will not be able to recoup any losses pending trial owing to the uncertainty of his position. But that uncertainty 'is no more than a necessary consequence of the existence of a claim which has not yet been adjudicated'.[49]

---

[47] For conflicting authority on whether the claimant should be forced to seek interim relief see *Blue Town Investments Ltd v Higgs & Hill plc* [1990] 1 WLR 696 (where the claimant was so forced in a right of light case) and *Oxy-Electric Ltd v Zainuddin* [1991] 1 WLR 115 (where the court refused, where a breach of covenant was alleged, to require the claimant to make such an election). In *Vardy v Banner New Homes*, unreported, 1998, the court preferred the latter authority, largely because the striking factors of delay and lack of merit in the claimants' claim which were present in the former case were not present in the instant case. It is suggested that both of the two latter cases are correct in not requiring the claimant to make an interim application. This is particularly so since the case management powers of the court under the CPR will allow claims to be managed in such a way as, for example, merits their urgency. A Part 23 application can be made at any time seeking directions for an early hearing. In addition, it is suggested that Art 6 of the Convention for the Protection of Human Rights and Fundamental Freedoms 1950 (the Convention) now part of Sch 1 to the Human Rights Act 1998 and in force since 2 October 2000, allows a claimant to decide how he wants to pursue his claim (within the rules) and should not be forced to make an application as a condition of pursuing that claim. See Chapter 20 below. See Practice Direction, Pt 25, para 5 for the terms of an order for an injunction unless the court orders otherwise. See n 48 below.

[48] As with claims for security for costs under CPR Pt 25, r 13 (which raises issues under Art 6 of the Convention) it may be argued that to require a claimant, or any other party, to give an undertaking which he is financially unable to give is a breach of Art 6. Hence the discretion of the court at the opening of the Practice Direction, Pt 25, para 5. For the nature of the undertaking and its enforcement, see *Cheltenham & Gloucester BS v Ricketts* [1993] 1 WLR 1545. For the practice and the problems thrown up by impecunious claimants, see CPR, Pt 25 and *Allen v Jambo Holdings* [1980] 1 WLR 1252. See *Mortimer v Bailey* [2004] EWCA Civ 1514, at para 30, per Peter Gibson, LJ. See **15.22** and **15.23** above.

[49] Per Hoffmann J in *Oxy-Electric v Zainuddin*, at n 47 above, at 120.

What the claimant may have to contemplate is the 'David and Goliath' situation of having to give an undertaking for many thousands of pounds in a case where the defendant is a builder, or developer and there are penalties on the contract and other costs following a delay in the execution of the projected development.

It is clear that in any case of anticipated enforcement of covenants *the claimant must be forewarned of the generally accepted need to give an undertaking in damages as the price of obtaining an injunction.* Moreover, it is not always prudent to avoid this issue by not seeking interim relief in view of the risk that either the defendant will simply carry on regardless.[50] *The defendant should be warned that unless he can obtain an undertaking in damages from the claimant (which is of some value) he will be out of pocket if at the hearing it turns out that the interim injunction should not have been granted.*

What do you have to show the court in order to obtain an interim injunction in restrictive covenant cases?

15.30

(1) In most respects applications for interim injunctions to enforce restrictive covenants are no different from other types of application for injunctions. You have to satisfy the court that:[51]
  (a) there is a serious question to be tried;[52]
  (b) the balance of convenience dictates the grant of the injunction;
  (c) the claimant can give the undertaking in damages where it is appropriate to require him to do so.

(2) In restrictive covenant cases, unless it is plain that the claimant does not have the benefit of the covenant, or that the defendant is not bound, there will usually be no dispute that there is a serious question to be tried. (It is, however, remarkable that in so many cases the question of whether the covenant is protected by registration is overlooked until the last minute, and only then does one side or the other realise that the covenant cannot be enforced.)

(3) As to the balance of convenience, in cases where the injunction is restraining building, there is less room for argument that the building work should be stopped than in a case where a trade is being carried on – albeit in breach.

---

[50] It should not be forgotten that it is a rule of practice (at least in the Chancery Division) that even where the defendant accepts that he should be bound by an interim Order until trial and gives an undertaking not, for example, to do the acts alleged to be in breach of covenant, the claimant must still give the undertaking in damages; at least in case where the claimant would otherwise be required to give it, or unless the contrary is agreed. See *The Chancery Guide 2002* (Court Service, 2002), para 5.37.

[51] See CPR, Pts 23 and 25 and the test based on *American Cyanamid v Ethicon* [1975] AC 396. In view of the way in which the courts now encourage the parties to identify and resolve issues in a claim at an early stage, and the speed with which claims proceed to a full hearing, the significance of the threefold test in *Cyanamid* may be somewhat lessened. However, at the interim stage, the court will be concerned to preserve the status quo, if that is the just course to take, and will often issue directions for the further conduct of the claim, eg as to an early hearing date where building work is in issue. See *Mortimer v Bailey*, n 26 above.

[52] Unless there is prima facie evidence of breach (actual or threatened) the court will dismiss the application; see the flowchart at pp 5–7 above; see also *Harbour Park Ltd v Arun DC* [1998] EGCS 150, for a case where there was no prima facie evidence of breach.

In *Gregory v Courtroyal Ltd* (unreported) 30 April 2002, Rimer J, the court refused to grant an interim injunction to restrain building work in breach of covenant as the work was substantially advanced, £2 million had already been spent on the development by the defendant, damages might be an adequate remedy to the claimants, and the claimants did not have the means to satisfy the defendants' losses if they had to stop work, which if ordered would seriously jeopardise their financial position. So there was less risk of injunction if the application for an interim injunction was refused than if it was granted.

(4)　The courts do not like defendants trying to 'steal a march' on the claimant and will take such conduct into account when deciding whether to grant the interim injunction.[53]

(5)　It is much harder to persuade a court to grant a mandatory injunction on an *interim* basis, for in order that the court can do so it must be as certain as it can be that at the trial it will appear that the mandatory interim injunction was rightly granted. See **15.26** above. In restrictive covenant disputes it will be very rare for such an interim order to be made save in exceptional cases. The view has been expressed recently to the effect that the court should consider whether the *injustice* suffered by the defendant (in a case where the injunction turned out to be wrongly granted) is greater than the injustice suffered by the claimant, if at trial it turned out that he was entitled to a mandatory injunction, having been refused it at the interlocutory stage.[54] In cases concerning covenants it may be difficult to assess where the greater injustice lies; where a building is to be knocked down the contrast between the two situations is extreme. In other cases (such as a breach of covenant relating to a wall) the contrast will be far less acute. In many cases money can satisfy the claimant, thereby making it less likely that a mandatory injunction will be granted.

(6)　The court will have regard to whether an award of damages will be an adequate remedy, if an injunction were refused.

---

[53]　*Shepherd Homes v Sandham* [1971] Ch 340 at p 349.

[54]　See *Shepherd Homes v Sandham*, above. For the 'injustice' argument see *Films Rover Ltd v Cannon film Sales Ltd* [1987] 1 WLR 670. See *Nottingham BS v Eurodynamics Systems* [1993] FSR 468 for the current approach. The principle of who will suffer the greater injustice has been applied in *Nottingham BS v Eurodynamics Systems* [1993] FSR 468 and in *Zockoll Group v Mercury Communications* [1998] FSR 354. In *Zockoll* the Court of Appeal held that the summary of principles in the *Nottingham BS* case was 'all the citation that should in future be necessary'. The summary is as follows: (1) As this is an interlocutory (interim) matter, the overriding consideration is which course is likely to involve the least risk of injustice if it turns out to be 'wrong' in the sense described by Hoffman J in *Films Rover*. (2) An Order which requires a party to take a positive step at the interim stage may well carry with it a greater risk of injustice, if it turns out to have been wrongly made, than an Order which merely prohibits action, preserving the status quo. (3) It is legitimate for the court to consider at the interim stage whether it feels a high degree of assurance that the claimant will be entitled to establish the right to that Order at trial. The greater the degree of assurance, the less the risk of an injustice if an interim mandatory injunction is granted. (4) But there may still be circumstances in which it is appropriate to grant an interim mandatory injunction, even where the court is unable to feel any high level of assurance that the claimant will establish this right. These circumstances will exist where the risk of injustice, if the injunction is refused, outweigh the risk of injustice if it is granted.

How to obtain an interim injunction

15.31 Reference should be made to the current edition of *Civil Court Service 2004*[55] for the practice and the forms required.

Costs of applications for interim injunctions

15.32 The usual practice is:

(1) If the claimant succeeds in obtaining interim relief he will get his costs as 'claimant's costs in the case', ie if he wins at trial he gets the costs of the interim application (and presumably the other costs of the action), but if he loses at trial he does not have to pay the defendant's costs of that application, although the claimant may have to pay the defendant's other costs of the action.

(2) If the claimant loses his application for interim relief the order will be 'defendant's costs in the case'. Thus if the defendant wins at trial he will get the costs of the interim application (and presumably the other costs of the action) from the claimant. If, however, the claimant wins at trial and gets an injunction he will get the costs of the action, but not his costs of the interim application.[56]

The 'usual practice' can only be a general guide in view of the discretion as to costs and the principles set out in CPR, Part 44. In some cases the court may be persuaded to reserve the question of costs over to final hearing. In other cases the costs may simply be ordered to be 'in the case' so that whoever wins at trial will get all his costs including the costs of the interim application. There is also to be borne in mind the factor of open pre-claim offers of undertakings and '*Calderbank*' and Part 36 letters which will affect the way in which the court will deal with costs at this stage – if not later at the final hearing.[57]

In any claim consideration must also be had to the court's powers to make orders for costs on an indemnity (as opposed to a standard) basis (CPR Part 44, rule 4) against non-parties (Part 48, rule 2) or against legal representatives (Part 48, rule 7). These rules apply not just where interim applications have been made, but also at, or after, final hearings of claims.

PART III: CLAIMS FOR DAMAGES, EITHER AT COMMON LAW, OR IN LIEU OF AN INJUNCTION

15.33 The grounds upon which damages for breach of a restrictive covenant may be awarded are:

(1) for breach of covenant at common law;

(2) for breach of covenant in equity where damages are awarded in lieu of an injunction.[58]

---

[55] (Jordan Publishing Ltd, 2004).
[56] See CPR, Pt 44, Practice Direction, Costs.
[57] See CPR, Pts 36 and 44.
[58] See **15.39** below.

It is worth noting that the original covenantee still has the right to claim damages for breach of covenant even though he may have sold the benefited land, by virtue of his contract with the covenantor.[59] But such damages will be nominal only and it is unlikely in practice that anyone will bother to take such action.

Why is there a difference?

15.34 The difference arses because of the historical distinction between the ability to enforce covenants at common law (eg between original parties, or where the original covenantor was being sued by an assignee of the benefit – the benefit running at common law) and the ability to enforce covenants in equity, which enabled the burden of the covenant to run. In the case of covenants enforceable at common law, damages were historically the only remedy, although since the fusion of law and equity in 1875 an injunction will also lie. In the case of covenants enforceable in equity, only equitable remedies lie, which consist of the injunction and since 1858, damages in lieu thereof.[60]

Does the difference matter?

15.35 It should not do, and in the vast majority of cases it does not, but there can be a distinction in some cases.

As will be seen below, where damages are awarded at common law for breach of covenant, such damages can only compensate for *past* breaches of covenant, and in practical terms this means the diminution in the value of the benefited land by reason of the breach. In contrast, when assessing damages in lieu of an injunction the court can take into account not only the effect of *future* breaches of covenant but also the fact that there is value in the ability to claim an injunction which in turn translates into the price of a release.

However, the contrast has now become muted, as recent authority[61] has suggested that a similar measure to that available in lieu of an injunction, may be applied in cases where *common law* damages are being sought. An instance of this new approach is where mere diminution in value would not be truly compensatory and where such damages *could* have been awarded in equity in lieu of an injunction.

The principles to be applied in awarding damages

15.36 The last paragraph shows that a distinction between damages at common law and in equity can emerge which is unhelpful and makes an understanding of this part of the law of covenants difficult.

From the point of view of the practitioner it is suggested that there should be no distinction in practice. Whether the claimant is suing to enforce as an original

---

59 See Chapter 6 for the scope of original 'liability'. Such a liability may be passed on under the indemnity covenant usually taken by the vendor/covenantor on a disposition of the burdened land, as to which see **4.24** above.

60 See **7.4** above for the distinction between the common law and equitable rules as to the enforceability of covenants.

61 *Gafford v Graham*, see n 27 above; *AG v Blake* [2001] 1 AC 268.

covenantee, or as a successor, against an original covenantor, or a successor, the principles governing an award of damages should be the same.

15.37 It seems from recent authority[62] that the courts will no longer regard whether the claimant is suing at common law, or in equity as a distinction of importance when it comes to the assessment of damages. This is a sensible approach.

On the basis of such recent authority, the principles of assessment can be stated thus:

(1) It is axiomatic that any award of damages for breach of covenant should be *compensatory* in its aim, based on the theory that the claimant should be put into the position he would be in had the covenant been observed or performed.[63]

(2) *Prima facie* the measure will be based on the diminution in value of the benefited land by reason of the breach, whether past or continuing. However, in this context, the concept of 'parasitic' damages should not be ignored. Damage to part of a piece of land may in fact cause the whole to be diminished in value. This is a concept which is well known in interference with light actions (easements) and there is no reason why a similar approach should not be adopted where a breach of covenant is the subject of the claim.[64]

(3) There may, however, be cases where the measure at (2) is not compensatory, either because it does not take full account of what the claimant has lost, or because it does not take into account the value of what he would have had if the covenant had been observed. The latter alternative may be translated into the right to enforce the covenant at any time by means of an injunction.

(4) In cases falling within (3) the court may award the claimant a sum which represents the amount the defendant would reasonably be willing to pay to secure the release from the covenant. That sum may be calculated by reference to a percentage of the defendant's profit, or by reference to some other benefit which accrues to the defendant from a release; eg a percentage of the uplift in value of his land freed from the covenant. What the defendant ought to be willing to pay (and the claimant ought to be prepared to accept) depends on the outcome of a hypothetical negotiation. The features of such a negotiation will vary from case to case. In *Amec Developments Ltd v Jury's Hotel Management (UK) Ltd* (2001) 82 P&CR 286 at paragraph 35, the court set out the sorts of factors which ought to be considered. But as the judge said under factor (n) 'at the end of the day the deal has to feel right'. This means that there are no set 'tariffs'; a point made at **15.38** below.[65]

(5) An award under (4) is capable of being made both at common law and in equity. At common law such damages reflecting the price of a release can

---

62 *Gafford v Graham* (1998) 77 P&CR 73.
63 See *McGregor on Damages* (Sweet & Maxwell, 17th edn, 2003), para 12.002–12.006 for the general principles.
64 See Hudson, '*Parasitic Damages for Loss of Light*', 39 Conv [NS] 116.
65 Recent authority on this area of law is also to be found in the following: *Attorney-General v Blake* [2001] 1 AC 268; *Amec Developments v Jury's Hotel Management (UK) Ltd* (2001) 82 P&CR 268; *Experience Hendrix v PPX Enterprises Inc* [2003] EWCA Civ 323; *Severn Trent Water v Barnes* [2004] EWCA Civ 570 and *Lane v O'Brien Homes Ltd* [2004] EWHC 303 (QB).

only be awarded where they are compensatory and if they could have been awarded in equity.

(6)   A claimant cannot recover damages based on the price of a release if at the date of the claim form the court *could not* have awarded an injunction as matter of jurisdiction, eg because it was not sought, or because the persons to whom any injunction would have been directed were not parties.[66] If the court *could* have granted an injunction, but chose not to do so because, for example, such an order would have been oppressive to the defendant, or because of the claimant's conduct, the measure under (4) is available.[67]

(7)   As a matter of defining the issues in the Particular of Claim, it is not necessary to claim either damages in lieu of an injunction (if the claimant is really seeking an injunction) or an injunction (if the claimant is really seeking damages in lieu – the chances of obtaining an injunction being remote) expressly in the claim form and particulars of claim within CPR, Parts 7 and 16. What is required is a clear indication of whether the claimant is seeking damages for past injury, or damages in substitution for an injunction; if the latter it is sensible to put forward how the price of the release is calculated.[68]

If damages are assessed as the price of a release, what will be the measure?

15.38

(1)   The starting point is to look at the anticipated net profit to be made from the development in breach. (Alternatively, the net development value of the land, that being the amount by which the value of the land is increased by virtue of the freedom from the covenant.)

(2)   The percentage to be applied to that is conventionally expressed as the 'Stokes' percentage, that being one third of the net profit or uplift.[69]

(3)   The percentage is not, however, immutable. The following fluctuations are recorded in the reported authorities:

'High Water Mark' 50 per cent (*Re SJC Construction Co Ltd's Application*[70])

---

[66]   As in *Surrey County Council v Bredero Homes* [1993] 1 WLR 1361, where the houses built in breach had been sold off by the defendant prior to the action, and the house owners were not parties; the court could not have awarded an injunction to the claimant in such a case, even if it had sought it, which it did not.

[67]   For authority on the principles in this paragraph, see, *Wrotham Park Estate Co v Parkside Homes*, above, *Jaggard v Sawyer* [1995] 1 WLR 269, and *Gafford v AH Graham*, at n 27 above. The rationale of refusing damages based on the price of a release expressed in *Surrey County Council v Bredero Homes* (above) was rejected by the Court of Appeal in the last two cases referred to above.

[68]   *Jaggard v Sawyer*, above, at 285, per Millett LJ. The clearer the case is put as regards damages in the particulars of claim the better. See CPR, Pt 16, r 4 and the Practice Direction, Pt 16, for what must be included in the particulars of claim.

[69]   See *Stokes v Cambridge Corporation* (1962) 13 P&CR 77. *See Amec Developments v Jury's Hotel Management (UK) Ltd*, at n 65 above, for the factors which ought to be considered by the hypothetical negotiation and the 'reality check' which should be applied to any resulting figures.

[70]   (1975) 29 P&CR 322. An application to modify a covenant under Law of Property Act 1925, s 84(1) where the issue was the compensation payable for such modification; see further Chapter 16 below. Note that in *R v Braintree DC ex parte Halls* (2000) 80 P&CR 266, CA, the council sought 90 per cent of the open market value of the building plot. A demand held unlawful as beyond the council's powers under the Housing Act 1985; see **10.5** above. See *Re Skupinski's Application*, LP/34/2003, decision of the President (30 November 2004), which considers the 'release' fee, see

'Low Water Mark' 5 per cent (*Wrotham Park Estate Co v Parkside Homes*[71]).

(4)   In other cases it may be difficult to apply a crude *Stokes* percentage and other measures are taken.

In *Gafford v Graham*[72] the Court of Appeal made an award of £25,000 based on the income generated by the business being carried on breach and the marriage value between the land and the business, that being a realistic guide to what the claimant would have demanded for a relaxation of the covenants. In *Jaggard v Sawyer*[73] the sum awarded as a fair ransom price was £6,250, where the injury to the claimant was small and where there was no element of speculative development.

(5)   In practice the claimant should be warned against over-estimating his expectation of recovery of a *Stokes* payment, whilst at the same time being advised that a *Stokes* percentage is at least a starting point. From the defendant's point of view he may be concerned, particularly in the context of speculative development, where time and money is at a premium, to reach a quick settlement, and he can at least point to the low percentage in *Wrotham Park*. It may be that if there have been payments in settlement of claims by other parties entitled to enforce these can be used as a precedent to show what the 'market value' of the release will be.[74] In practice both sides need to get their respective surveyors together to see if a sum can be agreed. It is in this context that the importance of testing the outcome of the hypothetical (if not actual) negotiation against the words of the judge in *Amec v Jury's Hotel*[75] that 'at the end of the day the deal has to feel right' is stressed. It is in this context that pre-claim (protocol) letters can be helpful as they can be used to set out the figures which a potential claimant will be seeking, without prejudice of course to any claim for an injunction.[76]

When will damages in lieu of an injunction be granted?

15.39   When the court has jurisdiction at the date of the claim form to grant an injunction, it can give damages in lieu, governed by the circumstances in existence at the date of the hearing, or if later, the date of the inquiry as to damages.[77]

The discretion to grant such damages is governed by the following 'good working rule' setting out the circumstances in which damages in lieu may be given:

(1)   where the injury to the claimant's legal rights is small;

---

nn 67–69 above, in assessing compensation in applications under s 84(1) of the Law of Property Act 1925; see **16.96** below.

[71]   [1974] 1 WLR 798.
[72]   Referred to at n 27 above.
[73]   Above at n 67.
[74]   This was the approach adopted in *Marine & General Mutual Life Assurance Society v St James' Real Estate Co Ltd* [1991] 2 EGLR 178 (a right of light claim) where the court used a figure reached in settlement with another person affected as good evidence of the 'ransom' price.
[75]   See **15.37** above.
[76]   Tactically, defendants can also use pre-claim letters to 'tempt' claimants or their advisers into making *open* statements that they will accept money in lieu of an injunction; for the effect of this, see *Gafford v Graham*, at **15.36** above.
[77]   See *Jaggard v Sawyer*, at n 67 above. As to the later assessment of damages see *Ward v Cannock Chase DC* [1986] Ch 546. The jurisdiction to grant damages in lieu of an injunction (or specific performance) which was formerly in Lord Cairn's Act 1858, is now contained in Supreme Court Act 1981, s 50.

(2)   one which is capable of being estimated in money;

(3)   one which is capable of being compensated by a small money payment;

(4)   one in which it would be oppressive to grant an injunction.

Other factors which may incline the court more towards the grant of an injunction than against it (even though the four factors above are present); for example where the defendant has tried to steal a march on the claimant.[78]

But care must be taken to advise a defendant that the idea that he has the right to 'buy off' the claimant with an offer of damages is wrong. It will fall to the defendant to show why the claimant's prima facie right to an injunction should not be granted. In effect the defendant must show that it would be oppressive to award an injunction against him.[79]

Finally, a warning on tax

15.40   The *tax treatment* of payments for a release (or damages for breach) should never be forgotten – whether for capital gains tax, or income tax. The moral here is to consult a tax specialist, as the complete details of potential charges to tax and traps for the unwary are beyond the scope of this book, but here are some short reminders of what to look for.

First, the tax treatment may not vary, even if the release is paid as damages, as opposed to a consensual price for a release. In principle whether a sum is paid in compromise of a claim under an agreed Order, or as a result of terms (eg in 'Tomlin' Order), or is paid under an Order of the court where no agreement was present, the capital sum may be liable to capital gains tax.[80]

15.41   Secondly, and in summary, practitioners should be aware of the following tax consequences of a release.

---

[78]   The four rules and this paragraph are taken from the well-known judgment of AL Smith J in *Shelfer v City of London Electric Lighting Co Ltd* [1895] 1 Ch 287, recently applied in *Jaggard v Sawyer* and *Gafford v Graham*, at n 27 above. See **15.36** above. See *Mortimer v Bailey* at n 27 above, for a recent example of a claim where the court awarded a mandatory injunction to pull down an extension and refused to grant damages in lieu.

[79]   The fact of oppression was the guiding factor in the decision by the Court of Appeal in *Gafford v Graham*, above, at n 27 in awarding damages in lieu. It is clear from that authority and from *Sefton v Tophams* [1965] Ch 1140 at 1169, that some special case needs to be shown by the defendant to avoid an injunction where there is jurisdiction to grant it. See *Mortimer v Bailey*, at n 27 above. See *Midtown v City of London Real Property Co*, at n 27 above, at paras 65–80, for recent examination of the 'Shelfer' principles. (Prohibitory injunction refused as oppressive to defendants to be prevented from pursuing a 'worthwhile and beneficial' development east of New Fetter Lane, London, EC4.) See **15.22** above for the principles on which injunctions will be granted.

[80]   See McGregor, *Damages* (Sweet & Maxwell, 17th ed, 2003), 14–062. Reference should also be made to the current version of the Inland Revenue *Capital Gains Manual* (on the Inland Revenue website): see www.inlandrevenue.gov.uk.

Capital gains tax

The release of the covenant will be a disposal of an asset, unless it is possible to claim principal private residence exemptions.[81]

Income tax

The real trap here may be the treatment of the release as taxable under ICTA 1988, section 776, which although seemingly bringing into charge artificial transactions in land, has brought into charge perfectly innocent transactions which could include releases of rights under covenants. It is, however, possible to ask for clearance under ICTA, section 776(1).[82]

VAT

In view of the exemption provisions contained in Schedule 9 (Group 1) to the VAT Act 1994 it is not thought likely that a release would attract VAT if granted by a trader in the course of his business. But, as with any tax point, it is wise to check.

Stamp Duty Land Tax and Restrictive Covenants

The charge to tax

Restrictive covenants are a chargeable interest within the Stamp Duty Land Tax regime, as set out in the Finance Act 2003 (as amended); see section 48(1) thereof. By section 43(3), releases, variations and creation of chargeable interests are all caught unless exempt. By section 49, a land transaction will be chargeable unless it is exempt. Where a Court order is made releasing, or varying, restrictive covenants, or making a declaration about them, provided that there is no consideration payable, there will be no Stamp Duty Land Tax consequences. (Note that by section 43(2) a land transaction falls within the scope of the charge to tax 'however the acquisition is effected, whether by act of the parties, by order of a court or other authority or by or under any statutory provision or by operation of law'.) Therefore, if a Court order is made, it is necessary to consider whether, or not consideration has passed. If no consideration passes, then it is exempt under Schedule 3, paragraph 1 ('A land transaction is exempt from charge if there is no chargeable consideration for the transaction'). 'Chargeable consideration' is defined by Schedule 4, paragraph 1, in the following terms:

> '1(1) The chargeable consideration for a transaction is, except as otherwise expressly provided, any consideration in money or money's worth given for the subject-matter of the transaction, directly or indirectly, by the purchaser or a person connected with him.'

---

[81]   See TCGA 1992, ss 21(1) (what is an asset) and s 222 (for principal private residence exemption). A release may also be chargeable under TCGA 1992, s 22(1)(a) as a disposal when a capital sum is received in return for exercising or not exercising a right. See also *Emmet*, Chapter 29, para 29.009. The cost is not an allowable expense for capital gains tax purposes: *Garner (IT) v Pounds Shipowners and Shipbreaking Ltd* [1998] BTC 495.

[82]   See *Page v Lowther* (1983) STC 799 for a perfectly innocent scheme for deferred consideration for development which was so caught.

Subsection (2) applies section 839 of the Taxes Act 1998 for the purposes of defining who is and who is not a connected person.

Consequently, if a court order is made, whether, or not by consent, (eg in a 'Tomlin Order') where money is to pass for a release, or a variation, then Stamp Duty Land Tax will be chargeable owing to the presence of chargeable consideration. Where an agreement, to release or vary a covenant is made by contract or deed, then Stamp Duty Land Tax will be payable on the consideration unless it is exempt within Schedule 3, paragraph 1, as one for no consideration.) (Note that the contract triggers the charge, even if completion is delayed; see sections 45 and 46, the latter including the operation of options.) The principles above will apply to Orders of the Lands Tribunal. It is not thought that an award of compensation under section 84 by that Tribunal is dutiable as the true nature of such an award is compensation for loss.

Exemption and relief

A compulsory purchase order, and therefore any release as a result of that order, will be exempt by virtue of section 60 of the Finance Act 2003, whether or not the order is made ultimately by agreement or not. The same would appear to apply if a covenant is acquired as a result of a Compulsory Purchase Order acquisition made under section 237 of the Town and Country Planning Act 1990. Section 106 agreements are exempt under section 61, as are modifications of such agreements under section 106A of the Town and Country Planning Act 1990. There is also relief from Stamp Duty Land Tax for charities, as set out in section 68 and Schedule 8 of the Finance Act 2003.

Administration

In respect of the administration of Stamp Duty Land Tax, regard must be had to Schedule 10 of the Finance Act 2003 and the Stamp Duty Land Tax (Administration) Regulations 2003.[83] Those familiar with the administration of Stamp Duty Land Tax will be aware that there is an obligation to submit a Land Transaction Return in the case of chargeable transactions. Where there is no consideration – and, therefore, the transaction is exempt under paragraph 1 of Schedule 3 – that is not a notifiable transaction, in view of the terms of sections 77(3) and (4). A restrictive covenant is not a 'major interest' in land under section 117 and in respect of chargeable transactions affecting restrictive covenants where tax is chargeable at the rate of 1 per cent or higher (ie at present where consideration is below £60,000) there is a duty to notify that transaction. It must not be forgotten that, even though the transaction may not be notifiable, there will be a requirement, if any document has to be lodged at the Land Registry (eg an order or deed), to comply with the self-certification obligation that no Land Transaction Return is required for the specific transaction; Form SDLT 60.[84]

---

[83]   SI 2003/2837.
[84]   For a full setting out of the law, see Reg Nock, *Stamp Duty Land Tax, The New Law* (Jordan Publishing Ltd, 2004) with periodic supplements.

15.42 Rectification of restrictive covenants and other remedies

Rectification

Instruments containing restrictive covenants are potentially rectifiable if the conditions for that remedy can be met. The essential ingredients are:

(i)   That rectification is the proper remedy. Thus, if the question is one of construction, that is the proper remedy rather than one seeking rectification.

(ii) There must be a mistake. The mistake may be common to both or all parties to the instrument, or to one only of them (or, at least, not all of them). In the case of the latter, the mistake is often called *unilateral* and, in the case of the former, it is often called *common.*

(iii) There must be a prior agreement between the parties. It need not be an enforceable contract. It is this agreement which has not been carried through into the instrument and it is, therefore, the instrument which requires rectification, not the agreement.

(iv) The agreement must have been continuing until the instrument was made.

(v)   The instrument which it is sought to rectify must fail to represent the agreement. The mistake can be one of fact, or a mistake as to the legal effect of words in the instrument. Where the mistake is one of law only (for example, as to the question whether there has been an annexation of the benefit of a covenant), it is less clear whether rectification can be used to correct that mistake.[85]

(vi) The instrument which it is sought to rectify must be accurately rectified. This means that it will only be possible to rectify the instrument if such an exercise will lead to a document which properly reflects the agreement between the parties subsisting at the date of the execution of the instrument.

(vii) The party seeking rectification must prove his case on the normal civil standard; that is to say, on the balance of probabilities. But, in reality, he may have a hard task because of the fact that he is seeking to go behind the terms of a written document which he has signed.

In the context of unilateral, as opposed to common mistake, a claimant can seek rectification on the footing that he has been the victim either of 'fraud' or conduct by the other party which has led the claimant into a false position. This is often a species of 'sharp practice'; for example, where the defendant knows of the mistake that the covenant has not been effectively annexed, but does nothing to correct the claimant's mistaken belief. Equity, therefore, comes to the rescue in such circumstances.[86]

---

[85]   See *Kleinwort Benson v Lincoln City Council* [1999] 2 AC 349. This is House of Lords' authority for the proposition that money paid under a mistake of *law* should be recoverable, at least in theory, and subject to any defences available, in the law of restitution. Therefore, by analogy, the rectification remedy ought to be available where there has been a mistake of law as to the terms and effect of an instrument.

[86]   For the classic setting out of what is required to prove unilateral mistake is a species of 'equitable fraud', see *Thomas Bates & Son Ltd v Wyndhams Lingerie Ltd* [1981] 1 WLR 505, *Commission for New Towns v Cooper* [1995] Ch 259, and *Swainland Builders Ltd v Freehold Properties Ltd* [2002] 2 EGLR 71 ([2002] EWCA Civ 560, at paras 33–34, per Peter Gibson LJ. For a full review of the law, see Snell's *Principles of Equity* (Sweet & Maxwell, 31st Edition, 2004), Chapter 14.

The specific points referable to the rectification of restrictive covenants

Where restrictive covenants are the potential subject of a rectification claim, the following questions should always be asked:

(i)   Is this a rectification, as opposed to a construction claim?

(ii) Are those who may have rights under the covenant parties, or (if not parties) have they been notified of this potential claim?

A particular problem arises where successors in title of the original parties may be the subject of a claim. In such a case, as the right to rectify an instrument may not bind a *bona fide* third party purchaser for value who takes under it (where he, in particular, has no notice of any claim at the time he acquired the interest), it is open to argument whether rectification should be available where the burden, or the benefit of the covenant (imposed by the original instrument which it is sought to rectify) has passed on to third parties.[87]

Of relevance here, in registered titles, is section 116 of the Land Registration Act 2002, which states:

> 'Section 116
>
> It is hereby declared for the avoidance of doubt that, in relation to registered land, each of the following:
>
> (a) an equity by estoppel, and
>
> (b) a mere equity,
>
> has effect from the time the equity arises as an interest capable of binding successors in title (subject to the rules about the effect of dispositions on priority).'

As stated above, a right to rectify an instrument is regarded as a 'mere equity' and is generally not thought to be capable of binding successors in title.[88] However, such a claim may be enforced against successors in title of the original parties provided the claim is not barred by the defence of a *bona fide* purchaser for value without notice.[89] The present position would, therefore, appear to be as follows.

Where the title to land is *registered*, section 116 of the Land Registration Act 2002, will cause any right to rectify as a mere equity to bind those who are the registered proprietors of the title. This section applies to mere equities which arose before and after the 13 October 2003.[90]

In *unregistered* titles there may still be doubt whether a right to rectify an instrument can bind a successor in title and it is suggested that the following principle should apply. In the light of *Blacklocks* (see n 89 above), it is possible to contend as follows. A purchaser of unregistered land (who will take the land

---

[87]   See Megarry & Wade, *The Law of Real Property* (Sweet & Maxwell, 6th edn, 1999), at paras 5-012 to 5-013, and Snell's *Principles of Equity*, Chapter 14.

[88]   See *Smith v Jones* [1954] 1 WLR 1089.

[89]   See *Blacklocks v JB Developments (Godalming) Ltd* [1982] Ch 183.

[90]   See *Ruoff & Roper on the Law and Practice of Registered Conveyancing* (Sweet & Maxwell, looseleaf), paragraph 15.031. Note also, a right to rectify a restrictive covenant may be an interest which overrides under either Schedule 1 or Schedule 3 Land Registration Act 2002 as an interest of a person in *actual occupation* (see *Ruoff & Roper* 10-012 and 17-011 for a full discussion of this issue).

subject to any DII Land Charges Register entries as to the burden, or will have the benefit of the covenant by annexation (see Chapter 8 above)), acquiring that land with those rights or obligations attached to it, will be subject to the 'mere equity' to rectify the instrument which imposes the benefit or the burden of the covenant. This is because a successor in title cannot, in other words, be in any better, or worse position, than his predecessor. So, a third party should take subject to, or with the benefit of, the right to rectify the instrument imposing the covenant. If there is any doubt about this the appropriate remedy may be a declaration under section 84(2) of the Law of Property Act 1925, see Chapter 15 above.

It should be noted that the rectification remedies discussed above are not the same as alteration of the Register under section 65 of, and Schedule 4 to, Land Registration Act 2002. However, if an order to alter an instrument which affects a registered restrictive covenant is made, the Land Registry will rectify the entry of that covenant under Schedule 4, paragraph 2, Land Registration Act 2002.

Other remedies

Specific performance

So far as a restrictive covenant may impose positive obligations on any party, the remedy of specific performance may be available. For example, where there is an obligation to submit plans of development for approval.[91]

Setting aside covenants on the basis of misrepresentation, fraud, or mistake

It is conceivable that remedies of this nature may be available where the evidence supports such a claim to set aside a restrictive covenant. In such cases, no doubt, the evidence will dictate the extent to which it is possible to allege either misrepresentation, or fraud, or mistake, which would allow the Court to set aside the covenant in question. The position of successors in title, who have no knowledge of the misrepresentation etc will have to be considered in the light of the observations made under **15.42** above, where the remedy of rectification is discussed.

---

[91]   See Snell's *Principles of Equity*, at n 86 above, Chapter 42.40.

Chapter 16

DISCHARGE AND MODIFICATION OF RESTRICTIVE COVENANTS UNDER LAW OF PROPERTY ACT 1925, SECTION 84(1) BY THE LANDS TRIBUNAL

INTRODUCTION

16.1 This chapter considers the means by which restrictive covenants can be discharged, or modified, appear to serve no useful function, or where they are a hindrance to economic activity on land which is (or which appears to be) burdened by them. There may be instances where all the parties whose interests which are affected can agree on the terms by which covenants can be removed or altered. But in other cases it is necessary to consider how this can be achieved where such agreement is not possible.

In such cases the jurisdiction to discharge or modify restrictive covenants is exercised by the Lands Tribunal under the Law of Property Act 1925, s 84(1) and this chapter is devoted to an examination of that jurisdiction. Note that this jurisdiction does not extend to section 106 agreements made under the Town and Country Planning Act 1990 (s 106A (10)). See Chapter 10 above.

HOW CAN A RESTRICTIVE COVENANT BE DISCHARGED OR MODIFIED?

16.2 Restrictive covenants over freehold land do not have a defined period of existence. Unlike covenants in leases where, at the end of the term, the covenants will cease to have effect, there is no automatic termination of the life of restrictive covenants which affect freehold land.[1] They are not usually subject to perpetuity rules – unlike certain other contractual agreements such as options – which limits their duration.[2] The fact that they are 'old' does not make them any the less effective. Covenants which have passed their centenary may be just as potent as those which are mere striplings by comparison. The mere fact of their existence can, therefore, operate as a potential hindrance to the economic development of

---

[1] In the context of landlord and tenant there may be an extension of the life of covenants in a lease by the various statutory means by which protection is given to landlords and tenants. But the point which is being made here is that ultimately covenants in leases have the prospect of termination, whereas those affecting freeholds are, like freeholds themselves, of potentially indefinite duration. See Chapter 19 below for an outline of the position as regards commonhold tenure.

[2] See **13.14**.

land; particularly where social, or environmental change has caused covenants to be regarded as obsolete.[3]

16.3   Unless use can be made of the planning, local government, or compulsory purchase legislation to 'override' covenants standing in the way of development (and as explained in Chapter 12 above there is a limited capacity to do this and at the cost of compensating those affected) there is no means by which covenants can be discharged, or their terms modified, other than with the agreement of all entitled to the benefit of them, or by using the jurisdiction under the Law of Property Act 1925, section 84(1).

For private individuals, or corporate developers, either securing the agreement of all concerned to a release, or making an application under section 84(1) which is successful, may be the only way to free land from the burden of covenants, or to alter that burden as a result of a modification. The procedure for seeking a declaration under the Law of Property Act 1925, section 84(2), which may be used in suitable cases to 'clear off' covenants which are no longer enforceable (see Chapter 15 above) may also be an option to consider.

Although insurance may sometimes be available (see Chapter 18 below), it may not be an option to take if the risk of enforcement is too great, or if the premium is too large.

It is, therefore, in such cases that the jurisdiction of the Lands Tribunal to discharge, or modify restrictive covenants can be considered and if thought fit, invoked.

THE LANDS TRIBUNAL AND SECTION 84(1)

16.4   The full text of section 84(1) and the subsections linked to it is found at Appendix 1.

In summary, the Lands Tribunal[4] will only discharge or modify restrictive covenants where it can be shown that *one* of four conditions are met, ie:

–   there is *agreement* between all entitled to the benefit of it that there should be a discharge or modification; or
–   the covenant is, in effect, *obsolete*; or
–   the covenant restricts reasonable use of land, confers no *practical benefit of substantial value or advantage* on those entitled to enforce it (or is contrary to the public interest) and the *loss* of the covenant can be *compensated in money*; or

---

[3]   A modern example is in the case of inner city redevelopment where restrictive covenants (and easements) can act as a disincentive to regeneration unless overcome. That is why the use of s 237 of the Town and Country Planning Act 1990 by local authorities may be of vital importance in order to extinguish adverse rights which would otherwise hinder development: see Chapter 12 above.

[4]   The address of the Lands Tribunal is Procession House, 55 Ludgate Hill, London, EC4M 7JW. (DX 149065 Ludgate Hill 2). Tel: 020 7029 9780 Fax 020 7029 9781. Website: www.landstribunal.gov.uk.

– *no injury* will be caused to those entitled to the benefit of the covenant by reason of its discharge or modification.

The jurisdiction is discretionary, so there is no 'right' to an order on any application being made. Therefore, as is pointed out at paragraph 16.105 below, an intending applicant should always consider the effect of his application at an early stage. This means, in particular, using the question whether the Tribunal is more likely to make an order for *discharge* of the restriction, or is more likely to make an order for *modification*.

In many cases, the latter will be more likely to be granted than the former.[5] From the applicant's point of view such an order will also achieve what he wants, eg an increase in permitted density, or a modification of the user covenant, to allow the proposed development. The Tribunal always has to consider whether, even when a ground under section 84(1) is made out, it should exercise its discretion to make any order, and if so, in what form. This is particularly important where the Tribunal has to address particular concerns of objection where restrictions are going to be modified: eg as to screening or privacy. In such cases, additional restrictions can be imposed: see **16.108** below.

WHO CAN APPLY?

16.5   Two classes of person may apply:

– 'any person interested in any freehold land affected by any restriction' (section 84(1))
– a person interested in leasehold land affected by any restriction, provided the lease (not being an missing lease) was granted for a term of more than 40 years, of which 25 years have already expired (section 84(12)).[6]

Application by leasehold owners

In each case it is the person with an interest in the burdened land who is going to be the applicant. In practical terms this will usually be the owner of the freehold to that land, or if the application is being made under section 84(12) it will be the person in whom the lease is vested.

16.6   Ignoring the freehold/leasehold distinction the class of applicants also encompasses:

– purchasers under an uncompleted contract;[7]
– a mortgagee;
– option holders;

---

[5]   See the guidance notes on the form of application at rr 12 and 13 of the Lands Tribunal Rules 1996, see Appendix 4.
[6]   See also in this context the jurisdiction to vary leases in Landlord and Tenant Act 1987, Pt IV. War damaged leasehold land is also excluded from this jurisdiction but this exclusion is now highly unlikely to arise in practice (Landlord and Tenant (War Damage) Act 1939, s 18(1) and (4)).
[7]   *Re Pioneer Properties* (1956) 7 P&CR 264.

–   joint applicants eg where a vendor of land is selling it for development and
      the purchaser under contract who is to carry it out, joins with the vendor in
      making the application. The latter usually has the greater financial interest in
      the success of the application. The contract may be conditional on its success,
      in which case both may be said to be equally interested in the outcome!

If a leaseholder wants to apply to vary the covenants on the freehold reversion
(with no doubt the approval of the reversioner) there seems no reason why as a
person 'interested' in the freehold, that lessee should not be able to apply.[8]

The problems posed by applicants who are original covenantors or where
covenants have been recently imposed and those covenants are the subject of the
application are dealt with at **16.114** below.

Note: two important conditions must be satisfied before the Lands Tribunal can
exercise its jurisdiction under section 84(1).

(1)   The *restriction* which it is sought to discharge or modify must be one which
      relates to the *user* of the land or the *building* thereon. It must be a restriction;
      ie negative and not positive. Thus restrictions which relate, for example, only
      to *personal* qualities of occupation and not user, will be outside the scope of
      section 84(1).[9]

(2)   Jurisdiction must not be excluded by the terms of subsection (7) (restrictions
      imposed on a gratuitous disposition, or made for a nominal consideration for
      public purposes) or subsections (11) and (11A) (Royal parks and gardens and
      other Crown and naval, military and air force purposes). The exclusion of the
      jurisdiction under section 84(7) must not be overlooked. It is often engaged
      when the potential applicant's title is derived from a 'gratuitous' disputation,
      for example, by a local authority to a university. (See also **16.93** below for
      other specific statutory examples where the jurisdiction under section 84(1) is
      excluded.)[10]

WHO CAN OBJECT?

16.7

(1)   Those who appear to be entitled to the benefit of the restriction. An objector
      will have to show that he is either the original covenantee, or that he has the
      benefit of the covenant as a result or any of these methods by which the
      benefit of a restrictive covenant may pass. Since the decision of the Court of
      Appeal in *Crest Nicholson v McAllister* [2004] EWCA Civ 410, even in the
      case of covenants imposed after 1925, whether annexation of the benefit is

---

[8]   In *Re Independent Television Authority's Application* (1961) 13 P&CR 222, the applicant was that
      body holding under an agreement for a lease for 5 years, with seemingly the freeholder's consent to
      the application.
[9]   On this question, see *Abbey Homesteads (Developments) Ltd v Northants County Council* [1986]
      1 EGLR 24; *Westminster City Council v Duke of Westminster* [1991] 4 All ER 136;
      Re Blumenthal's Application LP/34/2002 (decision 14 January 2004), approved by the Court of
      Appeal [2004] EWCA Civ 1688.
[10] See *Re Plumpton Parish Council's Application* (1962) 14 P&CR 234 for an example of
      an application excluded by section 84(7). Applied in *Re Robins' Application*, LP/17/2004 (decision
      of 16 February 2005).

achieved by section 78(1) of the Law of Property Act 1925 will require the objector to show that the land of the covenantee intended to be benefited can be easily ascertained (see Chapter 8 above). In this type of case, the objector will be the *freehold* owner of the land benefited (or which claims to be benefited) by the restrictive covenant.[11]

(2) It is also possible for a *tenant* of the land benefited by the restriction to object, for under section 78 a person with an estate derived from the freehold (a lease) can enforce a restrictive covenant taken for the benefit of that land.[12] In practice it may well often be the tenant who will be more concerned to object than the freeholder, unless the application is clearly going to diminish the value of the reversion. There may, however, be difficulties in the way of tenants who successfully object to the extent that the application is allowed only on payment of compensation, for if the tenant's interest is a short one the diminution in value may be negligible, although less difficulty will be encountered in measuring the loss of amenity, and in the solatium for the effect of building works, for example.[13] Equally, it may well be the case that the freeholder whose interest is subject to a long lease or a number of long leases will not suffer much by way of diminution by comparison with the tenant(s).[14]

In the past there have been suggestions (almost of 'moral outrage') that the Tribunal should be slow to allow applications made by original covenantors, and there should be a like degree of reluctance where covenants were imposed recently.

The present position is that such an applicant will face a very heavy burden, but there is no longer any 'moral indignation' in such applications. The fact that the original covenantor is the applicant (or the fact that the covenant is a recent one) is merely one of the matters (albeit an important one) which the Tribunal can and must take into account.[15]

16.8

(3) Those who have some right to enforce by virtue of a statute. They will be objecting as 'custodians of the public interest'; for example the National Trust, or a local authority entitled to enforce under the statute by virtue of which the covenant was imposed.[16]

---

[11] See *Re Felton Homes Ltd's Application* LP/3/2003 (decision 2 December 2004), at paras 46–48 for the approach of the Tribunal to evidence from 'supporters' of the objectors, who cannot be admitted as objectors under s 84 (3A).

[12] *Smith v River Douglas Catchment Board* [1949] 2 KB 500 establishes the proposition that a tenant can enforce. See **8.5** above.

[13] See **16.95** below for the measure of compensation.

[14] See *Re Vaizey* (1974) 28 P&CR 517.

[15] For the old view see *Ridley v Taylor* (1965) 16 P&CR 113; for the modern and current view, see *Jones v Rhys-Jones* (1974) 30 P&CR 451, as applied in *Re Beech* (1990) 59 P&CR 502. See *Re Farrow's Application* LP/18/2000 (decision 10 May 2001), where the applicant had the greater burden of proof as original covenantor; covenant entered into in 1988; and see *Re Wake's Application* LP/2/2001 (decision 17 June 2002). Covenant imposed 1981.

[16] See *Gee v National Trust* (1966) 17 P&CR 6; *Re Martin's Application* (1988) 57 P&CR 119; see Chapter 10 for statutory imposition of covenants

THE TIMING OF THE APPLICATION

16.8.1   Any application under section 84(1) should be made at a time when the grounds under the paragraphs of that subsection referred to below can be made out, or appear to be so made out. In addition, an application may be made under s 84(1) when a claim is brought to enforce a restrictive covenant, in effect as a 'contraclaim'. In accordance with section 84(9) the court may stay the claim to enforce and either give leave to the defendant in that claim to make the application to the Lands Tribunal under section 84(1), or (if that application has already been made at the time of the hearing of the application to stay the claim to enforce) give directions as to the future conduct of the claim to enforce, including the making of conditions on which the parties are to be subject as a term of allowing the stay.[17]

Finally, as the Lands Tribunal is *not* the correct forum to seek declarations as to the meaning, effect, or enforceability of restrictive covenants, such remedies must be sought under section 84(2) in the High Court (or the County Court, see Chapter 15 above). Therefore, whilst an application may be made under section 84(1) in the Lands Tribunal, that application may have to be adjourned pending the hearing of the High Court or County Court claim. (See **16.105** for procedural stages.) That is not to say, however, that (in order to determine an application before it) the Tribunal, will not decide whether a covenant is enforceable. This may be necessary as a preliminary step towards deciding whether or not to modify the restriction. An important function of the Tribunal in applications made under paragraph (a) is where one question the Tribunal has to ask is whether the main purpose of the application can still be served. That requires the Tribunal to consider, in turn, whether the restriction is enforceable.[18]

16.8.2   Relationship between Court claims and Lands Tribunal application.

In *Re Skupinski's application* (LP/34/2003, decision of November 2004), the Lands Tribunal had to consider whether or not an award of damages ordered to be paid in a claim brought in the Chancery Division of the High Court against the applicant in the Lands Tribunal, and prior to that application being made, estopped the applicant from seeking an award of compensation on a different basis from that adopted by the High Court. The President found that it did not, that decision being based on the negotiations between the agents for the parties in the Chancery claim, and the conduct of the parties. The general point to be made is that where a claim is brought in the High Court or County Court, to restrain a breach of covenant, that claim may be met by an application by the defendant to that claim with an

---

[17]   See *Luckies v Simon* [2003] 2 P&CR 30; see **15.24** above. See also *Re Skupinski*, LP/34/2003; decision of the President (30 November 2004).

[18]   See *Re Girls Day School Trust* (1872); *Re Skipton House, London W13* LP/19/1999 (2000). See also *Re Jilla's Application* [2000] 2 EGLR 99, where the Tribunal held that it must determine the meaning of a restriction in order to determine the application before it, and any terms to be implied by the wording of the restriction are part of its meaning; in that case, the implication was made that approval to building plans should not be unreasonably withheld; see *Re Jilla's Application*, at p 101 L–M. For recent authority on the link between the power of the court to construe an easement in the light of the Lands Tribunal's jurisdiction, see *Hotchkin v McDonald* [2004] EWCA Civ 519. See n 1, at **14.1** above.

application to the Lands Tribunal under section 84(1). In such a case the claim in the High Court or County Court, should be adjourned to allow the Lands Tribunal application to proceed. In this context, care should be taken by the parties and their agents to ensure that there is no estoppel which would lead to any findings or orders in the Court claim, or any negotiations between the parties or their agents being used against either of the parties in the Lands Tribunal application. See Stage 1 at **16.106** below.

ON WHAT GROUNDS CAN AN APPLICATION BE MADE?

Each ground is considered below.

Paragraph (a)

16.9

> *'that by reason of changes in the character of the property or the neighbourhood or other circumstances of the case which the Lands Tribunal may deem material, the restriction ought to be deemed obsolete'.*

There are generally two types of change which will lead to an application under this ground being contemplated.

First, where *social* changes make the restriction obsolete.

Secondly, where *environmental* changes have occurred which make the restriction obsolete.

An example of the former type will include the changed attitude to the sale of alcohol. An example of the latter will be the presence of flats amongst houses and a greater density of houses, or a mix of residential and non-residential uses.

There are two questions which have to be asked when an application is made under sub-paragraph (a).

In all cases each question has to be asked in relation to the development which is proposed.

Question 1

16.10 Have there been material changes in:

– the character of the land which is the subject of the application; or
– in the neighbourhood of it; or
– some other material change in circumstances

since the covenant which it is sought to discharge or vary was imposed?

Question 2

16.11 What was the original purpose of the covenant? If there have been changes identified in answer to Question 1, ought the covenant to be deemed obsolete in the sense that it no longer fulfils its original purpose (or is no longer capable of doing so)? The original purpose of the covenant may be apparent from the face of the document imposing it (eg a density, or user restriction) or it may be less easy to discover (eg the overall 'ethos' of a development scheme). It is the 'main purpose' which matters.[19]

The following material changes may lead to the original purpose of the covenant no longer being served and, therefore, being treated as obsolete.

– Changes in the character of the property, eg use in breach for many years as a shop and not a dwelling house; a hotel used as flats; a school used as flats.[20]

– Changes in the character of the neighbourhood. 'Neighbourhood' has a wide definition and may mean a larger area than the immediate neighbourhood of the property within the application. The question of what is the neighbourhood is a question of fact. It is usually the applicant who will point to a wide definition of the neighbourhood, thereby trying to get in as many changes since the covenant was imposed as possible. The objector, on the other hand, will try to limit the area of the neighbourhood so as to show that there are fewer changes which are not material.

– Other material circumstances which have changed; eg dormant schemes of development. These words (ie material circumstances) are to be read *eiusdem generis* (together with) the earlier words which refer to the land within the application or the neighbourhood. Planning matters alone will not amount to a material circumstance.

– the effect of large council estates.[21]

Practical tips for applications under sub-paragraph (a)

16.12

(1) Identify by means of a series of Ordnance maps (or, in user cases, plans showing the uses of property in the neighbourhood) the changes which will be relied upon as regards the application land. Mere neglect of that land will not be a change in character. Photographic evidence, both past and present may be of assistance. Local authorities will often have archive aerial photographs taken over a number of years (usually for planning purposes) and these can be used to show the changes in a neighbourhood. Ordnance Survey may also

---

[19] See *Re Girls Day School Trust (1872)*: *Re Skipton House*, at n 18 above, for an examination of what may be described as the 'main purpose' of a covenant or set of covenants; in that case use as a private dwelling house. See *Re Truman, Hanbury, Buxton & Co Ltd* [1956] 1 QB 261, at p 272, per Romer LJ, for an early statement that if the original purpose can no longer be achieved, he covenant may be regarded as 'obsolete' in s 84(1)(a). For recent authority on the question whether a restriction is obsolete falls to be considered in relation to the development that s proposed, see *Marcello's Developments Ltd*, LP/18/1999 and LP/31/2000 (2001), and the authorities referred to at paras 39–41 of the member in *Re Azfar's Application* LP/10/2000 (2000). It is suggested that there can be no 'partial' obsoleteness other than in the context of the particular development proposed and in respect of the particular restriction which it is sought to modify, or discharge, to enable that development to proceed: *Azfar's Application,* at para 41. See also *Re Hamden Homes' Application* LP/38/1999 (decision 12 December 2001).

[20] *Re Forestmere* (1980) 41 P&CR 390.

[21] *Re Truman* [1956] 1 QB 261 contains guidance on what is an obsolete covenant where the character of an estate has changed. Note that the restriction may be obsolete but the Lands Tribunal may replace it with a new one; *Re Forestmere,* at n 20 above.

be able to supply photographs taken during mapping (use the online facilities at www.ordancesurvey.co.uk).

(2)   Do the same thing as regards the changes to the neighbourhood – once you have tried to define it.

(3)   List the changes, eg conversion of large house to multiple accommodation; construction of industrial units; use of gardens for houses. Use colour-coded plans. Identify planning consents within the neighbourhood.

(4)   Identify the purpose of the covenant which is the subject of the application. Was it to protect a particular house which still warrants that protection? Was it to protect a larger area from development, which has now taken place? Was it to protect the amenity of an estate, or was it to protect purer commercial interests? In the former case the purpose may be more likely to be capable of fulfilment than in the latter, where the commercial interests (eg competition between trades) may have changed beyond recognition.

(5)   If the purpose has been identified (and there may be more than one) ask the vital question whether that purpose can no longer be carried out. An example would be the preservation of the integrity of a building scheme, where changes of use from purely residential to some hotel user has taken place. The purpose for which the original covenant was taken was to preserve the 'good character' of the original estate, and it may be debatable whether further hotel development would, in view of the changes which have already occurred, really make much difference. In such a case it can be argued that the original purpose of the covenants cannot be fulfilled. This problem is one which emerges from time to time in schemes dating from the nineteenth century in seaside towns in the south-west of England, such as Torbay and Torquay.

(6)   Beware the trap that can arise where the greater the changes in the neighbourhood, the greater the importance of the preservation of the covenant, rather than its discharge.[22] The previous example of the prolonged effect of changes in certain scheme covenants is one case where this trap can arise. It is also in this context that the 'thin end of the wedge' argument may be mustered; this is dealt with at **16.73** below.

(7)   In cases where there is evidence of acquiescence in a breach of covenant for many years, the Tribunal may find that a covenant is no longer enforceable by injunction, its main (or original) purpose can no longer be carried out. This means that an application will succeed under this paragraph.[23]

---

[22]   See *Re Davies's Application* (1971) 25 P&CR 115.

[23]   As it did in *Re Girls Day School Trust (1872); Re Skipton House*, at n 18 above. That was a case where there had been use of building for educational purposes (in breach of private dwelling house restriction) from 1945 without complaint until 2000, save for one letter written to oppose redevelopment in 1998 (when knowledge of the covenant came to the objector's notice). Modification allowed by the Lands Tribunal for use as an educational institution.

Illustrations of applications under subsection (a): section 84(1)(a): cases where applications succeeded

'by reason of changes in the character of the property ...'

16.13 REDUNDANT CINEMA CONTROLS OBSOLETE

Re Forestmere Properties Limited (1980) 41 P&CR 390. The *leaseholders* applied to modify or discharge covenants which obliged them to use a 1.41 acre site on Finchley Road, Northwest London on the fringe of Hampstead Garden suburbs exclusively for a cinema so that they could erect a block of flats upon it. As the cinema was defunct, the covenants in so far as they related to it were held to be obsolete and were modified so that residential flats could be built upon the site with the consent of the lessors.

16.14 CHANGES LEAD TO COVENANT NO LONGER FULFILLING ITS PURPOSE

Re Nichols' Application [1997] 1 EGLR 144. The applicants wished to erect a bungalow at the rear of 27, Elms Road, Stoneygate, Leicester although a covenant in a conveyance of the property prevented any building. The character of the property, which had previously formed part of the grounds of a neighbouring detached house, had changed such that it presently had the appearance of a separate building plot waiting for development. Moreover, the covenant had originally been imposed to protect the amenity of the neighbouring house and to increase the price of an another estate upon a subsequent sale. As the neighbouring house had been demolished and replaced by a nursing home and a new dwelling house had been built at its rear and the estate had already been sold, the covenant was deemed to be obsolete.

'by reason of changes in the character of the neighbourhood ...'

16.15 GROUNDS OF NEIGHBOURING HOUSES SOLD OFF FOR MODERN DEVELOPMENT

Re Briarwood Estates Limited (1979) 39 P&CR 419. A covenant contained in an underlease prevented the erection of more than three dwelling houses on the property known as Hill Top House, Grappenhall, Warrington. The applicants wished to divide the existing dwelling house into two and erect two further houses upon the property. At the date of the imposition of the restriction, the neighbourhood consisted of large houses in large grounds. However, as the grounds of neighbouring houses had recently been sold off as sites for modern dwellings the restriction was deemed to be obsolete and therefore modified so as to prevent the erection of more than four dwelling houses on the property.

16.16 DESTRUCTION OF BENEFIT OF MUTUAL RESTRICTIONS

Re Bradley Clare Estates Limited (1987) 55 P&CR 126. Covenants contained in an indenture prevented the applicants from erecting more than one house on the property known as No 14, the Street, Rustington, West Sussex and from using the property other than for residential purposes. The applicants wished to build sheltered housing units for the elderly. These restrictions were originally intended to ensure that the neighbourhood would not be developed other than for residential purposes. However, as a surgery had been built in the immediate neighbourhood, the benefit of the scheme of mutual restrictions had broken down and the restrictions were deemed to be obsolete.

Re Girls Day School Trust (1872); Re Skipton House, London W13. LP/19/1999 (2000). Long-term acquiescence in breach of covenant during use as a school. Skipton House, Cleveland Road, Ealing, London W13, so used since 1945. Original main purpose of the restriction, to use Skipton House as a private dwelling house, could not be served, so obsolete. Modification of relevant covenants allowed for use as an educational institution. (Application also successful under s 84(1)(aa) without an award of compensation.)

16.17 *'other material circumstances ...'*

CHANGES AS TO SOCIAL CONDITIONS AS TO EMPLOYMENT OF STAFF

Re Cox (1985) 51 P&CR 335. The freehold owner of Belfairs at Gun Hill, Chiddingly, East Sussex applied to discharge covenants which prohibited the use of Sunnyside, a building 19 feet from Belfairs, except by domestic staff employed in Belfairs so that an agricultural worker would be permitted to occupy Sunnyside. As there was no prospect that Sunnyside would ever be needed as a residence for Belfairs' domestic staff and persons who were unrelated to the occupiers of Belfairs occupied Sunnyside, the covenants were deemed to be obsolete. New restriction imposed limiting occupation or user to persons employed in agriculture.

16.18 MOTORWAY NETWORK AND OTHER BUILDINGS

Re Quaffers Limited (1988) 56 P&CR 142. Covenants in three conveyances forbade the use of property consisting of 0.86 acres of land in Worsley, Greater Manchester for trade or business and the sale of alcohol. The applicants wished to erect a hotel upon the property. The object of the restrictions was to protect the amenity of the land retained by the covenantee. As a network of motorways and a hotel had already been built within the immediate vicinity of the property, the amenity of the retained land could no longer be protected and the covenants were deemed to be obsolete.

16.19 BUILDING HAD ALREADY DESTROYED VIEW

Re Kennet Properties (1991) 72 P&CR 353. Covenants imposed under a building scheme for the development of an estate to the south of a road known as Fortis Green, Hornsey, London, forbade any building upon the paddock. The applicants wished to build 27 houses upon a site of 1.64 acres of land which formed part of the paddock. The original purpose of the covenants was to procure for the owners of each adjoining building plot an open view across his neighbour's land. As various housing developments, summer houses and a tennis club had already been built on the remainder of the paddock and impinged upon that view, the covenants were deemed to be obsolete.

Illustrations of applications under subsection (a): section 84(1)(a): cases where applications failed

16.20   LAND STILL CAPABLE OF AGRICULTURAL USE

Re Davies (1971) 25 P&CR 115. A covenant prevented any building within 100 yards of Loman House upon a site of 2.363 acres of land situated at West End, Somerton, Somerset. The applicant proposed to build 11 houses on the site. Although the surrounding land had changed in character from being agricultural to residential, the site, which had become neglected, was still capable of agricultural use and had to be retained as such in order to preserve the character of Loman House.

16.21   ONE HOUSE ONE PLOT STILL OBSERVED

Re Gossip (1972) 25 P&CR 215. The applicant was the freehold owner of two detached houses which were purchased as 2 lots and were known as numbers 20 and 22, Avenue Road, New Milton, Hampshire. These lots were subject to a covenant presenting the building of more than one private dwelling house upon each plot. Although the original plotting had not been followed consistently, the restriction pattern of one dwelling house to one plot had been observed and the residential estate had been developed at a comparatively low density such that the covenant was not deemed to be obsolete.[24]

16.22

ATTEMPT TO BUILD ON PUBLIC OPEN SPACE

Re Martin's Application (1988) 57 P&CR 119. A covenant in an agreement made with the local authority prevented the property situated at 228, Harley Shute Road, St. Leonards, East Sussex from being used other than as a public open space. The applicants wished to build a dwelling house for which they had obtained planning permission in the garden of the property. The purpose of the covenant was to prevent excessive density in the vicinity of the property. As the proposed house would create a cramped appearance in the neighbourhood and the inspector who had granted planning permission for the proposed development had not indicated how this appearance could be overcome, the purpose of the restriction could still be achieved and it was not obsolete.

16.23   ATTEMPT TO CONVERT RESIDENTIAL TO OFFICE USER

Re Houdret and Co Limited (1989) 58 P&CR 310. A covenant prevented the use of a grade II listed property known as St. Mary's House, 37, Market Place, Henley-on-Thames, Oxfordshire other than for residential purposes. The applicants wished to use the basement, ground and first floors of the property as offices. The purpose of the restriction (in a section 52 [now section 106] agreement) was to ensure that the property was used solely for residential purposes. This purpose could still be achieved as there was a demand in the market for its residential user notwithstanding the noise pollution levels and other inherent disadvantages from which the property continually suffered.

---

[24]   See also *Re Jilla's Application* [2000] 2 EGLR 99, where the purpose of the covenant, to protect against alterations to neighbouring houses, or building which would impact on the benefited land, was clearly capable of fulfilment. Changes elsewhere and alterations to other houses did not affect the potential impact on the covenantee's house.

16.24   LANGUAGE OF COVENANT IMPORTANT

Re Towner & Goddard (1989) 58 P&CR 316. An agreement under section 52 of the Town and Country Planning Act 1971 (now section 106) forbade any sort of erection on land forming part of the gardens of two properties situated in Cookham Dene Close, Chislehurst, Kent. The applicants proposed to erect two tennis courts with chain-link fencing all around their perimeter in the gardens of the properties. It was argued that the restriction should be deemed obsolete in so far as it prohibited the erection of tennis courts but that it could still apply to restrict the development of sheds, greenhouses and summer houses. This was rejected because a restriction cannot be deemed obsolete merely with regard to its effect rather than its language. However the application was still allowed under section 84(1)(c).

16.25

INFILLING MAY NOT DETRACT FROM THE QUALITY OF A NEIGHBOURHOOD

Re North (1997) 75 P&CR 117. A covenant contained in the conveyance of Garden Cottage, Winkfield Lane, Winkfield, Berkshire, prevented any building in the garden of the cottage without the consent of the neighbouring owner. The applicants proposed to erect a dwelling house and two garages in the garden. Despite some residential development, the neighbourhood had retained its attractive semi-rural character and had not materially changed. Thus, there was no need to examine the further question whether the restriction ought to be deemed to be obsolete. It was however found that the restriction's original purpose of protecting neighbouring land could still be achieved in any event.

For other recent instances of applications which failed under paragraph (a), see:

- *Re Harolds Application* LP/45/2002: decision of 3 December 2003 (15 Hough Top, Bromley, Leeds).
- *Re Coles' Application* LP/2/2003; decision of 16 February 2004 (Glenfalls, The Glen, Saltford, Bristol).
- *Re Boulton's Application* LP/31/2003; decision of 4 August 2004.
- *Re Camstead Ltd* LP/26/2003; decision of 18 October 2004.
- *Re Felton's Application* LP/3/2003; decision of 2 December 2004.
- *Re Bromley's Application* LP/51/2003; decision of 16 December 2004.

Paragraph (aa)

16.26

> *'that (in a case falling within subsection (1A) below) the continued existence thereof would impede some reasonable user of the land for public or private purposes or, as the case may be, would unless modified so impede such user.'*

> *'(1A) Subsection (1)(aa) above authorises the discharge or modification of a restriction by reference to its impeding some reasonable user of land in any case in which the Lands Tribunal is satisfied that the restriction, in impeding that user, either –*

> *(a)   does not secure to persons entitled to the benefit of it any practical benefits of substantial value or advantage to them; or*

> *(b)   is contrary to the public interest*

and that money will be an adequate compensation for the loss or disadvantage (if any) which any such person will suffer from the discharge or modification.

(1B) In determining whether a case is falling within subsection (1A) above, and in determining whether (in any such case or otherwise) a restriction ought to be discharged or modified, the Lands Tribunal shall take into account the development plan and any declared or ascertainable pattern for the grant or refusal of planning permissions in the relevant areas, as well as the period at which and context in which the restriction was created or imposed and any other material circumstance.'

16.27   When considering this ground of application the following questions are usually asked.[25]

Question 1

Is the proposed user reasonable?

In an application where it is by no means certain that the applicant will obtain planning consent for the proposed development he may not be able to persuade the Tribunal that the proposed user is reasonable.[26]

Question 2

Do the covenants impede that user?

Note: As to questions 1 and 2 where planning consent has been obtained for a definite project, few applicants will fail to satisfy these questions. In such circumstances the first two questions posed are the easiest hurdles to overcome when applying under sub-paragraph (aa).

Question 3

16.28   *Does impeding the proposed user secure practical benefits to the objector?*

Question 4

If the answer to question 3 is 'yes' are those benefits of substantial value or advantage?

Note: 'practical benefits' will include:

−   a view
−   peace and quiet
−   light[27]
−   the open character of the neighbourhood[28]

---

[25]   *Re Bass Ltd's Application* (1973) 26 P&CR 156 sets out the questions asked under this ground of application, which are paraphrased here.

[26]   *Re Hamden Homes' Application* LP/38/1999 (decision 12 December 2001). Applicant had not in fact got ownership, or even contractual rights over land necessary to implement development for which he had consent and uncertain whether the Local Planning Authority would grant consent for smaller scheme: Bell Lane, Little Chalfont, Bucks.

[27]   *Re North's Application* (1997) 75 P&CR 117; preservation of a view and light.

but not:

- bargaining power and the capacity to extract a ransom.[29] In *Re Zopats Developments' Application* (1966) 18 P&CR 156, the member phrased the usual expression of concern by objections to proposed developments as 'a case where the prospect terrifies while the reality will prove harmless'. In this context, if instructed for the applicant, always obtain permission at an early stage to view the development site from the objectors' land, rear windows etc. That is what the member will see on his view during the hearing!

Question 5

16.29 *Is impeding the proposed user contrary to the public interest?*

Note:

Only in rare cases, even where the application under paragraph (aa) is by a local, or public authority, is the answer likely to be yes. Such applications are rare in view of the powers given to local authorities to override covenants set out in Chapter 12 above.

It may well be that a proposal (eg to allow sheltered housing) is within the public interest. But the fact that this is so does not mean that the restriction (in impeding that user) is contrary to the public interest. It may be in the public interest to preserve certain elements of a neighbourhood, eg to preserve the types of amenity referred to under question 4 above. Only where the proposal *is so important* that it is almost an exceptional case, will such an argument succeed.[30]

16.30 In all cases the applicant will need to put before the Lands Tribunal the following evidence in order to satisfy sub-section l(A) and sub-section l(B):

- the planning matters referred to in subsection (1B). This evidence is very important and should not be overlooked, or its effect underestimated.
- But note that it is merely a *circumstance* which the Tribunal can and should take 'into account', it is not decisive.[31] This is a very important principle.
- the planning consent relating to the applicant's site.
- the pattern of the grant or refusal of planning consent in the 'relevant areas'; this term is not defined but would appear to include the areas both benefited and burdened by the covenant which is the subject of the application.[32]

---

[28] *Re Martins' Application* (1988) 57 P&CR 119; preservation of a public open space for that purpose.

[29] See *Gilbert v Spoor* [1983] Ch 27 and *Stannard v Issa* [1987] AC 175, on views and other practical benefits. See *Stockport MBC v Alwiyah Developments* (1983) 52 P&CR 278, for authority that bargaining power and its value in 'ransom' terms is not a *practical* benefit. Applied in *Re Wakes's Application* LP/2/2001 (decision 17 June 2002) (Protection of intensive farming operation opposite Applicant's land). See also *Re Zaineeb Al-Saeed's Application* (2002) (LP 41/1999). That decision is also important for summarising the other post application under s 84(1) on the Wimbledon House Estate, and the effect of such 'precedents').

[30] *Re SJC Construction Co Ltd's Application* (1974) 28 P&CR 200, may be an example of an exceptional case where there was an acute shortage of housing for the elderly; see also *Re Bradley Clare* (1987) 55 P&CR 126.

[31] *Re Martin's Application* [1988] 57 P&CR 119, at pp 124–125, per Fox LJ.

[32] See Lands Tribunal Rules, Practice Direction 14, Expert Evidence, as to the manner in which expert evidence is to be admitted, reproduced at Appendix 4 below.

In this context it is important to note that in applications under paragraph (aa), planning evidence is not going to be decisive save in rare cases, such as where there is a shortage of local housing land.[33] See the illustrations below for cases which show how this principle operates.

Question 6

16.31   *If either (a) the benefits secured by the covenants are not of substantial value or advantage or (b) if impeding the proposed user is contrary to the public interest, will money be adequate compensation?*

Note:

Compensation is dealt with under **16.95** below and reference should be made there for the principles upon which it is awarded. But at this stage it is necessary to have some idea of those principles in order to answer the question posed above. There is an element of circularity here, but it is unavoidable in view of the exercise which has to be carried out in order to see if the application under subsection (aa) will succeed.

For ease of reference, adequate compensation is defined in section 84(1) as either:

(1)   a sum to make up for any loss or disadvantage suffered by that person in consequence of the discharge or modification; or

(2)   a sum to make up for any effect which the restriction had, at the time when it was imposed, in reducing the consideration then received for the land affected by it.

16.32   The practical answer to question 6 is usually as follows.

–   If the Lands Tribunal has reached a provisional conclusion that the benefits secured by the covenants are not of substantial value, the compensation is likely to be small if assessed under section 84(1)(i). Such a conclusion would support an application under paragraph (aa). If, however, compensation were to be assessed on the alternative basis under section 84(1)(ii) the outcome is more speculative and there may be more room for argument on that measure that money will not be adequate compensation.[34]

–   In contrast, if the compensation could be shown to be substantial (at least on a provisional basis) that would tend to show that the benefit of the covenant is of substantial value, or advantage and the application is unlikely to succeed under subsection (aa).[35]

–   If the Lands Tribunal has reached a provisional conclusion that impeding the proposed user is contrary to public interest, the compensation may well be large, so that it is adequate to compensate for the loss of amenity.[36]

–   Where the objector is a statutory, or quasi-statutory body (eg local authorities, or the National Trust) acting as 'custodians of the public interest' it may be

---

[33]   As occurred in *Re SJC Construction Co Ltd's Application*, see n 30 above.

[34]   *Re Vaizey* (1974) 28 P&CR 517 – where the interest of the objector was in reversion to long leases.

[35]   See *Re Bushell* (1987) 54 P&CR 386, where £30,000 was said to represent the loss in value in the property with the benefit of a covenant to protect a view, and that led the Tribunal to conclude that the benefit of that covenant was of substantial view.

[36]   *Re SJC Construction Co Ltd*, at n 30 above.

impossible to show that money compensation will be adequate. In which case the application will fail under this ground, but may be successful under subparagraph (c) referred to below.[37]

16.33   *Practical tips for applications under paragraph (aa)*

– Identify, at an early stage, what are the practical benefits which are of substantial value, or advantage secured by the covenant which is the subject of the application. If you act for an objector this will be a crucial part of your opposition. If you act for the applicant your task will be to show either a lack of such benefits, or that the value or advantage is small and is capable of being the subject of adequate compensation.

– Identify and place clearly before the Tribunal the matters referred to in section 1(B). This means setting out the planning evidence, and the relevant evidence relating to the covenant itself. Consider why the covenant was imposed, and what was the context of such imposition. Is this a case of a tight scheme, or an isolated covenant?

– Consider what expert evidence will be required on any of the issues raised by the questions posed above, and particularly on the question of compensation and its adequacy, or otherwise.

Illustrations of applications made under paragraph (aa): section 84(1)(aa)

16.34   *(1) Is the proposed user reasonable?*

YES, WHERE PLANNING PERMISSION AND DETAILED PLANS ARE TO HAND[38]

Re Bass Limited (1973) 26 P&CR 156. A brewery based near City Road, Smethwick, Birmingham wished to use land subject to restrictions preventing its use other than for residential purposes as a loading area for lorries making deliveries to the brewery. Assuming the restrictions were not in place, the proposed user was considered to be reasonable as it had received planning permission and businesses within the Birmingham area had to be preserved. However, the proposal was not in the public interest because it was largely of the brewery's own making and the restrictions secured practical benefits for the objectors.

16.35   *Re North* (1997) 75 P&CR 117. Proposed user of a garden for the erection of a house and two garages in Winkfield, Berkshire (a residential neighbourhood) was a definite project which had been granted planning permission and was therefore reasonable. However, the restrictions secured practical benefits of a substantial value for the owners of a neighbouring house, Foliejon Garden House. Thus, the application failed.

---

[37]   As occurred in *Re Martins' Application* (1988) 57 P&CR 119. There a money payment would not have removed the adverse effect of the proposed development on a public open space which the local authority was entitled to enforce in the public interest.

[38]   *Re Barry* (1980) 41 P&CR 383.

16.36   NO, WHERE SCHEME COVENANTS ARE PRESENT

Re Bromor (1995) 70 P&CR 569. The applicant wished to demolish a semi-detached house in Drummond Drive, Stanmore, Middlesex so as to permit the construction of an access road for the proposed development of a triangular piece of land to the rear of the house. The house was subject to a covenant which prevented its use other than as a dwelling house. As the house was part of the Hill House estate where a building scheme existed, there was a great presumption that the covenant would be upheld and therefore a greater onus of proof upon the applicant. It was doubted whether the proposed user of the land was reasonable as in an earlier case (see *Fletcher* LP/56/1987) the construction of a roadway upon land where a house and garden already existed to serve development to the rear of the house was considered to be an unreasonable use of the subject land.

(2)   The continued existence of the covenants would impede the proposed user

16.37   It may be necessary to show that no *other* restriction will impede the proposed user.

(3)   Does impeding the user secure practical benefits to the objectors?

PRACTICAL BENEFITS

Note: these must be secured by the covenant and not, for example, by some indirect route, such as local authority policy.

16.38   *Re O'Reilly* (1993) 66 P&CR 485. The applicant wished to develop houses upon land in Arnhem Drive, Chatham which was sold subject to a restriction which provided that 'Not without the prior consent of the council in its capacity as vendor [was the applicant] to use the land or any part thereof otherwise than for the purpose of parking and garaging cars.' As the applicant could cease to use the land for off-street parking without being in breach of the restriction, such practical benefit as there was in providing off-street parking was not a benefit secured by the restriction.

16.39   VIEW

Gilbert v Spoor [1983] Ch 27. Restrictions gave residents benefit of preventing any interference, by erection of dwelling houses, with the view across the Tyne Valley from a certain part of The Centurion Way (the approach road), or from public seats situated thereon or from the vicinity of the seats. It was perfectly reasonable to say that the loss of a view just round the corner from the land may have an adverse effect on the land itself. See also *Re Farrow's Application* LP/18/2000, decision of 10 May 2001; view held to be a practical benefit; St Austin's Estate, Sheringham, Norfolk.

16.40   *Stockport Metropolitan Borough Council v Alwiyah Developments* (1983) 52 P&CR 278. Council claimed benefit of being able to provide 11 houses forming part of a larger estate in Romiley, Stockport, Cheshire with a view down to the Goyt Valley. Not a practical benefit secured by restrictions as no evidence that the view provided the council with an advantage in carrying out its duties as a housing authority in housing tenants or that the tenants of the relevant houses cared about the view.

16.41   *Re Purnell* (1987) 55 P&CR 133. Planning permission had been granted for a chalet-bungalow to be built in the garden of a dwelling in the Chelsfield Park Estate in Orpington, Kent. A restriction forbade the erection of more than one dwelling house per plot of land on the estate. The residents' association and its members would be injured if the restriction were to be modified as the neighbourhood would lose the advantage of its open development and therefore its almost unique character in the area.

16.42   QUIET

Re Wards Construction (Medway) Limited (1973) 25 P&CR 223. An application to erect a block of 12 flats on land in Gillingham, Kent. Restrictions so that could only build detached or semi-detached houses. Objectors had special reasons for wanting a feeling of space and quiet and were found to value space and quiet and light. The development proposal would blot out the sky and sunlight and the application was therefore refused. See also *Re Boulton's Application*; LP/31/2003, decision of 4 August 2004, effect of children, day care nursery on neighbouring properties and increased traffic and noise. Application refused.

16.43   LIGHT

Re North (1997) 75 P&CR 117. The restriction was of substantial benefit to the objectors as it prevented the deterioration of the view and the obstruction of light from and to the windows in the flank wall of the rear living room of Foliejohn Garden House.

Re Jilla's Application [2000] 2 EGLR 99. Protection to light and amenity secured by covenant requiring approval of building plans by neighbouring owner at 136 Hainault Road, Chigwell, Esssex. Application allowed under paragraph (aa) on payment of £10,000 (about 1.5 per cent of the value of No 136) as benefits secured by the restriction not of substantial value, or advantage and that payment adequate compensation for the loss or disadvantage caused by the modification.

16.44   PRIVACY, PUBLIC AMENITY, OPEN SPACE

Re Martins' Application (1988) 57 P&CR 119.[39] The restrictions were a practical benefit to the corporation in preventing detriment to the visual amenity of the area. The proposed house would be visually unacceptable because the width of the plot was inadequate and in the context of the relaxed density of houses in the area would constitute a cramped form of development. The cramped appearance would prejudice the amenities of the neighbourhood which the corporation had a duty to protect. See *Re Farrow's Application* LP/18/2000 (decision of 10 May 2001, above at **16.39**). See also *Re Hamden Homes' Application* (at **16.27** above) where wild birds in gardens, prospective roadways at rear of gardens, traffic noise and pollution held to be practical benefits of substantial value or advantage. See also *Re Marshall's Application* LP/32/2001; decision of 5 August 2003, where views from houses, and prospective overlooking of swimming pools, amounted to benefits within paragraph (aa) even though no evidence of diminution of value

---

[39]   And see *Re Barry*, at n 38 above.

bar a loss of £4,000 on the benefited property (2 The Courtway, Low Ackworth, West Yorkshire). See also *Re Diggens' Application* at **16.48** below.

16.45 THE PRESERVATION OF AN IDENTITY OF AN ESTABLISHED ESTATE

Re Collins and Others (1974) 30 P&CR 527. Stockton House Estate, Fleet, Hampshire subject to covenants within a building scheme which were of substantial advantage because they helped to maintain the ethos of the estate. The estate was suburban but the proposed development was urban in character due to its density and the numbers and types of roads. The development would also increase traffic, noise and involve loss of privacy and the felling of a high number of trees and shrubs. Moreover, some purchasers had specifically bought the properties in reliance upon the scheme of covenants. See also *Re Felton Homes Application*, LP/3/2003, decision of 2 December 2004. Application refused under (aa) because of need to protect effective system of covenants in Caldy Manor Estate, Wirral.

16.46 *Re Brierfield* (1976) 35 P&CR 124. 50, Manor Way, Onslow Village, Guildford was subject to a restriction that not more than an average of five houses to the acre were to be built and that Onslow Village Limited should determine the number of houses on each plot. Onslow Village Limited was under a moral obligation to their purchasers to safeguard the covenants and to safeguard the character of the village maintaining the standards of quality and density of housing in the area. The proposal would lead to the development of the whole frontage of Abbott's Close and Manor Way, and double the existing density of housing. The application therefore failed.

16.47 *Re Kalsi* (1993) 66 P&CR 313. Plot on Wentworth Estate, Virginia Water, Surrey with restriction of building to one house and lodge for use of servant or occupier. The construction of a two-storey house or a bungalow in the garden of the property was a reasonable user. The roads committee argued that the restriction was of practical benefit to them as custodian of the interests of the estate in preserving the system of covenants. This was accepted but neither the scheme of covenants, nor the committee's role would be rendered ineffective by the applicant's proposals. Therefore the restriction was modified so that the applicant was permitted to build a bungalow (but not a house) on the property. (Compare *Re Henman* (1970) 23 P&CR 102 below.)[40]

16.48 *Re Willis* (1997) 76 P&CR 97. Planning permission for change of use of council house in Castle Donington, Leicestershire as bed and breakfast establishment. Restriction forbade use of the house for any trade or business. The restriction did not secure practical benefits for the council by preventing a deterioration in the amenity of the area because the bed and breakfast user did not cause such deterioration. Moreover, the proposed development would not set a precedent for applications for further bed and breakfast use on the estate. Thus, the application would not undermine the scheme of covenants which was policed by the council as the custodian of the public interest for the benefit of the residents of the estate. *Re Diggens' Application* LP/27/1999; LP/25/2000, decision of

---

[40] The Wentworth Estate is governed by a Private Act, the Wentworth Estate Act 1964. But the fact that such an Act exists does not oust the jurisdiction of the Lands Tribunal under s 84(1).

25 November 2000) (preservation of density restriction, Seymour Road, St Albans, Herts).

Re Zaineeb Al-Saeed's Application (2002) (LP/41/1999), (Wimbledon House Estate, 44 Parkside). Preservation of statuesque, spaciousness, open character and prevention of unsuitable backland, or garden development by maintenance of density of one house per plot and evidence of precedent for backland, or garden development, were benefits of substantial advantage (see **16.28** above).

16.49 FREEDOM FROM TRAFFIC AND ALL THAT GOES WITH IT

Re Bass Limited (1973) 26 P&CR 156. Restrictions preventing use of land as loading and unloading area for deliveries to brewery secured a substantial benefit for the owners of premises on City Road, Smethwick as they prevented the noises, fumes, vibration, dirt and risk of accidents which was associated with the delivery lorries.

16.50 *Re Wallace and Co* (1993) 66 P&CR 124. The applicant wished to build a block of six garages on land to the rear of numbers 29–37 Perth Road, St. Leonards-on-Sea, East Sussex and upon which it had covenanted not to build at all. The proposed development would involve increased use by vehicles of the subject land and the access way thereto. The covenant provided the council with the benefit of being able to resist the proposed development in the interests of adjoining occupiers upon this basis.

Re Fairclough Homes' Application LP/30/2001, decision 8 June 2004; 60 Wigton Lane, Alwoodley, Leeds. Proposed plot development would cause more traffic movement and greater disturbance. Also out of accord with the residential character of the area.[41]

16.51 NOISE AND GENERALLY UNDESIRABLE SOCIAL ACTIVITY

Re Solarfilms (Sales) Limited (1993) 67 P&CR 110. Proposed user of a bungalow as a day nursery for children in Grane Park, Halingden, Lancashire. The covenants ensured that Grane Park retained its character as an exclusively residential enclave and avoided the traffic disturbance which would be caused by the user as a day nursery. See also *Re Wake's Application* (at **16.28** above) (protection from interference with intensive farming operation a practical benefit of substantial value secured by covenant).

16.52 FREEDOM FROM CARAVANS

Re Hopcraft (1993) 66 P&CR 475. Covenant preventing use of land at Lucky Lite Farm, Horndean, Waterlooville, Hampshire other than for agricultural and horticultural purposes. It was proposed to use the land for the storage of touring caravans. The public at large derived substantial benefit from the maintenance of the application land in its open and undeveloped state. The enjoyment of the public footpaths which offered extensive views of the countryside across the subject land would be seriously diminished if caravans were stored on the land. The covenant therefore secured a substantial benefit to the council as the custodian of the public interest.

---

[41] See also *Re Boulton's Application* (2004), referred to at **16.42** above.

16.53 NASTY CARPORTS AND OTHER UNAESTHETIC STRUCTURES

Re Livingstone (1982) 47 P&CR 462. The applicants wished to modify a covenant preventing any external alterations or additions to the front or side elevations of the property so that they could maintain the carport which they had erected at the side of their house in Ambroseden, near Bicester in Oxfordshire. The carport, which consisted of PVC roof sheeting on a steel frame, was an eyesore in that it could deteriorate and its roof sheeting could become discoloured. The covenant therefore secured practical benefits to Ambroseden Court Limited (the original covenantee) ás it could thereby prevent any deterioration of the visual amenity of the area. There can be no absolute definition of the words 'practical benefits'.[42]

(4) Are the practical benefits of substantial value or advantage?

16.54 This is a question of fact and degree. The right to build without being in breach of covenant is not a practical benefit: *Re Hydeshire* (1993) 67 P&CR 93.

Two questions:

(1) What interest does the objector have?
– freeholder in possession
– freeholder subject to a lease or licence

in the latter case, whether the covenants secure benefits of substantial value/advantage may be open to doubt. Much will depend on the value of the reversion and when it will fall into possession.

16.55 *Re Vaizey* (1974) 28 P&CR 517. Mrs Vaizey had let a block of flats on long leases such that her interest was limited to the freehold reversions of the flats and a freehold interest (in possession) of the common parts of the block of flats and the undeveloped parts of the protected land. Thus, the covenants secured no practical benefit for Mrs Vaizey and she could be adequately compensated for her loss.

But a reversionary freeholder may have a moral obligation to enforce which may be a benefit of substantial value to him: where building schemes exist, for example.

(2) What is substantial in terms of either value or advantage (if not both)?

Something which is of importance in money terms or in some other way which is of advantage to the landowner with the benefit of the covenant.

THE LOSS OF A VIEW HAS A VALUE

Re Carter (1973) 25 P&CR 542. Nuisance during building operations and partial loss of sea view valued at £200; partial loss of outlook over pleasant garden valued at £100.

---

[42] *Re Gaffney's Application* [1974] 35 P&CR 440; considered and applied in *Re Coles' Application* LP/2/2003 (decision 16 February 2004, 5 per cent diminution in value not substantial; application allowed under paragraph (aa) on payment of compensation). See **16.104** for the cases which show the 'range' of what is and is not 'substantial'.

THE PREVENTION OF 'INTOLERABLE NUISANCES' DURING BUILDING OPERATIONS OF PRACTICAL BENEFIT

16.56 *Re Tarhale Limited* (1990) 60 P&CR 368.

THE RIGHT TO VET PLANS

Re Reynolds (1987) 54 P&CR 121. The development of Woodside was allowed but as the garage of the property did not need to be built so close to Wharf Cottage, the objectors were awarded £500 in respect of minor changes to the development plans which could have been made for their benefit.

THE PRESERVATION OF THE 'ETHOS' OF AN ESTATE

16.57 A practical benefit of substantial advantage (even if not of value).

Re Collins and Others (1974) 30 P&CR 527. Preservation of Stockton House Estate, Fleet, Hampshire: see **16.45** above.

16.58 *Re Henman* (1970) 23 P&CR 102 (preservation of Wentworth Estate). The continuance of scheme of covenants secured benefits for Wentworth Estate Company and Roads Committee as elected representatives of the owners and would discourage others from using and 'in-filling' argument in attempting to develop their land.[43]

16.59 *Re Lee* (1996) 72 P&CR 439. Covenant preventing more than one house per plot formed part of a building scheme created in the 1960s in Hardwick Court, Pontefract, West Yorkshire. Applicant had planning permission to build another house in her garden. A building scheme establishes a system of local law applicable to the whole estate and creates a presumption that restrictions under it will be upheld and therefore a greater burden of proof on the applicant to show that the requirements of section 84 are met. Although the construction of the extra house was a reasonable user of land, the covenant secured one general and two specific benefits which were of substantial value to the objector who lived opposite the proposed development. The general benefit was enjoyed by all members of Hardwick Court and was the right to object to the intensification of development in contravention of the restriction and maintain the status quo. The specific benefits secured to the objector were the preservation of the present outlook from her property over the applicant's garden and the prevention of the increase in traffic and parking problems in the hammerhead at the end of Hardwick Court. However, the prevention of disturbance from building works which were estimated to last for approximately 6 months was not considered to be a benefit of substantial value or advantage.

(5) *Contrary to the public interest?*

16.60 This is an *alternative* to putting the application on the footing that the covenant does not secure any practical benefits of substantial value or advantage to those entitled to the benefit.

---

[43] The Wentworth Estate is governed by a Private Act, the Wentworth Estate Act 1964. See also *Re Kalsi* (1993) 66 P&CR 313, as stated at **16.47** above. The existence of the Private Act does not oust the jurisdiction of the Lands Tribunal under s 84(1).

Note: factors under 1B to be taken into account under this alternative head, just as before.

Only in some cases will this alternative succeed. Why?

(1)   In many cases the evidence re planning policy (admitted under IB) will show that such evidence is consistent with the terms of the restriction.

16.61   *Re Bass Ltd's Application* (1973) 26 P&CR 156. Applied in *Re Farrow's Application* (2001) LP/18/2000. The fact that planning consent was granted for a house but might be refused for a bungalow did not mean that the subsection was contrary to the public interest by preventing the erection of the house. The restriction was one that limited buildings to single stories. The applicant wanted to put up a house (two storeys) for which he had planning consent.

Re Mansfield DC (1976) 33 P&CR 141. Restriction on land for use as cattle market consistent with planning policy on land use. Planning permission for proposed use as leisure centre. Not contrary to public interest for cattle market user to continue. It may have been contrary to the public interest to enforce the covenant if the applicants could, for example, have shown that there was no suitable alternative site for the leisure centre and that it was wholly impracticable or uneconomic to continue the cattle market at the present site or indeed any other site. No such evidence upon the facts.

(2)   The fact that planning permission has been granted for the development which is in conflict with the covenant does not mean that the covenant, in stopping the proposed development, is contrary to the public interest.

16.62   *Re Davies* (1971) 25 P&CR 115. Planning permission means that a particular form of development is not contrary to the public interest, it does not mean that it is contrary to the public interest if the proposed development is not permitted. Planning permission sought for 11 houses on a site in Somerton. No evidence of public interest other than general evidence of a need to build houses to meet the demand from elsewhere in the county.

16.63   *Re Wallace and Co* (1993) 66 P&CR 124. Application to erect six garages for which planning permission had been granted on a plot of land to the rear of some terraced houses on Perth Road, St Leonards-on-Sea, East Sussex. Not contrary to the public interest to prevent the proposed development because there was no need for further off-street parking in the immediate area. On-street parking in Perth Road did not present any specific problem or danger.

16.64   *Re Hopcraft* (1993) 66 P&CR 475. Grant of planning permission merely a factor which Lands Tribunal can take into account in the exercise of its discretion. The Planning Acts and the Lands Tribunal's jurisdiction under the Law of Property Act 1925 were two separate regimes. The public interest required that the subject land be kept free from development rather than as a site for the storage of touring caravans. Although the occupants of touring caravans parked them in driveways or gardens in the district, there was no evidence that the owners left them there because of lack of storage sites.

16.65   *Re O'Reilly* (1993) 66 P&CR 485. Restriction which impeded the proposed development of land for six houses in Chatham was not contrary to the public interest. Although the development had been granted planning permission, there was no evidence of any need for housing in the area or that the removal or modification of the restriction would end or reduce vandalism in the area.

However, there may be cases where the public interest requirement can be made out, but those are likely to be rare.

Illustration of where the 'public interest' requirement was met

NEED FOR CARE HOMES

16.66 *Re Lloyd and Lloyd* (1993) 66 P&CR 112. Planning permission for change of use to community care home for psychiatric patients in Worthing area. This use was contrary to the restriction which permitted use as a school or boarding house. It was government policy to discharge psychiatric patients into community care and there was a desperate need for such a home in the Worthing area. Therefore public interest requirement met.

SHORTAGE OF HOUSING LAND

16.67 *Re SJC Construction Company Limited* (1974) 28 P&CR 200. Planning permission was granted for a two-storey block of flats to be built on land in Cheam. Restriction which permitted the erection of a single dwelling house upon the subject land. At the time of the application, a dwelling house which had previously been built upon the land had been demolished and the proposed flats had been constructed up to first-floor level. The restriction was contrary to the public interest because there was a scarcity of housing in the whole of the south-east of England including the area of Sutton and Cheam and the building work which had already been carried out would be wasted unless the restriction was modified.[44]

UNNECESSARY DEMOLITION OF HOUSING

16.68 *Re Fisher & Gimson (Builders) Limited* (1992) 65 P&CR 312. Application for discharge or modification of restriction providing that a third of an acre of land in Solihull, West Midlands, should only be used as garden land, so as to permit the retention of a house and garage erected there. The objectors had also commenced proceedings to enforce the restriction in the High Court and claimed mandatory orders that *inter alia* the house and garage be pulled down and demolished.

These proceedings had been adjourned to await the outcome of the application. If the restriction was enforced there was a real risk that important housing accommodation would be demolished and that was contrary to the public interest. As the restriction, therefore, impeded a reasonable user of the land contrary to the public interest, it was modified so as to permit the development retrospectively. Compensation of £6,000 was awarded to reflect price of release or by reference to other releases achieved by consent.

---

[44] This part of the decision was not challenged in the Court of Appeal: see (1975) 29 P&CR 322 at p 325. See **16.98** below for the question of compensation which was the issue before the Court of Appeal.

But compare:

16.69   *Re Hunt* (1996) 73 P&CR 126. A dwelling house had been erected in the rear garden of 251, Marlborough Road, Swindon pursuant to planning permission. This development was in breach of covenants under a building scheme whereby the erection of only one house was permitted per plot and each house had to be built within the building line. The development was obtrusive in relation to the remainder of the scheme area as it had been built well in advance of the building line and had a cramped appearance. Moreover, to allow the application would have the effect of opening the first breach in a carefully maintained scheme of development and would render it more difficult to oppose further subdivisions of lots with the consequent threat of increasing density and loss of character in the neighbourhood. Thus, the covenants secured a substantial practical benefit, namely the assurance of the continued integrity of the budding scheme. To pull the dwelling house down was not contrary to the public interest because there was no scarcity of land available for housing development in the area and a writ claiming an injunction to enforce the covenants had not been issued.

(5)   *Will money be adequate compensation?*

16.70   The Lands Tribunal must be satisfied that:

(1)   money is an adequate substitute for the loss arising from the discharge and modification; and
(2)   such money which the Lands Tribunal has power to award under section 84(1)(i) or (ii) (see below) is adequate compensation.

(See **16.95** below.)

Note: if no loss would be caused by discharge or modification, this question does not arise: *Re Willis* (1997) 76 P&CR 97; see above, at **16.48**.

Paragraph (b)

16.71

> *'that the persons of full age and capacity for the time being or from time to time entitled to the benefit of the restriction ... have agreed, either expressly or by implication, by their acts or omissions, to the same being discharged or modified'.*

This ground is unlikely to be relied on at the time of the application in view of the obvious point that if all the persons with the benefit are agreed that the discharge or modification should go ahead, they can achieve this end by deed.

But there are cases where at the date of the application it is possible that there will be a class of persons who, by the time of the hearing, have not lodged notices of objection, or have withdrawn those lodged. In such cases the applicant should rely on this ground as an alternative to his main ground.[45]

Even if there are no objectors the Lands Tribunal still has a discretion as to whether to discharge or modify.[46]

---

[45]   See **A7.8**.
[46]   *Re University of Westminster's Application* [1998] 3 All ER 1014, CA.

When relying on this ground, it is important in practice that any notice of application must make it clear to those upon whom it might be served, or to whom it might be directed, what will be the effect of any order the Tribunal may make on the application. Thus, where an application is made seeking discharge and modification in the alternative, the consequences of each alternative must be made clear in the notice of application. If there is room for misunderstanding about the effect of one, or other of the consequences of an order being made for one of the alternatives claimed, the Tribunal is entitled to refuse to exercise its discretion to refuse to make an order under subsection (b) in respect of that part of the application. It will refuse to make the order even though there may be no objection to it. It is, therefore, vital that the effect of alternative heads of application is made clear to potential objectors in any notice of application.[47] It may also be worth making a decision at an early stage, and certainly before the application is drawn and made, whether it is preferable to make the application for either discharge or modification and not both, even in the alternative. In many cases the application will be focussed on the need to modify, and the reality will be that discharge is not desired. This course, which requires an early decision to 'nail one's colours to the mast' may be wise in order to avoid any later difficulty of the type that arose in *Re University of Westminster*. The Form of Application now makes it clear that the grounds of application are to be set out clearly and that discharge and modification are *alternatives*.

Practical tips for applications under paragraph (b)

16.72

– Is it certain that all relevant consents are to hand? A failure to respond is not evidence of consent although it may be evidence of agreement by implication. Nor should such a failure be taken in all cases as implied consent. Where the application proceeds on such a basis the applicant should be prepared to prove his case on the other paragraphs which may be available in case the Tribunal is not satisfied that the objector has agreed 'by implication'. The important thing is that there must be an *agreement*; so leaving deeds of release with a party, or trying to *persuade* a party to agree will not bring paragraph (b) into play. See *Re Farrow's Application* LP/18/2000 (decision of 10 May 2001 at paragraphs 68–88 for a failure by the applicant to prove agreement). See also *Re Furnell and Pearce's Application* LP3&13/2001: decision of 12 July 2002 for the rejection of an application under paragraph (c) on the ground of 'implied acquiescence' and where no express consent had been given to the application to discharge a restriction.

– Has the application made it clear what the consequences of the relief sought are, particularly if there are alternatives between discharge and modification? The notice must be drawn so as to make it clear 'beyond the possibility of misunderstanding'.

– Is this a case where modification (as opposed to discharge) is really what is sought?

---

[47] It was the failure to make the effect of a discharge, as opposed to a modification, clear in the notice ('beyond the possibility of misunderstanding') which justified the Tribunal in *Re University of Westminster*, above, in refusing to make an order under para (b) for discharge; agreement to that part of the application could not be inferred from the absence of objection.

Illustrations of cases under paragraph 84(1)(b)

16.72.1 *Re Child Brothers, Limited* (1958) 10 P&CR 71. Application for the modification of covenants affecting 14.53 acres of land which was formerly part of the Whitstable Manor Estate, Whitstable so that 100 houses could be built. If a building scheme existed, it had been more honoured in the breach than in the observance. The permitted number of houses had been exceeded upon 14 out of the 22 plots of land. No building scheme was found to exist but in any event if such a scheme had existed the evidence of the general disregard of the covenants meant that they would have been impliedly waived under paragraph (b).

16.72.2 *Re Robinson and O'Connor* (1964) 16 P&CR 106. Restrictions imposed on the user of a shop in Timperley, Cheshire, for the benefit of two adjacent shops which forbade its use except for specified trades. Applicants wished to modify the restrictions so as to continue to use the shop as an off-licence (this use had commenced a year before the hearing). Although the objectors had indicated that they were generally willing to consider agreeing to such use and their solicitors had sent a letter in these terms, they had not given their irrevocable consent in writing to the user such that the application failed under paragraph (b).

16.72.3 *Re Goodban* (1970) 23 P&CR 110. Restriction prohibited erection of more than one detached or one pair of semi-detached dwelling houses on a site in Caversham, Reading. Application to permit the erection of four private dwelling houses on the site. The objectors did not have the benefit of the restrictions because no building scheme with mutual covenants existed. The benefit of the restriction vested in the Caversham Park Estate Company whose rights had been assigned to Davis Contractors Limited. The assignee consented to the proposed development and the restriction was therefore modified under paragraph (b).

16.72.4 *Re Fettishaw (No 2)* (1973) 27 P&CR 292. The applicants sought modification of certain restrictive covenants to enable them to erect a five-storey block of flats on a site in Wimbledon Hill Road, London SW19. After certain objectors had withdrawn from the proceedings, the applicants agreed terms with the remaining objectors upon the basis that the restrictions should be modified to permit a four-storey block of flats with parking space below the level of the ground floor, the applicants should enter new restrictive covenants with the objectors and also pay them a sum towards their costs. Thus, the objectors had expressly agreed to modify the covenants under paragraph (b) whilst any other persons who may potentially object, had by implication, by their failure to come forward despite the publicity given the application, agreed to the restrictions being modified.

16.72.5 *Re Dare and Beck* (1974) 28 P&CR 354. As all objectors entitled to the benefit of the restrictions had withdrawn their objections, the Lands Tribunal allowed the application to be amended to seek modification under paragraph (b). The restrictions were modified in accordance with the development plans annexed to the application under that paragraph.

16.72.6 *Re Lloyds Bank Limited* (1976) 35 P&CR 128. The bank applied as the administrators of the estate of the deceased owner of the bungalow in St. Briavels, Gloucestershire, to discharge covenants which applied to the land forming part of the curtilage of the bungalow. In about 1951, in breach of covenant, the deceased's predecessor in title built the bungalow which encroached upon protected land and was used to store trade materials for business. The objectors were unaware of these breaches until the date of the application and did not object to the retrospective modification of the covenants so as to allow the encroachment by the bungalow. However, they opposed the application to discharge the covenants. Although the objectors could be deemed to have condoned the breach both for the extension of the bungalow and for its use for trade purposes, their acquiescence could be met by modification and did not warrant a total discharge of the covenants.

16.72.7   *Re Cornick* (1994) 68 P&CR 372. Some 0.041 acres of land in Bridport, Dorset to be used for the construction of three dwelling-houses. Land subject to restriction that to be used exclusively for a jam factory. The objector did not object to the discharge of the covenant but claimed he was entitled to compensation. Therefore the restriction was discharged under paragraph (b). The objector was awarded compensation of £5,000 upon the basis that he would have obtained a higher price for the land from the applicant if no stipulation restricting the use of the site had been agreed at the time of the purchase.

16.72.8   *Re University of Westminster* [1998] 3 All ER 1014. The university applied to discharge or modify restrictions limiting the use of its buildings fronting Marylebone Road, London NW1, for specified educational uses so as to permit their use for general educational purposes. Although there were no objectors, the applicants were not entitled to an order for the discharge of the restrictions, either as of right or as the inevitable result of the exercise of the Tribunal's discretion. The Court of Appeal upheld the Tribunal in exercising its discretion as to whether or not to grant relief. Upon the facts of the case the Tribunal had correctly decided to modify the restrictions, rather than discharge them, having regard to the interests of those whom the restrictions may have been intended to protect and having regard to the fact that the application had not made it clear what the consequences of discharge (as opposed to modification) would be.

Paragraph (c)

16.73

> '*that the proposed discharge or modification will not injure the persons entitled to the benefit of the restriction*'.

When will this ground be used?

(1)   To stop vexatious or frivolous objections.[48]
(2)   As a long stop to prevent vexatious or frivolous objections.[49]
(3)   Where it can be shown that the proposed discharge or modification will not injure those entitled to the benefit. The emphasis is on the words *proposed discharge or modification*. It is not the proposed *development* which is being examined under this ground. Thus, it may be necessary to look at the scheme of the covenants. For example, in a development scheme the discharge or modification would cause the enforceability of the scheme to be vulnerable,

---

[48]   *Ridley v Taylor* [1965] 1 WLR 611; *Stockport MBC v Alwiyah Developments*, at **16.40** above.
[49]   *Ridley v Taylor*, above.

that would be an injury. An application in such a case, on this ground would fail. The replacement of one 'eyesore' with another would be objectionable if the effect would be to injure those with the benefit.[50] Local authorities with an interest in enforcing covenants as 'custodians of the public interest' will be entitled to oppose applications made under this subsection on the footing that they have an interest in preserving covenants which secure advantages to the inhabitants, such as amenity, or residential space.[51]

(4) Where there is evidence that the covenants that are the subject of the application are being used simply to extract money and not to control development, the Lands Tribunal may well conclude that there is no injury.

(5) In some cases the argument is raised that, whereas the instant application may not injure, its future effect may do so, for example in schemes of development. This is often known as the 'thin end of the wedge' argument.[52] This is a potentially serious argument to be dealt with on the merits of each case.[53] Whilst the Tribunal cannot bind itself to a future course of action, it will have regard to the scheme of covenants as a whole and to the maintenance of the integrity of such covenants. Thus, where an application threatens the integrity of such covenants, the preservation of such integrity is of substantial practical benefit to those with the benefit of the covenants, and if that is so, the argument that the application does not injure will fail. The Tribunal will also have regard to the fact that if the instant application succeeds, that may have an effect on future applications and the context in which they will be considered. The 'thin end of the wedge' argument is, therefore, to be looked at with care by both applicants and objectors. Such an argument will assist those objecting by showing that there are practical benefits of value or advantage when applications are made under subsection (aa) and in showing that there is injury under subsection (c). For the applicant the argument may be difficult to rebut, unless there are few properties affected by the covenants, or where there is no scheme.[54] See for a recent example of the greater burden faced by applicants where the application relates to building schemes, *Zaineeb Al-Saeed's Application* LP/41/1999: decision of 24 April 2002 (44, Parkside, Wimbledon, London SW19). That decision is important in the context of the significance and relevance of previous objection of the Tribunal in the same estate and consents etc in

---

[50] *Re Forestmere* (1980) 41 P&CR 390.

[51] See *Re Martins' Application* (1988) 57 P&CR 119, (open space); *Re Houdret* (1989) 58 P&CR 310 (residential as opposed to office user in town centre).

[52] See **16.85** below for further discussion of this point and the cases.

[53] *Re Emery* (1956) 8 P&CR 113; *Re Saviker (No 2)* (1973) 26 P&CR 441; *Cryer v Scott Bros (Sunbury) Ltd* (1986) 55 P&CR 183.

[54] See *McMorris v Brown* [1999] AC 142, for approval by the Privy Council of the approach taken by the Tribunal in *Re Snaith & Dodding's Application* (1995) 71 P&CR 104, which is summarised above. For an instance where there was no scheme and adjacent properties would not be affected by proposed development, see *Re Chapman* (1980) 42 P&CR 114, where the 'thin end of the wedge' argument was rejected. See also *Re Hextall's Application* (1998) 79 P&CR 382, (George Bartlett QC President) where the 'thin end of the wedge' argument was accepted in the context of covenants *not* part of a scheme. See *Re Hextall's Application*, per The President, at p 391, where it was held that the 'thin end of the wedge' argument was not confined to building scheme cases, although in such cases it is most likely to have application. See also *Re Pennington's Application* LP/22/2000 (decision 25 September 2001) for an example of the 'thin end of the wedge' argument being upheld in a scheme covenant case and in a 'high quality residential area'. See **16.85** for further examples below.

respect of the 'thin end of the wedge' argument. The Tribunal refused the application under paragraph (aa) as it would set a precedent as an example of the building of a new house on open garden land unconnected with an existing building and residential use. Cf *Re Forgac's Application* (1976) 32 P&CR 464 (on the same estate).

Practical tips for applications under subsection (c)

16.74

- Bearing in mind the burden of proving a lack of injury, if you are for the applicant, is my expert evidence going to stand up to scrutiny?
- Is this a case where the 'thin end of the wedge' argument has any merit? It is a potentially useful weapon for objectors. See **16.85** below.

Illustrations under section 84(1)(c)

When will this ground be used?

To STOP VEXATIOUS OR FRIVOLOUS OBJECTIONS

16.75   *Ridley v Taylor* [1965] 1 WLR 611. The general rule:

> 'My own view of paragraph (c) is that it is, so to speak, a long stop against vexatious objections to extended user ... [u]nder paragraph (c) the objection must be related to his [the plaintiff's] own proprietary interest. ... [The textbooks] suggest that paragraph (c) may be designed to cover the case of the, proprietorially speaking, frivolous objection. For my part I would subscribe to that view.'

Russell LJ held that the Lands Tribunal had incorrectly modified a restriction preventing the user of a dwelling house as five self-contained flats in Mayfair.

16.76   *Re Brown* (1977) 35 P&CR 254. The applicant wished to conduct alteration and extension works in accordance with conditional planning permission to the front of No 32, Stag Lane. Restriction preventing any alteration to existing building at No 32 for the benefit of the freeholder of No 34. Restrictions modified to allow renovation work because the objector's complaints that would interfere with light and air were 'trivial'. In fact the renovations would enhance the value of No 34 rather than affect it detrimentally.

16.77   *Re Pearson* (1978) 36 P&CR 285. The applicant wished to alter the barn in grounds of his dwelling house in Cubbington, Warwick and use as a nursing home. Restrictions in favour of occupiers of adjoining land preventing the use of the subject land except as a dwelling house and preventing any alteration to the existing buildings. Objectors claimed that if the application were granted, it would be more difficult for them to get planning permission for their own land for industrial purposes. As the objectors could not reasonably be expected to get planning permission in any event, the objectors did not suffer any prejudice by the discharge or modification of the restrictions to permit the alterations to the barn.

WHERE IT CAN BE SHOWN THAT THE PROPOSED DISCHARGE OR MODIFICATION WILL
NOT INJURE THOSE ENTITLED TO BENEFIT

16.78   *Re Beecham Group Limited* (1980) 41 P&CR 369. The applicant wished to
erect buildings upon a 10-acre site in Sompting, West Sussex for the manufacture
of desensitising vaccines. Site subject to a restriction that no buildings to be erected
save for purposes incidental to its use as playing fields. The District Council did
not own any land capable of being benefited by the restriction and did not object to
the development on aesthetic grounds. Thus it would not be injured by any
proposed modification.

16.79   *Re Chapman* (1980) 42 P&CR 114. The applicant wished to build a
dwelling house in a quarter of an acre of the garden of Mere Cottage, Old Woking
Road, Woking. Restriction prevented more than two houses (which already
existed) on the plot for the benefit of Nos 135 and 139, Old Woking Road.
The occupiers of Nos 135 and 139 would not be injured by the development
because it would be screened from their view by a line of trees and No 137 which
was interposed between the objectors' houses and Mere Cottage.

16.80   *Re Farmiloe* (1983) 48 P&CR 317. The applicant wished to convert a
coach house with 260 square yards of land on the Selly Hall Estate, Birmingham,
into a dwelling house. Land subject to a restriction requiring each dwelling house
to have a quarter of an acre of land. No evidence that any of the objectors would
suffer any direct detriment in the enjoyment of their properties or any immediate
diminution in their value. The increase in density of housing as a result of the
proposal was negligible and would result in an attractive improvement to Upland
Road. Restrictions modified to permit proposed development.

16.81   *Re Cox* (1985) 51 P&CR 335. The owner of Sunnyside, Chiddingly, East
Sussex wished to use an adjoining house known as Belfairs as a residence for an
agricultural worker. Restrictions that Sunnyside only to be used as a residence for
domestic staff of Belfairs and that not to be sold off or let separately from Belfairs.
The Council would not be injured by any proposed modification of the restrictions
since no new dwelling house was to be erected and therefore there was no breach
of planning policies applicable to the area.

16.82   *Re Towner & Goddard* (1989) 58 P&CR 316. Applicant proposed to build
tennis courts with chain-link perimeter fencing in gardens of Nos 1 and 2,
Cookham Dene Close, Chislehurst, Kent. The gardens formed part of the
metropolitan green belt and were subject to a restriction preventing any building in
the area. The council as custodian of the public interest claimed that the openness
of the view would be lost if the tennis courts were built. As the view was not open
but a view of houses and their gardens, the existence of tennis courts in the gardens
would not appear out of place and the council would not suffer injury.

16.83   *Re Hydeshire Limited* (1993) 67 P&CR 93. Applicant proposed to build
five houses on a site covering No 180, Jersey Road, Osterley. Covenants imposed
in 1922 and 1923 limited the number and type of houses to be built on land which
included the site of No 180. The 1923 covenant only permitted the erection of two
houses on No 180. The proposed development would result in a total of eight
detached houses on land including No 180, whilst a 1922 covenant permitted only
six. The owner of number 188 objected, as he was also proposing to build two

houses on the site of No 188. If the proposed development were completed *before* his own proposals were executed, he would be in breach of covenant in constructing two further houses on the site of No 188. Application succeeded under paragraph (aa) as the owner of No 188 did not have a practical benefit in seeking to preserve the right to build on his land without being in breach of covenant. The application would have succeeded under paragraph (c) in any event for the injury claimed by the objector was not as a result of the proposed modification but as a consequence of the objector's own failure to get his building done earlier at a time when the restriction would not have prohibited him.[55]

WHERE THERE IS EVIDENCE THAT THE COVENANTS ARE USED SIMPLY TO EXTRACT MONEY AND NOT TO CONTROL DEVELOPMENT

16.84 *Re Bennett and Tamarlin Limited* (1987) 54 P&CR 378. Restriction imposed on four-storey, end-of-terrace house and a three-storey mid-terrace house in Plymouth permitting their use only as private residence. Applicant proposed to use them for five self-contained flats and a maisonette. The trustees of the St Aubyn Discretionary Trust would not suffer any loss of amenity and there would be no diminution in value of any property retained by them. The trustees had been and were using the restrictions for a purpose for which they were not intended, namely to enable them to extract money as a consideration for agreeing to modifications of the restrictions. This loss of bargaining power was not a factor to be taken into account under paragraph (c).

ILLUSTRATIONS OF THE 'THIN END OF THE WEDGE ARGUMENT'[56] WHERE THE ARGUMENT WAS ACCEPTED

16.85 *Re Emery* (1956) 8 P&CR 113. Applicant proposed to build second house in grounds of property in Roundwood Park, Harpenden, Hertfordshire although a restriction permitted only one house on each plot. The objectors would be injured by the proposed development to the extent that the whole scheme and lay-out of the estate would be broken if the application were granted. Moreover, in time, many houses might be built upon vacant land forming part of the wood by the severance of existing plots or the mutual rearrangement of boundaries, if the application were allowed.

16.86 *Re Saviker (No 2)* (1973) 26 P&CR 441. Henry Boot Estates Limited laid out the Orchard Estates, Staines, for building purposes. Out of 240 plots, 92 remained unsold and were therefore vested in Boot which let them out. All the plots were subject to a restriction permitting only one house per plot for the benefit of Boot. A purchaser applied to build a second house on his plot. To allow the application would mean the beginning of the breakdown in Boot's system of 'one plot, one house' and therefore the basis upon which Boot sold houses to residents on the estate.

---

[55] See also *Re Furnell and Pearce's Application* LP/3&13/2001 (decision 12 July 2002), for a recent example where para (c) was satisfied on an application to modify a covenant so as to allow certain alterations which had been carried out and to permit the placing of satellite dishes. The Tribunal found that a court would have refused injunctive relief and that any damages would have been nominal.

[56] See para **16.73** above.

16.87 *Re Beech* (1990) 59 P&CR 502. Applicant proposed to use terraced house in Harborough Road, Kingsthorpe, Northampton, as an annex for adjoining solicitors' offices. Restriction preventing use other than for residential purposes. Necessary to consider council's position as owner of adjoining property, in the capacity of housing authority, and as local planning authority. Legitimate objective to seek to preserve residential enclave in predominantly commercial setting of Harborough Road and to oppose continuing process of conversion of property to non-residential uses. Moreover, if the scheme of covenants created upon the sale of council property to sitting tenants were breached once, it would be more difficult for other modifications to be resisted and reduce the availability of housing stock at the lower end of the market. Thus the restriction secured a substantial advantage to the council under paragraph (aa).

16.88 *Re Solarfilms (Sales) Limited* (1993) 67 P&CR 110. Applicant proposed to use bungalow in Grane Park, Haslingden, Lancashire as nursery school although restriction that must only be used as private residence. Restriction secured practical benefit and advantage to objectors under paragraph (aa) because it allowed them to preserve the character of Grane Park as an exclusively residential enclave, and without traffic problem. The 'thin end of the wedge argument' succeeded.

16.89 *Re Snaith and Dolding* (1995) 71 P&CR 104. Applicant proposed to build a second house in the curtilage of a house known as Westwood, Blackhall Lane, Sevenoaks and which formed part of the Wilderness Estate. The estate was subject to a building scheme of mutually binding covenants which *inter alia* permitted only one house on each plot. To allow the application would deprive the objectors of a substantial benefit secured by the covenants, namely the assurance of the integrity of the building scheme. The erection of the house would also alter the context in which further subdivisions of estate plots would be considered. Thus the objectors could preserve the integrity of the scheme and forestall further applications of a similar kind.[57]

16.90 *Re Hunt* (1996) 73 P&CR 126. A house had been built in advance of the building line in the garden of a plot forming part of a building scheme in Swindon. Restrictive covenants in the building scheme provided that only one house was to be built on each plot and that each house was to be within the building line. To grant the application would have the effect of opening the first breach in a carefully maintained and successful scheme of development, and would render it more difficult to resist further applications for the subdivision of plots with the consequent threats of increasing density and loss of character. The restrictions therefore secured a substantial practical benefit for the objectors, namely the assurance of the continued integrity of the building scheme.

See also *Re Fairclough Homes' Application* (2004) LP/30/2001, decision of 23 April 2004, where the proposed application for flat development would 'set a precedent' in a low density residential area and *Re Diggen's Application* (**16.48** above) where the argument was upheld even though there was no development scheme, and see *Re Hextall's Application* (1998) 79 P&CR 382, on the same issue (at **16.73**).

---

[57] Applied and considered in *Re Diggen's Application* (see **16.48** above).

16.91   *Re Willis* (1997) 76 P&CR 97. Semi-detached house in Castle Donington, Leicestershire was proposed to be used as a bed and breakfast establishment. Restrictions imposed by council upon the sale of property to the applicant prevented any use of the property for trade or business. The council claimed that if the application were allowed, it would be the 'thin end of the wedge' and would set a precedent for the introduction of further commercial uses onto the residential estate. As there were very few properties on the estate which were capable of being so converted and each application must be considered upon its own merits, the proposed modification did not set a precedent.

16.92   *Re Love and Love* (1993) 67 P&CR 101. Erection of garage in character with house and not detrimental to amenity of area, which was of no great architectural merit, permitted. 'Thin end of the wedge' argument rejected. This argument was also rejected in *Re Joyce's Application* LP/13/2002: decision of 3 February 2004; Brookside Road, Brockenhurst, Hants.

WHAT ARE THE PRINCIPAL MATTERS WHICH WILL AFFECT THE LANDS TRIBUNAL'S DISCRETION UNDER SECTION 84(1)

16.93

(1)   The Tribunal must have jurisdiction to entertain an application as one which falls within section 84(1). The covenant to be discharged or modified must be in the nature of a restriction on user.[58] Applications relating to covenants within subsections (7) and (11) of section 84 will not be entertained. In addition certain statutes expressly exclude the Lands Tribunal's jurisdiction.[59]

(2)   Where the applicant wants a temporary modification only, or a personal licence to act in breach of the restriction the Tribunal will decline jurisdiction.

(3)   The Tribunal will not rewrite the restriction, for example by inserting additional words which are unrelated to the need to modify.[60]

16.94   In applications under paragraph (aa) only the matters set out in sub-section (1B) of section 84:

- –   the development plan;
- –   local structure or unitary plans;

---

[58]   See *Re Milius* [1996] 1 EGLR 209 where the Tribunal questioned whether a covenant under Housing Act 1985, s 159, restricting the class of owner, fell within s 84(1) as a 'restriction ... as to the user [of the land].' See also *Westminster City Council v Duke of Westminster* [1991] 4 All ER 136. See **16.6** above.

[59]   See National Trust Act 1971, s 27 (and Chapter 10 above), Green Belt (London and Home Counties) Act 1938. In respect of the latter, see *R (on the application of O'Byrne) v Secretary of State for the Environment, Transport and the Regions* [2003] 1 All ER 15. See also Leasehold Reform Act 1967, ss 29–30; Forestry Act 1967, s 5(2)(b); Ancient Monument and Archaeological Areas Act 1979, s 17; Town and Country Planning Act 1990, ss 106 and 106a and restrictions imposed under the Defence Acts, or under the Land Powers (Defence) Act 1958, s 13. See statutes in Appendix 2.

[60]   Re *North's Application* (1997) 75 P&CR 117, the Tribunal refused to add words so as to imply a condition of reasonableness as to the granting of consent.

- the period and context in which the covenant was created or imposed (Where the covenant is part of a building scheme, or where it is clear that the covenants support a 'cohesive' approach to the maintenance of a certain standard or style of development, the greater the burden of proof on the applicant to show that the requirements of section 84 have been met);[61]
- the age of the covenant;
- whether the applicant is a recent, or original covenantor. Such an applicant may have to satisfy the Tribunal to a higher degree of proof but the emphasis nowadays may be more on the other matters referred to above.
- the planning consent for the proposed development on the land within the application. But note that this is merely a circumstance which the Tribunal can and should take into account, see **16.30** above.

WHAT COMPENSATION WILL THE LANDS TRIBUNAL AWARD?

Generally

16.95   The Lands Tribunal has a discretion in determining what sum by way of compensation it is just to award. That leads to the result that there is no hard and fast formula which governs the means by which compensation can be determined. Under section 84(1) there are two alternative heads and each requires the application of different principles. The text of the alternatives is as follows:

(1)   a sum to make up for any loss or disadvantage suffered by that person in consequence of the discharge or modification; or

(2)   a sum to make up for any effect which the restriction had, at the time when it was imposed, in reducing the consideration then received for the land affected by it.

Principles applicable under paragraph (i)

16.96

> *'a sum to make up for any loss or disadvantage suffered by that person in consequence of the discharge or modification'.*

This means that:

(1)   Any compensation given must be as a result of loss suffered as a consequence of the discharge, or modification of the restriction.

(2)   The mere existence of the jurisdiction under section 84 and the fact that its existence diminishes the ability of the covenantee to extract the price of a release from the covenantor (assuming the continued existence of the

---

[61]   See *Re Lee's Application* (1996) 72 P&CR 439 for a recent decision emphasising this important factor.

covenant) does not allow the Lands Tribunal to award compensation based on the loss of such bargaining power, or the opportunity to exercise it. Such loss is attributable to the failure of the covenantee to negotiate prior to an application to the Lands Tribunal by the covenantor. Such loss (attributable, in effect, to such failure) is not attributable to the making of any order by the Lands Tribunal.[62]

(3)   Thus, what is recoverable is often measured by reference to 'loss of amenity'.

There is no hard and fast formula for what governs the calculation of this sum, but, in practical terms this can include:

(1)   Diminution in value of the objector's land, or his interest in it

16.97   This may not always be substantial. It will be for the parties to adduce expert evidence from their valuers what such diminution is in terms of effect on the value of the benefited land. Again there is no hard and fast formula here, but within the scope of such diminution the following factors can be isolated and, where appropriate, can be given a value:

–   loss of the benefit of certain obvious amenities such as loss of a view;[63]

–   the loss of other benefits which can have an effect on value, even if no 'hard and fast' value can be placed on them. For example the effect of the potential increase in noise, or traffic, which development may bring. But where the effect on those with the benefit will be marked and where the benefits secured by the restriction are of substantial value (eg between 12 and 20 per cent of current values of the properties affected) the Tribunal will find that such benefits, being of substantial value, money will not be adequate compensation; the two matters run hand-in-hand; see *Re Azfar's Application*.[64]

(2)   What would be the price of a release?

16.98   This means the amount which those with the benefit of the covenant (which is the subject of the application) would have regarded as a fair price for a licence to carry out what is proposed, which but for the prospective exercise of the Tribunal's jurisdiction, would be in breach of it. The starting point is invariably an assessment of the net development value of the land the subject of the application. The second stage is to ask what proportion of that should be regarded as a fair price for a release.

---

[62]   *Stockport MBC v Alwiyah Developments* (1983) 52 P&CR 238. See *Re Jilla's Application* [2000] 2 EGLR 99, where approximately 1.5 per cent of the value of the property with the benefit of the covenant was awarded under paragraph (aa). The amount, £10,000 was held to be 'substantial value' in terms of the value of the benefits (light, amenity) secured by the covenant, and was adequate compensation for the loss or disadvantage suffered by the respondent by the modification which permitted the applicant to build the proposed extension. For a discussion of the assessment of compensation by reference to uplift in the value of the applicant's land by the President, George Bartlett QC, in a recent case, see *Re Skupinski*, at n 17 above.

[63]   *Gilbert v Spoor* (1983) Ch 27.

[64]   LP/10/2000 (decision 25 May 2001).

It is sometimes said that this requires compensation to be assessed by reference to a fixed percentage of the developer's gain. But this is not so for two reasons. First, it is important to note that the Tribunal must be satisfied that in any case where this approach is being advocated, those with the benefit would have obtained the price of a release on this basis. The fair price of a release will be dictated by the degree of loss of amenity. Secondly, the percentage itself is not fixed and its size must reflect all the factors which affect the circumstances in which the price of the release is being assessed. Although one third is described the '*Stokes*' percentage it is misleading to think that this is going to determine the award.[65]

The question may be put this way in order to try to assess the amount due:

> '*What would the outcome of friendly negotiations have been – assuming both sides had made a serious attempt to assess the net development value of the subject land?*'

Because the Tribunal has a wide discretion, it may go as high as 50 per cent of the developer's gain, as it did in *SJC Construction*, or it may go to a much lower percentage, such as 5 per cent. Equally, it may simply look at what has been agreed as the 'licence fee' in other cases in the locality where others have agreed releases or variations of the same covenants without invoking the Tribunal's jurisdiction.[66] Such 'comparables' may, therefore, be of some importance in establishing a benchmark for compensation under paragraph (i). Where loss of amenity is slight the fair price of consent will also be slight.[67]

(3)   A 'solatium' for the effect of building works

16.99   The Tribunal may decide that the effect of the discharge or modification is not such as to cause any loss to those with the benefit of the covenant in terms of diminution in the value of that land, however measured, but that proposed works of building which will be sanctioned by the discharge or modification will be a nuisance to those with the benefit while the works are being carried out. In such cases the Tribunal may award a sum designed to compensate those so affected for three months, or thereabouts, by nuisance caused by noise and dust, etc.

The amount is not going to be high. In *Re Gaffney's Application* (1974) 35 P&CR 440, £500 was described as generous. Allowing for inflation since then, an award of £4,000 may be a realistic ceiling. Less than this sum may be awarded in practice.

---

[65]   See *Re SJC Construction* (1975) 29 P&CR 322, for the way in which the Tribunal approaches this method of assessment. See **15.38** above, for the manner in which the courts have applied the 'licence' or release fee principle in the assessment of damages. The approach of both the Tribunal and the courts will often be the same. See *Re Skupinski's Application*, at n 17 above, where this measure was considered in the light of *SJC Construction*, and a 'Stokes' percentage was adopted at 33.3 per cent, see paras 20–37 of this decision.

[66]   As it did in *Re Fisher & Gimson* (1992) 65 P&CR 312.

[67]   *Stockport MBC v Alwiyah* (1983) 52 P&CR 278.

Principles applicable under paragraph (ii)

16.100

'a sum to make up for any effect which the restriction had, at the time when it was imposed, in reducing the consideration then received for the land affected by it'.

(1) Compensation has to be assessed by reference to the difference between the price paid for the burdened land subject to the restriction and the price which would have been payable for the same land free from any restriction.

(2) Unlike compensation under paragraph (i) where the person entitled to the benefit of the covenant suffers loss by reason of the discharge or modification, under paragraph (ii) compensation is based on the price or value of the applicant's land. Under paragraph (ii) the applicant should be effectively disgorging the saving he made when he bought the land subject to the restriction, as opposed to a purchase of the same land without it. But as is seen below, it is difficult to establish this 'saving'. The emphasis is, therefore, on the words 'a sum to make up for'. This means that the Tribunal may only be able to go part of the way (if it is able to proceed under paragraph (ii) at all) to establishing what effect the restriction had on the consideration part for the land.

16.101

(3) There are a number of problems inherent in any attempt to award compensation under paragraph (ii). They are:

– The burden lies on the objector to show that he is entitled to compensation under either paragraph (i) or (ii), but in the case of a claim under paragraph (ii) he must show that the price was reduced on account of the restriction. In many cases it may be impossible to show this. In fact in some cases, particularly in scheme covenants, the presence of the scheme and the 'select' nature of the estate may have increased the price of the land. Covenants may not, therefore, always be depreciatory in their effect on value. For a recent but unsuccessful attempt to obtain an award of compensation under paragraph (ii) see *Re Broomhead & Kidd's Application* LP/7/2001 (2003) which succeeded under paragraph (aa). The Tribunal had to consider evidence of value in 1967 (when the land subject to the covenants was sold) and accepted the applicant's evidence that the restriction had no effect on the price paid in 1967 for that land.

– No allowance is made for inflation or deflation. The measure is historic. So a price based on a purchase in 1935 or 1975 is compared with a price for the same land at that date without a restriction. Once again the stress is on the words 'a sum to make up for' the reduction.

– Quite apart from problems with historic evidence of value in many cases it may be impossible to show what the difference is, if any. Many residential estates are developed where restrictions are imposed and plots are sold at a price which can hardly be dissected to discover what lower price would have been paid at that time. Accordingly, the approach can only be one which adopts 'intelligent guesswork' or 'rough and ready inference'. However, it may be clear that land has a difference in value where for example the covenant allows a permitted density of houses and where the application to modify is seeking a double of the original permitted density.[68] The words 'a sum to make up for' are repeated to show that the approach to compensation under paragraph (ii) cannot be accurate, and the paragraph does not require it to be so.

Finally, it is important to remember that the Tribunal is not obliged to order compensation in every case where the covenant is discharged or modified. It is entitled to take the view that, if there is no evidence of loss or disadvantage, or any difference under paragraph (ii), it may decline to make any award of compensation.[69]

WILL THE COMPENSATION AWARDED VARY ACCORDING TO THE GROUND ON WHICH DISCHARGE OR MODIFICATION IS SOUGHT?

16.102   The following general principles apply so far as they emerge from the authorities.

Applications under paragraph (a)

(OBSOLETE COVENANTS)

16.103   A claim for loss or disadvantage under paragraph (i) is not likely to succeed if the covenant is obsolete. But a claim based on the difference in value of the land under paragraph (ii) above might well succeed.[70]

Applications under paragraph (aa)

(NO PRACTICAL BENEFITS, ETC)

16.104   If relief is granted on the basis that the covenant does not secure any practical benefit of substantial value or advantage (section 84 (1A)(a)) an award under paragraph (i) will usually be small in view of the lack of any substantial value or advantage in the covenant. See **16.54** above. If there are benefits of substantial value or advantage, the application under paragraph (aa) will fail.[71]

---

[68]   As to rough and ready inference see *Re Bowden* (1983) 47 P&CR 455 and *Re Cornick* (1994) 68 P&CR 372. For an instance of a clear difference in land value under this paragraph see *Re New Ideal Homes Ltd* (1978) 36 P&CR 476.

[69]   *Re Willis* (1997) 76 P&CR 97, at 113, is an example of this.

[70]   See *Re Quaffer's Application* (1988) 56 P&CR 142, for an example of this, where there was no loss or disadvantage suffered by the discharge of obsolete covenants and any loss of bargaining power as a result of the jurisdiction to discharge was not allowable, following *Stockport MBC v Alwiyah Developments*, noted at **16.96** above. For the facts of *Re Quaffer*, see the illustrations of applications under paragraph (a) above at **16.18**.

[71]   Compare the following cases *Re Jilla's Application* [2000] 2 EGLR 99 (diminution in value only 1.5 per cent of value (£10,000 in money terms) held not to be of substantial value) with *Re Azfar* LP/10/2000, where the benefits secured by the covenants were estimated as between 12 and 20 per cent of value and thus held substantial. In *Azfar* the application failed. A 10 per cent reduction in value was held substantial in *Re Fairclough Homes' Application* (2004) LP/30/2001 (decision 23 April 2004). But a 5 per cent reduction was held not substantial in *Re Cole's Application* (2004) (see **16.53** above).

However, by way of contrast, in some cases substantial compensation has been held to be adequate. The pattern is not altogether clear here and paragraph (ii) can be relied upon where there is a marked difference in original value.

If relief is granted under section (1A)(b) (contrary to the public interest) an award can clearly be granted under either paragraph (i) for the loss or disadvantage may well be substantial, or under paragraph (ii).

Applications under paragraph (b)

(CONSENT CASES)

If the affected parties consent there is no reason why an award cannot be made under paragraphs (i) or (ii).

Applications under paragraph (c)

(NO INJURY)

The same principles apply here as they do under applications under paragraph (a). As there is no injury no compensation is likely to be awarded under paragraph (i), there being no loss or disadvantage suffered in such a case. But, as under paragraph (a) there is still the possibility of an award under paragraph (ii).

Tactical advice in ALL applications

(1)   Only pursue the ground which has a realistic prospect of success. (Be wary especially of applying under paragraph (a); this ground is quite 'tight' and hard to prove.) Late amendments which make the case significantly different will be refused (*Re Bromley's Application*, LP/51/2003 (2004).
(2)   Seek a modification order, as opposed to one for a 'blanket' discharge.
(3)   Always inspect the land or property from both the applicant's and the respondent's side.

HOW CAN THE APPLICATION BE MADE AND WHAT ARE THE STAGES TO ITS FINAL DETERMINATION

16.105   The application must follow the procedure set out in the Lands Tibunal Rules 1996, principally Part V of those Rules (printed in Appendix 4). Also printed in Appendix 4 are the Practice Directions issued by the Tribunal (current at time of going to press). These should be followed at each stage where applicable.

In addition it is helpful for applicants to have sight of the explanatory information which can be obtained free from the Tribunal and which is updated from time to time.

The latest version of the Practice Directions and other information will be on the Lands Tribunal's website which is www.landstribunal.gov.uk.

16.106   The stages are as follows, with reference in parentheses in each stage to the relevant rules and the party primarily responsible for that stage, if not the Tribunal.

Whilst the CPR do not apply to the procedure in the Lands Tribunal, the Tribunal follows the procedures of the CPR and in particular adopts the overriding objective which ensures that cases are dealt with fairly and that includes, so far as practicable:

(1)   ensuring that the parties are on an equal footing;
(2)   saving expense;
(3)   dealing with the case in ways which are proportionate:
      (a)   as to the amount of money involved;
      (b)   to the importance of the case;
      (c)   to the complexity of the issues; and
      (d)   to the financial position of each party;
(4)   ensuring that it is dealt with expeditiously and fairly; and
(5)   allotting to it an appropriate share of the Tribunal's resources while taking into account the need to allot resources to other cases.

The Tribunal expects parties to assist it to further the overriding objective (see Practice Directions 2.1 and 2.2).

Stage 1

(APPLICANT: RULE 13)

Make the application noting the detail which is required under rule 13. The form prescribed is LPA together with LPB. See Appendix 7. See also the Fees Rules in Appendix 4. Current setting down fee (for issue) £200.

Consider:

–   Whether any remedy is needed in the High Court, or County Court, as to the meaning, or enforceability of the covenant.
–   If this is an application to stay an enforcement claim under section 84(9), what directions are needed in the Lands Tribunal pending the hearing of the enforcement claim.
–   Whether it is more appropriate to seek a modification order, as opposed to discharge of the restriction. In nine cases out of ten the former will be preferable.

Stage 2

(APPLICANT/LANDS TRIBUNAL: RULE 14)

Consider what notices/advertisements are required. The Tribunal will give directions as to service. (See precedent at A7.8.)

Stage 3

(OBJECTOR: RULE 15)

Lodge form of objection. The objector must use form LPD, Appendix A7.9. There is no fee for objecting.

Stage 4

(ALL PARTIES/LANDS TRIBUNAL: RULES 38 AND 39)

16.107   At this stage the applicant will need to certify that all objectors have lodged their objections and their title to object by showing that they have the benefit of the covenant within the application. The applicant must also certify whether and to what extent such objections are admitted. To the extent that such title is not admitted the objectors will have to show their title to object. Consider at this stage:

– whether any interim applications are required;
– case management; see Practice Direction 3; pre-trial review, rule 39;
– whether amendments are required;
– whether to exclude objectors who do not have title to object under section 84(3A); no appeal lies from any direction made under this provision;
– in complex cases, whether any decision is required under section 84(2) as to construction or enforceability of the restriction which is the subject of the application, thereby requiring the application to be suspended for the time being, rule 16. This is *mandatory* if either party applies for such a suspension: *Re Girl's Day School Trust (1872)* [2002] 2 EGLR 89. The Tribunal may have to make certain findings of construction in order to determine the application before it.[72]

Obtain orders and directions accordingly.

Stage 5

(ALL PARTIES: RULE 42)

16.108   Consider the use to be made of expert evidence. Obtain Orders and directions accordingly. Consider also the use of assessors under rule 29A if special knowledge is required by the Tribunal, but this is extremely rare.

Try to agree facts. It is wrong to instruct experts not to agree them.[73] See Practice Direction 14 for the duties of expert witnesses. Note: experts *must* direct themselves to the relevant terms and criteria of section 84. If they do not, there may be adverse cost consequences. Practice Direction 14 must be understood clearly and followed.

---

[72]   *Re Jilla's Application* [2000] 2 EGLR 99.
[73]   See the warning given in *Re Nichols' Application* (1997) 1 EGLR 144.

Stage 6

(ALL PARTIES)

Consider the extent to which orders and directions are required as to:

– disclosure: rule 34
– whether the default procedure under rule 46 should be used.
– arranging the hearing and venue. Practice Directions 9 and 10.
– permission to amend the application, which must be made in good time.

Note: An application under rule 43 for the hearing of a preliminary issue is not appropriate for applications under section 84(1) where there may be a question over who has the benefit of the restriction. In such cases directions are given as to the hearing by the Tribunal or by the Court of matters which require prior determination, such as the title to object, or construction under section 84(2) or 84(3A); see stage 4 above and Practice Direction 7, and 7.5 in particular. Note the rules as to documentation, bundles, skeleton arguments to be lodged prior to the hearing; Practice Direction 12.

Stage 7

(ALL PARTIES: RULES 17 AND 27)

Consider whether this is a case where the Lands Tribunal can make a determination without an oral hearing. (For example, where all parties are agreed, or where there are no objections to the application.)

Note: the simplified procedure under rule 28 is not used in applications under section 84.

Stage 8

(ALL PARTIES: RULES 29 AND 33)

Full hearing, which invariably includes a view by the Tribunal of the site. Procedure will usually follow that of a civil action. See Practice Directions 13–17.

As regards the view, it is always prudent for the applicant's advisers to obtain permission at an early stage, even pre-application, to inspect from the objector's land with an eye to the likely effect of the proposed development from that point of view.

Consent ought to be given to this and if difficulties are encountered apply to the Tribunal for permission to gain access. An objector could hardly oppose such an application.

WHAT ORDERS CAN THE LANDS TRIBUNAL MAKE?

As to the substance of the application:

(1) The Lands Tribunal may make an order in terms of the Application, or may dismiss it.

(2) The Lands Tribunal may make a 'provisional' order in terms that an order for modification will be made if certain new restrictions are accepted.[74]

(3) The Lands Tribunal may make an order under section 84(1C) imposing new restrictions for old.[75]

(4) The Lands Tribunal will in suitable cases make an order for payment of compensation within a specified time (which may be paid into court) and provide that until the compensation is paid the order for discharge is not to come into effect. The Lands Tribunal may order that the compensation will carry interest at such rate and for such period and calculated in such manner as the Tribunal directs; rule 32 applying Arbitration Act 1996, section 49.[76]

16.109 As to costs:

(1) Costs are entirely at the discretion of the Tribunal: rule 52. Practice Direction 20.

But, as the nature of the application under section 84(1) is one whereby the applicant is seeking to have removed or reduced rights which were conferred on the objector, or his predecessors, by force of contract, certain *specific* costs rules apply, which differ from 'ordinary' hostile property litigation. Applications under section 84(1) are not of that sort. Hence, whilst a successful objector who resists the application will normally get his costs, the converse rule does not always apply as regards the applicant if he is successful.[77] The conduct of the objector may be a significant factor in the Tribunal's determination of whether and if so to what extent he should pay the applicant's costs even where, prima facie, the objector may be able to point to factors in his favour.[78]

(2) Unless either party has made a *Calderbank* letter or a sealed offer as to costs under rule 44 (as to which see below) the practice is as follows:

---

[74] See *Re Cole's Application* LP/2/2003 (decision 16 February 2004), for a recent example to ensure protection by preservation of boundaries and tree screen.

[75] As it did in *Re Forestmere* (1980) 41 P&CR 390, where it removed controls relating to use of the land as a cinema and imposed new ones relating to residential restrictions.

[76] Appendix 4. For various types of costs orders see for example: (i) Partial success only by applicant, but points made by objectors which failed; applicant to pay two-thirds of objectors' costs: *Re Kalsi* (1993) 66 P&CR 313. (ii) Applicant succeeded on only one out of three grounds advanced. Unsuccessful grounds lengthened the hearing, but not substantially. Applicant's principal witness failed to address itself to s 84. Objector awarded one-sixth of what was sought at hearing. *Calderbank* offers made by applicant not enough, and on a wider basis than as ordered. No order as to costs. *Re Jilla's Application* [2000] 2 EGLR 99. (iii) Successful application, against largely misconceived objections and time spent on irrelevant matters *from* objectors; applicant awarded costs. *Re Girl's Day School Trust* (1872) LP/19/1999.

[77] See *Re Norfolk & Norwich University Hospital NHS Trust's Application* LP/41/2001, decision applied with approval in *Re Broomhead and Kidd's Application* LP/7/2001 (decision 13 March 2003); *Re Joyce's Application* LP/13/2002 (decision 3 February 2004); and in *Re Fairclough Home's Application* (2004), at n 71 above.

[78] *Re Norfolk and Norwich University Hospital*, above. See Practice Directions 20.1 and 20.4.

(a)   an applicant who loses normally pays the objector's costs, but an objector who loses and has acted reasonably may not always have to pay the applicant's costs;

(b)   an applicant who wins and does not have to pay any compensation can expect either to recover some or all of his costs from the objector(s) or, at least, an order that each side bears their own costs;

(c)   if the applicant wins (but has to pay compensation), he can expect to have to pay the objector's costs, unless there are grounds for saying that there should be no order as to costs; for example where the application was substantially taken up by a claim to compensation which failed;

(d)   the scale of costs will be on the High Court scale and unless the case is a simple one, or the costs relate to an interim application (where there may be summary assessment) costs will be the subject of detailed assessment (unless agreed) under rule 52 (Practice Direction 20.8). Indemnity costs (as opposed to standard basis costs) assessment may be appropriate if the conduct of any party is so bad as to warrant it.[79]

(e)   the practice set out above may vary to reflect the hostile nature of the application (the more hostile the application, the more likely there will be adverse orders as to costs) and additionally orders for costs may be made to reflect the conduct of the parties; for example penalising those who change their position 'mid-stream.' The way in which applications are conducted, both before and during the application, will be reflected in the order made as to costs. This is in line with CPR Part 44, rule 3 where conduct is a specific factor in determining where the burden of costs should lie. But, one relevant and important point is that in this jurisdiction the applicant is seeking to have removed from the objector's particular property, rights which he has. Thus if the objector is successful he ought to get his costs. If unsuccessful, he ought not to have to pay the applicant's costs unless he has acted unreasonably.[80]

See Practice Directions 20.2 and 20.4, which states that the 'general rule' as to costs does not apply in view of the nature of the application under section 84, as set out in the text above.

16.110

(3)   The use of *Calderbank* letters and *sealed offers* under rule 44 must always be considered in an application before the Lands Tribunal. In practice, in applications under section 84 the use of sealed offers is rare and *Calderbank* letters are used and are encouraged to be used. Practice Direction 20.7.

Certain points are worth bearing in mind as to such offers – however made.

–   they must be unconditional;

–   any offer should be directed at influencing the exercise of the Lands Tribunal's discretion in respect of costs. The main protection given by them is by showing that such offers, if accepted, would have shortened, if not avoided, the hearing;

[79] See *Re Farrow's Application* (2001), LP/18/2000 (decision 10 May 2001), for a 'weak' case (but not a hopeless one) where failure by the applicant did not lead to an assessment on the indemnity basis as sought by the respondent.

[80] *Re Fairclough Homes' Application*, decision on costs, at n 71 above.

–   offers are important where, for example, payment of compensation will only arise if the Lands Tribunal decides to modify, and the only issue is whether there should be modification, compensation being agreed.[81]

It is important to consider *Calderbank* offers where the applicant can put forward an alternative restriction, or where an offer of compensation can be made.

(4)   See Practice Directions 19–20 generally, on fees and costs.

It is the usual practice of the Tribunal to invite submissions on costs at the conclusion of the hearing on the basis of the decision going one way, or another. If the issue as to costs is complicated, there may have to be a costs only hearing after the decision has been issued. Written submissions on costs are invariably invited and exchanged between parties in advance and will always assist the Tribunal (Practice Direction 20.8).

IMPORTANT POINTS TO REMEMBER WHEN THE ORDER OF THE LANDS TRIBUNAL HAS BEEN OBTAINED

16.111   Either party may need to consider an *appeal* to the Court of Appeal.[82]

An appeal may be on a point of law only.

Permission to appeal is needed from the Court of Appeal. This must be requested in the appellant's notice under CPR, Part 52, rule 4(1).

The notice must be filed at the Court of Appeal within 28 days after the *decision* of the Tribunal. (This means that when the decision is given and not a later date when any final order is made. Note that the 28 days includes 'non working' days.) The Tribunal usually states the date on which its decision is given. For full procedural rules on appeals see CPR, Part 52 and Part 52 PD. (It would seem that an appeal on a question of costs only does not lie from the Tribunal.) There is no longer any requirement for the Tribunal to state a case as it formerly was required to do.[83]

16.112   If there is to be no appeal:

(1)   In unregistered titles:
–   The order must be kept with the title deeds and, if there is modification which requires an entire vacation of the registered covenant, application should be made to the Land Charges Registry for removal of the D(ii) entry.
–   If there is modification which does not require vacation the person entitled to the benefit of the covenant should re-register the covenant as modified by lodging the order at the Land Charges Registry and requesting variation of the entry of the covenant. It is important at this stage if no other to ensure that the order of the Tribunal is correctly drawn up; see (c) below as to the practice as to the order.

---

[81]   While CPR Pt 36 does not apply in the Tribunal, the 'modern culture' of making sensible offers at the right time, and not just at the eleventh hour, has its place in this jurisdiction. For a recent example of the effect of sealed and *Calderbank* offers, see *Re Joyce's Application* (2004), LP/13/2002.

[82]   See Land Tribunal Act 1949, ss 3(4) and 11(a).

[83]   See *Re Girl's Day School Trust (1872) v Dadak & Ors* [2002] 1 P&CR 4.

(b)   In registered titles:
   -   In respect of the *benefited land*, unless in the very rare instance of the benefit being entered on that title, nothing needs to be done. If, exceptionally, the benefit is entered, the order should be lodged with the certificate to that title for the appropriate entry to be made so as to reflect the order.
   -   In respect of the burdened land, application is made under section 84(8) of the Law of Property Act 1925 and section 65 of and Schedule 4 to the Land Registration Act 2002 to have the entry modified so as to reflect the order. Where a discharge occurs the whole entry may be cancelled. Where there is evidence that the *benefit* has been entered the Land Registry may require production of the certificate of title to the benefited title to make a mirror entry on that title. The need for a check on the terms of the order is repeated.
(c)   It is usually the practice of the Tribunal to send a draft of the proposed order to the parties for their approval or comments before it is finally drawn up. This is the opportunity to ensure that there are no errors in it which would be incorporated in any entry on the Land Charges Register, or on the title to property registered at the Land Registry. This practice will invariably apply where the application can proceed without the need for a hearing, in which case the applicant gets a draft of the proposed order for approval or comment once the application has been determined.[84]

HOW LONG DOES IT TAKE FOR AN APPLICATION IN THE LANDS TRIBUNAL TO BE DETERMINED?

16.113   Where there is no objection, applications can be disposed of within three months from inception to determination.

Where there is objection, the length of time taken will depend upon the urgency of the application, and the manner in which the parties proceed. In broad terms, the time taken from starting the application will be equivalent to that of a civil action in the High Court. At present that is between 25 and 40 weeks on average.

The Tribunal aims to despatch its decision to all parties within two months from the close of the hearing in the vast majority of cases. There are a minority of cases where special factors apply which mean that this time is exceeded. In some cases (rare) the decision can be given *ex tempore*, either in full, or briefly with reasons to follow, usually within one week.

---

[84]   Arbitration Act 1996, s 57, subs (3)–(7) and for enforcement see s 66 thereof, both provisions being at Appendix 4 and see Rule 32 (application of the Arbitration Act 1996) of the Lands Tribunal Rules 1996, also at Appendix 4.

MISCELLANEOUS

16.114   The Lands Tribunal has jurisdiction where granted to discharge or modify statutory covenants; see Chapter 10 and the statutes in Appendix 2.

The right of the covenantor to make an application under section 84 is not easily restricted. It is not a right which can be excluded as public policy would prevent that.

In some cases, particularly in development agreements, an application to the Lands Tribunal (if made) may be expressed so as to trigger the payment of money. In a case where a pure restriction is imposed, there seems no reason why the covenantor or his successor should not apply under section 84 to modify or discharge that restriction.

However, if the covenant is drawn in such a way as to trigger a payment of money on any application, no application under section 84 could be made in respect of such a covenant because it would not be a restriction as to the *user of land* within section 84(1); see **16.94** above.

Chapter 17

PRACTICAL DRAFTING POINTS

17.1   The preceding chapters in this book have dealt with the existence, validity and enforceability of restrictive covenants which are already in being. This chapter devotes a little attention to the creation of restrictive covenants.

PRELIMINARIES

17.2   It is always going to be the case that the context in which covenants are imposed and the instructions given to the draughtsman will govern the terms of the covenants. A set of covenants to control a new housing development will differ from covenants imposed on the sale of a plot of land for one house in the former grounds of a larger house. Likewise restrictions as to trading, or use of land or buildings may have to be quite specific. For example, it may be desirable to limit the use of land for agricultural purposes, but with a proviso for the release of that covenant on payment of a sum geared to the difference between agricultural and housing value. We are not concerned here with the means by which the obligation to pay may be secured, but the importance of drafting a covenant which cannot be evaded and which is clear in terms of the restriction imposed.

The starting point will invariably be a set of instructions and some precedents. They can be used as a starting point, as with all precedents, but can never be regarded as the model, at least as to the terms of the restrictions themselves. The form of the precedents should, however, be used where they define how the benefit of the covenants is to run.

17.3   Finally, a word about plain English. The Plain English Campaign deserves credit for improving the quality of many legal documents.[1] It had been an aim in writing this book to produce a set of covenant precedents which conformed to the aims of that campaign. That aim proved difficult for two reasons. First, the law of restrictive covenants, particularly that concerned with the running of the benefit, demands that certain forms of words are used, and these appear almost to have been elevated to terms of legal science.[2] This may be an overstatement but it was felt to be too radical (and possibly dangerous) to produce a set of forms which might satisfy the Plain English Campaign but which might fail the tests set by the rigours of the law. Secondly, many of the modern forms do use language which is clearer and more direct. In terms of the obligations which are specified in Appendix 7 the precedents attempt to meet these difficulties as best they can.

---

[1]   The author acknowledges the assistance he has derived from the Campaign's handbook *Language on Trial, The Plain English Guide to Legal Writing*.

[2]   For example, the words so that 'the benefit may be annexed to'.

POINTS TO WATCH

17.4 Where covenants are to be used never use the word 'stipulation', and the verb 'to covenant' must be used in the operative part.[3]

Covenants can be expressed to be entered into jointly and severally, and there is no harm in saying so, even though section 81(l) of the Law of Property Act 1925 has made it unnecessary to do so since 1 January 1926.[4]

Consider with care how the benefit is to be annexed and to what land and how that land is to be identified and who is to enforce the covenant; is the right to be given to the owners for the time being so as to allow them to enforce within section 56 of the Law of Property Act 1925?[5] The best way to achieve this is to use words of annexation and to define the benefited land by reference to a (clear) plan.[6]

Limit liability to ownership of the burdened land and possession of it – particularly if the covenants themselves could impose vicarious liability by virtue of words such as 'permit' and 'suffer'.[7]

17.5 The covenants themselves should be directed at what is permitted or not as the case may be. Modern forms will do this. Older forms are to be avoided; references to soapboilers and fellmongers are really out of place these days. Define nuisances by reference to words such as 'activity which would materially affect the use and enjoyment of the [benefited land]'. Or in relation to covenants against noise define what is not allowed by reference to the latest BSI or ISO standard.

If the obligations are to be qualified with obligations not to withhold consent unreasonably, or to approve plans within a given period, say so.

If a scheme of development is to be imposed state that this is intended.[8] Consider whether a power to vary should be inserted; these can affect the existence of a scheme.[9]

Avoid putting positive covenants in the same schedule as restrictive ones.

17.6 Avoid uncertainty of drafting or of terminology so that the covenant is unenforceable.

If there are any parts of covenants which might be thought to be uncertain in their effect or operation, keep them in a separate paragraph in the schedule so that the court can sever them.

Consider the restrictions required in the context carefully.

---

[3]   For the danger created in doing so, see **1.2** above.
[4]   While on the subject of unnecessary words, the frequently ignored Law of Property Act 1925, s 61 treats the singular as including the plural and the masculine the feminine etc, thereby saving some space in 'definitions' clauses.
[5]   See **6.8** above.
[6]   See Precedents at Appendix 7. This is particularly important since the decision of the Court of Appeal in *Crest Nicholson v McAllister* [2004] EWCA Civ 410.
[7]   See **14.19** above.
[8]   See Precedents at Appendix 7.
[9]   See **8.31** above.

17.7 Where land use is to be restricted in respect of residential buildings consider:

–   Is the building (to be built) not to be used other than as a private dwelling house?
–   Is the same to be in the occupation of one family?
–   Is no trade or business to be carried on at the property?
–   What about detached houses – as opposed to semi-detached ones?
–   Are fences to be permitted beyond a certain point, or is it to be an open plan development with no structures or erections beyond that point?
–   What about aerials and satellite dishes, protection of trees, and the parking of cars, caravans, trailers and boats?
–   What about preventing the growth of the dreaded *Cupressus Leylandii*, or any trees above a certain height or beyond a certain point?

Where specific uses are to be prevented, or sole uses are to be permitted, consider:

–   Is the use to be restricted to the traditional concepts such as the retail shop or garage, or some other business?
–   Do you want to prevent the use of land for access to some business, or in some other way to facilitate it?[10]
–   Do you want to define use by reference to the Use Classes order?
–   In rural areas, where developments are taking place, often using existing farmhouses and buildings, they may want protection against intensive pig rearing, chicken houses and muck heaps – amongst other things capable of sending the temperature up between farmers and their neighbours.

17.8 Where plans are to be approved or consents or variations granted, say by whom they are to be given, providing for alternatives or substitutes, and make any provisos (such as consent not to be unreasonably withheld) express. If necessary list the factors which might be relevant.[11]

In the rare cases where covenants are to be recreated following unity of seisin, use a form of words which makes it clear that this is to occur.[12]

Finally, a short word on the Precedents in Appendix 7.

17.9 These are merely suggestions. Many readers will have a favoured choice of published, or 'in house', forms. But as precedents are good servants but bad masters, occasional references to other sources can keep the relationship between the user and the supplier of such forms fresh.

---

[10]   See *Elliott v Safeway Stores plc* [1995] 1 WLR 1396, for an instance where the covenant was not drawn in such a way so as to prevent use of land for access to a business. See *Jarvis Homes v Marshall* [2004] EWCA Civ 839 where the contrary result was reached by the Court of Appeal, on different covenants and facts. See also *GLN (Copenhagen) Southern Ltd v Tunbridge Wells DC* [2004] EWCA Civ, for a recent discussion on access and ancillary user.

[11]   See the approach to assignment of leases in the amended provisions of the Landlord and Tenant Act 1927, s 19, s 19(1A) where the criteria for reasonableness can be set out in the lease.

[12]   See **13.9** and Precedent **A7.5**.

Chapter 18

INSURING RESTRICTIVE COVENANTS

18.1   Imagine the distress of your client if their development site or property was rendered valueless through restrictive covenants being enforced. Problems of this nature probably occur more often than you realise as many cases are not reported in the press. The purpose of this chapter is to explore insurance as a potential solution to the problems created by restrictive covenants affecting freehold land by looking at the availability of insurance, underwriting considerations, costs and the scope of policy cover.

Restrictive covenant indemnity insurance is underwritten by a number of insurance companies and underwriters in the UK. It can provide a quick and cost effective solution and covers the named insured and successors in title including in some cases mortgagees and lessees against the enforcement or attempted enforcement of restrictive covenants.

THE AVAILABILITY OF INSURANCE

18.2   As a general principle insurance is provided when the restrictive covenants are unable to be cleared from the title by legal remedy. There are a number of issues which affect the availability of restrictive covenant insurance.

Cover for breach of covenants

18.3   It is available for those who are breaching covenants or are going to breach covenants by some form of development or change of use relating to land and not for those who are seeking to enforce their benefit of a covenant. Those seeking to enforce a right such as a restrictive covenant may find that they are covered under a legal expenses insurance policy if they have one.

Freehold covenants

Restrictive covenant indemnities are generally available to cover covenants affecting freehold titles. Where leasehold covenants have been imposed, the covenantee, being the landlord, is usually known and available to negotiate a deed of variation and as a golden rule leasehold covenants are uninsurable.

However, insurance is sometimes provided for leasehold covenants contained in older long leases where the landlord is missing and would have given consent under the terms of the lease if he had not been missing.

Restrictive not positive

The insurance is available for restrictive covenants only. There may be an element of uncertainty. For example, the requirement to maintain an area of land not built upon, on the face of it, is a positive covenant but would be interpreted as limiting the use of the site. If it is unclear, the underwriter will consider the intention rather than the wording.

If the covenant is positive, insurance will not be offered as a solution as such covenants are only enforceable between the two parties to the deed and may not be binding on a successor in title automatically.

The use of the property

18.4   A restrictive covenant indemnity policy will usually specify the proposed use of the land or property. There are very few limitations as to the uses which may be insured. They can range from a minor change of use or development, eg one house being in a rear garden, to the development of a large industrial complex. Insurance is also available for a continuation of an existing use which is in breach of covenant. As the breach has already occurred this is regarded as a lesser risk by the underwriter than a new breach of a covenant in the near future.

Geographical area

The majority of policies are issued for restrictive covenants burdening land in England and Wales. Insurers will also consider other areas such as Northern Ireland, the Channel Islands and Scotland where different legal considerations apply.

Unknown covenants

Insurance is also available for the potential breach of unknown restrictive covenants. This may occur where deeds have been lost or destroyed or the land has been registered with possessory title and there is an entry on the Charges Register showing that the property is subject to any restrictive covenants that exist.

Not always an alternative to negotiation

Insurance will not be offered to cover every possible situation where restrictive covenants are being breached. If the deed imposing the covenant is only a few years old, the covenantee still exists and is in a position to offer a release, insurers are unlikely to accept the risk. Similarly, in areas where attempts are often made to enforce covenants by residents (particularly where there are building schemes) or where the benefit of a covenant could be claimed by neighbours by annexation cover may not be available.

Residual risks

18.5 Once negotiations with the beneficiary of the covenant have commenced it is generally too late to seek insurance to cover the risk of enforceability by that particular party. However, if there is a residual risk because the benefit has annexed to owners of the surrounding land, insurance may be offered once the release has been completed usually on the basis that claims from the *Releasor* are excluded from the cover provided by the policy.

As an underwriter considers each restrictive covenant enquiry individually it is good practice to submit a proposal at an early stage in the conveyancing procedure to see whether insurance is likely to be available or whether some other legal remedy is necessary.

WHY INSURE?

18.6 There are a number of reasons why people choose to insure restrictive covenants. Alternatives to insurance include: self insurance, compulsory purchase, negotiation with the covenantees and application to the Lands Tribunal or court action. However, a restrictive covenant indemnity can be useful in providing a quick and permanent solution.

Generally, insurance transfers the risk of diminution in the value of the property owing to the enforcement of restrictive covenants from the property owner to the Insurer. A single premium is paid and in return the policy is issued in perpetuity. Financial compensation (including legal costs and expenses) is payable to the insured in the event of the covenants being enforced and the use or development of the property not continuing.

Lenders and mortgagees often require the additional security afforded by insurance and loans may be subject to restrictive covenant indemnity insurance being in place. In certain circumstances specific bespoke policies can be written to cover any individual parties interested in the property.

The CML *Lender's Handbook* indicates that lenders are now more risk averse than previously was the case. Whereas, in certain circumstances, a client may perceive that the risk of enforcement of a restrictive covenant is something that he is prepared to take on himself and self insure, his lender may not be prepared to take the same risk. In these cases it is sometimes feasible for insurers to offer bespoke policies covering the interests of the lender only, thereby satisfying the criteria of the *Lender's Handbook*.

Bespoke policies may be considered, for example, when acting for a tenant who intends to lease a property and use it for a specific purpose which is in breach of an existing restriction. The tenant may, if the restriction is enforced, be dispossessed of the property but still contractually liable to his landlord under the terms of his lease for payments due under the terms of the lease. The commercial tenant may also want to consider loss of profits, fit-out costs and other capital expenses that may not be recoverable if it/he is dispossessed of the property. These losses can often be covered as additional heads of cover in a Restrictive Covenant Indemnity policy.

A practitioner needs to advise his client of the terms of any Restrictive Covenant Indemnity Policy that he arranges on that client's behalf. It may therefore be necessary to adapt an Insurer's standard policy wording to cover any concerns his client may have about the cover offered, the conditions and terms of the policy, and anything else to comply with his duty of full disclosure to the Insurer and his duty of care to his client.

18.7   A policy may unlock the development potential of site and increase the value of it. A site which is subject to restrictive covenants that potentially prevent a proposed development will be worth more if there is a restrictive covenant indemnity in force which enables the development to proceed and a change of use of the site.

A restrictive covenant indemnity is an option available to the client when consultation with the covenantee is impossible. The covenantees and/or the extent of the land with the benefit may be unknown especially if the covenants are old. Also, the benefit may have annexed to many different parties in cases where the land has been split up and sold.

Insurance is an alternative to making an application to the Lands Tribunal or the High Court. Any application to the Tribunal or Court can be a fairly long and expensive process and there is no guarantee of success. In some cases insurance may be available even if the matter is not suitable for the Tribunal or Court.

18.8   Finally, by suggesting that restrictive covenants are insured the practitioner is providing the most complete advice to clients and should hopefully reduce the risk of a negligence claim if covenants are subsequently enforced.

UNDERWRITING AND INFORMATION REQUIRED

18.9   The insurance company or broker will usually supply a checklist or proposal form showing the information required to consider the risk of insuring restrictive covenants. All information supplied to the Insurer is treated as the proposal for insurance. Any material facts which come to light during the solicitor's usual conveyancing investigations or during the planning process must be supplied to the Insurer to make certain that the practitioner is not at fault for non-disclosure which could lead to the policy being avoided at a later date.

The underwriter takes into account both legal and practical information when deciding whether to insure and the terms and premium that will apply. When looking at a proposal for insurance consideration is given to the nature of the covenants, the surrounding area and the local reaction to any plans to change the use of, or to develop the property.

Not all of the information shown below will have to be supplied in every case. The amount of detail required by the underwriter will depend upon the likely enforceability of the covenants and the area concerned.

The covenants

18.10   It is useful for the Insurer to see a copy of the original deed which imposed the restrictive covenants as the shortened version contained in the Land Registry office copies does not automatically clarify the exact nature of the covenants. For example, where a building scheme exists it is not always immediately clear from the office copy entries. Also, the information in the Charges Register is unlikely to detail the precise position or extent of the land affected by covenants or the land that has the benefit of the restriction.

The key elements of the deed which the underwriter will take into account are the age, the covenantees, the enforceability of the restrictive covenants and the stipulations.

(1)   Age

It would normally be expected that recent covenants (eg those imposed within the last 25 to 30 years) would be less attractive to the underwriter as a risk than older covenants. However, age is not a factor which is considered alone. It is not uncommon for nineteenth century covenants to be the subject of insurance claims. Conversely, numerous sites which are potentially breaching restrictive covenants imposed in the 1980s and early 1990s have been insured and the developments completed without claims occurring.

(2)   The covenantees

18.11   The proposer should provide the underwriter with as much information as possible regarding the original covenantees or where relevant, the specific estate concerned as it is essential for risk assessment, particularly for more complex cases.

Local solicitors, or estate agents may be aware of the existence of specific covenantees and the need to obtain releases or approval for developments from them. If the covenantee is a company, a search should be supplied to show whether the company still exists, has been dissolved, or taken over.

Some insurance companies retain records showing whether particular covenantees, or estates still exist and are problematic, meaning that negotiation with them is necessary.

One of the major headaches for Insurers occurs where covenantees, or estates have in the past given their approval or those which having been dormant for some time suddenly decide that the covenants are of interest. However, many covenantees will have long since sold their estates and will not have an interest in the area concerned. Records built up over the years by Insurers can be invaluable in such cases.

(3)   The enforceability of the covenants

18.12   The covenanting clause is considered in conjunction with the current use of the property, the area and the proposed insured use. The underwriter will look at the deed which imposed the covenants (if available) or the office copy entries in detail to consider whether in his opinion the covenants are likely to be enforceable and whether additional information is needed. If the benefit of the restrictive covenants appears to have annexed to land surrounding the site in question the underwriter may require office copy entries of surrounding properties to be supplied.

Building schemes are some of the most difficult cases to underwrite, particularly in view of the high level of enforceability and, as shown above, the fact that a building scheme exists may not be immediately evident from the information supplied.

If counsel's opinion has been sought, a copy should be supplied to the Insurer with a copy of the instructions to counsel as in some cases it may improve their view of the risk. The underwriter will not request counsel's opinion as a matter of course but will occasionally do so if there are other adverse features.

Proposals for restrictive covenant indemnities where covenants are likely to be enforceable are treated prudently. Obviously, there are some risks for which insurance will not be provided.

(4)   Stipulations

18.13   Common stipulations for which insurance is required include:

–   density restrictions, eg two houses per plot;
–   height restrictions;
–   building lines;
–   limitations as to the use of the property, eg no alcohol sales and 'a private dwellinghouse';
–   approval of plans.

As with enforceability of covenants, the stipulations will be considered by the underwriter in conjunction with the proposed use of the property and the surrounding area.

The property and surrounding area

18.14   A detailed description of the property is required and often a plan is attached to the policy document to clearly identify the property being insured.

The Insurer will consider the previous and proposed use of the property and any development plans to assess whether it conforms to the character of the neighbourhood. Difficulties can occur when a proposed use is new to the area and does not 'fit in' with its surroundings. For example, commercial developments such as nursing homes in residential areas can prove unpopular with local residents and may consequently make the restrictive covenant risk unattractive to the underwriter.

One defence which is sometimes valid if a claim occurs is that an area has changed significantly since the covenants were imposed so that in practice, they are no longer relevant. Old OS plans may be requested in some cases to see how much an area has changed particularly where the covenants are relatively old. An up-to-date OS plan of the property and those immediately surrounding it can also prove useful in some cases.

A change of use of the property requiring a planning application

18.15 Most insurance underwriters will only offer 'post-planning' cover, ie will either offer cover where the planning process for the property's change of use has been finalised, or will offer cover prior to the planning process but conditional upon there being no material changes in circumstance or material objections to the change of use prior to risk being assumed.

Some underwriters will however offer a 'pre-planning' cover – that is that they will assume the risk prior to the planning application being made for the future change of use. This type of cover can be particularly beneficial to a developer which wants to or is required to acquire a site immediately by virtue of an unconditional purchase contract.

In order to consider granting pre-planning cover, an underwriter would need to see a copy of the planning history of the site, a proposed site layout or an indication of what the Insured has in mind for his development, confirmation that what is proposed accords with the local development plan for the area, information as to whether the covenants have already been breached before, and if so how and when, and what reaction this caused as far as enforcement of the breach is concerned.

If the planning history reveals that there is a recent planning permission granted affecting the site, an underwriter may wish to see any letters of objection in respect of that planning application. Where pre-planning cover is granted the Insured can take comfort in knowing that any future objection in the planning process which raises any insured covenant will be covered by the policy and treated as a claim under that policy.

Local reaction

Where cover is required 'post planning', the Insurer will ask to see copies of any responses (including supportive letters) or objections to the planning application. This is useful as it helps to assess the reaction to the development of those who may have the benefit of the covenants. The number and nature of objections and any concerted reaction from Residents' Associations or other local groups are a good guide to the popularity or otherwise of the proposed use. Any other letters which are received by the client which are in opposition to the proposed development should also be submitted to the underwriter for consideration. It may be that objections refer to the existence of restrictive covenants but those who know about their existence are unable/unwilling to enforce them. Such objections may preclude the availability of insurance, but not always.

Lack of objection to planning applications may lead to a false sense of security particularly as it is not normal practice for planners to take restrictive covenants into account. Insurers have had claims in cases where there were no significant objections to the planning application but the letter of protest is received once the development works have commenced.

On the other hand, there are some cases with many strong objections where the underwriter is still able to provide insurance. In such situations, a detailed appraisal of the legal position and a favourable counsel's opinion can help to make a difference.

Summary

18.16

Availability of Insurance	Underwriting Considerations	Information Required
Cover for breach of covenants	Restrictive covenants	Deed or office copies
Freehold covenants	Age	The covenantees
Restrictive not positive	Covenantees	Are the covenants registered enforceable?
Geographical area: mainly England and Wales	Enforceability Stipulations	OS plans of property and surrounding land
Unknown covenants	Property and surrounding area	Use of property
Residual risks	Local reaction	Development plans
Insurance is not always an alternative to negotiation		Objections to planning permission

The costs

18.17 It is general practice for underwriters to take into account the full value of a site once it has been developed and base the premium rate on this. Most claims tend to occur in the early stages of development. However, costs can still be substantial. Legal expenses alone can easily extend to tens of thousands of pounds. Lenders and any future purchaser of the property will usually insist that the indemnity is for the full value of the property.

Risks are considered individually by the underwriter and because each case is different, restrictive covenant indemnity insurance does not lend itself to standard rating. As a rough guide, for a restrictive covenant indemnity where you are insuring the full value of a property for £1,000,000 you could expect to pay anything from £1,000 to £5,000. In some cases, where there are unattractive features an excess may be applied, ie the Insured pays the first £X.

POLICY COVER

18.18 A number of companies provide restrictive covenant insurance as part of a portfolio of legal indemnities. Individual policy wordings vary but in practice there are a number of standard features. As an example, a copy of the Stewart Title standard wording can be found at Appendix 5.

(1) The policy covers a defined 'insured use' and contains a description of the property insured in an attached schedule.
(2) Cover operates following the attempted enforcement of any insured restrictive covenants.
(3) Options available in the event of a valid claim being made include the following:
  – defence of the allegation by seeking to prove that the covenants are not enforceable;
  – compensating a person who shows he has the benefit of the covenants and can enforce them thus allowing the development to proceed or the use to continue;
  – indemnity to the Insured, if it proves impossible to proceed with the insured use and/or development.

The method of settling the claim will depend upon the circumstances of the individual case, the time that the claim is made and progress in any development. Claim handling is usually the function of the Insurer in all instances and the Insured should advise the Insurer immediately that it is perceived that there will be a claim made.

18.19

(4) Key features of the indemnity to the Insured are as follows:
  – *Diminution/Loss in market value.* Where it is not possible to find an acceptable solution to allow development to proceed, the Insured is compensated for the diminution in market value of the property with and without the covenants. In the most serious cases, the residual value may be very low.
  – *Cost of works/fees.* By the time covenants are successfully enforced considerable costs may have been incurred. Indemnity is provided for the cost of works already undertaken prior to the enforcement action and architects' and surveyors' fees.

18.20

  – *Demolition costs.* Where necessary, the costs of demolishing the buildings on the site and restoring the property to its original condition are paid.
  – *Costs and expenses (incurred with Insurer's prior consent).* This may include legal fees incurred in defence of the claim, compensation payable to a successful claimant and costs awarded against the insured.
(5) Policy exceptions. Claims are excluded if the Insured decides to approach the parties believed to have the benefit of the covenant or makes an application to the Lands Tribunal. As we have already seen, these are potential solutions

to restrictive covenants but insurance is an alternative. Such actions could easily provoke a claim.

18.21

(6) Limits of indemnity. Most underwriters will look to insure risks based on the full developed value of the property once works are complete. Lower limits can be considered but lenders will often insist on cover for the full value, or at least the amount of the advance secured against the property. The maximum amount payable under the policy is the limit of indemnity.

(7) Unusual features compared to other insurance contracts. Unlike most insurance contracts, the policies are single premium, usually without time limit and cover automatically passes to successors in title. In addition, mortgagees and lessees are normally included without further payment.

18.22

(8) Extensions of cover. The standard policy does not include cover for loss of rent or other consequential losses such as loss of profits. Insurers will consider adding such extensions in some cases as secondary heads of cover supplemental to the primary cover.

In conclusion, restrictive covenants are a complex legal area and can prove to be an expensive and real trap for the unwary. Problems can arise when you least expect them and it is not always the obvious cases which lead to claims.

It is certainly worth asking whether insurance is available. Initial reactions and often decisions can be given by the underwriter upon receipt of fairly basic information. Insurance provides a quick and cost effective solution to the problem and has the potential to provide financial recompense if the worst happens.

DUE DILIGENCE

18.23

With the increasing popularity of Restrictive Covenant Indemnity Policies practitioners should consider the sufficiency of the policy provided to them as part of the title deduced.

Some questions that might be considered include:

- Is the policy still valid?
- Have there been any claims made against the policy and who by?
- What was the result of the claim?
- Is the amount of cover sufficient for the buyer's purpose – does it need to be increased?
- Is the buyer's use of the property covered by the policy?
- What was the proposal for the policy and is the proposal still valid for what the buyer wants to use the property for?
- Is there anything in the title that has not been covered by insurance that should have been?

- Have the terms and conditions of the policy been adhered to by the current Insured and will the Insured's successor (your client) be able to adhere to them?
- Does the seller have the original policy document and will this be handed over on completion?
- Does the buyer want to have his own 'splinter' policy rather than share part of an existing policy? If not, what endorsement is needed to recognise the buyer's interest in the property?
- Who is defined as 'insured' and does it include successors in title, lenders and/or tenants and their respective successors in title?
- Is the policy written in perpetuity, or is it for a limited period?
- Has the description of the property covered changed over time and is it still recognisable as title numbers and addresses change?

Chapter 19

RESTRICTIVE COVENANTS AND COMMONHOLD TITLE

INTRODUCTION

19.1 On 27 September 2004 the law relating to commonhold titles came into force. From that date, it became possible to own land 'commonhold'. What is significant about the law of commonhold is that, whilst it is a new form of ownership, applicable only in England and Wales, it is not a new form of estate in land. The fundamental point which lies at the heart of commonhold ownership, is that it is still a *freehold* title.[1] Because commonhold ownership is of a freehold estate, the rules relating to the rights and liabilities under the law of restrictive covenants will, in the majority of cases, continue to apply. The way in which those rules will apply has been set out in the earlier chapters of this book. However, some of the practical aspects of the way in which commonhold titles will be set up and will operate may lead to questions arising when restrictive covenants are being considered. That is why an outline knowledge of how commonhold ownership is required when advising on restrictive covenants. This chapter is not a full explanation of the law relating to commonhold. A reader seeking such an explanation should refer to the textbooks on commonhold which are now on the market.

19.2 It is worth pointing out at this stage that as (at the time of writing) the law relating to commonhold had only just come into force, there may well be changes in the first few months and years which the system 'beds down' and it is not inconceivable that both parliament and the courts will have to address themselves to issues which arise when the relevant legislation and rules are under scrutiny. That said, it would appear from the legislation and rules that the system created is reasonably straightforward (it is certainly designed to be so) and indications at this early stage suggest that commonhold ownership *may* become the preferred title in certain situations; for example, in the case of new built residential blocks of flats.[2] But only time will tell and the market may be slow to adopt this 'new' form of ownership.

---

[1] That is to say, an estate in fee simple, absolute in possession, as defined by s 1(1)(a) of the Law of Property Act 1925. That is significant because, unless a commonhold title is brought to an end (as to which see below), the tenure will not have a limited life and that is why commonhold is more attractive than leasehold tenure where the term of years will obviously have a date for its termination inherent in it.

[2] The attraction lies in the fact that the units are held freehold with no problems created by leases which may eventually become unmortgageable; and, of course, there is no threat of termination by, for example, forfeiture. However, as appears from **19.18–19.22** below, a major disincentive to the creation and adoption of commonhold is the effect of winding up on a commonhold scheme.

19.3   This chapter contains the following topics.

(1)   An outline of commonhold ownership.
(2)   How restrictive covenants will operate when titles are owned in commonhold.
(3)   Aspects of restrictive covenants and commonhold which may require careful analysis in the future. Areas are highlighted where the law and practice may not be entirely clear, and where questions arise on the face of the new commonhold scheme to which the answers, at present, may not be conclusive.

AN OUTLINE OF COMMONHOLD OWNERSHIP

19.4   The relevant legislation is contained in Part I of, and Schedules 1–5 to, the Commonhold and Leasehold Reform Act 2002 ('the 2002 Act'). As is ever the case with modern legislation, the meat on the bones of the 2002 Act is to be found in the rules made under that Act by delegated legislation. The principal rules are to be found in the Commonhold Regulations 2004; SI 2004/1829.[3] Also of importance in this context is the Land Registry's own Practice Note (No 60), which is an invaluable guide and is to be found on the Land Registry website, with other up-to-date material, as added and modified from time to time; see www.landregistry.gov.uk.

19.5   Within this outline, there are certain key requirements which will be found in any commonhold scheme.

These are:

(i)   The title must be freehold; see section 1 of the 2002 Act.
(ii)   The land must be registered at the Land Registry; see section 2 of the 2002 Act.[4]
(iii) Some types of land *cannot* be held commonhold. For example, agricultural land, leasehold land, flying freeholds, and freeholds subject to reverter, such as under the School Sites Act 1841; see section 4 of the 2002 Act.
(iv)   The freehold owner (or owners, if more than one) must consent to the application to register the freehold title in commonhold. The same applies to any leaseholder with a term granted of more than 21 years, and to any chargee; see section 3 of the 2002 Act and Regulations 3–5 of the 2004 Regulations.[5]

---

[3]   There are additional statutory instruments dealing with such matters as registration, principally the Commonhold (Land Registration Rules) 2004; SI 2004/1830.

[4]   Thus, an application for commonhold ownership will require an application for first registration if the title is unregistered.

[5]   This is an important requirement when converting existing developments to commonhold. The requirement that there be 100 per cent consent of those who have, for example, leasehold interests, may well be an impediment in practice to 'conversion' of existing developments.
       Note also that commonhold ownership is not restricted to residential development. There is no reason in theory why commonhold should not apply to commercial developments; for example, units in industrial estates. However, in such cases, the capital cost of acquisition of a freehold to such a unit may be unattractive. It is not generally possible to create leases of more than 7 years of a registered commonhold unit; see s 17 of the 2002 Act and reg 11 of the 2004 Regulations. It is not possible to create leases of more than 21 years in non-residential commonhold units; see s 18 of the 2002 Act.

19.6 Key features of commonhold ownership will be:

- The existence of *commonhold units*. Each such unit is held freehold by the *commonhold unit holder*; see sections 11–13 of the 2002 Act. (There may be more than one such holder.)
- The existence of a *Commonhold Association*. This is a company limited by guarantee, in which each commonhold unit holder will be a member. The 2002 Act and the 2004 Regulations define strictly the Memorandum and Articles of that Association. The Association owned the freehold as to *the common parts*. The common parts are defined by section 25 of the 2002 Act as 'every part of the commonhold [itself defined by plans at the Land Registry] which is not for the time being a commonhold unit in accordance with the Commonhold Community Statement'.
- The *Commonhold Community Statement* is the agreement which regulates the use of the units and of the common parts; section 26. It is this feature of commonhold which is significant because, unlike the case of ordinary freehold ownership where positive covenants do not run against successors,[6] a Commonhold Community Statement will oblige commonhold unit holders and the Commonhold Association to observe *positive* covenants. These will be enforceable between all unit holders and the Commonhold Association. It is also the case that the Commonhold Community Statement *must* make provision for the insurance of the common parts and their repair and maintenance. This is, therefore, a very important document. It is this local law which will impose the obligations which will remain – and will continue to remain – at the heart of any commonhold scheme.

In practice, commonhold ownership will work in the following way.

In new developments

19.7 The freehold owner (eg the developer) will seek registration of the freehold as a commonhold; section 7 of the 2002 Act. Initially, all the units and the common parts are registered in the developer's name. Each unit will get a separate title number at the Land Registry before it is sold. This means that, once there is a sale with completion, an ordinary Form TR1 can be used on that completion. The common parts are also registered at the Land Registry under a separate title. The developer will also have to incorporate the Commonhold Association and will have sent the relevant documents (including the Memorandum and Articles of Association of the Commonhold Association) to the Land Registry in order to satisfy the Land Registry that it can register the title commonhold. (See the terms of Schedule 1 to the 2002 Act.) There is a transitional period (see section 8 of the 2002 Act) between the registration referred to above and the sale of the first unit. This allows the developer to go back on a commonhold scheme. For example, he can convert back to an 'ordinary' freehold granting, for example, long leases of each flat. But once the first unit is sold, that period ceases and the common parts are automatically vested in the Commonhold Association, and each commonhold unit will remain vested in the developer's name until it is sold and transferred to the

---

6   See Chapter 3 above.

new commonhold unit holder. Once all the units are sold, there will be one title at the Land Registry for the common parts and separate titles at the Land Registry for each unit. Each unit is freehold and is, therefore, freely transferable. Each unit holder must be a member of the Commonhold Association.

In existing developments[7]

19.8   The consent of *all* those with an interest in leases granted for more than 21 years is required. It is important to note this absolute requirement, and the same requirement applies to chargees. In practice, it may well be difficult to achieve. All existing leases will be extinguished under section 9(3)(f) of the 2002 Act. This means that, whatever the term, even leases granted for not more than 21 years will be extinguished and this, in turn, means that generally the consent of such a person will be required as well; see the 2004 Regulations (Regulation 3(1)(d)).[8]

So, in new developments, each unit holder will become a member of the Commonhold Association and be subject to the rules of the Commonhold Community Statement and will have a freehold commonhold unit.

The practical outcome

19.9   In the case of a residential block of flats, which (for the sake of this example) is called 'Magnate House', commonhold ownership will mean that, in practical terms:

(i)   The common parts will be held freehold by the Commonhold Association. The name of that association must end with 'Commonhold Association Limited'; for example, 'Magnate House Commonhold Association Limited'. That will have its own registered title number; for example 'Land Registry No LN12345'. The common parts cannot be charged, save by a unanimous resolution of the Commonhold Association; see sections 28 and 29 of the 2002 Act.

(ii)   Each flat owner will have a freehold title to his or their unit; for example:

LN12346 – Flat 1 Magnate House
LN12347 – Flat 2 Magnate House, etc.

The unit can be transferred freely (as with any other freehold); section 15(2) of the 2002 Act. The 2004 Regulations provide for notice to the Commonhold Association; Commonhold Community Statement, paragraph 4.7.

(iii) Each flat owner will be a member of the 'Magnate House Commonhold Association Limited'.

(iv)   Magnate House Commonhold Association Limited must have a Commonhold Community Statement. This Commonhold Community Statement must comply with the terms of the 2004 Regulations, as set out in annex 1 to those

---

[7]   These principles may apply to both freehold as well as leasehold 'conversions'.

[8]   The consent of such a person will not be required if a lease permitted by the 2002 Act is being granted back to the occupier on the same terms as the old one; see reg 3(2) of the 2004 Regulations. This is referred to as a 'compulsory lease'. See also reg 11(2), where the term is limited to 7 years: so, this may not always be possible because in some cases the term being extinguished will be longer than the 7-year period offered.

Regulations. This will also require the unit holder to comply with his obligations, as well as enjoying rights conferred, and will require the unit holder to pay a commonhold assessment referable to the costs incurred by the Commonhold Association to meet the expenses of that association; for example, insurance, repair, maintenance and legal costs.[9]

Transfers of commonhold units are made in the normal way as regards any freehold. As already stated, the Commonhold Community Statement requires notice to the Commonhold Association to be given on transfer. Rules also apply to the notification of new members of the Commonhold Association to it.

Termination of the commonhold

19.10   The 2002 Act provides for methods of bringing commonhold ownership to an end; see sections 43–56 of the 2002 Act. This is dealt with in detail at **19.17** below.

How restrictive covenants will operate when the title is held commonhold

19.11   As the title is freehold, as is stated at **19.1** opening this chapter, all the existing law relating to restrictive covenants will apply. The restrictive covenants on the freehold title prior to registration as a commonhold will be carried forward onto the register of not only the common parts' title but also to each of the unit holder's titles. This means that the rules relating to the benefit and burden applicable to restrictive covenants will continue to apply. Thus, taking the example above of 'Magnate House', 'Magnate House' may be subject to restrictive covenants imposed for the benefit of adjoining land. The owner of that adjoining land can enforce the restrictive covenants against the freeholder of 'Magnate House'. This will include (after a commonhold registration) not only the Commonhold Association but all the unit holders. There are, however, practical limits to this, as set out below. Unit holders will not be able to enforce restrictive covenants between themselves, nor can the Commonhold Association claim the benefit of covenants unless they are plainly for the benefit of the common parts. At **19.13–19.16** below there is a further examination of some of the issues raised by this outline.

19.12   Further analysis reveals that some aspects of commonhold law will require consideration where commonhold title is encountered and where there are restrictive covenants. The reader should note that this part of this Chapter is not concerned with the obligations which may be binding as between unit holders and the Commonhold Association, so far as those obligations stem from the Commonhold Community Statement. As has already been pointed out, this is an entirely separate document, created and defined by the terms of the 2002 Act and the 2004 Regulations. The Commonhold Community Statement will, in the vast majority of cases, have nothing to do with any restrictive covenants which may be

---

[9]   The detail of this is set out in the 2004 Regulations. They also set out in detail what is to happen in the event of non-payment of the assessment; see also ss 31–40 of the 2002 Act.

binding, or which may benefit the underlying freeholds in respect of which commonhold is enjoyed.

19.13   This analysis, therefore, reveals points which should be noted and these are summarised below. These are:

(i)   Where the existing freehold title is vested in both the Commonhold Association (as to its title) and the unit holders (as to their title). This will mean that there are a number of freeholders who may be able to claim the benefit, as well as be subject to the burden, of any covenant. If there is litigation, thought will need to be given to who should be the claimant and who should be the defendant, or defendants. There should also be consideration as to representative parties under CPR Part 19. This is particularly the case as regards defendants.

(ii)   The relationship between the Commonhold Community Statement and the obligations between the Commonhold Association and the unit holders, and any restrictive covenants on the title, may sometimes arise. There should not be any conflict. The Commonhold Community Statement will have to be drawn so as to comply with the statutory rules and it is suggested, it will also have to be drawn with any restrictive covenants in mind, so far as there are special obligations on any of the unit holders and the Commonhold Association. As has already been suggested, there should be no need to create separate restrictive covenants of the traditional variety in addition to the obligations defined in the Commonhold Community Statement. At this stage, it is hard to speculate, but, whilst the Regulations do not outlaw the creation of such restrictive covenants, it is considered that there is no *need* to create them. It has already been pointed out that the significance of commonhold – and, in particular, the way in which the Commonhold Community Statement operates – is that it allows positive obligations to be enforced as between freehold owners. This is not the case in ordinary freehold ownership.[10]

(iii)   The definition of both the benefited and the burdened land will have to be carried over onto the Commonhold Association and unit holders' titles by the Land Registry. The Land Registry ought to be able to get this right; for example, where part of the land in the commonhold development is shaded pink and subject to covenants, or is part of a building scheme. It will be necessary for practitioners to check the titles once the Land Registry has registered them, particularly as regards each commonhold title of the units. Some units – and indeed some common parts – may cross the boundary of the freehold where covenants do or do not affect the title. (This should, in reality, be no more difficult, or different, from the case where there are titles on a freehold reversion which are referred to on the title of a lease.)

(iv)   The extinguishment of leases under section 9 may cause restrictive covenants which are defined by reference to a term to be extinguished.[11]

(v)   The enforcement of restrictive covenants already on the title as between the Commonhold Association and unit holders, and as between unit holders and

---

[10]   See *Rhone v Stephens* [1994] 1 AC 310 and **1.5** above.

[11]   See **7.16** and *Golden Lion Hotel (Hunstanton) Ltd v Carter* [1965] 1 WLR 1189. In cases where there has been extinguishment under s 9, there should be no question but that the lease has been brought to an end and, therefore, liability under any covenant goes with it.

themselves, will only arise if it is plain that the freehold is affected by covenants which, for example, affect only *part* of the development which is subject to the commonhold ownership. Thus, for example, if a covenant was imposed over the original freehold for the entirety of 'Magnate House' – which is now held commonhold by the Commonhold Association and 100 unit holders – and if the benefit is vested next door, then clearly it is *only* the next door owner who can enforce the covenant. A unit holder cannot enforce the covenant and will need to rely on the Commonhold Community Statement; for example, if there is conduct by another unit holder, or the Commonhold Association, which might otherwise amount to a breach of covenant. The Commonhold Community Statement should, in fact, contain terms to oblige the commonhold unit holders and the Commonhold Association to observe the covenants on the freehold; see Regulation 15 in Schedule 3 to the 2004 Regulations, and also see part 1, paragraph 1.1.3, which states that the rights and duties under the Commonhold Community Statement are in addition to those under the general law. What is equally clear is that, if, for example, *part* of 'Magnate House' is subject to covenants in respect of which the other part had the benefit (and assuming that those covenants had not been extinguished when the freehold became vested in the developer),[12] then it is conceivable that one group of unit holders *might* be able to enforce a restrictive covenant against another group of unit holders if the former could prove that they had the benefit, and if it could also be proved that the latter had the burden. It is anticipated that this is likely to be a rare occurrence and in the vast majority of cases the Commonhold Community Statement can be relied on to enforce good order in the development. If there is to be litigation engaged in by the Commonhold Association, the costs of that litigation should be recoverable under the annual Commonhold Assessment which arises under the Commonhold Community Statement. There may well be a question in commonhold ownership as to whether or not the factual benefit of a restrictive covenant can be claimed by each unit holder, or just some of them. As has already been pointed out at Chapter 8 above, where a potential claimant has the factual benefit of a covenant (in terms of evidence)[13] this may well be a matter of evidence. In the example given above of 'Magnate House', the size of the development may be such that unit holders on one side of the development may not be affected by potential breaches of covenant by a neighbour on the other side of the development. Once again, it is suggested that not all the freehold unit holders need to be brought into any proceedings and that there should be representative claimants or defendants, as has been suggested above.

Applications to the Lands Tribunal

19.14 The rules set out in Chapter 16 above will continue to apply, so far as there are applications made by or against freeholds held in commonhold. However, it would seem that (in the case of any such application) there will need to be, either the joinder of all the unit holders and the Commonhold Association, or

---

[12] See *Re Tiltwood* [1978] Ch 269 and Chapter 13 above.
[13] See *Marten v Flight Refuelling* [1962] Ch 115.

representation of a representative sample of such parties in any application under section 84 Law of Property Act 1925. Otherwise, it would be difficult – if not impossible – for the Lands Tribunal to discharge, or modify covenants under that jurisdiction. The same will be true of any consensual release, or such other agreement, made by parties to covenants. In such cases all will need to join in. It would appear that, in view of the fact that covenants are carried forward onto the unit holder's title, all the unit holders will need to join in such a release.[14]

New covenants?

19.15 As has already been suggested, it is not impossible but it is likely to be inappropriate that fresh restrictive covenants should be imposed on each unit. At one stage, it was contemplated that this right should be specifically barred by the regulations but the current form of regulations do not specifically bar that right. The reason that the creation of fresh restrictive covenants on each unit is unlikely is because, as has already been stated, the Commonhold Community Statement will deal with the entirety of the rights and obligations as between the Commonhold Association and the unit holders.

Summary

19.16 In summary, therefore, the unit holders and the Commonhold Association will be bound and will have the benefit of two sets of rules. First, those in any *restrictive covenants* which affect the freehold. Secondly, those which are set out in the Commonhold Community Statement. It is also significant that the rules in the *Commonhold Community Statement* are specifically enforceable as between the parties thereto and there is a specific application of compulsory dispute resolutions. The latter fact is one major difference between the enforcement of restrictive covenants where there is no such automatic requirement.

The effect on restrictive covenants of the termination of the commonhold

Overview

19.17 The provisions as regards the termination of a commonhold ownership are not only complex but are unsatisfactory in some respects. Examples of the latter are given below, but the reader is referred to the detailed textbooks for the more specific examples of what can happen on the termination of commonhold ownership. It is sufficient to say, for present purposes, that, as the basis of any commonhold is the Commonhold Association, without that Association being in existence, commonhold cannot exist. It follows that as the Commonhold Association is a company limited by guarantee, that company may be wound up (in

---

[14] In fact, in practice, it may be prudent under the current system of leasehold titles for leaseholders to join in releasing covenants where there are covenants to which they might conceivably have the benefit under s 78 of the Law of Property Act 1925, bearing in mind the ability of leaseholders to enforce covenants as the owner of legal estate and having regard to the authority of *Smith and Snipes Hall Farm v River Douglas Catchment Board* [1949] 2 KB 500, referred to at **8.5** above.

the normal way applicable to any company) either voluntarily, or compulsorily. After winding up a company is dissolved and the Commonhold Association is no exception to this principle. The 2002 Act provides for what is to happen in each of the circumstances at sections 43–55. Different consequences will apply according to whether or not the termination is one which is voluntary, or is one where the Court winds up the Commonhold Association.

Voluntary winding up

19.18   In the case of a voluntary winding up, a *termination statement* will need to specify what will happen to the freehold in each commonhold unit; sections 47–49 of the 2002 Act. (In the case of winding up by the Court, a *Succession Order* is made dealing with the ownership of the common parts.) The principal difference is that – in the former instance, namely a voluntary winding up – by section 49(3) of the 2002 Act, the freehold to each unit will be vested in the Commonhold Association which is being wound up.

19.19   The practical effect of these events in a voluntary winding up on unit holders and their mortgagees is, at this stage, by no means clear. Commentators and authors have indicated that it will be necessary (so far as the rules allow) in the Commonhold Community Statement and in the Articles of Association of the Commonhold Association to make some provision for what is to happen after the termination and the end of the commonhold. From the perspective of those with an interest in restrictive covenants, as it is unlikely that there will be restrictive covenants created as between the unit holders and the Commonhold Association (or between themselves), termination should not affect any of the restrictive covenants which are already on the freehold title. They will continue to exist. If there are any 'new' restrictive covenants created as between the unit holders and the Commonhold Association, those would come to an end on the termination of the commonhold. The position as regards termination of leases referred to at n 11 would seem to be analogous.) As has already been pointed out, any existing interests on the freehold title, such as existing restrictive covenants, will be preserved when – at least in the case of a voluntary winding up – the Commonhold Association becomes the registered proprietor of each unit under section 49(3) of the 2002 Act, or whoever becomes the registered proprietor of the freeholds of each unit according to the terms of the Termination Statement. It is likely, in practice, that the statement made (under section 47(1)(a)) will transfer the freehold vested in the Commonhold Association by section 49(3) to a third party and that third party is likely to grant long leases of the units. If that does not happen, there will have to be a sale of the development with each unit holder taking a share in the net surplus. That is considered, at this stage, to be an unattractive option and is one major potential weakness in the whole scheme of commonhold ownership. That said, none of this will affect the benefit, or burden of any covenants affecting the freehold of the development. These will continue in effect so far as they were created prior to the inception of the commonhold ownership. It is suggested that the 'collapse' of the freehold units on termination of the commonhold scheme – with the closure of the registers to each unit as freehold commonhold units – should not affect the existence and continuance of those covenants; it will be up to the Land Registry to take such action as appears to be appropriate to give effect to any termination statement; see section 49(4) of the 2002 Act and also see Land Registry Forms CM5 and CM6 used in these circumstances.

19.20   In summary, therefore, whilst the termination on a voluntary winding up of the Commonhold Association does pose some serious and practical problems for the commonhold unit holders, there would appear to be no difficulty as regards the continuation of the enforceability of any restrictive covenants imposed on the titles prior to the creation of the commonhold scheme. So far as new commonhold title unit holders may have created covenants, then, on the vesting of the unit holders' titles in the Commonhold Association on the winding up, those covenants would appear to come to an end; see *Re Tiltwood* cited above at note 12 above.

Winding up by the Court

19.21   Where the Commonhold Association is wound up by the Court, instead of a termination statement there is a Succession Order made by the Court under section 51 of the 2002 Act. That will allow a successor Commonhold Association to be registered as the registered proprietor of the common parts, as successor to old Commonhold Association, which was, of course, insolvent; see Land Registry Form CM6. The commonhold will carry on as before and none of this will affect the enforceability of restrictive covenants over any freehold of the common parts or unit holders. Where a Succession Order is not made, on the winding up of the Commonhold Association the commonhold does not come to an end. The liquidator takes control of the Commonhold Association. He must then inform the Chief Registrar that section 54 of the 2002 Act applies; section 54(2) thereof. Unlike a voluntary winding up, there is no *automatic* termination of the commonhold. So, the Commonhold Community Statement continues to bind unit holders between themselves and the liquidator. At some stage, however, the commonhold may have to be terminated and, under section 55(4), the Chief Registrar has power to reflect the completion of the winding up and the dissolution of the Commonhold Association by ensuring as soon as reasonably practicable that 'the freehold land in respect of which the Commonhold Association exercises functions ceases to be registered as a freehold estate in commonhold land'. This would appear to mean (quite apart from the problems which the effect of the termination of the commonhold will create between unit holders) that, as regards restrictive covenants on the freehold owned by Commonhold Association, these will continue to bind the land and any benefit will also be enforceable if the usual tests for annexation, etc, are satisfied.[15] If, as appears likely, on the termination of the commonhold and before the winding up is complete, the commonhold titles to the unit will be cancelled (there being no successor) in the absence of any new restrictive covenants entered into between the unit holders or the Commonhold Association (rare, for the reasons given above) there will be no further consequences. The covenants which formerly bound the freehold will continue to do so and the benefit will be for the same period as before. In any case of termination of commonhold (whether voluntarily or by the Court) in the rare instance where *new* covenants have been created as between unit holders and the Commonhold Association (and where there is no succession) it would seem that

---

[15]   See Chapter 8 above.

any new such restrictive covenants will be extinguished for two reasons. First, because, on the vesting of the units in the Commonhold Association on a voluntary winding up under section 49(3), the benefit and the burden will be in one person.[16] Secondly, on the determination of the freehold in the units, there is no estate on which those restrictive covenants can depend for their existence. See note 12, **19.19** and **19.20** above.

19.22 However, it is an open question as to what may happen if all the unit holders and the Commonhold Association covenant with a neighbouring freeholder after the creation of the commonhold scheme. Thus, to take the example given above, if the Magnate House Commonhold Association Limited and/or the one hundred unit holders in 'Magnate House' covenant for the benefit of the neighbouring property that *x* or *y* shall or shall not occur, what is the consequence of the termination of the commonhold ownership scheme? It is suggested that, as the freehold of the development (formerly commonhold) will continue as a *freehold*, however owned, the burden or the benefit of the covenants annexed or attached, or binding on the freehold will continue. It may well be that the termination statement, or the succession order can allow for this continuation, although that is by no means clear at this stage. Where there is no succession order, the Chief Land Registrar will want to continue the entries on the freehold (although it is no longer held commonhold) where it is plain that those entries bind that freehold. One final factor may enter into the answer to this question. Under the Human Rights Act 1998 the court may need to construe the 2002 Act and any regulations made thereunder in such a way so as to prevent a breach of Convention rights. These rights (if engaged) are anticipated to be those arising under Article 8 of the Convention (respect for the home) and under Article 1 of the First Protocol to the Convention (peaceful enjoyment of possessions). This means that, for example, the neighbour to 'Magnate House' has the benefit of a restrictive covenant entered into by all the commonhold unit holders and the Commonhold Association. He has the legitimate right to expect the benefit of that covenant to continue to be enforceable against the freehold to 'Magnate House', notwithstanding the termination of any commonhold scheme under the terms of the 2002 Act.[17] The benefit of a restrictive covenant could be held to be in the same category and the Courts are obliged under section 3 of the Human Rights Act to construe the 2002 Act in such a way as is consistent with convention rights; see *Ghaidan v Godin Mendoza* [2004] 3 WLR 113.

---

[16]   See *Re Tiltwood* [1978] Ch 269, at Chapter 13 above.

[17]   *Re Stretch v United Kingdom* [2004] 03 Estates Gazette 100; in that case it was held by the European Court of Human Rights that Art 1 of the First Protocol (peaceful enjoyment of possessions) was breached by a local authority which asserted that it had no power to grant an option to renew a lease. It was held by the Court that 'possessions' within the First Protocol could include a claim in respect of which the applicant had a legitimate expectation of obtaining effective enjoyment of a property right. See also *PW & Co v Milton Gate Investments* [2004] Ch 142. See also construction of ss 141–142 of the Law of Property Act 1925 to accord with Art 1 of the First Protocol in the context of enforcement of covenants by a head lessee against the sub-lessee where the head lease has determined. See Chapter 20 below.

CONCLUSION

19.23   As was pointed out at the beginning of this chapter, the law relating to the ownership of a freehold in commonhold is new and there will, no doubt, be developments once commonhold ownership comes into use to any appreciable extent. As commonhold ownership is only a different way of holding a freehold title, it is clear that all the rules affecting the running of restrictive covenants for and against specific titles will continue to apply. Whilst there may be some specific issues arising, such as when there is litigation with a potential plethora of claimants or defendants, these issues can be managed within the existing rules relating to civil litigation. As the relationship between the unit holders and the Commonhold Association will be governed by the Commonhold Community Statement, and as it should be extremely rare for fresh restrictive covenants to be created as between those parties, commonhold ownership should not pose any particular difficulties in the context of restrictive covenants.

Chapter 20

THE HUMAN RIGHTS ACT 1998 AND RESTRICTIVE COVENANTS

OVERVIEW

20.1 The Human Rights Act came into force in the United Kingdom on 2 October 2000. It gives effect to certain rights set out in the European Convention for the Protection of Human Rights and Fundamental Freedoms 1950 and in the Protocols to it. By virtue of the Act, those rights which are contained in Schedule 1 to the Act are enforceable as a matter of domestic law within the United Kingdom. Those rights are referred to in this chapter as 'the Convention Rights'. The Human Rights Act 1998 is referred to in this chapter as 'the 1998 Act'.

The effect of the 1998 Act on the domestic law of the United Kingdom has, within a period (at the time of writing) of just over 4 years, been immense. This is because the Convention Rights affect, or have the capacity to affect, a large spectrum of rights, obligations and responsibilities at all levels of society. Convention Rights apply between individuals and public authorities (eg central and local government – but not just those bodies) and indirectly affect private claims between individuals because of the effect of section 3 of the 1998 Act, as explained below. This chapter is not intended to be an outline of the relevant law under the 1998 Act and, for that purpose, the reader is referred to specialist text books on the subject.[1] The aim of this chapter is to highlight certain aspects of the law which have been created by the 1998 Act and to consider that law, so far as may be applicable, to the law of restrictive covenants over freehold land. It should be pointed out at this stage that, whilst the 1998 Act extends over the United Kingdom, the law of restrictive covenants dealt with in this book is applicable only to England and Wales. So far as Convention Rights may have a bearing on restrictive covenants, or in respect of other forms of land obligations in Northern Ireland and Scotland, recourse will be needed to the terms of the local law in those parts of the United Kingdom for an assessment of the situation there.

AN OVERVIEW OF THE HUMAN RIGHTS ACT 1998

20.2 Before examining the relationship between the 1998 Act and the law of restrictive covenants, it is necessary to set out very briefly the effect of the 1998 Act. There are four broad headings which fall within this summary.

---

[1] For example, see Lester and Pannick, *Human Rights Law and Practice* (Butterworths, 2nd edn, 2004).

First, the Courts have to take into account decisions and opinions of the European Court of Human Rights (section 2).

Secondly, so far as it is possible to do so, the Courts must interpret and give effect to primary and subordinate legislation (whenever enacted) in a way which is compatible with the Convention Rights (sections 3 and 6). The Convention Rights are now part of the law of the UK, as mentioned above.

Thirdly, if necessary (and effectively as a last resort), the Courts may have to make a declaration of incompatibility where primary legislation is not compatible with a Convention Right, so far as it has been construed under section 3 to be incompatible with that Right (see section 4 of the Act).

Fourthly and finally, there is the overriding obligation on public authorities under section 6 of the 1998 Act not to act in a way which is incompatible with a Convention Right. What is and is not a Public Authority has received a broad interpretation from the Courts. However, there is still room for doubt and argument about the meaning of these words.[2] This obligation applies to the Courts (who are a public authority under section 6(3)) who must decide all cases before them (whether brought under common law or under statute) compatibly with Convention Rights, save as excluded from doing so by section 6(2).

To the above there must be added certain qualifications which affect the way in which Convention Rights will be applied and, if necessary, upheld. Again, in very broad summary form, there must first be a fair balance struck between the general interest of the community and the protection of the fundamental rights of an individual. Secondly, the doctrine of proportionality is applied. This operates so as to balance the interests of the State and the individual. If rights are to be limited, there must be an important and rational reason to do so. Thirdly and finally, it is for the individual to show a breach of Convention Rights. Where there is a *prima facie* breach of such rights, it is for the State to show that any restriction of those rights is justified by law and is necessary in a democratic society; for example, to protect the rights of others. Some rights are qualified (eg, Article 8, so that in those cases it may be harder to prove a breach of Convention Rights). This means, in practice, that the Courts will interpret Convention Rights broadly, whilst taking a narrow view of the interpretation of any exceptions to those rights. Fourthly, the State is allowed a 'margin of appreciation' when consideration is given to the question whether there has been an infringement of a Convention Right. The application of the 'margin of appreciation' is subject to a number of different factors. All of them are based on the principle that there must be a balance struck between the competing requirements of the State and the individual. Much will depend on the nature of the Convention Right as to how far the 'margin of appreciation' will be taken into account. For example, freedom of expression (under Article 10) may be less susceptible to the principle of the 'margin of appreciation' than, for example, the right to peaceful enjoyment of possessions under Article 1 of the First Protocol.[3] The 'margin of appreciation' does not apply to the obligation of the United Kingdom Courts to consider and apply the 1998 Act where necessary under

---

[2]　　The recent authority of *Aston Cantlow Parochial Church Council v Wallbank* [2004] 1 AC 546, sets out (in summary form) the approach to what is, and what is not, a public authority.

[3]　　*R v East Sussex County Council ex parte Reprotech (Pebsham) Ltd* [2003] 1 WLR 348.

section 3. That is an absolute obligation. The 'margin of appreciation' does, however, have a bearing on whether or not there has been a breach of rights.[4]

CONVENTION RIGHTS WHICH MAY BE RELEVANT IN THE CONTEXT OF RESTRICTIVE COVENANTS

The following Convention Rights would appear to fall within this description.

Article 6 – The right to a fair trial

20.3 Article 6(1) is relevant here.[5] Little needs to be said about this Convention Right in the context of restrictive covenants. If there is to be litigation over a restrictive covenant, then the determination of the parties' rights under the Civil Procedure Rules (whether between individuals, or between an individual and the State, or a public body or authority) will invariably conform to the principle of procedural fairness and the resolution of such a dispute. Where rights are being acquired, for example under section 237 of the Town and Country Planning Act 1990, and the local authority has to pay compensation for the acquisition of that right, it is also the case that the procedures for resolving any issues over compensation should be – and indeed are – scrupulously fair. In addition, the presence of Judicial Review under CPR Part 54 will satisfy Article 6, in that it allows access to a Court where the decision of an Administrative Body is being impugned. There can be no suggestion that the Procedural Rules in either the Civil Courts, or in the Lands Tribunal, do not strike a fair balance between the parties, who must be able to present their cases on an equal footing. This right is often referred to as that of 'equality of arms' and would appear to be present in the context of any litigation over restrictive covenants. The only area of any doubt is that which concerns the requirement of the undertaking in damages to be given if an interim injunction is being sought (see **15.28** and **15.29** below). There is an argument for saying that this requirement offends the equality of arms principle. However, the requirement that the undertaking should be give is by no means an inflexible one. Furthermore, it is a requirement which is designed to operate in the interest of the defendant and to avoid the obvious unfairness in an outcome where the defendant is out of pocket after an interim injunction has been discharged. At present the rules of procedure, and the way in which civil claims are determined would appear to satisfy Article 6(1).

---

[4] See Blackstone's *Guide to the Human Rights Act 1998* (Oxford University Press, 3rd edn, 2003), Chapter 3, for a useful summary of the provisions of the 1998 Act and their application. Those provisions relating to remedies, etc (eg s 7) are not referred to in this chapter.

[5] '6.1 In the determination of his civil rights and obligations or of any criminal charge against him, everyone is entitled to a fair and public hearing within a reasonable time by an independent and impartial tribunal established by law. Judgment shall be pronounced publicly but the press and public may be excluded from all or part of the trial in the interest of morals, public order or national security in a democratic society, where the interests of juveniles or the protection of the private life of the parties so require, or to the extent strictly necessary in the opinion of the Court in special circumstances where publicity would prejudice the interests of justice.'

Article 8

'Everyone has the right to respect for his private and family life, his home and his correspondence.

...

There shall be no interference by a Public Authority with the exercise of this right except such as is in accordance with the law and is necessary in a Democratic society in the interests of national security, public safety, or the economic well-being of the country, for the prevention of disorder or crime, for the protection of health or morals, or for the protection of the rights and freedoms of others.'

20.4   This is a very wide-ranging Convention Right. It has been found to extend over a large number of interests, from sexual freedom to personal correspondence, and to the home environment. The qualification in paragraph 2 is important. That expressly recognises the margin of appreciation, if not the doctrine of proportionality, in cases where the legitimate interest of the State must take precedence. A recent example of the application of the latter principles is *Lough v First Secretary of State*[6] where it was held (per Pill LJ, at paragraph 43) as follows:

'(a) Article 8 is concerned to prevent intrusions into a person's private life and home, and in particular arbitrary intrusions, and that is the background against which alleged breaches are to be considered. (b) Respect for the home has an environmental dimension in that the law must offer protection to the environment of the home. (c) Not every loss of amenity involves a breach of Article 8(1). The degree of seriousness required to trigger lack of respect for the home will depend on the circumstances, but it must be substantial. (d) The contents of Article 8(2) throw light on the extent of the right in Article 8(1), but infringement of Article 8(1) does not necessarily arise upon a loss of amenity, and the reasonableness and appropriateness of measures taken by the public authority are relevant in considering whether the respect required by Article 8(1) has been accorded. (e) It is also open to the public authority to justify an interference in accordance with Article 8(2), but the principles to be applied are broadly similar in the context of the two parts of the Article. (f) When balances are struck, the competing interests of the individual, other individuals, and the community as a whole must be considered. (g) The public authority concerned is granted a certain margin of appreciation in determining the steps to be taken to ensure compliance with Article 8. (h) The margin of appreciation may be wide when the implementation of planning policies is to be considered.'

The significant word in paragraph 1 of Article 8 is that of 'respect'. This means that because Article 8 is a qualified right and, as appears above from the judgment in *Lough*, not all interference will be a breach of that Convention Right. In broad terms, cases where a breach has been found have been where, for example, the interference with the Convention Right under Article 8 has been unlawful, or where the rights of the family are so important that interference with those rights by the State is not proportionate. First impressions suggest that Article 8 may have a direct bearing on restrictive covenant matters in the following situations given by way of example. First, where enforcement of a covenant by a Public Authority would require the family to be dispossessed of its home. Secondly, where the acquisition of a right under section 237 of the Town and Country Planning

---

6   [2004] 1 WLR 2557. Leave to appeal to the House of Lords refused by the House [2004] 1 WLR 2892.

Act 1990 might lead to a loss of privacy. However, in both examples, *Lough* would suggest that Article 8 is not engaged because of the effect of Article 8(2).[7] In each case neither the right of possession, nor privacy are absolute rights.

Article 1 of the First Protocol

'Protection of Property

Every natural or legal person is entitled to the peaceful enjoyment of his possessions. No-one shall be deprived of his possessions except in the public interest and subject to the conditions provided for by law and by the General Principles of International Law. The preceding provisions shall not, however, in any way impair the right of a State to enforce such laws as it deems necessary to control the use of property in accordance with the general interest or to secure the payment of taxes or other contributions or penalties.'

20.5 The key word in this Article is 'possessions'. Authority has given this word a very wide meaning. It does, however, require the claimant to show that he *has* that 'possession' and the mere expectation of a future right would not necessarily fall within the meaning of the Article.[8] It is suggested that the following interests will fall within the scope of the word 'possessions':

(i) The right to enforce the benefit of a restrictive covenant, as vested in the potential claimant.

The reason for this conclusion is because the benefit of the covenant may be seen as an interest in property which is vested in the claimant.[9]

(ii) The right to compensation if the benefit is acquired by a Public Authority, for example under section 237 of the Town and Country Planning Act 1990.

The reason for this conclusion is that the right to compensation is, *once due,* a right which can be claimed under statute.[10]

It is important to note that the Article has three ingredients. First, the general principle of the peaceful enjoyment of property. Secondly, the right not to be deprived of those possessions, save as set out in the Article; ie where public

---

[7] See also the significant House of Lords' decision in *Harrow London Borough Council v Qazi* [2004] 1 AC 983, where it was held that, in the context of a right to possession of the home, the right to respect for the home did not stop those entitled to proprietary, or contractual rights of possession from exercising those rights within the law. In the light of *Lough v First Secretary of State*, it is difficult to conceive of a situation where the conduct of a Public Authority in relation to an individual who has either the benefit, or is subject to the burden, of a restrictive covenant, engages Art 8. This means that it is unlikely that s 3 of the Human Rights Act will oblige the Court to interpret legislation in such a way so as to be in conformity with a Convention Right. This point, however, is considered further below.

[8] See *Marckx v Belgium* [1979] 2 EHRR 330; *Inze v Austria* [1987] 10 EHRR 394; *Petrovic v Austria* [1998] 33 EHRR 307; *Ghaidan v Godin-Mendoza* [2004] 3 WLR 113; *Ram v Ram* [2004] EWCA Civ 1452. For a useful summary, see Blackstone, at n 4 above, at 8.18–8.19.4.

[9] See Chapter 8 above.

[10] See Chapter 12 above. However, note that there is a considerable body of authority as to whether rights conferred by statute (eg pension and social security benefits) are possessions within the Article. It is suggested that once a right to compensation has accrued it is within the scope of possessions; this appears to have been accepted in *S v United Kingdom*, at n 20 below.

interest prevails and where the conditions provided for by law and International law allow it. Finally, the control by the State of the use of property in accordance with the general interest.[11]

What seems reasonably clear is that, in the context of restrictive covenants, Article 1 can have the following application. First, as the benefit of a restrictive covenant is within the scope of 'possessions', *deprivation* of it by a Public Authority may be within the scope of the Article. However, a Public Authority is allowed to appropriate a right to enforce a covenant, if the right which is sought to be exercised is within the principles of proportionality. It is suggested that, as the operation of section 237 of the Town and Country Planning Act 1990 is safeguarded by the need for a Local Authority to satisfy a Court that it is necessary to acquire, or appropriate land and associated rights for planning purposes, it would be very hard to prove that a fair balance between individual and the State has not been struck.[12] It is also important to note that the provision in Paragraph 2 of the Article which allows deprivation of right under the conditions provided for by section 237 and associated sections of Town and Country Planning Act 1990 may prevent any challenge under this Article.[13] To this must, of course, be added the factor of the payment of compensation under section 10 of the Compulsory Purchase Act 1965. It is, therefore, suggested that, in the context – and in particular in the context of the authorities such as *Lough v First Secretary of State* (above) – it would be extremely hard to persuade a court that, in so far as a public authority is seeking to do so within the law, deprivation of the right to enforce the benefit of a covenant could be said to be in breach of Article 1. However, circumstances could arise whereby a public authority with limited powers entered into an agreement to confer the benefit of a restrictive covenant on the beneficiary of that agreement. If that beneficiary had legitimate expectations of being able to enforce the restrictive covenant, that fact would amount to 'possessions' and a deprivation of that right (for example, by the assertion by the limited body that it had acted *ultra vires*), might amount to a breach of Article 1.[14]

---

[11] See *Aston Cantlow Parochial Church Council v Wallbank* [2004] 1 AC 546, at p 571, para 67, per Lord Hope of Craighead, adopting the conventional 'three element' approach to the Art set out in *Sporrong & Lönnroth v Sweden* [1982] 5 EHRR 35, and *James v United Kingdom* [1986] 8 EHRR 123.

[12] See Chapter 12 above. See *R (Trailer and Marina) (Leven) Ltd v Secretary of State for Environment, Food and Rural Affairs, The Times*, 28 December 2004, for an example where statutory control struck the right balance. In *Midtown v City of London Real Property Co* [2005] EWHC 33 (Ch), at paras 49–50, the Judge declined to decide the 1998 Act arguments which had been placed before him under s 237 of the Town and Country Planning Act 1990.

[13] However, as there are no defined procedures for determining whether, or not it is proper to interfere with private rights (eg covenants and easements) (as opposed to material factors in planning or public law) once the land has been acquired, or appropriated, it may be argued that the interference with the private rights is not under 'conditions provided for by law' as Art 1 requires. The fact that the exercise of the discretion under s 237 is subject to judicial review may not be a complete answer to the argument that there are 'conditions provided for by law'. It is also material to note that a restrictive interpretation of the powers under s 237 ought to prevail in order that there is no undue interference with Convention rights, especially under Art 1. The restrictive interpretation of s 237 adopted in *Midtown v City of London Real Property Co* (above) led the Court to a conclusion which avoided the need to deal with extensive argument on the compatibility or otherwise with Convention rights and the need to apply s 3 of the 1998 Act. But it seems to the author that there is room for considerable debate here on whether far s 237, when exercised, is compliant or not.

[14] See *Stretch v United Kingdom* [2003] ECHR [2004] 03 *Estates Gazette* 100.

The overall conclusion under Article 1 is that it seems hard to see how there can be a breach of that Article in the vast majority of cases where a Local Authority, or other public authority, may be exercising statutory powers; for example, under section 237 of the Town and Country Planning Act 1990.

The interpretation obligation under section 3 of the 1998 Act is dealt with below.

THE IMPORTANCE OF SECTION 3 OF THE 1998 ACT

20.6 The chapter, so far, has been considering the specific Articles referred to above in the context of conduct by public authorities. What has not yet been considered is the obligation on the Courts under section 3 of the 1998 Act to give effect, so far as it is possible to do so, when interpreting domestic legislation (whether enacted before or after 2 October 2000) so as to give effect to Convention Rights. This interpretation obligation applies in respect of claim whether or not the litigants are public authorities. The section 3 obligation, therefore, applies Convention Rights *indirectly* to private litigants and upon public authorities. This is because the obligation under section 3 leads to an outcome where, so far as is possible Convention Rights are upheld. A wide construction is permitted.[15]

It is in the context of the Courts' obligations under section 3 that there may be a fertile ground for argument that legislative provisions which govern the enforcement of restrictive covenants may not be in conformity with Convention Rights and, therefore, should be construed, so far as possible, so as to be in conformity with them.

As has already been pointed out in this book, there are two aspects to any restrictive covenant. The first is the burden of the covenant and the second is the benefit.

The burden of a covenant

20.7 So far as the *burden* of the covenant is concerned, the principal statutory provision which deals with the running of the burden is section 79 of the Law of Property Act 1925, together with the various statutory provisions set out in Chapter 7 of this book which relate to the registration of covenants. As the burden of a covenant could neither be regarded as 'possessions' nor falling within the scope of Article 8 (the right to respect for private and family life and the home), it is hard to see how a court would be obliged to construe existing legislation so as to give effect to either Article 8 of the Convention, or Article 1 of the First Protocol. It has already been pointed out by reference to the extract from *Lough v First Secretary of State* at **20.4** above that, even if it could be said that enforcement of a restrictive covenant might lead, for example, to dispossession, or certainly interference with the home (eg so far as there might have to be an order to pull down works carried out in breach of contract) that would not necessarily be a breach of any Convention Rights. This is principally because Article 8(1) is qualified by Article 8(2). It is also suggested that, if somebody acquires land subject to properly registered interests, including the burden of restrictive covenants, that would be the 'ordinary

---

15 See *Ghaidan v Godin-Mendoza* [2004] 3 WLR 113 and *Wilson v First County Trust* [2004] 1 AC 816, at p 842 (para 61). See Lester and Pannick, at n 1 above, at 2.3.

incident' of the ownership of land and, so far as those incidents might have a negative effect on the owner, such effect should not be regarded as contrary to any Convention Right.[16] It is, therefore, hard to conceive of a case where the ordinary incidence of ownership of land and the statutory effect of section 79 of the Law of Property Act 1925 and the other statutes in the Land Charges Act and the Land Registration Act would have to be construed in such a way so as to cause the burden of a restrictive covenant to be avoided. It would have to be an exceptional case, so as to operate outside the usual rule that there is a narrow public interest in respect of the person who is bound, and a wider public interest in respect of upholding registered obligations, such as restrictive covenants.[17]

The benefit of a covenant

20.8   When considering the benefit of a restrictive covenant, and rights arising from the *benefit* of such a covenant, there may, however, be greater scope for arguing that section 78 of the Law of Property Act 1925 should be interpreted in such a way so as not to infringe either Article 8, or Article 1 of the First Protocol. The latter article is more likely to apply if at all. Such an obligation would require a Court to construe section 78(1) in such a way so as, for example, to allow a claimant to succeed in an argument that the benefit had passed to him by annexation, notwithstanding a failure to observe the strict terms of that section, as interpreted in *Crest Nicholson v McAllister* [2004] EWCA Civ 410 (see **8.18** above). At present, it seems hard to suggest that there is really any way in which section 78(1) can be construed other than as stated by Chadwick LJ, in that case. But, why should not a modern and purposive construction of section 78(1) lead to a wider conclusion in favour of annexation? Section 3 of the 1998 Act requires the Court to adopt such a construction if there is a prospect of incompatibility. The starting point is, therefore, that section 78(1) prevents the claimant from asserting a right to the benefit of the covenant. That benefit is possession within Article 1. (Or the inability to enforce may affect family life or the home within Article 8.) So section 78(1) should be construed under section 3 of the 1998 Act so as to allow the benefit to be enforced. The only difficulty in such an argument is this. Unlike cases where the claimant has been deprived of rights such as possession, or the benefit of an option,[18] or the right to enforce covenants as between head landlord and sub-tenant,[19] in a case where a claimant is seeking to establish the right to enforce a restrictive covenant, the whole purpose of the examination of section 78(1) is to determine whether the property right is there *in*

---

[16]   See *Aston Cantlow Parochial Church Council v Wallbank* [2004] 1 AC 546, at pp 602–603, para 171, per Lord Roger of Earlsferry, where he extracted the judgment of Ferris J, at first instance. Ferris J, regarded the liability to repair a Chancel (which was the liability which arose in that case) as one of the incidents of the ownership of Rectorial property. He said: 'It is, of course, an unusual incident because it does not amount to a charge on the land, it is not limited to the value of the land and imposes a personal liability on the owner of the land. But in principle I do not find it possible to distinguish it from the liability which would attach to the owner of land which is purchased subject to a mortgage, restrictive covenant or other encumbrance created by a predecessor in title.' Note the reference there to 'restrictive covenant'.

[17]   For recent examples of striking a fair balance between rights of parties with conflicting interests, see, in the context of bankruptcy, *Ram v Ram* [2004] EWCA Civ 1452 and *Barca v Mears*, Chancery Division, Nicholas Strauss QC, 24 September 2004.

[18]   As in *Stretch v United Kingdom*, see n 14 above.

[19]   See *PW & Co v Milton Gate Investments* [2004] Ch 142. See below.

the first place.[20] It is, therefore, suggested that, on this footing there is no obvious way for construing section 78(1) of the Law of Property Act 1925 so as to require a wider set of rules derived from Convention Rights to allow the benefit of the covenant to be claimed.[21] A contrary view might suggest that there is some scope for the application of a wider interpretation of section 78(1) of the Law of Property Act 1925 so as to be in conformity with the right to the peaceful enjoyment of possessions. This is based on the principle that the right to enforce ('possessions') is there at the outset (or at least it has been true since 2 October 2000). Therefore, the terms of section 78(1) should be construed in such a way *so as to allow that right to be fulfilled*. This argument relies, by analogy, on *Stretch v United Kingdom* (see note 13 above), where it was accepted by the United Kingdom Government that the option, of which Mr Stretch had the benefit and in respect of which he had a legitimate expectation of it being exercised, was void from the outset. As it was void from the outset, just as a covenant might be said to be subject to section 78(1) from the outset, the logical starting point in *Stretch* means that it is possible to regard a property right as one which *can* be subject to the effect of section 3 of the 1998 Act. This means that the view expressed here has validity if the property right which Article 1 is sought to protect is regarded as capable of full enjoyment without the statutory limitation under section 78(1) attached to it. Otherwise there would be circularity and section 3 could never be applies. In *PW & Co v Milton Gate* (see note 8 above), the rights of the defendant (the freeholder) were subject to the terms of sections 139, 141 and 142 of the Law of Property Act 1925. A head lease had been terminated by the exercise of a break clause. At common law, and indeed as a result of the terms of sections 139, 141 and 142 of the Law of Property Act 1925, the freeholder would not be able to enforce the rent covenants against the sub-lessees after the collapse of the intermediate head lease. The Court held that the defendant's legitimate expectations were possession of the demised property (subject to the Landlord and Tenant Act 1954) and the ability to enforce the rent covenants against the sub-lessees. The Court construed sections 141 and 142 (under section 3 of the 1998 Act) so as to allow the rent covenants to be enforced directly as between the freeholder and the sub-tenants, notwithstanding the determination of the Head Lease and the lack of privity of estate between the defendant and the sub-tenant. This case supports the contrary view, just expressed, that possessions should be regarded at the first stage of any consideration of section 3 of the 1998 Act in their fullest sense, without the constraint of the domestic statute. It is then the task of the Court to examine whether or not the effect of the statute is to deprive the Applicant of his Convention Right (in this case, under Article 1 'Possessions') and to construe, so far as possible, the relevant

---

[20] See *Wilson v First County Trust* [2003] UK HL 40; [2004] 1 AC 816.

[21] In *S v United Kingdom* (Application No 10741/1984) [1984] 41 DR 226, the Applicant had received a sum of money (£350) for the extinguishment of the benefit of rights under restrictive covenants in Northern Ireland. The sum had been awarded by the Lands Tribunal in Northern Ireland under what is now s 237 of the Town and Country Planning Act 1990 and s 10 of the Compulsory Purchase Act 1965. The Applicant sought to contend before the European Commission of Human Rights that she would have received a full release or ransom price for the release had it not been for the terms of the relevant statutory provision. (See **12.4** above, for the limits on the right to recovery.) There was held to be no breach of convention rights under Art 8 or, more specifically, under Art 1 of the First Protocol, as whilst the compensation might have been seen as inadequate, the purpose of the legislation was to acquire such rights for the greater public good. Thus, the Applicant's interest had to be sacrificed to that greater good.

domestic statute so as to allow the Applicant the enjoyment of that right. It is suggested that a narrow interpretation of rights (including the right to enforce a restrictive covenant) is one which begs the question whether or not the domestic statute which prevents the enforcement is one which is itself preventing the enjoyment of a Convention Right.

It must, however, be stressed that there can be no certainty in this area of the law and the two rival contentions, so far as they have been set out above, are no more than one way of approaching the question whether or not there is scope to argue that the Court may at a future date have to construe section 78(1) of the Law of Property Act 1925 in the light of section 3 of the 1998 Act, and in order to give effect to a Convention Right; in particular, that under Article 1 of the First Protocol.

CONCLUSION

20.9   As is said at the outset of this chapter, the effect of the application of Convention Rights to the domestic law of this country for the past 4 years or more has been immense and will, no doubt, continue to increase. It is, therefore, difficult to engage in anything more than speculation about the likely effect of Convention Rights and the 1998 Act on the law of restrictive covenants, so far as they affect freehold land.

It is appropriate that those advising in this area of law should at least consider this issue from two principal aspects. First, where Public Authorities are concerned, whether or not they are in breach of their responsibility under section 6 of the 1998 Act in so far as the exercise of their powers is an interference with the Convention Rights of the individual. The second aspect is that of the interpretation of legislation, which touches upon restrictive covenants, and the extent to which there may be incompatibility with Convention Rights requiring the Court to construe that legislation, so far as is possible, to accord with the rights. This can involve purely private claims. At present, under both heads, the law on restrictive covenants does not appear to be a particularly fertile ground for the application of the 1998 Act. It remains, however, a matter for conjecture as to how far, in the development of this jurisprudence, arguments can be maintained which would stand some prospect of success in any litigation and in particular in relation to questions arising over whether a party has the benefit of a restrictive covenant and the right, therefore, to invoke Article 8 of the Convention, or Article 1 of the First Protocol.

APPENDICES

APPENDICES

Appendix 1 – Statutory Material (extracts)

A1.1 Conveyancing and Law of Property Act 1881

58

(1) A covenant relating to land of inheritance, or devolving on the heir as special occupant, shall be deemed to be made with the covenantee, his heirs and assigns, and shall have effect as if heirs and assigns were expressed.

(2) A covenant relating to land not of inheritance, or not devolving on the heir as special occupant, shall be deemed to be made with the covenantee, his executors, administrators, and assigns, and shall have effect as if executors, administrators, and assigns were expressed.

(3) This section applies only to covenants made after the commencement of this Act. (January 1, 1882.)

A1.2 Law of Property Act 1925

56 Persons taking who are not parties and as to indentures

(1) A person may take an immediate or other interest in land or other property, or the benefit of any condition, right of entry, covenant or agreement over or respecting land or other property, although he may not be named as a party to the conveyance or other instrument.

(2) A deed between parties, to effect its objects, has the effect of an indenture though not indented or expressed to be an indenture.

78 Benefit of covenants relating to land

(1) A covenant relating to any land of the covenantee shall be deemed to be made with the covenantee and his successors in title and the persons deriving title under him or them, and shall have effect as if such successors and other persons were expressed.

For the purposes of this subsection in connexion with covenants restrictive of the user of land 'successors in title' shall be deemed to include the owners and occupiers for the time being of the land of the covenantee intended to be benefited.

(2) This section applies to covenants made after the commencement of this Act, but the repeal of section fifty-eight of the Conveyancing Act 1881 does not affect the operation of covenants to which that section applied.

79 Burden of covenants relating to land

(1) A covenant relating to any land of a covenantor or capable of being bound by him, shall, unless a contrary intention is expressed, be deemed to be made by the covenantor on behalf of himself his successors in title and the persons deriving title under him or them, and, subject as aforesaid, shall have effect as if such successors and other persons were expressed.

This subsection extends to a covenant to do some act relating to the land, notwithstanding that the subject-matter may not be in existence when the covenant is made.

(2) For the purpose of this section in connexion with covenants restrictive of the user of land 'successors in title' shall be deemed to include the owners and occupiers for the time being of such land.

(3) This section applies only to covenants made after the commencement of this Act.

80 Covenants binding land

(1) A covenant and a bond and an obligation or contract [made under seal after 31st December 1881 but before the coming into force of section 1 of the Law of Property (Miscellaneous Provisions) Act 1989 or executed as a deed in accordance with that section after its coming into force], binds the real estate as well as the personal estate of the person making the same if and so far as a contrary intention is not expressed in the covenant, bond, obligation, or contract.

This subsection extends to a covenant implied by virtue of this Act.

(2) Every covenant running with the land, whether entered into before or after the commencement of this Act, shall take effect in accordance with any statutory enactment affecting the devolution of the land, and accordingly the benefit or burden of every such covenant shall vest in or bind the persons who by virtue of any such enactment or otherwise succeed to the title of the covenantee or the covenantor, as the case may be.

(3) The benefit of a covenant relating to land entered into after the commencement of this Act may be made to run with the land without the use of any technical expression if the covenant is of such a nature that the benefit could have been made to run with the land before the commencement of this Act.

(4) For the purposes of this section, a covenant runs with the land when the benefit or burden of it, whether at law or in equity, passes to the successors in title of the covenantee or the covenantor, as the case may be.

Amendments – (Set out as reprinted with amendments in the Law of Property Act 1969, s 28(1), Sch 3); Law of Property (Miscellaneous Provisions) Act 1989, s 1, Sch 1, para 4, with effect from 31 July 1990, SI 1990/1175.

84 Power to discharge or modify restrictive covenants affecting land

(1) The Lands Tribunal shall (without prejudice to any concurrent jurisdiction of the court) have power from time to time, on the application of any person interested in any freehold land affected by any restriction arising under covenant or otherwise as to the user thereof or the building thereon, by order wholly or partially to discharge or modify any such restriction on being satisfied –

(a)   that by reason of changes in the character of the property or the neighbourhood or other circumstances of the case which the Lands Tribunal may deem material, the restriction ought to be deemed obsolete; or

(aa)   that (in a case falling within subsection (1A) below) the continued existence thereof would impede some reasonable user of the land for public or private purposes or, as the case may be, would unless modified so impede such user; or

(b)   that the persons of full age and capacity for the time being or from time to time entitled to the benefit of the restriction, whether in respect of estates in fee simple or any lesser estates or interests in the property to which the benefit of the restriction is annexed, have agreed, either expressly or by implication, by their acts or omissions, to the same being discharged or modified; or

(c)   that the proposed discharge or modification will not injure the persons entitled to the benefit of the restriction.

and an order discharging or modifying a restriction under this subsection may direct the applicant to pay to any person entitled to the benefit of the restriction such sum by way of consideration as the Tribunal may think it just to award under one, but not both, of the following heads, that is to say, either –

(i)   a sum to make up for any loss or disadvantage suffered by that person in consequence of the discharge or modification; or

(ii)   a sum to make up for any effect which the restriction had, at the time, when it was imposed, in reducing the consideration then received for the land affected by it.

(1A) Subsection (1)(aa) above authorises the discharge or modification of a restriction by reference to its impeding some reasonable user of land in any case in which the Lands Tribunal is satisfied that the restriction, in impeding that user, either –

(a)   does not secure to persons entitled to the benefit of it any practical benefits of substantial value or advantage to them; or

(b)   is contrary to the public interest;

and that money will be an adequate compensation for the loss or disadvantage (if any) which any such person will suffer from the discharge or modification.

(1B) In determining whether a case is one falling within subsection (1A) above, and in determining whether (in any such case or otherwise) a restriction ought to be discharged or modified, the Lands Tribunal shall take into account the development plan and any declared or ascertainable pattern for the grant or refusal of planning permissions in the relevant areas, as well as the period at which and context in which the restriction was created or imposed and any other material circumstances.

(1C) It is hereby declared that the power conferred by this section to modify a restriction includes power to add such further provisions restricting the user of or the building on the land affected as appear to the Lands Tribunal to be reasonable in view of the relaxation of the existing provisions, and as may be accepted by the applicant; and the Lands Tribunal may accordingly refuse to modify a restriction without some such addition.

(2) The court shall have power on the application of any person interested –

(a)   to declare whether or not in any particular case any freehold land is, or would in any given event be, affected by a restriction imposed by any instrument; or

(b)   to declare what, upon the true construction of any instrument purporting to impose a restriction, is the nature and extent of the restriction thereby imposed and whether the same is, or would in any given event be, enforceable and if so by whom.

Neither subsections (7) and (11) of this section nor, unless the contrary is expressed, any later enactment providing for this section not to apply to any restrictions shall affect the operation of this subsection or the operation for purposes of this subsection of any other provisions of this section.

(3) The Lands Tribunal shall, before making any order under this section, direct such enquiries, if any, to be made of any government department or local authority, and such notices, if any, whether by way of advertisement or otherwise, to be given to such of the persons who appear to be entitled, to the benefit of the restriction intended to be discharged, modified, or dealt with as, having regard to any enquiries, notices or other proceedings previously made, given or taken, the Lands Tribunal may think fit.

(3A) On an application to the Lands Tribunal under this section the Lands Tribunal shall give any necessary directions as to the persons who are or are not to be admitted (as appearing to be entitled to the benefit of the restriction) to oppose the application, and no appeal shall lie against any such direction; but rules under the Lands Tribunal Act 1949 shall make provision whereby, in cases in which there arises on such an application (whether or not in connection with the admission of persons to oppose) any such question as is referred to in subsection (2)(a) or (b) of this section, the proceedings on the application can and, if the rules so provide, shall be suspended to enable the decision of the court to be obtained on that question by an application under that subsection, or by rules of court.

(5) Any order made under this section shall be binding on all persons, whether ascertained or of full age or capacity or not, then entitled or thereafter capable of becoming entitled to the benefit of any restriction, which is thereby discharged, modified or dealt with, and whether such persons are parties to the proceedings or have been served with notice or not.

(6) An order may be made under this section notwithstanding that any instrument which is alleged to impose the restriction intended to be discharged, modified, or dealt with, may not have been produced to the court or the Lands Tribunal, and the court or the Lands Tribunal may act on such evidence of that instrument as it may think sufficient.

(7) This section applies to restrictions whether subsisting at the commencement of this Act or imposed thereafter, but this section does not apply where the restriction was imposed on the occasion of a disposition made gratuitously or for a nominal consideration for public purposes.

(8) This section applies whether the land affected by the restrictions is registered or not […].

(9) Where any proceedings by action or otherwise are taken to enforce a restrictive covenant, any person against whom the proceedings are taken, may in such proceedings apply to the court for an order giving leave to apply to the Lands Tribunal under this section, and staying the proceedings in the meantime.

(11) This section does not apply to restrictions imposed by the Commissioners of Works under any statutory power for the protection of any Royal Park or Garden or to restrictions of a like character imposed upon the occasion of any enfranchisement effected before the commencement of this Act in any manner vested in His Majesty in right of the Crown or the Duchy of Lancaster, nor (subject to subsection (11A) below) to restrictions created or imposed –

   (a)   for naval, military or air force purposes,
   [(b)   for civil aviation purposes under the powers of the Air Navigation Act 1920, of section 19 or 23 of the Civil Aviation Act 1949 or of section 30 or 41 of the Civil Aviation Act 1982.]

(11A) Subsection (11) of this section –

   (a)   shall exclude the application of this section to a restriction falling within subsection (11)(a), and not created or imposed in connection with the use of any land as an aerodrome, only so long as the restriction is enforceable by or on behalf of the Crown; and
   (b)   shall exclude the application of this section to a restriction falling within subsection (11)(b), or created or imposed in connection with the use of any land as an aerodrome, only so long as the restriction is enforceable by or on behalf of the Crown or any public or international authority.

(12) Where a term of more than forty years is created in land (whether before or after the commencement of this Act) this section shall, after the expiration of twenty-five years of the

term, apply to restrictions, affecting such leasehold land in like manner as it would have applied had the land been freehold:

Provided that this subsection shall not apply to mining leases.

Amendments – Land Registration Act 2002, ss 133, 135, Sch 11, para 2(1), (5), Sch 13, with effect from 13 October 2003, SI 2003/1725; Civil Aviation Act 1982, s 109, Sch 15, para 1, with effect from 27 August 1982.

Notices

196 Regulations respecting notices

(1) Any notice required or authorised to be served or given by this Act shall be in writing.

(2) Any notice required or authorised by this Act to be served on a lessee or mortgagor shall be sufficient, although only addressed to the lessee or mortgagor by that designation, without his name, or generally to the persons interested, without any name, and notwithstanding that any person to be affected by the notice is absent, under disability, unborn, or unascertained.

(3) Any notice required or authorised by this Act to be served shall be sufficiently served if it is left at the last-known place of abode or business in the United Kingdom of the lessee, lessor, mortgagee, mortgagor, or other person to be served, or, in case of a notice required or authorised to be served on a lessee or mortgagor, is affixed or left for him on the land or any house or building comprised in the lease or mortgage, or, in case of a mining lease, is left for the lessee at the office or counting-house of the mine.

(4) Any notice required or authorised by this Act to be served shall also be sufficiently served, if it is sent by post in a registered letter addressed to the lessee, lessor, mortgagee, mortgagor; or other person to be served, by name, at the aforesaid place of abode or business, office, or counting-house, and if that letter is not returned [by the postal operator (within the meaning of the Postal Services Act 2000) concerned] undelivered; and that service shall be deemed to be made at the time at which the registered letter would in the ordinary course be delivered.

(5) The provisions of this section shall extend to notices required to be served by any instrument affecting property executed or coming into operation after the commencement of this Act unless a contrary intention appears.

(6) This section does not apply to notices served in proceedings in the court.

Amendments – SI 2001/1149, art 3(1), Sch 1, para 7, with effect from 26 March 2001.

198 Registration under the Land Charges Act 1925, to be notice

(1) The registration of any instrument or matter [in any register kept under the Land Charges Act 1972 or any local land charges register] shall be deemed to constitute actual notice of such instrument or matter, and of the fact of such registration, to all persons and for all purposes connected with the land affected, as from the date of registration or other prescribed date and so long as the registration continues in force.

(2) This section operates without prejudice to the provisions of this Act respecting the making of further advances by a mortgagee, and applies only to instruments and matters required or authorised to be registered [in any such register].

Amendments – Local Land Charges Act 1975, s 17(2), Sch 1, with effect from 1 August 1977, SI 1977/984, art 2.

199 Restrictions on constructive notice

(1) A purchaser shall not be prejudicially affected by notice of –

    (i)   any instrument or matter capable of registration under the provisions of the Land Charges Act 1925, or any enactment which it replaces, which is void or not enforceable as against him under that Act or enactment, by reason of the non-registration thereof;

    (ii)   any other instrument or matter or any fact or thing unless –

        (a) it is within his own knowledge, or would have come to his knowledge if such inquiries and inspections had been made as ought reasonably to have been made by him; or

        (b) in the same transaction with respect to which a question of notice to the purchaser arises, it has come to the knowledge of his counsel, as such, or of his solicitor or other agent, as such, or would have come to the knowledge of his solicitor or other agent, as such, if such inquiries and inspections had been made as ought reasonably to have been made by the solicitor or other agent.

(2) Paragraph (ii) of the last subsection shall not exempt a purchaser from any liability under, or any obligation to perform or observe, any covenant, condition, provision, or restriction contained in any instrument under which his title is derived, mediately or immediately; and such liability or obligation may be enforced in the same manner and to the same extent as if that paragraph had not been enacted.

(3) A purchaser shall not by reason of anything in this section be affected by notice in any case where he would not have been so affected if this section had not been enacted.

(4) This section applies to purchases made either before or after the commencement of this Act.

A1.3   Land Registration Act 2002

11 Freehold estates

(1) This section is concerned with the registration of a person under this Chapter as the proprietor of a freehold estate.

(2) Registration with absolute title has the effect described in subsections (3) to (5).

(3) The estate is vested in the proprietor together with all interests subsisting for the benefit of the estate.

(4) The estate is vested in the proprietor subject only to the following interests affecting the estate at the time of registration –

    (a)   interests which are the subject of an entry in the register in relation to the estate,

    (b)   unregistered interests which fall within any of the paragraphs of Schedule 1, and

    (c)   interests acquired under the Limitation Act 1980 (c 58) of which the proprietor has notice.

(5) If the proprietor is not entitled to the estate for his own benefit, or not entitled solely for his own benefit, then, as between himself and the persons beneficially entitled to the estate, the estate is vested in him subject to such of their interests as he has notice of.

(6) Registration with qualified title has the same effect as registration with absolute title, except that it does not affect the enforcement of any estate, right or interest which appears from the register to be excepted from the effect of registration.

(7) Registration with possessory title has the same effect as registration with absolute title, except that it does not affect the enforcement of any estate, right or interest adverse to, or in derogation of, the proprietor's title subsisting at the time of registration or then capable of arising.

PART 3
DISPOSITION OF REGISTERED LAND

Effect of dispositions on priority

28   Basic rule

(1) Except as provided by sections 29 and 30, the priority of an interest affecting a registered estate or charge is not affected by a disposition of the estate or charge.

(2) It makes no difference for the purposes of this section whether the interest or disposition is registered.

29   Effect of registered dispositions: estates

(1) If a registrable disposition of a registered estate is made for valuable consideration, completion of the disposition by registration has the effect of postponing to the interest under the disposition any interest affecting the estate immediately before the disposition whose priority is not protected at the time of registration.

(2) For the purposes of subsection (1), the priority of an interest is protected –

    (a)   in any case, if the interest –
        (i) is a registered charge or the subject of a notice in the register,
        (ii) falls within any of the paragraphs of Schedule 3, or
        (iii) appears from the register to be excepted from the effect of registration, and
    (b)   in the case of a disposition of a leasehold estate, if the burden of the interest is incident to the estate.

(3) Subsection (2)(a)(ii) does not apply to an interest which has been the subject of a notice in the register at any time since the coming into force of this section.

(4) Where the grant of a leasehold estate in land out of a registered estate does not involve a registrable disposition, this section has effect as if –

    (a)   the grant involved such a disposition, and
    (b)   the disposition were registered at the time of the grant.

PART 4
NOTICES AND RESTRICTIONS

Notices

32 Nature and effect

(1) A notice is an entry in the register in respect of the burden of an interest affecting a registered estate or charge.

(2) The entry of a notice is to be made in relation to the registered estate or charge affected by the interest concerned.

(3) The fact that an interest is the subject of a notice does not necessarily mean that the interest is valid, but does mean that the priority of the interest, if valid, is protected for the purposes of sections 29 and 30.

34 Entry on application

(1) A person who claims to be entitled to the benefit of an interest affecting a registered estate or charge may, if the interest is not excluded by section 33, apply to the registrar for the entry in the register of a notice in respect of the interest.

(2) Subject to rules, an application under this section may be for –

    (a)   an agreed notice, or
    (b)   a unilateral notice.

(3) The registrar may only approve an application for an agreed notice if –

    (a)   the applicant is the relevant registered proprietor, or a person entitled to be registered as such proprietor,
    (b)   the relevant registered proprietor, or a person entitled to be registered as such proprietor, consents to the entry of the notice, or
    (c)   the registrar is satisfied as to the validity of the applicant's claim.

(4) In subsection (3), references to the relevant registered proprietor are to the proprietor of the registered estate or charge affected by the interest to which the application relates.

35 Unilateral notices

(1) If the registrar enters a notice in the register in pursuance of an application under section 34(2)(b) ('a unilateral notice'), he must give notice of the entry to –

    (a)   the proprietor of the registered estate or charge to which it relates, and
    (b)   such other persons as rules may provide.

(2) A unilateral notice must –

    (a)   indicate that it is such a notice, and
    (b)   identify who is the beneficiary of the notice.

(3) The person shown in the register as the beneficiary of a unilateral notice, or such other person as rules may provide, may apply to the registrar for the removal of the notice from the register.

36 Cancellation of unilateral notices

(1) A person may apply to the registrar for the cancellation of a unilateral notice if he is –

    (a)   the registered proprietor of the estate or charge to which the notice relates, or

    (b)   a person entitled to be registered as the proprietor of that estate or charge.

(2) Where an application is made under subsection (1), the registrar must give the beneficiary of the notice notice of the application and of the effect of subsection (3).

(3) If the beneficiary of the notice does not exercise his right to object to the application before the end of such period as rules may provide, the registrar must cancel the notice.

(4) In this section –

    'beneficiary', in relation to a unilateral notice, means the person shown in the register as the beneficiary of the notice, or such other person as rules may provide;

    'unilateral notice' means a notice entered in the register in pursuance of an application under section 34(2)(b).

37 Unregistered interests

(1) If it appears to the registrar that a registered estate is subject to an unregistered interest which –

    (a)   falls within any of the paragraphs of Schedule 1, and

    (b)   is not excluded by section 33,

he may enter a notice in the register in respect of the interest.

(2) The registrar must give notice of an entry under this section to such persons as rules may provide.

(4) If an order under this section includes a direction under subsection (3), the registrar must make such entry in the register as rules may provide.

(5) The court may make the exercise of its power under subsection (3) subject to such terms and conditions as it thinks fit.

PART 6
REGISTRATION: GENERAL

Alteration of register

65   Alteration of register

Schedule 4 (which makes provision about alteration of the register) has effect.

103   Indemnities

Schedule 8 (which makes provision for the payment of indemnities by the registrar) has effect.

132   General interpretation

(1) In this Act –

    'adjudicator' means the Adjudicator to Her Majesty's Land Registry;

    'caution against first registration' means a caution lodged under section 15;

'cautions register' means the register kept under section 19(1);

'charge' means any mortgage, charge or lien for securing money or money's worth;

'demesne land' means land belonging to Her Majesty in right of the Crown which is not held for an estate in fee simple absolute in possession;

'land' includes –

(a)   buildings and other structures,

(b)   land covered with water, and

(c)   mines and minerals, whether or not held with the surface;

'land registration rules' means any rules under this Act, other than rules under section 93, Part 11, section 121 or paragraph 1, 2 or 3 of Schedule 5;

'legal estate' has the same meaning as in the Law of Property Act 1925;

'legal mortgage' has the same meaning as in the Law of Property Act 1925;

'mines and minerals' includes any strata or seam of minerals or substances in or under any land, and powers of working and getting any such minerals or substances;

'registrar' means the Chief Land Registrar;

'register' means the register of title, except in the context of cautions against first registration;

'registered' means entered in the register;

'registered charge' means a charge the title to which is entered in the register;

'registered estate' means a legal estate the title to which is entered in the register, other than a registered charge;

'registered land' means a registered estate or registered charge;

'registrable disposition' means a disposition which is required to be completed by registration under section 27;

'requirement of registration' means the requirement of registration under section 4;

'sub-charge' means a charge under section 23(2)(b);

'term of years absolute' has the same meaning as in the Law of Property Act 1925;

'valuable consideration' does not include marriage consideration or a nominal consideration in money.

Schedules

Schedule 1

Unregistered Interests Which Override First Registration

Sections 11 and 12

Leasehold estates in land

1   A leasehold estate in land granted for a term not exceeding seven years from the date of the grant, except for a lease the grant of which falls within section 4(1)(d), (e) or (f).

Interests of persons in actual occupation

2   An interest belonging to a person in actual occupation, so far as relating to land of which he is in actual occupation, except for an interest under a settlement under the Settled Land Act 1925.

Easements and profits a prendre
3   A legal easement or profit a prendre.

Customary and public rights
4   A customary right.

5   A public right.

Local land charges
6   A local land charge.

Mines and minerals
7   An interest in any coal or coal mine, the rights attached to any such interest and the rights of any person under section 38, 49 or 51 of the Coal Industry Act 1994.

8   In the case of land to which title was registered before 1898, rights to mines and minerals (and incidental rights) created before 1898.

9   In the case of land to which title was registered between 1898 and 1925 inclusive, rights to mines and minerals (and incidental rights) created before the date of registration of the title.

Miscellaneous
10 A franchise.

11 A manorial right.

12 A right to rent which was reserved to the Crown on the granting of any freehold estate (whether or not the right is still vested in the Crown).

13 A non-statutory right in respect of an embankment or sea or river wall.

14 A right to payment in lieu of tithe. …

[15 A right acquired under the Limitation Act 1980 before the coming into force of this Schedule.]

[16 A right in respect of the repair of a church chancel.]

Prospective amendment: Paragraphs in italics prospectively repealed by Land Registration Act 2002, Land Registration Act 2002 (Commencement No 4) Order 2003, SI 2003/1725).

Amendments: Paragraph inserted: Land Registration Act 2002, s 134(2), Sch 12, para 7, with effect from 13 October 2003 to 13 October 2006 (Land Registration Act 2002, s 134(2), Sch 12, para 7, Land Registration Act 2002 (Commencement No 4) Order 2003, SI 2003/1725); Paragraph inserted: Land Registration Act 2002 (Transitional Provisions) (No 2) Order 2003, SI 2003/2431, with effect from 13 October 2003 to 13 October 2013 (Land Registration Act 2002 (Commencement No 4) Order 2003, SI 2003/1725, Land Registration Act 2002 (Transitional Provisions) (No 2) Order 2003, SI 2003/2431).

Schedule 3

Unregistered Interests Which Override Registered Dispositions

Sections 29 and 30

Leasehold estates in land
1   A leasehold estate in land granted for a term not exceeding seven years from the date of the grant, except for –

(a)   a lease the grant of which falls within section 4(1)(d), (e) or (f);
(b)   a lease the grant of which constitutes a registrable disposition.

Interests of persons in actual occupation

2   An interest belonging at the time of the disposition to a person in actual occupation, so far as relating to land of which he is in actual occupation, except for –

  (a)   an interest under a settlement under the Settled Land Act 1925;
  (b)   an interest of a person of whom inquiry was made before the disposition and who failed to disclose the right when he could reasonably have been expected to do so;
  (c)   an interest –
      (i)   which belongs to a person whose occupation would not have been obvious on a reasonably careful inspection of the land at the time of the disposition, and
      (ii) of which the person to whom the disposition is made does not have actual knowledge at that time;
  (d)   a leasehold estate in land granted to take effect in possession after the end of the period of three months beginning with the date of the grant and which has not taken effect in possession at the time of the disposition.

[2A—(1) An interest which, immediately before the coming into force of this Schedule, was an overriding interest under section 70(1)(g) of the Land Registration Act 1925 by virtue of a person's receipt of rents and profits, except for an interest of a person of whom inquiry was made before the disposition and who failed to disclose the right when he could reasonably have been expected to do so.

(2) Sub-paragraph (1) does not apply to an interest if at any time since the coming into force of this Schedule it has been an interest which, had the Land Registration Act 1925 (c 21) continued in force, would not have been an overriding interest under section 70(1)(g) of that Act by virtue of a person's receipt of rents and profits.]

Amendments: Paragraph inserted: Land Registration Act 2002, s 134(2), Sch 12, para 8, with effect from 13 October 2003 (Land Registration Act 2002, Sch 12, para 8, Land Registration Act 2002 (Commencement No 4) Order 2003, SI 2003/1725).

Easements and profits a prendre

3—(1) A legal easement or profit a prendre, except for an easement, or a profit a prendre which is not registered under the Commons Registration Act 1965 (c 64), which at the time of the disposition –

  (a)   is not within the actual knowledge of the person to whom the disposition is made, and
  (b)   would not have been obvious on a reasonably careful inspection of the land over which the easement or profit is exercisable.

(2) The exception in sub-paragraph (1) does not apply if the person entitled to the easement or profit proves that it has been exercised in the period of one year ending with the day of the disposition.[1]

Customary and public rights

4   A customary right.

5   A public right.

Local land charges

6   A local land charge.

---

[1]   Words in italics not in force until 13 October 2006: Land Registration Act 2002, s 134(2), Sch 12, para 10.

Mines and minerals

7   An interest in any coal or coal mine, the rights attached to any such interest and the rights of any person under sections 38, 49 or 51 of the Coal Industry Act 1994.

8   In the case of land to which title was registered before 1898, rights to mines and minerals (and incidental rights) created before 1898.

9   In the case of land to which title was registered between 1898 and 1925 inclusive, rights to mines and minerals (and incidental rights) created before the date of registration of the title.

Miscellaneous

10   A franchise.

11   A manorial right.

12   A right to rent which was reserved to the Crown on the granting of any freehold estate (whether or not the right is still vested in the Crown).

13   A non-statutory right in respect of an embankment or sea or river wall.

14   A right to payment in lieu of tithe. ...

[15 A right under paragraph 18(1) of Schedule 12.]

[16 A right in respect of the repair of a church chancel.]

Prospective amendments: Paragraphs in italics prospectively repealed by Land Registration Act 2002, s 117(1), with effect from 13 October 2013 (Land Registration Act 2002, s 117(1), Land Registration Act 2002 (Commencement No 4) Order 2003, SI 2003/1725).

Amendments: Paragraph inserted: Land Registration Act 2002, 134(2), Sch 12, para 11, with effect from 13 October 2003 (Land Registration Act 2002, Sch 12, para 11, Land Registration Act 2002 (Commencement No 4) Order 2003, SI 2003/1725); Paragraph inserted: Land Registration Act 2002 (Transitional Provisions) (No 2) Order 2003, SI 2003/2431, with effect from 13 October 2003 to 13 October 2013 (Land Registration Act 2002 (Commencement No 4) Order 2003, SI 2003/1725, Land Registration Act 2002 (Transitional Provisions) (No 2) Order 2003, SI 2003/2431).

Schedule 4

Alteration of the Register

Section 65

Introductory

1   In this Schedule, references to rectification, in relation to alteration of the register, are to alteration which –

(a)   involves the correction of a mistake, and
(b)   prejudicially affects the title of a registered proprietor.

Alteration pursuant to a court order

2—(1) The court may make an order for alteration of the register for the purpose of –

(a)   correcting a mistake,
(b)   bringing the register up to date, or
(c)   giving effect to any estate, right or interest excepted from the effect of registration.

(2) An order under this paragraph has effect when served on the registrar to impose a duty on him to give effect to it.

3—(1) This paragraph applies to the power under paragraph 2, so far as relating to rectification.

(2) If alteration affects the title of the proprietor of a registered estate in land, no order may be made under paragraph 2 without the proprietor's consent in relation to land in his possession unless –

    (a)   he has by fraud or lack of proper care caused or substantially contributed to the mistake, or

    (b)   it would for any other reason be unjust for the alteration not to be made.

(3) If in any proceedings the court has power to make an order under paragraph 2, it must do so, unless there are exceptional circumstances which justify its not doing so.

(4) In sub-paragraph (2), the reference to the title of the proprietor of a registered estate in land includes his title to any registered estate which subsists for the benefit of the estate in land.

4   Rules may –

    (a) make provision about the circumstances in which there is a duty to exercise the power under paragraph 2, so far as not relating to rectification;

    (b) make provision about the form of an order under paragraph 2;

    (c) make provision about service of such an order.

Alteration otherwise than pursuant to a court order

5   The registrar may alter the register for the purpose of –

    (a)   correcting a mistake,

    (b)   bringing the register up to date,

    (c)   giving effect to any estate, right or interest excepted from the effect of registration, or

    (d)   removing a superfluous entry.

6—(1) This paragraph applies to the power under paragraph 5, so far as relating to rectification.

(2) No alteration affecting the title of the proprietor of a registered estate in land may be made under paragraph 5 without the proprietor's consent in relation to land in his possession unless –

    (a)   he has by fraud or lack of proper care caused or substantially contributed to the mistake, or

    (b)   it would for any other reason be unjust for the alteration not to be made.

(3) If on an application for alteration under paragraph 5 the registrar has power to make the alteration, the application must be approved, unless there are exceptional circumstances which justify not making the alteration.

(4) In sub-paragraph (2), the reference to the title of the proprietor of a registered estate in land includes his title to any registered estate which subsists for the benefit of the estate in land.

7   Rules may –

    (a)   make provision about the circumstances in which there is a duty to exercise the power under paragraph 5, so far as not relating to rectification;

    (b)   make provision about how the register is to be altered in exercise of that power;

    (c)   make provision about applications for alteration under that paragraph, including provision requiring the making of such applications;

(d)   make provision about procedure in relation to the exercise of that power, whether on application or otherwise.

Rectification and derivative interests

8   The powers under this Schedule to alter the register, so far as relating to rectification, extend to changing for the future the priority of any interest affecting the registered estate or charge concerned.

Costs in non-rectification cases

9—(1) If the register is altered under this Schedule in a case not involving rectification, the registrar may pay such amount as he thinks fit in respect of any costs or expenses reasonably incurred by a person in connection with the alteration which have been incurred with the consent of the registrar.

(2) The registrar may make a payment under sub-paragraph (1) notwithstanding the absence of consent if –

(a)   it appears to him –
    (i) that the costs or expenses had to be incurred urgently, and
    (ii) that it was not reasonably practicable to apply for his consent, or
(b)   he has subsequently approved the incurring of the costs or expenses.

Schedule 8 – Indemnities

Section 103

Entitlement

1—(1) A person is entitled to be indemnified by the registrar if he suffers loss by reason of –

(a)   rectification of the register,
(b)   a mistake whose correction would involve rectification of the register,
(c)   a mistake in an official search,
(d)   a mistake in an official copy,
(e)   a mistake in a document kept by the registrar which is not an original and is referred to in the register,
(f)   the loss or destruction of a document lodged at the registry for inspection or safe custody,
(g)   a mistake in the cautions register, or
(h)   failure by the registrar to perform his duty under section 50.

(2) For the purposes of sub-paragraph (1)(a) –

(a)   any person who suffers loss by reason of the change of title under section 62 is to be regarded as having suffered loss by reason of rectification of the register, and
(b)   the proprietor of a registered estate or charge claiming in good faith under a forged disposition is, where the register is rectified, to be regarded as having suffered loss by reason of such rectification as if the disposition had not been forged.

(3) No indemnity under sub-paragraph (1)(b) is payable until a decision has been made about whether to alter the register for the purpose of correcting the mistake; and the loss suffered by reason of the mistake is to be determined in the light of that decision.

Mines and minerals

2   No indemnity is payable under this Schedule on account of –

(a)   any mines or minerals, or

(b)   the existence of any right to work or get mines or minerals,

unless it is noted in the register that the title to the registered estate concerned includes the mines or minerals.

Costs

3—(1) In respect of loss consisting of costs or expenses incurred by the claimant in relation to the matter, an indemnity under this Schedule is payable only on account of costs or expenses reasonably incurred by the claimant with the consent of the registrar.

(2) The requirement of consent does not apply where –

(a)   the costs or expenses must be incurred by the claimant urgently, and

(b)   it is not reasonably practicable to apply for the registrar's consent.

(3) If the registrar approves the incurring of costs or expenses after they have been incurred, they shall be treated for the purposes of this paragraph as having been incurred with his consent.

4—(1) If no indemnity is payable to a claimant under this Schedule, the registrar may pay such amount as he thinks fit in respect of any costs or expenses reasonably incurred by the claimant in connection with the claim which have been incurred with the consent of the registrar.

(2) The registrar may make a payment under sub-paragraph (1) notwithstanding the absence of consent if –

(a)   it appears to him –
      (i)   that the costs or expenses had to be incurred urgently, and
      (ii) that it was not reasonably practicable to apply for his consent, or

(b)   he has subsequently approved the incurring of the costs or expenses.

Claimant's fraud or lack of care

5—(1) No indemnity is payable under this Schedule on account of any loss suffered by a claimant –

(a)   wholly or partly as a result of his own fraud, or

(b)   wholly as a result of his own lack of proper care.

(2) Where any loss is suffered by a claimant partly as a result of his own lack of proper care, any indemnity payable to him is to be reduced to such extent as is fair having regard to his share in the responsibility for the loss.

(3) For the purposes of this paragraph any fraud or lack of care on the part of a person from whom the claimant derives title (otherwise than under a disposition for valuable consideration which is registered or protected by an entry in the register) is to be treated as if it were fraud or lack of care on the part of the claimant.

Valuation of estates etc

6   Where an indemnity is payable in respect of the loss of an estate, interest or charge, the value of the estate, interest or charge for the purposes of the indemnity is to be regarded as not exceeding –

(a)   in the case of an indemnity under paragraph 1(1)(a), its value immediately before rectification of the register (but as if there were to be no rectification), and

(b)   in the case of an indemnity under paragraph 1(1)(b), its value at the time when the mistake which caused the loss was made.

Determination of indemnity by court

7—(1) A person may apply to the court for the determination of any question as to –

    (a)   whether he is entitled to an indemnity under this Schedule, or

    (b)   the amount of such an indemnity.

(2) Paragraph 3(1) does not apply to the costs of an application to the court under this paragraph or of any legal proceedings arising out of such an application.

Time limits

8   For the purposes of the Limitation Act 1980 –

    (a)   a liability to pay an indemnity under this Schedule is a simple contract debt, and

    (b)   the cause of action arises at the time when the claimant knows, or but for his own default might have known, of the existence of his claim.

Interest

9   Rules may make provision about the payment of interest on an indemnity under this Schedule, including –

    (a)   the circumstances in which interest is payable, and

    (b)   the periods for and rates at which it is payable.

Recovery of indemnity by registrar

10—(1) Where an indemnity under this Schedule is paid to a claimant in respect of any loss, the registrar is entitled (without prejudice to any other rights he may have) –

    (a)   to recover the amount paid from any person who caused or substantially contributed to the loss by his fraud, or

    (b)   for the purpose of recovering the amount paid, to enforce the rights of action referred to in sub-paragraph (2).

(2) Those rights of action are –

    (a)   any right of action (of whatever nature and however arising) which the claimant would have been entitled to enforce had the indemnity not been paid, and

    (b)   where the register has been rectified, any right of action (of whatever nature and however arising) which the person in whose favour the register has been rectified would have been entitled to enforce had it not been rectified.

(3) References in this paragraph to an indemnity include interest paid on an indemnity under rules under paragraph 9.

Interpretation

11—(1) For the purposes of this Schedule, references to a mistake in something include anything mistakenly omitted from it as well as anything mistakenly included in it.

    (2) In this Schedule, references to rectification of the register are to alteration of the register which –

    (a)   involves the correction of a mistake, and

    (b)   prejudicially affects the title of a registered proprietor.

A1.4   Land Registration Rules 2003 (SI 2003/1417)

35 First registration – entry of burdens

(1) On first registration the registrar must enter a notice in the register of the burden of any interest which appears from his examination of the title to affect the registered estate.

(2) This rule does not apply to –

(a)   an interest that under section 33 or 90(4) of the Act cannot be protected by notice,

(b)   a public right,

(c)   a local land charge,

(d)   an interest which appears to the registrar to be of a trivial or obvious character, or the entry of a notice in respect of which would be likely to cause confusion or inconvenience.

Covenants

64 Positive covenants

(1) The registrar may make an appropriate entry in the proprietorship register of any positive covenant that relates to a registered estate given by the proprietor or any previous proprietor of that estate.

(2) Any entry made under paragraph (1) must, where practicable, refer to the instrument that contains the covenant.

(3) If it appears to the registrar that a covenant referred to in an entry made under paragraph (1) does not bind the current proprietor of the registered estate, he must remove the entry.

65 Indemnity covenants

(1) The registrar may make an appropriate entry in the proprietorship register of an indemnity covenant given by the proprietor of a registered estate in respect of any restrictive covenant or other matter that affects that estate or in respect of a positive covenant that relates to that estate.

(2) Any entry made under paragraph (1) must, where practicable, refer to the instrument that contains the indemnity covenant.

(3) If it appears to the registrar that a covenant referred to in an entry made under paragraph (1) does not bind the current proprietor of the registered estate, he must remove the entry.

81 Application for an agreed notice

(1) Subject to paragraph (2), an application for the entry in the register of an agreed notice (including an agreed notice in respect of any variation of an interest protected by a notice) must be –

(a)   made in Form AN1,

(b)   accompanied by the order or instrument (if any) giving rise to the interest claimed or, if there is no such order or instrument, such other details of the interest claimed as satisfy the registrar as to the nature of the applicant's claim, and

(c)   accompanied, where appropriate, by –

(i) the consent referred to in section 34(3)(b) of the Act, and, where appropriate, evidence to satisfy the registrar that the person applying for, or consenting to the entry of, the notice is entitled to be registered as the proprietor of the registered estate or charge affected by the interest to which the application relates, or

(ii) evidence to satisfy the registrar as to the validity of the applicant's claim.

(2) Paragraph (1) does not apply to an application for the entry of a matrimonial home rights notice made under rule 82.

83 Application for entry of a unilateral notice

An application for the entry in the register of a unilateral notice must be in Form UN1.

84 Entry of a notice in the register

(1) A notice under section 32 of the Act must be entered in the charges register of the registered title affected.

(2) The entry must identify the registered estate or registered charge affected and, where the interest protected by the notice only affects part of the registered estate in a registered title, it must contain sufficient details, by reference to a plan or otherwise, to identify clearly that part.

(3) In the case of a notice (other than a unilateral notice), the entry must give details of the interest protected.

(4) In the case of a notice (other than a unilateral notice) of a variation of an interest protected by a notice, the entry must give details of the variation.

(5) In the case of a unilateral notice, the entry must give such details of the interest protected as the registrar considers appropriate.

85 Removal of a unilateral notice

(1) An application for the removal of a unilateral notice from the register under section 35(3) of the Act must be in Form UN2.

(2) The personal representative or trustee in bankruptcy of the person shown in the register as the beneficiary of a unilateral notice may apply under section 35(3) of the Act; and if he does he must provide evidence to satisfy the registrar as to his appointment as personal representative or trustee in bankruptcy.

(3) If the registrar is satisfied that the application is in order he must remove the notice.

86 Cancellation of a unilateral notice

(1) An application to cancel a unilateral notice under section 36 of the Act must be made in Form UN4.

(2) An application made under section 36(1)(b) of the Act must be accompanied by –

(a) evidence to satisfy the registrar of the applicant's entitlement to be registered as the proprietor of the estate or charge to which the unilateral notice the subject of the application relates, or

(b) a conveyancer's certificate that the conveyancer is satisfied that the applicant is entitled to be registered as the proprietor of the estate or charge to which the unilateral notice the subject of the application relates.

(3) The period referred to in section 36(3) of the Act is the period ending at 12 noon on the fifteenth business day after the date of issue of the notice or such longer period as the registrar may allow following a request under paragraph (4), provided that the longer period never exceeds a period ending at 12 noon on the thirtieth business day after the issue of the notice.

(4) The request referred to in paragraph (3) is one by the beneficiary to the registrar setting out why the longer period referred to in that paragraph should be allowed.

(5) If a request is received under paragraph (4) the registrar may, if he considers it appropriate, seek the views of the person who applied for cancellation and if after considering any such views and all other relevant matters he is satisfied that a longer period should be allowed he may allow such period (not exceeding a period ending at 12 noon on the thirtieth business day after the issue of the notice) as he considers appropriate, whether or not the period is the same as any period requested by the beneficiary.

(6) A request under paragraph (4) must be made before the period ending at 12 noon on the fifteenth business day after the date of issue of the notice under section 36(2) of the Act has expired.

(7) A person entitled to be registered as the beneficiary of a notice under rule 88 may object to an application under section 36(1) of the Act for cancellation of that notice and the reference to the beneficiary in section 36(3) includes such a person.

87 Cancellation of a notice (other than a unilateral notice or a matrimonial home rights notice)

(1) An application for the cancellation of a notice (other than a unilateral notice or a matrimonial home rights notice) must be in Form CN1 and be accompanied by evidence to satisfy the registrar of the determination of the interest.

(2) Where a person applies for cancellation of a notice in accordance with paragraph (1) and the registrar is satisfied that the interest protected by the notice has come to an end, he must cancel the notice or make an entry in the register that the interest so protected has come to an end.

(3) If the interest protected by the notice has only come to an end in part, the registrar must make an appropriate entry.

88 Registration of a new or additional beneficiary of a unilateral notice

(1) A person entitled to the benefit of an interest protected by a unilateral notice may apply to be entered in the register in place of, or in addition to, the registered beneficiary.

(2) An application under paragraph (1) must be –

(a)   in Form UN3, and
(b)   accompanied by evidence to satisfy the registrar of the applicant's title to the interest protected by the unilateral notice.

(3) Subject to paragraph (4), if an application is made in accordance with paragraph (2) and the registrar is satisfied that the interest protected by the unilateral notice is vested –

(a)   in the applicant, the registrar must enter the applicant in the register in place of the registered beneficiary, or
(b)   in the applicant and the registered beneficiary, the registrar must enter the applicant in addition to the registered beneficiary.

(4) Except where one of the circumstances specified in paragraph (5) applies, the registrar must serve notice of the application on the registered beneficiary before entering the applicant in the register.

(5) The registrar is not obliged to serve notice on the registered beneficiary if –

    (a)   the registered beneficiary signs Form UN3 or otherwise consents to the application, or

    (b)   the applicant is the registered beneficiary's personal representative and evidence of his title to act accompanies the application.

(6) In this rule, 'registered beneficiary' means the person shown in the register as the beneficiary of the notice at the time an application is made under paragraph (1).

PART 12
ALTERATIONS AND CORRECTIONS

126 Alteration under a court order – not rectification

(1) Subject to paragraphs (2) and (3), if in any proceedings the court decides that –

    (a)   there is a mistake in the register,
    (b)   the register is not up to date, or
    (c)   there is an estate, right or interest excepted from the effect of registration that should be given effect to,

it must make an order for alteration of the register under the power given by paragraph 2(1) of Schedule 4 to the Act.

(2) The court is not obliged to make an order if there are exceptional circumstances that justify not doing so.

(3) This rule does not apply to an alteration of the register that amounts to rectification.

127 Court order for alteration of the register – form and service

(1) An order for alteration of the register must state the title number of the title affected and the alteration that is to be made, and must direct the registrar to make the alteration.

(2) Service on the registrar of an order for alteration of the register must be made by making an application for the registrar to give effect to the order, accompanied by the order.

128 Alteration otherwise than pursuant to a court order – notice and enquiries

(1) Subject to paragraph (5), this rule applies where an application for alteration of the register has been made, or where the registrar is considering altering the register without an application having been made.

(2) The registrar must give notice of the proposed alteration to –

    (a)   the registered proprietor of any registered estate,
    (b)   the registered proprietor of any registered charge, and
    (c)   subject to paragraph (3), any person who appears to the registrar to be entitled to an interest protected by a notice,

where that estate, charge or interest would be affected by the proposed alteration, unless he is satisfied that such notice is unnecessary.

(3) The registrar is not obliged to give notice to a person referred to in paragraph (2)(c) if that person's name and his address for service under rule 198 are not set out in the individual register in which the notice is entered.

(4) The registrar may make such enquiries as he thinks fit.

(5) This rule does not apply to alteration of the register in the specific circumstances covered by any other rule.

129 Alteration otherwise than under a court order – evidence

Unless otherwise provided in these rules, an application for alteration of the register (otherwise than under a court order) must be supported by evidence to justify the alteration.

130 Correction of mistakes in an application or accompanying document

(1) This rule applies to any alteration made by the registrar for the purpose of correcting a mistake in any application or accompanying document.

(2) The alteration will have effect as if made by the applicant or other interested party or parties –

(a)   in the case of a mistake of a clerical or like nature, in all circumstances,

(b)   in the case of any other mistake, only if the applicant and every other interested party has requested, or consented to, the alteration.

195   Payment of interest on an indemnity

(1) Subject to paragraph (4), interest is payable on the amount of any indemnity paid under Schedule 8 to the Act for the period specified in paragraph (2) at the rate specified in paragraph (3).

(2) Interest is payable –

(a)   where paragraph 1(1)(a) of Schedule 8 applies, from the date of the rectification to the date of payment,

(b)   where any other sub-paragraph of paragraph 1(1) of Schedule 8 applies, from the date the loss is suffered by reason of the relevant mistake, loss, destruction or failure to the date of payment,

but excluding any period or periods where the registrar or the court is satisfied that the claimant has not taken reasonable steps to pursue with due diligence the claim for indemnity or, where relevant, the application for rectification.

(3) Interest is payable at the applicable rate or rates set for court judgment debts.

(4) Interest is payable in respect of an indemnity on account of costs or expenses within paragraph 3 of Schedule 8 from the date when the claimant pays them to the date of payment.

(5) A reference in this rule to a period from a date to the date of payment excludes the former date but includes the latter date.

Appendix 2 – Statutory Material (extracts)

A2.1   Town and Country Planning Act 1990

106 Planning obligations

[(1) Any person interested in land in the area of a local planning authority may, by agreement or otherwise, enter into an obligation (referred to in this section and sections 106A and 106B as 'a planning obligation'), enforceable to the extent mentioned in subsection (3) –

(a)   restricting the development or use of the land in any specified way;

(b)   requiring specified operations or activities to be carried out in, on, under or over the land;

(c)   requiring the land to be used in any specified way; or

(d)   requiring a sum or sums to be paid to the authority on a specified date or dates or periodically.

(2) A planning obligation may –

(a)   be unconditional or subject to conditions;

(b)   impose any restriction or requirement mentioned in subsection (1)(a) to (c) either indefinitely or for such period or periods as may be specified; and

(c)   if it requires a sum or sums to be paid, require the payment of a specified amount or an amount determined in accordance with the instrument by which the obligation is entered into and, if it requires the payment of periodical sums, require them to be paid indefinitely or for a specified period.

(3) Subject to subsection (4) a planning obligation is enforceable by the authority identified in accordance with subsection (9)(d) –

(a)   against the person entering into the obligation; and

(b)   against any person deriving a title from that person.

(4) The instrument by which a planning obligation is entered into may provide that a person shall not be bound by the obligation in respect of any period during which he no longer has an interest in the land.

(5) A restriction or requirement imposed under a planning obligation is enforceable by injunction.

(6) Without prejudice to subsection (5), if there is a breach of a requirement in a planning obligation to carry out any operations in, on, under or over the land to which the obligation relates, the authority by whom the obligation is enforceable may –

(a)   enter the land and carry out the operations; and

(b)   recover from the person or persons against whom the obligation is enforceable any expenses reasonably incurred by them in doing so.

(7) Before an authority exercise their power under subsection (6)(a) they shall give not less than 21 days' notice of their intention to do so to any person against whom the planning obligation is enforceable.

(8) Any person who wilfully obstructs a person acting in the exercise of a power under subsection (6)(a) shall be guilty of an offence and liable on summary conviction to a fine not exceeding level 3 on the standard scale.

(9) A planning obligation may not be entered into except by an instrument executed as a deed which –

    (a)   states that the obligation is a planning obligation for the purposes of this section;

    (b)   identifies the land in which the person entering into the obligation is interested;

    (c)   identifies the person entering into the obligation and states what his interest in the land is; and

    (d)   identifies the local planning authority by whom the obligation is enforceable.

(10) A copy of any such instrument shall be given to the authority so identified.

(11) A planning obligation shall be a local land charge and for the purposes of the Local Land Charges Act 1975 the authority by whom the obligation is enforceable shall be treated as the originating authority as respects such a charge.

(12) Regulations may provide for the charging on the land of –

    (a)   any sum or sums required to be paid under a planning obligation; and

    (b)   any expenses recoverable by a local planning authority under subsection (6)(b),

and this section and sections 106A and 106B shall have effect subject to any such regulations.

(13) In this section 'specified' means specified in the instrument by which the planning obligation is entered into and in this section and section 106A 'land' has the same meaning as in the Local Land Charges Act 1975.]

Amendments – Planning and Compensation Act 1991, s 12(1), with effect from 25 October 1991, this section to be repealed by the Planning and Compulsory Purchase Act 2004, ss 118(1), 120, Sched 6, paras 1, 5, Sch 9, enforcement date pending at time of publication.

[106A   Modification and discharge of planning obligations]

[(1) A planning obligation may not be modified or discharged except –

    (a)   by agreement between the authority by whom the obligation is enforceable and the person or persons against whom the obligation is enforceable; or

    (b)   in accordance with this section and section 106B.

(2) An agreement falling within subsection (1)(a) shall not be entered into except by an instrument executed as a deed.

(3) A person against whom a planning obligation is enforceable may, at any time after the expiry of the relevant period, apply to the local planning authority by whom the obligation is enforceable for the obligation –

    (a)   to have effect subject to such modifications as may be specified in the application; or

    (b)   to be discharged.

(4) In subsection (3) 'the relevant period' means –

    (a)   such period as may be prescribed; or

    (b)   if no period is prescribed, the period of five years beginning with the date on which the obligation is entered into.

(5) An application under subsection (3) for the modification of a planning obligation may not specify a modification imposing an obligation on any other person against whom the obligation is enforceable.

(6) Where an application is made to an authority under subsection (3), the authority may determine –

(a)   that the planning obligation shall continue to have effect without modification;
(b)   if the obligation no longer serves a useful purpose, that it shall be discharged; or
(c)   if the obligation continues to serve a useful purpose, but would serve that purpose equally well if it had effect subject to the modifications specified in the application, that it shall have effect subject to those modifications.

(7) The authority shall give notice of their determination to the applicant within such period as may be prescribed.

(8) Where an authority determine that a planning obligation shall have effect subject to modifications specified in the application, the obligation as modified shall be enforceable as if it had been entered into on the date on which notice of the determination was given to the applicant.

(9) Regulations may make provision with respect to –

(a)   the form and content of applications under subsection (3);
(b)   the publication of notices of such applications;
(c)   the procedures for considering any representations made with respect to such applications; and
(d)   the notices to be given to applicants of determinations under subsection (6).

(10) Section 84 of the Law of Property Act 1925 (power to discharge or modify restrictive covenants affecting land) does not apply to a planning obligation.]

Amendments – Planning and Compensation Act 1991, s 12(1), with effect from 25 October 1991, this section to be repealed by the Planning and Compulsory Purchase Act 2004, ss 118(1), 120, Sched 6, paras 1, 5, Sch 9, enforcement date pending at time of publication.

[106B Appeals]

[(1) Where a local planning authority –

(a)   fail to give notice as mentioned in section 106A(7); or
(b)   determine that a planning obligation shall continue to have effect without modification,

the applicant may appeal to the Secretary of State.

(2) For the purposes of an appeal under subsection (1)(a), it shall be assumed that the authority have determined that the planning obligation shall continue to have effect without modification.

(3) An appeal under this section shall be made by notice served within such period and in such manner as may be prescribed.

(4) Subsections (6) to (9) of section 106A apply in relation to appeals to the Secretary of State under this section as they apply in relation to applications to authorities under that section.

(5) Before determining the appeal the Secretary of State shall, if either the applicant or the authority so wish, give each of them an opportunity of appearing before and being heard by a person appointed by the Secretary of State for the purpose.

(6) The determination of an appeal by the Secretary of State under this section shall be final.

(7) Schedule 6 applies to appeals under this section.]

Amendments – Planning and Compensation Act 1991, s 12(1), with effect from 25 October 1991, this section to be repealed by the Planning and Compulsory Purchase Act 2004, ss 118(1), 120, Sched 6, paras 1, 5, Sch 9, enforcement date pending at time of publication.

237 Power to override easements and other rights

(1) Subject to subsection (3), the erection, construction or carrying out, or maintenance of any building or work on land which has been acquired or appropriated by a local authority for planning purposes (whether done by the local authority or by a person deriving title under them) is authorised by virtue of this section if it is done in accordance with planning permission, notwithstanding that it involves –

    (a)   interference with an interest or right to which this section applies, or

    (b)   a breach of a restriction as to the user of land arising by virtue of a contract.

(2) Subject to subsection (3), the interests and rights to which this section applies are any easement, liberty, privilege, right or advantage annexed to land and adversely affecting other land, including any natural right to support.

(3) Nothing in this section shall authorise interference with any right of way or right of laying down, erecting, continuing or maintaining apparatus on, under or over land which is –

    (a)   a right vested in or belonging to statutory undertakers for the purpose of the carrying on of their undertaking, or

    (b)   a right conferred by or in accordance with the [electronic communications code]on the operator of [an electronic communications code network]

(4) In respect of any interference or breach in pursuance of subsection (1), compensation –

    (a)   shall be payable under section 63 or 68 of the Lands Clauses Consolidation Act 1845 or under section 7 or 10 of the Compulsory Purchase Act 1965, and

    (b)   shall be assessed in the same manner and subject to the same rules as in the case of other compensation under those sections in respect of injurious affection where –

        (i)   the compensation is to be estimated in connection with a purchase under those Acts, or

        (ii)   the injury arises from the execution of works on land acquired under those Acts.

(5) Where a person deriving title under the local authority by whom the land in question was acquired or appropriated –

    (a)   is liable to pay compensation by virtue of subsection (4), and

    (b)   fails to discharge that liability,

the liability shall be enforceable against the local authority.

(6) Nothing in subsection (5) shall be construed as affecting any agreement between the local authority and any other person for indemnifying the local authority against any liability under that subsection.

(7) Nothing in this section shall be construed as authorising any act or omission on the part of any person which is actionable at the suit of any person on any grounds other than such an interference or breach as is mentioned in subsection (1).

Amendments – Communications Act 2003, s 406(1), Sch 17, para 103(1)(b), (2)(a), (b), with effect from 25 July 2003.

A2.2   Local Government Act 1972

122 Appropriation of land by principal councils

(1) Subject to the following provisions of this section, a principal council may appropriate for any purpose for which the council are authorised by this or any other enactment to acquire land by agreement any land which belongs to the council and is no longer required for the purpose for which it is held immediately before the appropriation; but the appropriation of land by a council by virtue of this subsection shall be subject to the rights of other persons in, over or in respect of the land concerned.

(2) A principal council may not appropriate under subsection (1) above any land which they may be authorised to appropriate under [section 229 of the Town and Country Planning Act 1990] (land forming part of a common, etc) unless—

(a)   the total of the land appropriated in any particular common, ... or fuel or field garden allotment (giving those expressions the same meanings as in [the said section 229]) does not in the aggregate exceed 250 square yards, and

(b)   before appropriating the land they cause notice of their intention to do so, specifying the land in question, to be advertised in two consecutive weeks in a newspaper circulating in the area in which the land is situated, and consider any objections to the proposed appropriation which may be made to them, ...

[(2A)   A principal council may not appropriate under subsection (1) above any land consisting or forming part of an open space unless before appropriating the land they cause notice of their intention to do so, specifying the land in question, to be advertised in two consecutive weeks in a newspaper circulating in the area in which the land is situated, and consider any objections to the proposed appropriation which may be made to them.

(2B)   Where land appropriated by virtue of subsection (2A) above is held—

(a)   for the purposes of section 164 of the Public Health Act 1875 (pleasure grounds); or

(b)   in accordance with section 10 of the Open Spaces Act 1906 (duty of local authority to maintain open spaces and burial grounds),

the land shall by virtue of the appropriation be freed from any trust arising solely by virtue of its being land held in trust for enjoyment by the public in accordance with the said section 164 or, as the case may be, the said section 10.]

(3) ...

(4) Where land has been acquired under this Act or any other enactment or any statutory order incorporating the Lands Clauses Acts and is subsequently appropriated under this section, any work executed on the land after the appropriation has been effected shall be treated for the purposes of section 68 of the Lands Clauses Consolidation Act 1845 and section 10 of the Compulsory Purchase Act 1965 as having been authorised by the enactment or statutory order under which the land was acquired.

(5), (6)   ...

Amendments: Sub-s (2): words omitted repealed by the Local Government, Planning and Land Act 1980, ss 118, 194, Sch 23, para 12(1), Sch 34, Part XIII; words in square brackets substituted by the Planning (Consequential Provisions) Act 1990, s 4, Sch 2, para 28(1); Sub-ss (2A), (2B): inserted by the Local Government, Planning and Land Act 1980, s 118, Sch 23, para 12(2); Sub-ss (3), (5), (6): repealed by the Local Government, Planning and Land Act 1980, ss 118, 194, Sch 23, para 13, Sch 34, Part XIII.

Modification: By virtue of the Environment Act 1995, s 65, Sch 8, para 1(1) (and subject to para 1(2) thereto) this section has effect as if a National Park authority were a principal council and the relevant Park were the authority's area.

A2.3   National Trust Act 1937

8 Power to enter into agreements restricting use of land

Where any person is willing to agree with the National Trust that any land or any part thereof shall so far as his interest in the land enables him to bind it be made subject either permanently or for a specified period to conditions restricting the planning development or use thereof in any manner the National Trust may if it thinks fit enter into an agreement with him or accept a covenant from him to that effect and shall have power to enforce such agreement or covenant against persons deriving title under him in the like manner and to the like extent as if the National Trust were possessed of or entitled to or interested in adjacent land and as if the agreement or covenant had been and had been expressed to be entered into for the benefit of that adjacent land.

Amendments – Statute Law (Repeals) Act 2004, Repealed, in relation to the Isle of Man, with effect from 22 July 2004.

A2.4   National Trust Act 1971

27 Restrictions for protection of Trust property

Section 84 of the Law of Property Act 1925 (which contains power to discharge or modify restrictive covenants affecting land) shall not apply to restrictions imposed (whether before or after the passing of this Act) for the purpose of –

(a)   preserving; or
(b)   protecting or augmenting the amenities of; or
(c)   securing the access to and enjoyment by the public of;

any property which is or becomes inalienable by or under section 21 (Certain property of Trust to be inalienable) of the Act of 1907 or by section 8 (Mansion and lands to be inalienable by National Trust) of the National Trust Act 1939.

A2.5   National Parks and Access to the Countryside Act 1949

16 Agreements with Nature Conservancy for establishment of nature reserves

(1) [The Nature Conservancy Council] may enter into an agreement with every owner, lessee and occupier of any land, being land as to which it appears to [the Nature Conservancy Council] expedient in the national interest that it should be managed as a nature reserve, for securing that it shall be so managed.

(2) Any such agreement may impose such restrictions as may be expedient for the purposes of the agreement on the exercise of rights over the land by the persons who can be bound by the agreement.

(3) Any such agreement –

(a)   may provide for the management of the land in such manner, the carrying out thereon of such work and the doing thereon of such other things as may be expedient for the purposes of the agreement;

(b)   may provide for any of the matters mentioned in the last foregoing paragraph being carried out, or for the cost thereof being defrayed, either by the said owner or other persons, or by [the Nature Conservancy Council], or partly, in one way and partly in another;

(c)   may contain such other provisions as to the making of payments by [the Nature Conservancy Council], and in particular for the payment by them of compensation for the effect of the restrictions mentioned in the last foregoing subsection, as may be specified in the agreement.

(4) Section two of the Forestry Act 1947 (which empowers tenants for life and other limited owners to enter into forestry dedication covenants) shall apply to any such agreement; and where section seventy-nine of the Law of Property Act 1925 (which provides that unless a contrary intention is expressed the burden of a covenant runs with the land) applies, subsections (2) and (3) of section one of the said Act of 1947 (which provide for enforcement against persons other than the covenantor) shall apply to any such restrictions as are mentioned in subsection (2) of this section, but with the substitution for references to the Forestry Commissioners of references to [the Nature Conservancy Council].

(5) The following provisions shall have effect in the application of this section to Scotland –

(a)   a limited owner of land shall have power to enter into agreements under this section relating to the land;

(b)   the Trusts (Scotland) Act 1921, shall have effect as if among the powers conferred on trustees by section four thereof (which relates to the general powers of trustees) there were included a power to enter into agreements under this section relating to the trust estate or any part thereof;

(c)   subsection (2) of section three of the Forestry Act 1947, shall apply to an agreement under this section to which an owner or limited owner of land or a trustee acting under the last foregoing paragraph is a party as it applies to a forestry dedication agreement, with the substitution for the reference to the Forestry Commissioners of a reference to [Scottish Natural Heritage];

(d)   the expression 'owner' includes any person empowered under this subsection to enter into agreements relating to land;

(e)   subsection (4) shall not apply.

Amendments—Nature Conservancy Council Act 1973, s 1(1)(b), (7), Sch 1, para 1, with effect from 25 July 1973, Natural Heritage (Scotland) Act 1991, s 4(6), Sch 2, para 1(3), with effect from 1 April 1992.

A2.6   Green Belt (London and Home Counties) Act 1938

22 Enforcement of Covenants

(1) Where the owner of Green Belt land or a parish council in whom Green Belt land is vested has either before or after the commencement of this Act entered into or by virtue of this Act become subject to any covenant with a local authority restrictive of the user of such land the local authority shall have power to enforce such covenant against persons deriving title under such owner or parish council in the like manner and to the like extent as if the local authority were possessed of adjacent land capable of being benefited by such covenant and as if such covenant had been expressed to be entered into for the benefit of such adjacent land.

(2) Section 84 (Power to discharge or modify restrictive covenants affecting land) of the Law of Property Act 1925 shall not apply to a restriction imposed by a deed or covenant

made or entered into for the purposes of and after the commencement of this Act or to any deed or covenant which was made or entered into before such commencement but which is expressed to be made in contemplation of the passing of this Act and in which it is provided that the said section shall not apply.

A2.7   City of London (Various Powers) Act 1960

33 Undertakings and agreements binding successive owners

(1) Every undertaking given by or to the Corporation to or by the owner of a legal estate in land and every agreement made between the Corporation and any such owner being an undertaking or agreement –

    (a)   given or made under seal either on the passing of plans or otherwise in connection with the land; and

    (b)   expressed to be given or made in pursuance of this section;

shall be binding not only upon the Corporation and any owner joining in the undertaking or agreement but also upon the successors in title of any owner so joining and any person claiming through or under them.

(2) Such an undertaking or agreement shall be treated as a local land charge for the purposes of the Land Charges Act 1925 as amended by the Law of Property (Amendment) Act 1926.

(3) Any person upon whom such an undertaking or agreement is binding shall be entitled to require from the Corporation a copy thereof.

A2.8   Land Powers (Defence) Act 1958

13   Acquisition of land for oil installations

The Minister of Power may acquire by agreement, or, subject to the provisions of Part I of the Second Schedule to this Act, may by order provide that Part II of that Schedule shall have effect for the purpose of the acquisition by him of—

    (a)   any land required for the construction of oil installations which in his opinion are essential for the defence of the realm;

    (b)   any land on or under which there are oil installations which, immediately before the passing of this Act, were government war works for the purposes of Part II of the Requisitioned Land and War Works Act 1945;

    (c)   any easement over or right restrictive of the user of any other land, being an easement or right which in the opinion of that Minister is essential to the full enjoyment of any land on or under which such an oil installation as is mentioned in either of the two foregoing paragraphs is to be or has been constructed.

A2.9   Leasehold Reform Act 1967

19 Retention of management powers for general benefit of neighbourhood

(1) Where, in the case of any area which is occupied directly or indirectly under tenancies held from one landlord (apart from property occupied by him or his licensees or for the time being unoccupied), the Minister on an application made within the two years beginning with the commencement of this Part of this Act grants a certificate that, in order to maintain adequate standards of appearance and amenity and regulate redevelopment in the area in the event of tenants acquiring the landlord's interest in their house and premises under this Part

of this Act, it is in the Minister's opinion likely to be in the general interest that the landlord should retain powers of management in respect of the house and premises or have rights against the house and premises in respect of the benefits arising from the exercise elsewhere of his powers of management, then the High Court may, on an application made within one year of the giving of the certificate, approve a scheme giving the landlord such powers and rights as are contemplated by this subsection.

For purposes of this section 'the Minister' means as regards areas within Wales and Monmouthshire the Secretary of State, and as regards other areas the Minister of Housing and Local Government.

(2) The Minister shall not give a certificate under this section unless he is satisfied that the applicant has, by advertisement or otherwise as may be required by the Minister, given adequate notice to persons interested, informing them of the application for a certificate and its purpose and inviting them to make representations to the Minister for or against the application within a time which appears to the Minister to be reasonable; and before giving a certificate the Minister shall consider any representations so made within that time, and if from those representations it appears to him that there is among the persons making them substantial opposition to the application, he shall afford to those opposing the application, and on the same occasion to the applicant and such (if any) as the Minister thinks fit of those in favour of the application, an opportunity to appear and be heard by a person appointed by the Minister for the purpose, and shall consider the report of that person.

(3) The Minister in considering whether to grant a certificate authorising a scheme for any area, and the High Court in considering whether to approve a scheme shall have regard primarily to the benefit likely to result from the scheme to the area as a whole (including houses likely to be acquired from the landlord under this Part of this Act), and the extent to which it is reasonable to impose, for the benefit of the area, obligations on tenants so acquiring their freeholds; but regard may also be had to the past development and present character of the area and to architectural or historical considerations, to neighbouring areas and to the circumstances generally.

(4) If, having regard to the matters mentioned in subsection (3) above, to the provision which it is practicable to make by a scheme, and to any change of circumstances since the giving of the certificate under subsection (1), the High Court think it proper so to do, then the High Court may be order –

(a) exclude from the scheme any part of the area certified under that subsection; or
(b) declare that no scheme can be approved for the area;

and before submitting for approval a scheme for an area so certified a person may, if he sees fit, apply to the High Court for general directions as to the matters proper to be included in the scheme and for a decision whether an order should be made under paragraph (a) or (b) above.

(5) Subject to subsections (3) and (4) above, on the submission of a scheme to the High Court, the High Court shall approve the scheme either as originally submitted or with any modifications proposed or agreed to by the applicant for the scheme, if the scheme (with those modifications, if any) appears to the court to be fair and practicable and not to give the landlord a degree of control out of proportion to that previously exercised by him or to that required for the purposes of the scheme; and the High Court shall not dismiss an application for the approval of a scheme, unless either –

(a) the Court makes an order under subsection (4)(b) above; or
(b) in the opinion of the Court the applicant is unwilling to agree to a suitable scheme or is not proceeding in the manner with due despatch.

(6) A scheme under this section may make different provision for different parts of the area, and shall include provision for terminating or varying all or any of the provisions of the scheme, or excluding part of the area, if a change of circumstances makes it appropriate, or for enabling it to be done by or with the approval of the High Court.

(7) Except as provided by the scheme, the operation of a scheme under this section shall not be affected by any disposition or devolution of the landlord's interest in the property within the area or part of that property; but the scheme –

    (a)   shall include provision for identifying the person who is for the purposes of the scheme to be treated as the landlord for the time being; and

    (b)   may include provision for transferring, or allowing the landlord for the time being to transfer, all or any of the powers and rights conferred by the scheme on the landlord for the time being to a local authority or other body, including a body constituted for the purpose.

In the following provisions of this section references to the landlord for the time being shall have effect, in relation to powers and rights transferred to a local authority or other body as contemplated by paragraph (b) above, as references to that authority or body.

(8) Without prejudice to any other provision of this section, a scheme under it may provide for all or any of the following matters –

    (a)   for regulating the redevelopment, use or appearance of property of which tenants have acquired the landlord's interest under this Part of this Act; and

    (b)   for empowering the landlord for the time being to carry out work for the maintenance or repair of any such property or carry out work to remedy a failure in respect of any such property co comply with the scheme, or for making the operation of any provisions of the scheme conditional on his doing so or on the provision or maintenance by him of services, facilities or amenities of any description; and

    (c)   for imposing on persons from time to time occupying or interested in any such property obligations in respect of maintenance or repair of the property or of property used or enjoyed by them in common with others, or in respect of cost incurred by the landlord for the time being on any matter referred to in this paragraph or in paragraph (b) above;

    (d)   for the inspection from time to time of any such property on behalf of the landlord for the time being, and for the recovery by him of sums due to him under the scheme in respect of any such property by means of a charge on the property;

and the landlord for the time being shall have, for the enforcement of any change imposed under the scheme, the same powers and remedies under the Law of Property Act 1925 and otherwise as if he were a mortgagee by deed having powers of sale and leasing and of appointing a receiver.

(9) A scheme under this section may extend to property in which the landlord's interest is disposed of otherwise than under this Part of this Act (whether residential property or not), so as to make that property, or allow it to be made, subject to any such provision as is or might be made by the scheme for property in which tenants acquire the landlord's interest under this Part of this Act.

(10) A certificate given or scheme approved under this section shall (notwithstanding section 2(a) or (b) of the Local Land Charges Act 1975) be a local land charge and for the purposes of that Act the landlord for the area to which it relates shall be treated as the originating authority as respects such charge; and where a scheme is registered in the appropriate local land charges register –

(a)   the provisions of the scheme relating to property of any description shall, so far as they respectively affect the persons from time to time occupying or interested in that property, be enforceable by the landlord for the time being against them, as if each of them had covenanted with the landlord for the time being to be bound by the scheme; and

(b)   in relation to a house and premises in the area section 10 above shall have effect subject to the provisions of the scheme, and the price payable under section 9 shall be adjusted accordingly.

[(10A) Section 10 of the Local Land Charges Act 1975 shall not apply in relation to schemes which, by virtue of this section, are local land charges.]

(11) Subject to subsections (12) and (13) below, a certificate shall not be given nor a scheme approved under this section for any area except on the application of the landlord.

(12) Where, on a joint application made by two or more persons as landlords of neighbouring areas, it appears to the Minister –

(a)   that a certificate could in accordance with subsection (1) above be given as regards those areas, treated as a unit, if the interests of those persons were held by a single person; and

(b)   that the applicants are willing to be bound by any scheme to co-operate in the management of their property in those areas and in the administration of the scheme;

the Minister may give a certificate under this section for those areas as a whole; and where a certificate is given by virtue of this subsection, this section shall apply accordingly, but so that any scheme made by virtue of the certificate shall be made subject to conditions (enforceable in such manner as may be provided by the scheme) for securing that the landlords and their successors co-operate as aforesaid.

(13) Where it appears to the Minister –

(a)   that a certificate could be given under this section for any area or areas on the application of the landlord or landlords; and

(b)   that any body of persons is so constituted as to be capable of representing for purposes of this section the persons occupying or interested in property in the area or areas (other than the landlord or landlords), or such of them as are or may become entitled to acquire their landlord's interest under this Part of this Act, and is otherwise suitable;

then on an application made by that body either alone or jointly with the landlord or landlords a certificate may be granted accordingly; and where a certificate is so granted, whether to a representative body alone or to a representative body jointly with the landlord or landlords –

(i)   an application for a scheme in pursuance of the certificate may be made by the representative body alone or by the landlord or landlords alone or by both jointly and, by leave of the High Court, may be proceeded with by the representative body or by the landlord or landlords though not the applicant or applicants; and

(ii)   without prejudice to subsection (7)(b) above, the scheme may, with the consent of the landlord or landlords or on such terms as to compensation or otherwise as appear to the High Court to be just, confer on the representative body any such rights or powers under the scheme as might be conferred on the landlord or landlords for the time being, or enable the representative body to participate in the administration of the scheme or in the management by the landlord or landlords of his or their property in the area or areas.

(14) Where a certificate under this section has been given for an area, or an application for one is pending, then subject to subsection (15) below if (before or after the making of the application or the giving of the certificate) a tenant of a house in the area gives notice of his desire to have the freehold under this Part of this Act –

(a)   no further proceedings need to be taken in relation to the notice beyond those which appear to the landlord to be reasonable in the circumstances; but

(b)   the tenant may at any time withdraw the notice by a further notice in writing given to the landlord, and section 9(4) above shall not apply to require him to make any payment tot he landlord in respect of costs incurred by reason of the notice withdrawn.

(15) Subsection (14) above shall cease to have effect by virtue of an application for a certificate if the application is withdrawn or the certificate refused, and shall cease to have effect as regards the whole or part of an area to which a certificate relates –

(a)   on the approval of a scheme for the area or that part of it; or

(b)   on the expiration of one year from the giving of the certificate without an application having been made to the High Court for the approval of a scheme for the area or that part of it, or on the withdrawal of an application so made without a scheme being approved; or

(c)   on an order made under subsection (4) above with respect to the area or that part of it, or an order dismissing an application for the approval of a scheme for the area or that part of it, becoming final.

Amendments – Local Land Charges Act 1975, s 17(2), Sch 1, with effect from 1 August 1977.

A2.10   Leasehold Reform, Housing and Urban Development Act 1993

Chapter IV
Estate management schemes in connection with enfranchisement

69   Estate management schemes

(1) For the purposes of this Chapter an estate management scheme is a scheme which (subject to sections 71 and 73) is approved by a leasehold valuation tribunal under section 70 for an area occupied directly or indirectly under leases held from one landlord (apart from property occupied by him or his licensees or for the time being unoccupied) and which is designed to secure that in the event of tenants –

(a)   acquiring the landlord's interest in their house and premises ('the house') under Part I of the Leasehold Reform Act 1967 by virtue of the provisions of section 1AA of that Act (as inserted by paragraph 1 of Schedule 9 to the Housing Act 1996), or

(b)   acquiring the landlord's interest in any premises ('the premises') in accordance with Chapter I of this Part of this Act [in circumstances in which, but for section 117(1) of the Commonhold and Leasehold Reform Act 2002 and the repeal by that Act of paragraph 3 of Schedule 9 to the Housing Act 1996, they would have been entitled to acquire it by virtue of the amendments of that Chapter made by that paragraph],] the landlord will –

> (i) retain powers of management in respect of the house or premises, and
have rights against the house or premises in respect of the benefits arising from the exercise elsewhere of his powers of management.

(2)   In estate management scheme may make different provision for different parts of the area of the scheme, and shall include provision for terminating or varying all or any of the provisions of the scheme, or excluding part of the area, if a change of circumstances makes it appropriate, or for enabling it to be done by or with the approval of a leasehold valuation tribunal.

(3)   Without prejudice to any other provision of this section, an estate management scheme may provide for all or any of the following matters –

(a)   for regulating the redevelopment, use or appearance of property in which tenants have acquired the landlord's interest as mentioned in subsection (1)(a) or (b);

(b)   for empowering the landlord for the time being to carry out works of maintenance, repair, renewal or replacement in relation to any such property or carry out work to remedy a failure in respect of any such property to comply with the scheme, or for making the operation of any provisions of the scheme conditional on his doing so or on the provision or maintenance by him of services, facilities or amenities of any description;

(c)   for imposing on persons from time to time occupying or interested in any such property obligations in respect of the carrying out of works of maintenance, repair, renewal or replacement in relation to the property or property used or enjoyed by them in common with others, or in respect of costs incurred by the landlord for the time being on any matter referred to in this paragraph or in paragraph (b) above;

(d)   for the inspection from time to time of any such property on behalf of the landlord for the time being, and for the recovery by him of sums due to him under the scheme in respect of any such property by means of a charge on the property;

and the landlord for the time being shall have, for the enforcement of any charge imposed under the scheme, the same powers and remedies under the Law of Property Act 1925 and otherwise as if he were a mortgagee by deed having powers of sale and leasing and of appointing a receiver.

(4)   Except as provided by the scheme, the operation of an estate management scheme shall not be affected by any disposition or devolution of the landlord's interest in the property within the area of the scheme or in parts of that property; but the scheme –

(a)   shall include provision for identifying the person who is for the purposes of the scheme to be treated as the landlord for the time being; and

(b)   shall also include provision for transferring, or allowing the landlord for the time being to transfer, all or any of the powers and rights conferred by the scheme on the landlord for the time being to a local authority or other body, including a body constituted for the purpose.

(5)   Without prejudice to the generality of paragraph (b) of subsection (4), an estate management scheme may provide for the operation of any provision for transfer included in the scheme in accordance with that paragraph to be dependent –

(a)   on a determination of a leasehold valuation tribunal effecting or approving the transfer;

(b)   on such other circumstances as the scheme may provide.

(6)   An estate management scheme may extend to property in which the landlord's interest is disposed of otherwise than as mentioned in subsection (1)(a) or (b) (whether residential

property or not), so as to make that property, or allow it to be made, subject to any such provision as is or might be made by the scheme for property in which tenants acquire the landlord's interest as mentioned in either of those provisions.

(7)   In this Chapter references to the landlord for the time being shall have effect, in relation to powers and rights transferred to a local authority or other body as contemplated by subsection (4)(b) above, as references to that authority or body.

Amendments – Sub-s (1): paras (a), (b) substituted by the Housing Act 1996, s 118(2). Date in force (in relation to England): 26 July 2002 (except in relation to applications for collective enfranchisement in respect of which notice was given under s 13 hereof, or where applications were made for an order under s 26 hereof, before that date): see SI 2002/1912, arts 1(2), 2(b)(i), Sch 2, para 1; Sub-s (1): in para (b) words from 'in circumstances in' to 'by that paragraph' in square brackets substituted by the Commonhold and Leasehold Reform Act 2002, s 117(2). Date in force (in relation to Wales): 1 January 2003 (except in relation to applications for collective enfranchisement in respect of which notice was given under s 13 hereof, or where applications were made for an order under s 26 hereof, before that date): see SI 2002/3012, arts 1(2), 2(b)(i), Sch 2, para 1.

70 Approval by leasehold valuation tribunal of estate management scheme

(1)   A leasehold valuation tribunal may, on an application made by a landlord for the approval of a scheme submitted by him to the tribunal, approve the scheme as an estate management scheme for such area falling within section 69(1) as is specified in the scheme; but any such application must (subject to section 72) be made within the period of [two years beginning with the coming into force of section 118 of the Housing Act 1996].

(2)   A leasehold valuation tribunal shall not approve a scheme as an estate management scheme for any area unless it is satisfied that, in order to maintain adequate standards of appearance and amenity and regulate redevelopment within the area in the event of tenants acquiring the interest of the landlord in any property as mentioned in section 69(1)(a) or (b), it is in the general interest that the landlord should retain such powers of management and have such rights falling within section 69(1)(i) and (ii) as are conferred by the scheme.

(3)   In considering whether to approve a scheme as an estate management scheme for any area, a leasehold valuation tribunal shall have regard primarily to –

(a)   the benefit likely to result from the scheme to the area as a whole (including houses or premises likely to be acquired from the landlord as mentioned in section 69(1)(a) or (b)); and

(b)   the extent to which it is reasonable to impose, for the benefit of the area, obligations on tenants so acquiring the interest of their landlord;

but the tribunal shall also have regard to the past development and present character of the area and to architectural or historical considerations, to neighbouring areas and to the circumstances generally.

(4)   A leasehold valuation tribunal shall not consider any application for it to approve a scheme unless it is satisfied that the applicant has, by advertisement or otherwise, given adequate notice to persons interested –

(a)   informing them of the application for approval of the scheme and the provision intended to be made by the scheme, and

(b)   inviting them to make representations to the tribunal about the application within a time which appears to the tribunal to be reasonable.

(5)   In subsection (4) 'persons interested' includes, in particular, in relation to any application for the approval of a scheme for any area ('the scheme area') within a conservation area –

(a)   each local planning authority within whose area any part of the scheme area falls, and

(b)   if the whole of the scheme area is in England, the Historic Buildings and Monuments Commission for England.

[(6)   Where the application is to be considered in an oral hearing, the tribunal shall afford to any person making representations under subsection (4)(b) about the application an opportunity to appear at the hearing.]

(7)   Subject to the preceding provisions of this section, a leasehold valuation tribunal shall, after considering the application, approve the scheme in question either –

(a)   as originally submitted, or

(b)   with any relevant modifications proposed or agreed to by the applicant,

if the scheme (with those modifications, if any) appears to the tribunal –

(i)   to be fair and practicable, and

(ii)   not to give the landlord a degree of control out of proportion to that previously exercised by him or to that required for the purposes of the scheme.

(8)   In subsection (7) 'relevant modifications' means modifications relating to the extent of the area to which the scheme is to apply or to the provisions contained in it.

(9)   If, having regard to –

(a)   the matters mentioned in subsection (3), and

(b)   the provision which it is practicable to make by a scheme,

the tribunal thinks it proper to do so, the tribunal may declare that no scheme can be approved for the area in question in pursuance of the application.

(10)   A leasehold valuation tribunal shall not dismiss an application for the approval of a scheme unless –

(a)   it makes such a declaration as is mentioned in subsection (9); or

(b)   in the opinion of the tribunal the applicant is unwilling to agree to a suitable scheme or is not proceeding in the matter with due despatch.

[(10A)   Any person who makes representations under subsection (4)(b) about an application for the approval of a scheme may appeal from a decision of the tribunal in proceedings on the application.]

(11)   A scheme approved under this section as an estate management scheme for an area shall be a local land charge, notwithstanding section 2(a) or (b) of the Local Land Charges Act 1975 (matters which are not local land charges), and for the purposes of that Act the landlord for that area shall be treated as the originating authority as respects any such charge.

(12)   Where such a scheme is registered in the appropriate local land charges register –

(a)   the provisions of the scheme relating to property of any description shall so far as they respectively affect the persons from time to time occupying or interested in that property be enforceable by the landlord for the time being against them, as if each of them had covenanted with the landlord for the time being to be bound by the scheme; and

(b)   in relation to any acquisition such as is mentioned in section 69(1)(a) above, section 10 of the Leasehold Reform Act 1967 (rights to be conveyed on enfranchisement) shall have effect subject to the provisions of the scheme, and the price payable under section 9 of that Act shall be adjusted so far as is appropriate (if at all); and

(c)   in relation to any acquisition such as is mentioned in section 69(1)(b) above, section 34 of, and Schedule 7 to, this Act shall have effect subject to the provisions of the scheme, and any price payable under Schedule 6 to this Act shall be adjusted so far as is appropriate (if at all).

(13) Section 10 of the Local Land Charges Act 1975 (compensation for non-registration etc) shall not apply to schemes which, by virtue of subsection (11) above, are local land charges.

(14) In this section and in section 73 'conservation area' and 'local planning authority' have the same meaning as in the Planning (Listed Buildings and Conservation Areas) Act 1990; and in connection with the latter expression –

(a)   the expression 'the planning Acts' in the Town and Country Planning Act 1990 shall be treated as including this Act; and

(b)   paragraphs 4 and 5 of Schedule 4 to the Planning (Listed Buildings and Conservation Areas) Act 1990 (further provisions as to exercise of functions by different authorities) shall apply in relation to functions under or by virtue of this section or section 73 of this Act as they apply in relation to functions under section 69 of that Act.

Amendments: Sub-s (1): words from 'two years beginning' to 'Housing Act 1996' in square brackets substituted by the Housing Act 1996, s 118(3). Sub-s (6): substituted by the Commonhold and Leasehold Reform Act 2002, s 176, Sch 13, paras 12, 13(1), (2). Date in force (in relation to England): 30 September 2003 (except in relation to any application made to a LVT or any proceedings transferred to a LVT by a county court before that date): see SI 2003/1986, arts 1(2), 2(c)(i), Sch 2, para 13. Date in force (in relation to Wales): 30 March 2004 (except in relation to any application made to a LVT or any proceedings transferred to a LVT by a county court before 31 March 2004): see SI 2004/669, art 2(c)(i), Sch 2, para 13; Sub-s (10A): inserted by the Commonhold and Leasehold Reform Act 2002, s 176, Sch 13, paras 12, 13(1), (3). Date in force (in relation to England): 30 September 2003 (except in relation to any application made to a LVT or any proceedings transferred to a LVT by a county court before that date): see SI 2003/1986, arts 1(2), 2(c)(i), Sch 2, para 13. Date in force (in relation to Wales): 30 March 2004 (except in relation to any application made to a LVT or any proceedings transferred to a LVT by a county court before 31 March 2004): see SI 2004/669, art 2(c)(i), Sch 2, para 13.

71 Applications by two or more landlords or by representative bodies

(1) Where, on a joint application made by two or more persons as landlords of neighbouring areas, it appears to a leasehold valuation tribunal –

(a)   that a scheme could in accordance with subsections (1) and (2) of section 70 be approved as an estate management scheme for those areas, treated as a unit, if the interests of those persons were held by a single person, and

(b)   that the applicants are willing to be bound by the scheme to co-operate in the management of their property in those areas and in the administration of the scheme,

the tribunal may (subject to the provisions of section 70 and subsection (2) below) approve the scheme under that section as an estate management scheme for those areas as a whole.

(2) Any such scheme shall be made subject to conditions (enforceable in such manner as may be provided by the scheme) for securing that the landlords and their successors co-operate as mentioned in subsection (1)(b) above.

(3) Where it appears to a leasehold valuation tribunal –

(a)   that a scheme could, on the application of any landlord or landlords, be approved under section 70 as an estate management scheme for any area or areas, and

(b)   that any body of persons –

(i) is so constituted as to be capable of representing for the purposes of the scheme the persons occupying or interested in property in the area or areas (other than the landlord or landlords or his or their licensees), or such of them as are or may become entitled to acquire their landlord's interest as mentioned in section 69(1)(a) or (b), and

(ii) is otherwise suitable,

an application for the approval of the scheme under section 70 may be made to the tribunal by the representative body alone or by the landlord or landlords alone or by both jointly and, by leave of the tribunal, may be proceeded with by the representative body or by the landlord or landlords despite the fact that the body or landlord or landlords in question did not make the application.

(4)   Without prejudice to section 69(4)(b), any such scheme may with the consent of the landlord or landlords, or on such terms as to compensation or otherwise as appear to the tribunal to be just –

(a)   confer on the representative body any such rights or powers under the scheme as might be conferred on the landlord or landlords for the time being, or

(b)   enable the representative body to participate in the administration of the scheme or in the management by the landlord or landlords of his or their property in the area or areas.

(5)   Where any such scheme confers any rights or powers on the representative body in accordance with subsection (4) above, section 70(11) and (12)(a) shall have effect with such modifications (if any) as are provided for in the scheme.

72 Applications after expiry of two-year period

(1)   An application for the approval of a scheme for an area under section 70 (including an application in accordance with section 71(1) or (3)) may be made after the expiry of the period mentioned in subsection (1) of that section if the Secretary of State has, not more than six months previously, consented to the making of such an application for that area or for an area within which that area falls.

(2)   The Secretary of State may give consent under subsection (1) to the making of an application ('the proposed application') only where he is satisfied –

(a)   that either or both of the conditions mentioned in subsection (3) apply; and

(b)   that adequate notice has been given to persons interested informing them of the request for consent and the purpose of the request.

(3)   The conditions referred to in subsection (2)(a) are –

(a)   that the proposed application could not have been made before the expiry of the period mentioned in section 70(1); and

(b)   that –

(i) any application for the approval under section 70 of a scheme for the area, or part of the area, to which the proposed application relates would probably have been dismissed under section 70(10)(a) had it been made before the expiry of that period; but

(ii) because of a change in any of the circumstances required to be considered under section 70(3) the proposed application would, if made following the giving of consent by the Secretary of State, probably be granted.

(4)   A request for consent under subsection (1) must be in writing and must comply with such requirements (if any) as to the form of, or the particulars to be contained in, any such request as the Secretary of State may by regulations prescribe.

(5)   The procedure for considering a request for consent under subsection (1) shall be such as may be prescribed by regulations made by the Secretary of State.

73 Applications by certain public bodies

(1)   Where it appears to a leasehold valuation tribunal after the expiry of the period mentioned in section 70(1) that a scheme could, on the application of any landlord or landlords within that period, have been approved under section 70 as an estate management scheme for any area or areas within a conservation area, an application for the approval of the scheme under that section may, subject to subsections (2) and (3) below, be made to the tribunal by one or more bodies constituting the relevant authority for the purposes of this section.

(2)   An application under subsection (1) may only be made if—

(a)   no scheme has been approved under section 70 for the whole or any part of the area or areas to which the application relates ('the scheme area'); and

(b)   any application which has been made in accordance with section 70(1), 71(1) or 71(3) for the approval of a scheme for the whole or any part of the scheme area has been withdrawn or dismissed; and

(c)   no request for consent under section 72(1) which relates to the whole or any part of the scheme area is pending or has been granted within the last six months

(3)   An application under subsection (1) above must be made within the period of six months beginning –

(a)   with the date on which the period mentioned in section 70(1) expires, or

(b)   if any application has been made as mentioned in subsection (2)(b) above, with the date (or, as the case may be, the latest date) on which any such application is withdrawn or dismissed,

whichever is the later; but if at any time during that period of six months a request of a kind mentioned in subsection (2)(c) above is pending or granted, an application under subsection (1) above may, subject to subsection (2) above, be made within the period of –

(i)   six months beginning with the date on which the request is withdrawn or refused, or

(ii)   twelve months beginning with the date on which the request is granted

as the case may be.

(4)   A scheme approved on an application under subsection (1) may confer on the applicant or applicants any such rights or powers under the scheme as might have been conferred on the landlord or landlords for the time being.

(5)   For the purposes of this section the relevant authority for the scheme area is –

(a)   where that area falls wholly within the area of a local planning authority—
(i)that authority; or
(ii)subject to subsection (6), that authority acting jointly with the Historic Buildings and Monuments Commission for England ('the Commission'); or
(iii)subject to subsection (6), the Commission; or

(b)   in any other case –
(i)   all of the local planning authorities within each of whose areas any part of the scheme area falls, acting jointly; or
(ii)   subject to subsection (6), one or more of those authorities acting jointly with the Commission; or
(iii)   subject to subsection (6), the Commission.

(6)   The Commission may make, or join in the making of, an application under subsection (1) only if—

  (a)   the whole of the scheme area is in England; and
  (b)   they have consulted any local planning authority within whose area the whole or any part of the scheme area falls.

(7)   Where a scheme is approved on an application under subsection (1) by two or more bodies acting jointly, the scheme shall, if the tribunal considers it appropriate, be made subject to conditions (enforceable in such manner as may be provided by the scheme) for securing that those bodies co-operate in the administration of the scheme.

(8)   Where a scheme is approved on an application under subsection (1)—

  (a)   section 70(11) and (12)(a) shall (subject to subsection (9) below) have effect as if any reference to the landlord, or the landlord for the time being, for the area for which an estate management scheme has been approved were a reference to the applicant or applicants; and
  (b)   section 70(12)(b) and (c) shall each have effect with the omission of so much of that provision as relates to the adjustment of any such price as is there mentioned.

(9)   A scheme so approved shall not be enforceable by a local planning authority in relation to any property falling outside the authority's area; and in the case of a scheme approved on a joint application made by one or more local planning authorities and the Commission, the scheme may provide for any of its provisions to be enforceable in relation to property falling within the area of a local planning authority either by the authority alone, or by the Commission alone, or by the authority and the Commission acting jointly, as the scheme may provide.

(10)   For the purposes of –

  (a)   section 9(1A) of the Leasehold Reform Act 1967 (purchase price on enfranchisement) as it applies in relation to any acquisition such as is mentioned in section 69(1)(a) above, and
  (b)   paragraph 3 of Schedule 6 to this Act as it applies in relation to any acquisition such as is mentioned in section 69(1)(b) above (including that paragraph as it applies by virtue of paragraph 7 or 11 of that Schedule),

it shall be assumed that any scheme approved under subsection (1) and relating to the property in question had not been so approved, and accordingly any application for such a scheme to be approved, and the possibility of such an application being made, shall be disregarded.

(11)   Section 70(14) applies for the purposes of this section.

74 Effect of application for approval on claim to acquire freehold

(1)   Subject to subsections (5) and (6), this subsection applies where –

  (a)   an application ('the scheme application') is made for the approval of a scheme as an estate management scheme for any area or a request ('the request for consent') is made for consent under section 72(1) in relation to any area, and
  (b)   whether before or after the making of the application or request—

       (i)   the tenant of a house in that area gives notice of his desire to have the freehold under Part I of the Leasehold Reform Act 1967
       (ii)   a notice is given under section 13 above in respect of any premises in the area, [and

(c)   in the case of an application for the approval of a scheme as an estate management scheme, the scheme would extend to the house or premises if acquired in pursuance of the notice.]

(2)   Where subsection (1) applies by virtue of paragraph (b)(i) of that subsection, then –

(a)   no further steps need be taken towards the execution of a conveyance to give effect to section 10 of the 1967 Act beyond those which appear to the landlord to be reasonable in the circumstances; and

(b)   if the notice referred to in subsection (1)(b)(i) ('the tenant's notice') was given before the making of the scheme application or the request for consent, that notice may be withdrawn by a further notice given by the tenant to the landlord.

(3)   Where subsection (1) applies by virtue of paragraph (b)(ii) of that subsection, then –

(a)   if the notice referred to in that provision ('the initial notice') was given before the making of the scheme application or the request for consent, the notice may be withdrawn by a further notice given by the nominee purchaser to the reversioner;

(b)   unless the initial notice is so withdrawn, the reversioner shall, if he has not already given the *nominee purchaser* [RTE company] a counter-notice under section 21, give *him* [it] by the date referred to in subsection (1) of that section a counter-notice which complies with one of the requirements set out in subsection (2) of that section (but in relation to which subsection (3) of that section need not be complied with); and

(c)   no proceedings shall be brought under Chapter I in pursuance of the initial notice otherwise than under section 22 or 23, and, if the court under either of those sections makes an order requiring the reversioner to give a further counter-notice to the *nominee purchaser* [RTE company], the date by which it is to be given shall be such date as falls two months after subsection (1) above ceases to apply;

but no other counter-notice need be given under Chapter I, and (subject to the preceding provisions of this subsection) no further steps need be taken towards the final determination (whether by agreement or otherwise) of the terms of the proposed acquisition by the *nominee purchaser* [RTE company] beyond those which appear to the reversioner to be reasonable in the circumstances.

(4)   If the tenant's notice or the initial notice is withdrawn in accordance with subsection (2) or (3) above, section 9(4) of the 1967 Act or (as the case may be) section 33 above shall not have effect to require the payment of any costs incurred in pursuance of that notice.

(5)   Where the scheme application is withdrawn or dismissed, subsection (1) does not apply at any time falling after –

(a)   the date of the withdrawal of the application, or

(b)   the date when the decision of the tribunal dismissing the application becomes final,

as the case may be; and subsection (1) does not apply at any time falling after the date on which a scheme is approved for the area referred to in that subsection, or for any part of it, in pursuance of the scheme application.

(6)   Where the request for consent is withdrawn or refused, subsection (1) does not apply at any time falling after the date on which the request is withdrawn or refused, as the case may be; and where the request is granted, subsection (1) does not apply at any time falling more than six months after the date on which it is granted (unless that subsection applies by virtue of an application made in reliance on the consent).

(7)   Where in accordance with subsection (5) or (6), subsection (1) ceases to apply as from a particular date, it shall do so without prejudice to –

(a)   the effect of anything done before that date in pursuance of subsection (2) or (3); or

(b)   the operation of any provision of this Part, or of regulations made under it, in relation to anything so done.

(8)   If, however, no notice of withdrawal has been given in accordance with subsection (3) before the date when subsection (1) so ceases to apply and before that date either—

(a)   the reversioner has given the *nominee purchaser* [RTE company] a counter-notice under section 21 complying with the requirement set out in subsection (2)(a) of that section, or

(b)   section 23(6) would (but for subsection (3) above) have applied to require the reversioner to give a further counter-notice to the *nominee purchaser* [RTE company],

the reversioner shall give a further counter-notice to the nominee purchaser [RTE company] within the period of two months beginning with the date when subsection (1) ceases to apply.

(9)   Subsections (3) to (5) of section 21 shall apply to any further counter-notice required to be given by the reversioner under subsection (8) above as if it were a counter-notice under that section complying with the requirement set out in subsection (2)(a) of that section; and sections 24 and 25 shall apply in relation to any such counter-notice as they apply in relation to one required by section 22(3).

(10)   In this section –

'the 1967 Act' means the Leasehold Reform Act 1967; and

'the *nominee purchaser* [RTE company]' and 'the reversioner' have the same meaning as in Chapter I of this Part of this Act;

and references to the approval of a scheme for any area include references to the approval of a scheme for two or more areas in accordance with section 71 or 73 above.

Amendments: Sub-s (1): in para (b) words omitted repealed, and para (c) inserted, by the Housing Act 1996, s 118(4). Sub-s (3): words 'nominee purchaser' in italics in each place they occur repealed and subsequent words in square brackets substituted by the Commonhold and Leasehold Reform Act 2002, s 124, Sch 8, paras 2, 30(1), (2). Date in force: to be appointed: see the Commonhold and Leasehold Reform Act 2002, s 181(1); Sub-s (3): in para (b) word 'him' in italics repealed and subsequent word in square brackets substituted by the Commonhold and Leasehold Reform Act 2002, s 124, Sch 8, paras 2, 30(1), (3). Date in force: to be appointed: see the Commonhold and Leasehold Reform Act 2002, s 181(1); Sub-s (8): words 'nominee purchaser' in italics in each place they occur repealed and subsequent words in square brackets substituted by the Commonhold and Leasehold Reform Act 2002, s 124, Sch 8, paras 2, 30(1), (2). Date in force: to be appointed: see the Commonhold and Leasehold Reform Act 2002, s 181(1); Sub-s (10): in definition 'the nominee purchaser' words 'nominee purchaser' in italics repealed and subsequent words in square brackets substituted by the Commonhold and Leasehold Reform Act 2002, s 124, Sch 8, paras 2, 30(1), (2). Date in force: to be appointed: see the Commonhold and Leasehold Reform Act 2002, s 181(1).

75 Variation of existing schemes

(1)   Where a scheme under section 19 of the Leasehold Reform Act 1967 (estate management schemes in connection with enfranchisement under that Act) includes, in pursuance of subsection (6) of that section, provision for enabling the termination or variation of the scheme, or the exclusion of part of the area of the scheme, by or with the approval of the High Court, that provision shall have effect –

(a)   as if any reference to the High Court were a reference to a leasehold valuation tribunal, and

(b)   with such modifications (if any) as are necessary in consequence of paragraph (a).

(2)   A scheme under that section may be varied by or with the approval of a leasehold valuation tribunal for the purpose of, or in connection with, extending the scheme to property within the area of the scheme in which the landlord's interest may be acquired as mentioned in section 69(1)(a) above.

(3)   Where any such scheme has been varied in accordance with subsection (2) above, section 19 of that Act shall apply as if the variation had been effected under provisions included in the scheme in pursuance of subsection (6) of that section (and accordingly the scheme may be further varied under provisions so included).

(4)   ...

(5)   ...

Amendment: Sub-ss (4), (5): repealed by the Commonhold and Leasehold Reform Act 2002, s 180, Sch 14Date in force (in relation to England): 30 September 2003 (except in relation to any application made to a LVT or any proceedings transferred to a LVT by a county court before that date): see SI 2003/1986, arts 1(2), 2(c)(iv), Sch 1, Pt I, Sch 2, para 13 thereto. Date in force (in relation to Wales): 30 March 2004 (except in relation to any application made to a LVT or any proceedings transferred to a LVT by a county court before 31 March 2004): see SI 2004/669, art 2(c)(iv), Sch 1, Pt I, Sch 2, para 13.

A2.11   Forestry Act 1967

5 Forestry dedication convenants and agreements

(1) The provisions of this section shall have effect with a view to allowing land to be devoted to forestry by means of agreements entered into with the Commissioners, being agreements to the effect that the land shall not, except with the previous consent in writing of the Commissioners or, in the case of dispute, under direction of the Minister [as regards England and Wales and the Scottish Ministers as regards Scotland], be used otherwise than for the growing of timber or other forest products in accordance with the rules or practice of good forestry or for purposes connected therewith; and in this Act –

(a)   'forestry dedication covenant' means a covenant to the said effect entered into with the Commissioners in respect of land in England or Wales without an intention being expressed contrary to the application of section 79 of the Law of Property Act 1925 (under which covenants relating to land are, unless the contrary is expressed, deemed to be made on behalf of the covenantor, his successors in title and persons deriving title under him or them); and

(b)   'forestry dedication agreement' means an agreement to the said effect entered into with the Commissioners in respect of land in Scotland by a person who is the proprietor thereof for his own absolute use or is empowered by this section to enter into the agreement.

(2) Where land in England or Wales is subject to a forestry dedication covenant –

(a)   the Commissioners shall, as respects the enforcement of the covenant against persons other than the covenantor, have the like rights as if they had at all material times been the absolute owners in possession of ascertained land adjacent to the land subject to the covenant and capable of being benefited by the covenant, and the covenant had been expressed to be for the benefit of that adjacent land; and

(b)   section 84 of the Law of Property Act 1925 (which enables the Lands Tribunal to discharge or modify respective covenants) shall not apply to the covenant.

(3) (*Applies to Scotland only.*)

(4) Schedule 2 to this Act shall have effect to empower limited owners, trustees and others to enter into forestry dedication covenants or agreements and to provide for matters arising on their doing so.

Amendments – SI 1999/1747, art 3, Sch 12, Pt II, para 4(1), (6), with effect from 1 July 1999.

A2.12   Countryside Act 1968

15 Areas of special scientific interest

(1) This section has effect as respects land […] which is or forms part of an area which in the opinion of the [Nature Conservancy Council] (in this section referred to as 'the Council') is of special interest by reason of its flora, fauna, or geological or physiographical features.

(2) Where, for the purpose of conserving those flora, fauna or geological or physiographical features, it appears to the Council expedient […] to do so, the Council may enter into an agreement with the owners, lessees or occupiers of any such land [(or of any adjacent [other] land)] which imposes restrictions on the exercise of rights over land by the persons who can be bound by the agreement.

(3) Any such agreement –

(a)   may provide for the carrying out on the land of such work and the doing thereon of such other things as may be expedient for the purposes of the agreement,

(b)   may provide for any of the matters mentioned in paragraph (a) above being carried out, or for the cost thereof being defrayed, either by the owners or other persons, or by the Council, or partly in one way and partly in another, and

(c)   may contain such other provisions as to the making of payments by the Council as may be specified in the agreement.

(4) Where section 79 of the Law of Property Act 1925 (burden of covenant running with the land) applies to any such restrictions as are mentioned in subsection (2) of this section, the Council shall have the like rights as respects the enforcement of the restrictions as if the Council had at all material times been the absolute owner in possession of ascertained land adjacent to the land in respect of which the restriction is sought to be enforced, and capable of being benefited by the restriction, and the restriction had been expressed to be for the benefit of that adjacent land.

Section 84 of the Law of Property Act 1925 (discharge or modification of restrictive covenants) shall not apply to such a restriction.

(5) Schedule 2 to the Forestry Act 1967 (powers of tenants for life and other limited owners to enter into forestry dedication covenants or agreements) shall apply to any agreement made in pursuance of this section as it applies to such a covenant or agreement.

(6) (*Applies to Scotland only.*)

[(6A) In this section references to 'the Nature Conservancy Council' or 'the Council' are references to [English Nature], [Scottish National Heritage] or the Council, according as the land in question is in England, Scotland or Wales.]

(7) The Act of 1949 shall have effect as if this section were included in Part III of that Act.

Amendments – Wildlife and Countryside Act 1981, ss 72(8), 73, Sch 17, Part I, with effect from 30 November 1981; Nature Conservancy Council Act 1973, s 1(1)(b), Sch 1, para 9, with effect from 25 July 1973; Environmental Protection Act 1990, s 132, Sch 9, para 4(2), with effect from 5 November 1990; Countryside and Rights of Way Act 2000, ss 75(3), (4), Sch 8, para 1(c)(i) with effect from 30 January 2001; Natural Heritage (Scotland) Act 1991, s 4, Sch 2, para 3, with effect from 1 April 1992.

A2.13   Greater London Council (General Powers) Act 1974

16   Undertakings and agreements binding successive owners

(1) Every undertaking given to a local authority by the owner of any legal estate in land and every agreement made between a local authority and any such owner being an undertaking or agreement –

    (a)   given or made under seal in connection with the land; and

    (b)   expressed to be given or made in pursuance of this section;

shall be enforceable not only against the owner joining in the undertaking or agreement but also against the successors in title of any owner so joining and any person claiming through or under them.

(2) Such an undertaking or agreement shall be treated as a local land charge for the purposes of the Land Charges Act 1925.

(3) Any person against whom such an undertaking or agreement is enforceable shall be entitled to require a copy thereof from the local authority without payment.

(4) Any charge on the land which by virtue of this section is enforceable in the manner described in subsection (1) of this section shall, for the purposes of subsection (1) of section 32 of the Building Societies Act 1962 (which prohibits advances by building societies on second mortgage), be deemed not to be a prior mortgage within the meaning of that subsection.

(5)

    (a)   The enactments specified in Part III of Schedule 2 to this Act are hereby repealed.

    (b)   The enactments specified in Part II of Schedule 3 to this Act are hereby repealed so far as they relate to any part of Greater London.

(6) Any undertaking or agreement which by virtue of an enactment included in Part III of Schedule 2 or Part II of Schedule 3 to this Act was, immediately before the passing of this Act, binding on any successors in title of any owner joining in such undertaking or agreement and on any person claiming through or under them shall, notwithstanding the repeal of that enactment, continue to be so binding and enforceable as if such undertaking or agreement were expressed to be given or made in pursuance of this section.

(7) In this section 'local authority' means the Council or a borough council [or the London Residuary Body].

Amendments – SI 1990/1765, art 4(4), with effect from 21 September 1990.

A2.14   Ancient Monuments and Archaeological Areas Act 1979

Agreements concerning ancient monuments, etc

17 Agreement concerning ancient monuments and land in their vicinity

(1) The Secretary of State may enter into an agreement under this section with the occupier of an ancient monument or of any land adjoining or in the vicinity of an ancient monument.

[(1A) The Commission may enter into an agreement under this section with the occupier of an ancient monument situated in England or of any land so situated which adjoins or is in the vicinity of an ancient monument so situated.]

(2) A local authority may enter into an agreement under this section with the occupier of any ancient monument situated in or in the vicinity of their area or with the occupier of any and adjoining or in the vicinity of any such ancient monument.

(3) Any person who has an interest in an ancient monument or in any land adjoining or in the vicinity of an ancient monument may be a party to an agreement under this section in addition to the occupier.

(4) An agreement under this section may make provision for all or any of the following matters with respect to the monument or land in question, that is to say –

(a)	the maintenance and preservation of the monument and its amenities;
(b)	the carrying out of any such work, or the doing of any such other thing, in relation to the monument or land as may be specified in the agreement;
(c)	public access to the monument or land and the provision of facilities and information or other services for the use of the public in that connection;
(d)	restricting the use of the monument or land;
(e)	prohibiting in relation to the monument or land the doing of any such thing as may be specified in the agreement; and
(f)	the making by the Secretary of State or [the Commission or the local authority (as the case may be)] of payments in such manner, of such amounts and on such terms as may be so specified (and whether for or towards the cost of any work provided for under the agreement or in consideration of any restriction, prohibition or obligation accepted by any other party thereto);

and may contain such incidental and consequential provisions as appear to the Secretary of State or [the Commission or the local authority (as the case may be)] to be necessary or expedient.

(5) Where an agreement under this section expressly provides that the agreement as a whole or any restriction, prohibition or obligation arising thereunder is to be binding on the successors of any party to the agreement (but not otherwise), then, as respects any monument or land in England or Wales, every person deriving title to the monument or land in question from, through or under that party shall be bound by the agreement, or (as the case may be) by that restriction, prohibition or obligation, unless he derives title by virtue of any disposition made by that party before the date of the agreement.

(6) (*Applies to Scotland only.*)

[(7) Section 84 of the Law of Property Act 1925 (c 20) (power of Lands Tribunal to discharge or modify restrictive covenant) shall not apply to an agreement under this section.]

(8) Nothing in any agreement under this section to which the Secretary of State is a party shall be construed as operating as a scheduled monument consent.

[(9) References to an ancient monument in subsection (1A) above, and in subsection (3) above so far as it applies for the purposes of subsection (1A), shall be construed as if the reference in section 61(12)(b) of this Act to the Secretary of State were to the Commission.]

[(10) References in this section to an ancient monument situated in England include any such monument situated in, on or under the seabed within the seaward limits of the United Kingdom territorial waters adjacent to England; and an order under section 33(10) of the National Heritage Act 1983 (orders determining limits of waters adjacent to England) applies for the purposes of this subsection as it applies for the purposes of section 33(9) of that Act.]

Amendments – National Heritage Act 1983, s 33, Sch 4, para 43, with effect from 1 April 1984; Title Conditions (Scotland) Act 2003, s 128(1), Sch 14, para 8, with effect from 28 November 2004; National Heritage Act 2002, s 2(2), with effect from 1 July 2002.

A2.15   Highways Act 1980

35   Creation of walkways by agreement

(1) An agreement under this section may be entered into –

    (a)   by a local highway authority, after consultation with the council of any non-metropolitan district in which the land concerned is situated;

    (b)   by a [non-metropolitan] district council, either alone or jointly with the local highway authority, after consultation with the local highway authority.

(2) An agreement under this section is an agreement with any person having an interest in any land on which a building is, or is proposed to be, situated, being a person who by virtue of that interest has the necessary power in that behalf –

    (a)   for the provision of ways over, through or under parts of the building, or the building when constructed, as the case may be, or parts of any structure attached, or to be attached, to the building; and

    (b)   for the dedication by that person of those ways as footpaths subject to such limitations and conditions, if any, affecting the public right of way thereover as may be specified in the agreement and to any rights reserved by the agreement to that person and any person deriving title to the land under him.

A footpath created in pursuance of an agreement under this section is referred to below as a 'walkway'.

(3) An agreement under this section may make provision for –

    (a)   the maintenance, cleansing and drainage of any walkway to which the agreement relates;

    (b)   the lighting of such walkway and of that part of the building or structure which will be over or above it;

    (c)   the provision and maintenance of support for such walkway;

    (d)   entitling the authority entering into the agreement or, where the agreement is entered into jointly by a [non-metropolitan] district council and a local highway authority, either of those authorities to enter on any building or structure in which such walkway will be situated and to execute any works necessary to secure the performance of any obligation which any person is for the time being liable to perform by virtue of the agreement or of subsection (4) below;

(e)   the making of payments by the authority entering into the agreement or, where the agreement is entered into jointly by a [non-metropolitan] district council and a local highway authority, either of those authorities to any person having an interest in the land or building affected by the agreement;

(f)   the termination, in such manner and subject to such conditions as maybe specified in the agreement, of the right of the public to use such walkway;

(g)   any incidental and consequential matters.

(4) Any covenant (whether positive or restrictive) contained in an agreement under this section and entered into by a person having an interest in any land affected by the agreement shall be binding upon persons deriving title to the land under the covenantor to the same extent as it is binding upon the covenantor notwithstanding that it would not have been binding upon those persons apart from the provisions of this subsection, and shall be enforceable against those persons by the local highways authority.

(5) A covenant contained in an agreement under this section and entered into by a person having an interest in any land affected by the agreement is a local land charge.

(6) Where an agreement has been entered into under this section the appropriate authority may make byelaws regulating –

(a)   the conduct of persons using any walkway to which the agreement relates;

(b)   the times at which any such walkway may be closed to the public;

(c)   the placing or retention of anything (including any structure or projection) in, on or over any such walkway.

(7) For the purposes of subsection (6) above, 'the appropriate authority' means –

(a)   where the agreement was entered into by a local highway authority, that authority;

(b)   where the agreement was entered into by a [non-metropolitan] district council alone, that council;

(c)   where the agreement was entered into by a [non-metropolitan] district council jointly with the local highway authority, the local highway authority;

but in cases falling within paragraph (c) above the local highway authority shall before making any byelaw consult the district council, and in exercising his power of confirmation the Minister shall have regard to any dispute between the local highway authority and the district council.

(8) Not less than 2 months before an authority propose to make byelaws under subsection (6) above they shall display in a conspicuous position on or adjacent to the walkway in question notice of their intention to make such byelaws.

(9) A notice under subsection (8) above shall specify the place where a copy of the proposed byelaws may be inspected and the period, which shall not be less than 6 weeks from the date on which the notice was first displayed as aforesaid, within which representations may be made to the authority, and the authority shall consider any representations made to them within that period.

(10) The Minister of the Crown having power by virtue of section 236 of the Local Government Act 1972 to confirm byelaws made under subsection (6) above may confirm them with or without modifications; and if he proposes to confirm them with modifications he may, before confirming them, direct the authority by whom they were made to give notice of the proposed modifications to such persons and in such manner as may be specified in the direction.

(11) Subject to subsection (12) below, the Minister after consulting such representative organisations as he thinks fit, may make regulations –

(a)   for preventing any enactment or instrument relating to highways or to things done on or in connection with highways from applying to walkways which have been, or are to be, created in pursuance of agreements under this section or to things done on or in connection with such walkways;

(b)   for amending, modifying or adapting any such enactment or instrument in its application to such walkways;

(c)   without prejudice to the generality of paragraphs (a) and (b) above, for excluding, restricting or regulating the rights of statutory undertakers, [...] [[...] and the operators of [electronic communications code networks] to place] and maintain apparatus in, under, over, along or across such walkways;

(d)   without prejudice as aforesaid, for defining the circumstances and manner in which such walkways may be closed periodically or temporarily or stopped up and for prescribing the procedure to be followed before such a walkway is stopped up.

(12) Regulations under this section shall not exclude the rights of statutory undertakers, [...] [[...] or the operators of [electronic communications code networks] to place] and maintain apparatus in, under, along or across any part of a walkway, being a part which is not supported by any structure.

(13) Without prejudice to subjection (11) above, regulations under this section may make different provisions for different classes of walkways and may include such incidental, supplemental and consequential provisions (and, in particular, provisions relating to walkways provided in pursuance of agreements made before the coming into operation of the regulations) as appear to the Minister to be expedient for the purposes of the regulations.

(14) Nothing in this section is to be taken as affecting any other provision of this Act, or any other enactment, by virtue of which highways may be created.

Amendments – Local Government Act 1985, s 8, Sch 4, para 9, with effect from 1 April 1986; Water Act 1989, s 190, Sch 27, Pt I, with effect from 1 September 1989, Telecommunications Act 1984, s 109, Sch 4, para 76, with effect from 5 August 1984; Communications Act 2003, s 406(1), Sch 17, para 53, with effect from 25 July 2003.

A2.16   Wildlife and Countryside Act 1981

39 Management agreements with owners and occupiers of land

(1) A relevant authority may, for the purpose of conserving or enhancing the natural beauty or amenity of any land which is [...] within their area or promoting its enjoyment by the public, make an agreement (in this section referred to as a 'management agreement') with any person having an interest in the land with respect to the management of the land during a specified term or without limitation of the duration of the agreement.

(2) Without prejudice to the generality of subsection (1), a management agreement –

(a)   may impose on the person having an interest in the land restrictions as respects the method of cultivating the land, its use for agricultural purposes or the exercise of rights over the land and may impose obligations on that person to carry out works or agricultural or forestry operations or do other things on the land;

(b)   may confer on the relevant authority power to carry out works for the purpose of performing their functions under the 1949 Act and the 1968 Act; and

(c)   may contain such incidental and consequential provisions (including provisions for the making of payments by either party to the other) as appear to the relevant authority to be necessary or expedient for the purposes of the agreement.

(3) The provisions of a management agreement with any person interested in the land shall, unless the agreement otherwise provides, be binding on persons deriving title under or from that person and be enforceable by the relevant authority against those persons accordingly.

(4) Schedule 2 to the Forestry Act 1967 (power for tenant for life and others to enter into forestry dedication covenants) shall apply to management agreements as it applies to forestry dedication covenants.

(5) In this section 'the relevant authority' means –

(a)   [...]
[(aa)   as respects land within the Broads, the Broads Authority;]
(b)   [...]
(c)   as respects any other land, the local planning authority.
[(d)   as respects any land in England, the Countryside Agency;
(e)   as respects any land in Wales, the Countryside Council for Wales;
(f)   as respects land in any area of outstanding natural beauty designated under section 82 of the Countryside and Rights of Way Act 2000 for which a conservation board has been established under section 86 of that Act, that board].

(6) The powers conferred by this section on a relevant authority shall be in addition to and not in derogation of any powers conferred on such an authority by or under any enactment.

Amendments – Countryside and Rights of Way Act 2000, ss 96(a), (b), 102, Sch 16, Pt VI, with effect from, (in relation to England), 1 April 2001; (in relation to Wales), 1 May 2001; Environment Act 1995, s 120, Sch 24, with effect from, 28 July 1995; Norfolk and Suffolk Broads Act 1988, s 2(5), (6), Sch 3, Pt I, with effect from 1 April 1089; Local Government Act 1985, ss 7, 102, Sch 3, para 7, Sch 17, with effect from 1 April 1986.

A2.17   Local Government (Miscellaneous Provisions) Act 1982

33 Enforceability by local authorities of certain covenants relating to land

(1) The provisions of this section shall apply if a principal council (in the exercise of their powers under section 111 of the Local Government Act 1972 or otherwise) and any other person are parties to an instrument under seal which –

[(a)   is executed for the purpose of securing the carrying out of works on land in the council's area in which the other person has an interest, or
(b)   is executed for the purpose of regulating the use of or is otherwise connected with land in or outside the council's area in which the other person has an interest,

and which is neither executed for the purpose of facilitating nor connected with the development of the land in question.]

(2) If, in a case where this section applies –

(a)   the instrument contains a covenant on the part of any person having an interest in land, being a covenant to carry out any works or do any other thing on or in relation to that land, and
(b)   the instrument defines the land to which the covenant relates, being land in which that person has an interest at the time the instrument is executed, and
(c)   the covenant is expressed to be one to which this section or section 126 of the Housing Act 1974 (which is superseded by this section) applies,

the covenant shall be enforceable (without any limit of time) against any person deriving title from the original covenant in respect of his interest in any of the land defined as mentioned in paragraph (b) above and any person deriving title under him in respect of any lesser interest in that land as if that person had also been an original covenanting party in respect of the interest for the time being held by him.

(3) Without prejudice to any other method of enforcement of a covenant falling within subsection (2) above, if there is a breach of the covenant in relation to any of the land to which the covenant relates, then, subject to subsection (4) below, the principal council who are a party to the instrument in which the covenant is contained may –

    (a)   enter on the land concerned and carry out the works or do anything which the covenant requires to be carried out or done or remedy anything which has been done and which the covenant required not to be done; and

    (b)   recover from any person against whom the covenant is enforceable (whether by virtue of subsection (2) above or otherwise) any expenses incurred by the council in exercise of their powers under this subsection.

(4) Before a principal council exercise their powers under subsection (3)(a) above they shall give not less than 21 days notice of their intention to do so to any person –

    (a)   who has for the time being an interest in the land on or in relation to which the works are to be carried out or other thing is to be done; and

    (b)   against whom the covenant is enforceable (whether by virtue of subsection (2) above or otherwise).

(5) If a person against whom a covenant is enforceable by virtue of subsection (2) above requests the principal council to supply him with a copy of the covenant, it shall be their duty to do so free of charge.

(6) The Public Health Act 1936 shall have effect as if any reference to that Act in –

    (a)   section 283 of that Act (notices to be in writing; forms of notices, etc.),

    (b)   section 288 of that Act (penalty for obstructing execution of Act), and

    (c)   section 291 of that Act (certain expenses recoverable from owners to be a charge on the premises; power to order payment by instalments),

included a reference to subsections (1) to (4) above and as if any reference in those sections of that Act –

    (i)   to a local authority were a reference to a principal council; and

    (ii)   to the owner of the premises were a reference to the holder of an interest in land.

(7) Section 16 of the Local Government (Miscellaneous Provisions) Act 1976 shall have effect as if references to a local authority and to functions conferred on a local authority by any enactment included respectively references to such a board as is mentioned in subsection (9) below and to functions of such a board under this section.

(8) In its application to a notice or other document authorised to be given or served under subsection (4) above or by virtue of any provision of the Public Health Act 1936 specified in subsection (6) above, section 233 of the Local Government Act 1972 (service of notices by local authorities) shall have effect as if any reference in that section to a local authority included a reference to the Common Council of the City of London and such a board is mentioned in the following subsection.

(9) In this section –

    (a)   'principal council' means the council of a county, district or London borough, a board constituted in pursuance of section 1 of the Town and Country Planning Act 1971 or reconstituted in pursuance of Schedule 17 to the Local

Government Act 1972, the Common Council of the City of London ... the Inner London Education Authority or a joint authority established by Part IV of the Local Government Act 1985; and

(b) 'area' in relation to such a board means the district for which the board is constituted or reconstituted, in relation to the Inner London Education Authority means the Inner Education Area, and in relation to such a joint authority means the area for which the authority was established.

(10) Section 126 of the Housing Act 1974 (which is superseded by this section) shall cease to have effect; but in relation to a covenant falling within subsection (2) of that section, section 1(1)(d) of the Local Land Charges Act 1975 shall continue to have effect as if the reference to the commencement of that Act had been a reference to the coming into operation of the said section 126.

Amendments – Planning and Compensation Act 1991,s 32, Sch 7, para 6, with effect from 25 October 1991 (SI 1991/2272).

A2.18   Allotments Act 1950

12 Abolition of contractual restrictions on keeping hens and rabbits

(1) Notwithstanding any provision to the contrary in any lease or tenancy or in any covenant, contract or undertaking relating to the use to be made of any land, it shall be lawful for the occupier of any land to keep, otherwise than by way of trade or business, hens or rabbits in any place on the land and to erect or place and maintain such buildings or structures on the land as are reasonably necessary for that purpose:

Provided that nothing in this subsection shall authorise any hen or rabbits to be kept in such a place or in such a manner as to be prejudicial to health or a nuisance or affect the operation of any enactment.

A2.19   Pastoral Measure 1983

62 Power to impose and enforce covenants

(1) Without prejudice to any restriction or requirement in a redundancy scheme or a pastoral scheme to which section 46 or section 47 applies, the Commissioners or the diocesan board of finance may, in exercising their powers under this Part to sell, give, exchange or let or, as the case may be, to let or license any building or land, include in the conveyance, lease or other instrument such covenants imposing conditions and requirements as to the use of the building or land concerned as the Commissioners or board think necessary or expedient to give effect to the provisions of the scheme or otherwise to secure the suitable use of the building or land; and, in a case where the land is sold, given or exchanged, any such covenants shall be enforceable as if the Commissioners or board were the owners of adjacent land and the covenants were expressed to be entered into for the benefit of that adjacent land, and in the case of covenants of a positive character as if they were negative.

(2) Where any such covenant is subsequently varied or released by agreement, any sum of money received by a diocesan board of finance in consideration of the variation or release of a covenant imposed by the board shall be paid to the Commissioners and section 51(5) shall apply in relation to the sum so paid, and in relation to any sum of money received by the Commissioners in consideration of the variation or release of a covenant imposed by them, as it applies in relation to the proceeds of any sale or exchange under section 51(2), (3) or (4).

[(3) Section 84 (except subsection (2)) of the Law of Property Act 1925 (which enables the Lands Tribunal to discharge or modify restrictions affecting land) shall not apply in relation to conditions and requirements imposed under subsection (1).]

Amendments – Pastoral (Amendment) Measure 1994, s 8(3), with effect from 1 April 1994.

A2.20   Housing Act 1985

Enforceability of covenants, etc

609   Enforcement of covenants against owner for the time being

Where –

(a)   a local housing authority have disposed of land held by them for any of the purposes of this Act and the person to whom the disposal was made has entered into a covenant with the authority concerning the and, or

(b)   an owner of any land has entered into a covenant with the local housing authority concerning the land for the purposes of any of the provisions of this Act,

the authority may enforce the covenant against the persons deriving title under the covenantor, notwithstanding that the authority are not in possession of or interested in any land for the benefit of which the covenant was entered into, in like manner and to the like extent as if they had been possessed of or interested in such land.

610   Power of court to authorise conversion of house into flats

(1) The local housing authority or a person interested in [any premises] may apply to the county court where –

(a)   owing to changes in the character of the neighbourhood in which the [premises] [are situated, they] cannot readily be let as a single [dwelling-house] but could readily be let for occupation if converted into two or more [dwelling-houses], or

(b)   planning permission has been granted under Part III of [the Town and Country Planning Act 1990] (general planning control) for the use of the [premises] as converted into two or more separate dwelling-houses instead of as a single dwelling-house,

and the conversion is prohibited or restricted by the provisions of the lease of the [premises], or by a restrictive covenant affecting the [premises], or otherwise.

(2) The court may, after giving any person interested an opportunity of being heard, vary the terms of the lease or other instrument imposing the prohibition or restriction, subject to such conditions and upon such terms as the court may think just.

Amendments – Planning (Consequential Provisions) Act 1990, s 4, Sch 2, para 71(5), with effect from 24 August 1990; Local Government and Housing Act 1989, s 165, Sch 9, Part V, para 88, with effect from 1 April 1990.

Appendix 3 – Statutory Material (extracts)

A3.1   Land Charges Act 1972

PRELIMINARY

1 The registers and the index

(1) The registrar shall continue to keep at the registry in the prescribed manner the following registers, namely –

    (a)   a register of land charges;
    (b)   a register of pending actions;
    (c)   ...;
    (d)   ...;
    (e)   ...,

and shall also continue to keep there an index whereby all entries made in any of those registers can readily be traced.

(2) Every application to register shall be in the prescribed form and shall contain the prescribed particulars.

[(3) Where any charge or other matter is registrable in more than one of the registers kept under this Act, it shall be sufficient if it is registered in one such register, and if it is so registered the person entitled to the benefit of it shall not be prejudicially affected by any provision of this Act as to the effect of non-registration in any other such register.

(3A) Where any charge or other matter is registrable in a register kept under this Act and was also, before the commencement of the Local Land Charges Act 1975, registrable in a local land charges register, then, if before the commencement of the said Act it was registered in the appropriate local land charges register, it shall be treated for the purposes of the provisions of this Act as to the effect of non-registration as if it had been registered in the appropriate register under this Act; and any certificate setting out the result of an official search of the appropriate local land charges register shall, in relation to it, have effect as if it were a certificate setting out the result of an official search under this Act.]

(4) ...

(5) An office copy of an entry in any register kept under this section shall be admissible in evidence in all proceedings and between all parties to the same extent as the original would be admissible.

(6) Subject to the provisions of this Act, registration may be vacated pursuant to an order of the court.

[(6A) The county courts have jurisdiction under subsection (6) above –

    (a)   ...;
    (b)   ...;
    (c)   in the case of a land charge of Class A, Class B, Class C(iv), Class D(ii), Class D(iii) or Class E if the capital value of the land affected does not exceed £30,000;
    (d)   ...;
    (e)   ...

(6B) [...]

(7) In this section 'index' includes any device or combination of devices serving the purpose of an index.

Amendments – Local Land Charges Act 1975, s 17(1)(a), with effect from 1 August 1977; County Courts Act 1984, s 148(1), Sch 2, para 16, with effect from 1 August 1984; SI 1991/724, art 2(6), (8), Schedule, Pt I, with effect from 1 July 1991; Family Law Act 1996, s 66(1), Sch 8, para 46, with effect from 1 October 1997 (SI 1997/1892, art 3(1)(b)).

2 The register of land charges

(1) If a charge on or obligation affecting land falls into one of the classes described in this section, it may be registered in the register of land charges as a land charge of that class.

(2) ...

    (a)   ...
    (b)   ...

(3) ....

(4) A Class C land charge is any of the following [(not being a local land charge)], namely –

    (i)   ...;
    (ii)   ...;
    (iii)   a general equitable charge;
    (iv)   an estate contract;

and for this purpose –

    (i)   ...;
    (ii)   ...;
    (iii)   ...
        (a) ...
        (b) ...
        (c) ...
        (d) ...;

    (iv)   an estate contract is a contract by an estate owner or by a person entitled at the date of the contract to have a legal estate conveyed to him to convey or create a legal estate, including a contract conferring either expressly or by statutory implication a valid option to purchase, a right of pre-emption or any other like right.

(5) A Class D land charge is any of the following [(not being a local land charge)], namely –

    (i)   ...;
    (ii)   a restrictive covenant;
    (iii)   an equitable easement;

and for this purpose –

    (i)   ...];
    (ii)   a restrictive covenant is a covenant or agreement (other than a covenant or agreement between a lessor and a lessee) restrictive of the user of land and entered into on or after 1st January 1926;

(iii)   an equitable easement is an easement, right or privilege over or affecting land created or arising on or after 1st January 1926, and being merely an equitable interest.

(6) ....

(7) ...].

(8) ....

(9) [...]

Amendments – Local Land Charges Act 1975, ss 17(1)(b), 19, Sch 2, with effect from 1 August 1977; Finance Act 1975, s 52(1), Sch 12, paras 2, 18(1), (2), with effect from 13 March 1975; Inheritance Tax Act 1984, s 276, Sch 8, para 3(1)(a), (b), with effect from 1 January 1985; Trusts of Land and Appointment of Trustees Act 1996, s 25(1), Sch 3, para 12(2), with effect from 1 January 1997; Family Law Act 1996, s 66(1), Sch 8, para 47, with effect from 1 October 1997; Finance Act 1977, s 59, Sch 9, with effect from 29 July 1977.

3 Registration of land charges

(1) A land charge shall be registered in the name of the estate owner whose estate is intended to be affected.

[(1A) Where a person has died and a land charge created before his death would apart from his death have been registered in his name, it shall be so registered notwithstanding his death.]

(2) A land charge registered before 1st January 1926 under any enactment replaced by the Land Charges Act 1925 in the name of a person other than the estate owner may remain so registered until it is registered in the name of the estate owner in the prescribed manner.

(3) ....

(4) The expenses incurred by the person entitled to the charge in registering a land charge of Class A, Class B or Class C (other than an estate contract) or by the Board in registering an Inland Revenue charge shall be deemed to form part of the land charge, and shall be recoverable accordingly on the day for payment of any part of the land charge next after such expenses are incurred.

(5) Where a land charge is not created by an instrument, short particulars of the effect of the charge shall be furnished with the application to register the charge.

(6) ....

(7) ....

(8) ...].

Amendments – Law of Property (Miscellaneous Provisions) Act 1994, s 15(2), with effect from 1 July 1995; Finance Act 1975, s 52, Sch 12, paras 2, 18(1), (4), with effect from 13 March 1975; Companies Act 1989, s 107, Sch 16, para 1(2), (3), with effect from 1 January 1993; Companies Consolidation (Consequential Provisions) Act 1985, s 30, Sch 2, with effect from 1 July 1985;

4 Effect of land charges and protection of purchasers

(1) ....

(2) ....

(3) ....

(4) ....

(5) A land charge of Class B and a land charge of Class C (other than an estate contract) created or arising on or after 1 January 1926 shall be void as against a purchaser of the land charged with it, or of any interest in such land, unless the land charge is registered in the appropriate register before the completion of the purchase.

(6) An estate contract and a land charge of Class D created or entered into on or after 1st January 1926 shall be void as against a purchaser for money or money's worth [(or, in the case of an Inland Revenue charge, a purchaser within the meaning of [the Inheritance Tax Act 1984)]] of a legal estate in the land charged with it, unless the land charge is registered in the appropriate register before the completion of the purchase.

(7) After the expiration of one year from the first conveyance occurring on or after January 1, 1926 of a land charge of Class B or Class C created before that date the person entitled to the land charge shall not be able to enforce or recover the land charge or any part of it as against a purchaser of the land charged with it, or of any interest in the land, unless the land charge is registered in the appropriate register before the completion of the purchase.

(8) ....

Amendments – Finance Act 1975, s 52, Sch 12, paras 2, 18(1), (5), with effect from 13 March 1975; Inheritance Tax Act 1984, s 276, Sch 8, para 13, with effect from 1 January 1985.

SEARCHES AND OFFICIAL SEARCHES

9 Searches

(1) Any person may search in any register kept under this Act on paying the prescribed fee.

(2) Without prejudice to subsection (1) above, the registrar may provide facilities for enabling persons entitled to search in any such register to see photographic or other images or copies of any portion of the register which they may wish to examine.

10 Official searches

(1) Where any person requires search to be made at the registry for entries of any matters or documents, entries of which are required or allowed to be made in the registry by this Act, he may make a requisition in that behalf to the registrar, which may be either –

(a) a written requisition delivered at or sent by post to the registry; or
(b) a requisition communicated by teleprinter, telephone or other means in such manner as may be prescribed in relation to the means in question, in which case it shall be treated as made to the registrar if, but only if, he accepts it;

and the registrar shall not accept a requisition made in accordance with paragraph (b) above unless it is made by a person maintaining a credit account at the registry, and may at his discretion refuse to accept it notwithstanding that it is made by such a person.

(2) The prescribed fee shall be payable in respect of every requisition made under this section; and that fee –

(a) in the case of a requisition made in accordance with subsection (1)(a) above, shall be paid in such manner as may be prescribed for the purposes of this paragraph unless the requisition is made by a person maintaining a credit account at the registry and the fee is debited to that account;
(b) in the case of a requisition made in accordance with subsection (1)(b) above, shall be debited to the credit account of the person by whom the requisition is made.

(3) Where a requisition is made under subsection (1) above and the fee payable in respect of it is paid or debited in accordance with subsection (2) above, the registrar shall thereupon make the search required and –

    (a)   shall issue a certificate setting out the result of the search; and

    (b)   without prejudice to paragraph (a) above, may take such other steps as he considers appropriate to communicate that result to the person by whom the requisition was made.

(4) In favour of a purchaser or an intending purchaser, as against persons interested under or in respect of matters or documents entries of which are required or allowed as aforesaid, the certificate, according to its tenor, shall be conclusive, affirmatively or negatively, as the case may be.

(5) If any officer, clerk or person employed in the registry commits, or is party or privy to, any act of fraud or collusion, or is wilfully negligent, in the making of or otherwise in relation to any certificate under this section, he shall be guilty of an offence and shall be liable on conviction on indictment to imprisonment for a term not exceeding two years, or on summary conviction to imprisonment for a term not exceeding three months or to a fine not exceeding [the prescribed sum], or to both such imprisonment and fine.

(6) Without prejudice to subsection (5) above, no officer, clerk or person employed in the registry shall, in the absence of fraud on his part, be liable for any loss which may be suffered –

    (a)   by reason of any discrepancy between –

        (i) the particulars which are shown in a certificate under this section as being the particulars in respect of which the search for entries was made, and

        (ii) the particulars in respect of which a search for entries was required by the person who made the requisition; or

    (b)   by reason of any communication of the result of a search under this section made otherwise than by issuing a certificate under this section.

Amendments – Magistrates' Courts Act 1980, s 32(2), with effect from 6 July 1981.

MISCELLANEOUS AND SUPPLEMENTARY

11 Date of effective registration and priority notices

(1) Any person intending to make an application for the registration of any contemplated charge, instrument or other matter in pursuance of this Act or any rule made under this Act may give a priority notice in the prescribed form at least the relevant number of days before the registration is to take effect.

(2) Where a notice is given under subsection (1) above, it shall be entered in the register to which the intended application when made will related.

(3) If the application is presented within the relevant number of days thereafter and refers in the prescribed manner to the notice, the registration shall take effect as if the registration had been made at the time when the charge, instrument or matter was created, entered into, made or arose, and the date at which the registration so takes effect shall be deemed to be the date of registration.

(4) Where –

    (a)   any two charges, instruments or matters are contemporaneous; and

    (b)   one of them (whether or not protected by a priority notice) is subject to or dependent on the other; and

(c)   the latter is protected by a priority notice,

the subsequent or dependent charge, instrument or matter shall be deemed to have been created, entered into or made, or to have arisen, after the registration of the other.

(5) Where a purchaser has obtained a certificate under section 10 above, any entry which is made in the register after the date of the certificate and before the completion of the purchase, and is not made pursuant to a priority notice entered on the register on or before the date of the certificate, shall not affect the purchaser if the purchase is completed before the expiration of the relevant number of days after the date of the certificate.

(6) The relevant number of days is –

(a)   for the purposes of subsections (1) and (5) above, fifteen;
(b)   for the purposes of subsection (3) above, thirty;

or such other number as may be prescribed; but in reckoning the relevant number of days for any of the purposes of this section any days when the registry is not open to the public shall be excluded.

12 Protection of solicitors, trustees, etc.

A solicitor, or a trustee, personal representative, agent or other person in a fiduciary position, shall not be answerable –

(a)   in respect of any loss occasioned by reliance on an office copy of an entry in any register kept under this Act;
(b)   for any loss that may arise from error in a certificate under section 10 above obtained by him.

13 Saving for overreaching powers

(1) The registration of any charge, annuity or other interest under this Act shall not prevent the charge, annuity or interest being overreached under any other Act, except where otherwise provided by that other Act.

(2) The registration as a land charge of a puisne mortgage or charge shall not operate to prevent that mortgage or charge being overreached in favour of a prior mortgagee or a person deriving title under him where, by reason of a sale or foreclosure, or otherwise, the right of the puisne mortgagee or subsequent chargee to redeem is barred.

14 Exclusion of matters affecting registered land or created by instruments necessitating registration of land

(1) This Act shall not apply to instruments or matters required to be registered or re-registered on or after 1st January 1926, if and so far as they affect registered land, and can be protected under the [Land Registration Act 2002].

(2) Nothing in this Act imposes on the registrar any obligation to ascertain whether or not an instrument or matter affects registered land.

(3) Where an instrument executed on or after 27th July 1971 conveys, grants or assigns an estate in land and creates a land charge affecting that estate, this Act shall not apply to the land charge, so far as it affects that estate, if under [section 7 of the Land Registration Act 2002 (effect of failure to comply with requirement of registration)] the instrument will, unless the necessary application for registration under that Act is made within the time allowed by or under [section 6 of that Act], become void so far as respects the conveyance, grant or assignment of that estate.

Amendments – Land Registration Act 2002, s 133, Sch 11, para 10(1), (2), (3)(a), (b), with effect from 13 October 2003 (SI 2003/1725, art 2(1)).

15 Application to the Crown

(1) This Act binds the Crown, but nothing in this Act shall be construed as rendering land owned by or occupied for the purposes of the Crown subject to any charge to which, independently of this Act, it would not be subject.

(2) References in this Act to restrictive covenants include references to any conditions, stipulations or restrictions imposed on or after January 1, 1926, by virtue of section 137 of the Law of Property Act 1922, for the protection of the amenities of royal parks, gardens and palaces.

16 General rules

(1) The Lord Chancellor may, with the concurrence of the Treasury as to fees, make such general rules as may be required for carrying this Act into effect, and in particular –

  (a)   as to forms and contents of applications for registration, modes of identifying where practicable the land affected, requisitions for and certificates of official searches, and regulating the practice of the registry in connection therewith;

  (b)   for providing for the mode of registration of a land charge (and in the case of a puisne mortgage, general equitable charge, estate contract, restrictive covenant or equitable easement by reference to the instrument imposing or creating the charge, interest or restriction, or an extract from that instrument) and for the cancellation without an order of court of the registration of a land charge, on its cesser, or with the consent of the person entitled to it, or on sufficient evidence being furnished that the land charge has been overreached under the provisions of any Act or otherwise;

  (c)   for determining the date on which applications and notices shall be treated for the purposes of section 11 of this Act as having been made or given;

  (d)   for determining the times and order at and in which applications and priority notices are to be registered;

  (e)   for varying the relevant number of days for any of the purposes of section 11 of this Act;

  (f)   for enabling the registrar to provide credit accounting facilities in respect of fees payable by virtue of this Act;

  (g)   for treating the debiting of such a fee to a credit account maintained at the registry as being, for such purposes of this Act or of the rules as may be specified in the rules, payment of that fee;

  (h)   for the termination or general suspension of any credit accounting facilities provided under the rules or for their withdrawal or suspension in particular cases at the discretion of the registrar;

  (j)   for requiring the registrar to take steps in relation to any instrument or matter in respect of which compensation has been claimed under section 25 of the Law of Property Act 1969 which would be likely to bring that instrument or matter to the notice of any person who subsequently makes a search of the registers kept under section 1 of this Act or requires such a search to be made in relation to the estate or interest affected by the instrument or matter; and

  (k)   for authorising the use of the index kept under this Act in any manner which will serve that purpose, notwithstanding that its use in that manner is not otherwise authorised by or by virtue of this Act.

(2) The power of the Lord Chancellor, with the concurrence of the Secretary of State, to make [rules under section [412 of the Insolvency Act 1986]] shall include power to make rules as respects the registration and re-registration of a petition in bankruptcy under section 5 of this Act and [a bankruptcy order] under section 6 of this Act, as if the registration and re-registration were required [by [Parts VIII to XI] of that Act].

Amendments – Insolvency Act 1985, s 235, Sch 8, para 21, with effect from 29 December 1986; Insolvency Act 1986, s 439(2), Sch 14, with effect from 29 December 1986.

17 Interpretation

(1) In this Act, unless the context otherwise requires –

...;

...;

'conveyance' includes a mortgage, charge, lease, assent, vesting declaration, vesting instrument, release and every other assurance of property, or of an interest in property, by any instrument except a will, and 'convey' has a corresponding meaning;

'court' means the High Court, or the county court in a case where that court has jurisdiction;

...;

'estate owner', 'legal estate', 'equitable interest' [...], 'charge by way of legal mortgage', [and 'will'] have the same meanings as in the Law of Property Act 1925;

...;

'land' includes land of any tenure and mines and minerals, whether or not severed from the surface, buildings or parts of buildings (whether the division is horizontal, vertical or made in any other way) and other corporeal hereditaments, also a manor, an advowson and a rent and other incorporeal hereditaments, and an easement, right, privilege or benefit in, over or derived from land, but not an undivided share in land, and 'hereditament' means real property which, on an intestacy occurring before 1st January 1926, might have devolved on an heir;

...;

...;

'prescribed' means prescribed by rules made pursuant to this Act;

'purchaser' means any person (including a mortgagee or lessee) who, for valuable consideration, takes any interest in land or in a charge on land, and 'purchase' has a corresponding meaning;

'registrar' means the Chief Land Registrar, 'registry' means Her Majesty's Land Registry, and 'registered land' has the same meaning as in the [Land Registration Act 2002];

'tenant for life', 'statutory owner', 'vesting instrument' and 'settlement' have the same meanings as in the Settled Land Act 1925.

(2) For the purposes of any provision in this Act requiring or authorising anything to be done at or delivered or sent to the registry, any reference to the registry shall, if the registrar so directs, be read as a reference to such office of the registry (whether in London or elsewhere) as may be specified in the direction.

(3) Any reference in this Act to any enactment is a reference to it as amended by or under any other enactment, including this Act.

Amendments – Trusts of Land and Appointment of Trustees Act 1996, s 25(2), Sch 4; for savings in relation to entailed interests created before the commencement of that Act, and savings consequential upon the abolition of the doctrine of conversion, see s 25(4), (5) thereof, with effect from 1 January 1997; Finance Act 1975, s 52(1), Sch 12, paras 2, 18(1), (6), with effect from 13 March 1975; Land

Registration Act 2002, s 133, Sch 11, para 10(1), (4), with effect from 13 October 2003 (SI 2003/1725, art 2(1)).

18 Consequential amendments, repeals, savings, etc

(1) ....

(2) [...]

(3) ...

(4) [...]

(5) In so far as any entry in a register or instrument made or other thing whatsoever done under any enactment repealed by this Act could have been made or done under a corresponding provision in this Act, it shall have effect as if made or done under that corresponding provision; and for the purposes of this provision any entry in a register which under section 24 of the Land Charges Act 1925 had effect as if made under that Act shall, so far as may be necessary for the continuity of the law, be treated as made under this Act.

(6) Any enactment or other document referring to an enactment repealed by this Act or to an enactment repealed by the Land Charges Act 1925 shall, as far as may be necessary for preserving its effect, be construed as referring, or as including a reference, to the corresponding enactment in this Act.

(7) Nothing in the foregoing provisions of this section shall be taken as prejudicing the operation of section 38 of the Interpretation Act 1889 (which relates to the effect of repeals).

Amendments – Local Land Charges Act 1975, s 19(1), Sch2, with effect from 1 August 1997; Statute Law (Repeals) Act 2004, with effect from 22 July 2004.

19 Short title, commencement and extent

(1) This Act may be cited as the Land Charges Act 1972.

(2) This Act shall come into force on such day as the Lord Chancellor may by order made by statutory instrument appoint; and different days may be so appointed for different purposes.

(3) This Act extends to England and Wales only.

Schedules

(not printed here)

A3.2   Local Land Charges Act 1975

DEFINITION OF LOCAL LAND CHARGES

1 Local land charges

(1) A charge or other matter affecting land is a local land charge if it falls within any of the following descriptions and is not one of the matters set out in section 2 below –

(a)   any charge acquired either before or after the commencement of this Act by a local authority [or National Park authority], water authority [sewerage undertaker] or new town development corporation under the Public Health Acts 1936 and 1937, [...] the Public Health Act 1961 or [the Highways Act 1980 (or any Act repealed by that Act)] [or the Building Act 1984], or any similar charge acquired by a local authority [or National Park authority] under any other Act, whether passed before or after this Act, being a charge that is binding on successive owners of the land affected;

(b)   any prohibition of or restriction on the use of land –

    (i)   imposed by a local authority [or National Park authority] on or after 1st January 1926 (including any prohibition or restriction embodied in any condition attached to a consent, approval or licence granted by a local authority on or after that date), or

    (ii) enforceable by a local authority [or National Park authority] under any covenant or agreement made with them on or after that date,
          being a prohibition or restriction binding on successive owners of the land affected;

(c)   any prohibition of or restriction on the use of land –

    (i)   imposed by a Minister of the Crown or government department on or after the date of the commencement of this Act (including any prohibition or restriction embodied in any condition attached to a consent, approval or licence granted by such a Minister or department on or after that date), or

    (ii) enforceable by such a Minister or department under any covenant or agreement made with him or them on or after that date, being a prohibition or restriction binding on successive owners of the land affected;

(d)   any positive obligation affecting land enforceable by a Minister of the Crown, government department or local authority [or National Park authority] under any covenant or agreement made with him or them on or after the date of the commencement of this Act and binding on successive owners of the land affected;

(e)   any charge or other matter which is expressly made a local land charge by any statutory provision not contained in this section.

(2) For the purposes of subsection (1)(a) above, any sum which is recoverable from successive owners or occupiers of the land in respect of which the sum is recoverable shall be treated as a charge, whether the sum is expressed to be a charge on the land or not.

[(3) For the purposes of this section and section 2 of this Act, the Broads Authority shall be treated as a local authority [or National Park authority].]

Amendments – Environment Act 1995, s 78, Sch 10, para 14, with effect from 23 November 1995; Water Act 1989, s 190, Sch 25, para 52, with effect from 1 September 1989; Highways Act 1980, s 343(2), Sch 24, para 26, with effect from 1 January 1981; Building Act 1984, s 133(1), Sch 6, para 16, with effect from 1 December 1984; Norfolk and Suffolk Broads Act 1988, s 21, Sch 6, para 14, with effect from 1 April 1989;

2 Matters which are not local land charges

The following matters are not local land charges –

(a)   a prohibition or restriction enforceable under a covenant or agreement made between a lessor and a lessee;

(b)   a positive obligation enforceable under a covenant or agreement made between a lessor and a lessee;

(c)   a prohibition or restriction enforceable by a Minister of the Crown, government department or local authority [or National Park authority] under any covenant or agreement, being a prohibition or restriction binding on successive owners of the land affected by reason of the fact that the covenant or agreement is made for the benefit of land of the Minister, government department or local authority [or National Park authority];

(d)   a prohibition or restriction embodied in any bye-laws;

(e)   a condition or limitation subject to which planning permission was granted at any time before the commencement of this Act or was or is (at any time) deemed to be granted under any statutory provision relating to town and country planning, whether by a Minister of the Crown, government department or local authority [or National Park authority];

(f)   a prohibition or restriction embodied in a scheme under the Town and Country Planning Act 1932 or any enactment repealed by that Act;

(g)   a prohibition or restriction enforceable under a forestry dedication covenant entered into pursuant to section 5 of the Forestry Act 1967;

(h)   a prohibition or restriction affecting the whole of any of the following areas –
   (i)   England, Wales or England and Wales;
   (ii) England, or England and Wales, with the exception of, or of any part of, Greater London;
   (iii) Greater London.

Amendments – Environment Act 1995, s 78, Sch 10, para 14, with effect from 23 November 1995.

3 Registering authorities, local land charges registers, and indexes

(1) Each of the following local authorities –

   (a)   the council of any district;
   [(aa) a Welsh county council;
   (ab)   a county borough council;]
   (b)   the council of any London borough; and
   (c)   the Common Council of the City of London,

shall be a registering authority for the purposes of this Act.

(2) There shall continue to be kept for the area of each registering authority –

   (a)   a local land charges register, and
   (b)   an index whereby all entries made in that register can readily be traced,

and as from the commencement of this Act the register and index kept for the area of a registering authority shall be kept by that authority.

[(3) Neither a local land charges register nor an index such as is mentioned in subsection (2)(b) above need be kept in documentary form.]

(4) For the purposes of this Act the area of the Common Council of the City of London includes the Inner Temple and the Middle Temple.

Amendments – Local Government (Wales) Act 1994, s 66(6), Sch 16, para 49, with effect from 3 April 1995; Local Government (Miscellaneous Provisions) Act 1982, s 34(a), with effect from 13 July 1982.

4 The appropriate local land charges register

In this Act [...], unless the context otherwise requires, 'the appropriate local land charges register', in relation to any land or to a local land charge, means the local land charges register for the area in which the land or, as the case may be, the land affected by the charge is situated or, if the land in question is situated in two or more areas for which local land charges registers are kept, each of the local land charges registers kept for those areas respectively.

Amendments – Interpretation Act 1978, s 25(1), Sch 3, with effect from 1 January 1979.

5 Registration

(1) Subject to subsection (6) below, where the originating authority as respects a local land charge are the registering authority, it shall be their duty to register it in the appropriate local land charges register.

(2) Subject to subsection (6) below, where the originating authority as respects a local land charge are not the registering authority, it shall be the duty of the originating authority to apply to the registering authority for its registration in the appropriate local land charges register and upon any such application being made it shall be the duty of the registering authority to register the charges accordingly.

(3) The registration in a local land charges register of a local land charge, or of any matter which when registered becomes a local land charge, shall be carried out by reference to the land affected or such part of it as is situated in the area for which the register is kept.

(4) In this Act, 'the originating authority', as respects a local land charge, means the Minister of the Crown, government department, local authority or other person by whom the charge is brought into existence or by whom, on its coming into existence, the charge is enforceable; and for this purpose –

(a)   where a matter that is a local land charge consists of or is embodied in, or is otherwise given effect by, an order, scheme or other instrument made or confirmed by a Minister of the Crown or government department on the application of another authority the charge shall be treated as brought into existence by that other authority; and

(b)   a local land charge brought into existence by a Minister of the Crown or government department on an appeal from a decision or determination of another authority or in the exercise of powers ordinarily exercisable by another authority shall be treated as brought into existence by that other authority.

(5) The registration of a local land charge may be cancelled pursuant to an order of the court.

(6) Where a charge or other matter is registrable in a local land charges register and before the commencement of this Act was also registrable in a register kept under the Land Charges Act 1972, then, if before the commencement of this Act it was registered in a register kept under that Act, there shall be no duty to register it, or to apply for its registration, under this Act and section 10 below shall not apply in relation to it.

6 Local authority's right to register a general charge against land in certain circumstances

(1) Where a local authority have incurred any expenditure in respect of which, when any relevant work is completed and any requisite resolution is passed or order is made, there will arise in their favour a local land charge (in this section referred to as 'the specific charge'), the following provisions of this section shall apply.

(2) At any time before the specific charge comes into existence, a general charge against the land, without any amount being specified, may be registered in the appropriate local land charges register by the registering authority if they are the originating authority and, if they

are not, shall be registered therein by them if the originating authority make an application for that purpose.

(3) A general charge registered under this section shall be a local land charge, but section 5(1) and (2) above shall not apply in relation to such a charge.

(4) If a general charge is registered under this section pursuant to an application by the originating authority, they shall, when the specific charge comes into existence, notify the registering authority of that fact, and any such notification shall be treated as an application (subject to subsection (5) below) for the cancellation of the general charge and the registration of the specific charge.

(5) Where a general charge is registered under this section its registration shall be cancelled within such period starting with the day on which the specific charge comes into existence, and not being less than 1 year, as may be prescribed, and the specific charge shall not be registered before the general charge is cancelled.

(6) If the registration of the general charge is duly cancelled within the period specified in subsection (5) above and the specific charge is registered forthwith upon the cancellation or was discharged before the cancellation, then, for the purposes of section 10 below, the specific charge shall be treated as having come into existence at the time when the general charge was cancelled.

7 Effect of registering certain financial charges

A local land charge falling within section 1(1)(a) above shall, when registered, take effect as if it had been created by a deed of charge by way of legal mortgage within the meaning of the Law of Property Act 1925, but without prejudice to the priority of the charge.

SEARCHES

8 Personal searches

(1) Any person may search in any local land charges register on paying the prescribed fee.

[(1A) If a local land charges register is kept otherwise than in documentary form, the entitlement of a person to search in it is satisfied if the registering authority makes the portion of it which he wishes to examine available for inspection in visible and legible form.]

(2) Without prejudice to [subsections (1) and (1A)] above, a registering authority may provide facilities for enabling persons entitled to search in the authority's local land charges register to see photographic or other images or copies of any portion of the register which they may wish to examine.

Amendments – Local Government (Miscellaneous Provisions) Act 1982, s 34(b), (c), with effect from 13 July 1982.

9 Official searches

(1) Where any person requires an official search of the appropriate local land charges register to be made in respect of any land, he may make a requisition in that behalf to the registering authority.

(2) A requisition under this section must be in writing, and for the purposes of serving any such requisition on the Common Council of the City of London section 231(1) of the Local

Government Act 1972 shall apply in relation to that Council as it applies in relation to a local authority within the meaning of that Act.

(3) The prescribed fee shall be payable in the prescribed manner in respect of every requisition made under this section.

(4) Where a requisition is made to a registering authority under this section and the fee payable in respect of it is paid in accordance with subsection (3) above, the registering authority shall thereupon make the search required and shall issue an official certificate setting out the result of the search.

Amendments – Local Government and Housing Act 1989, ss 158, 194, Sch 12, Pt II, prospectively repealed as from a day to be appointed.

10 Compensation for non-registration or defective official search certificate

(1) Failure to register a local land charge in the appropriate local land charges register shall not affect the enforceability of the charge but where a person has purchased any land affected by a local land charge, then –

(a)   in a case where a material personal search of the appropriate local land charges register was made in respect of the land in question before the relevant time, if at the time of the search the charge was in existence but not registered in that register; or

[(aa)   in a case where the appropriate local land charges register kept otherwise than in documentary form and a material personal search of that register was made in respect of the land in question before the relevant time, if the entitlement to search in that register conferred by section 8 above was not satisfied as mentioned in subsection (1A) of that section; or]

(b)   in a case where a material official search of the appropriate local land charges register was made in respect of the land in question before the relevant time, if the charge was in existence at the time of the search but (whether registered or not) was not shown by the official search certificate as registered in that register,

the purchaser shall (subject to section 11(1) below) be entitled to compensation for any loss suffered by him [in consequence].

(2) At any time when rules made under this Act make provision for local land charges registers to be divided into parts then, for the purposes of subsection (1) above –

(a)   a search (whether personal or official) of a part or parts only of any such register shall not constitute a search of that register in relation to any local land charge registrable in a part of the register not searched; and

(b)   a charge shall not be taken to be registered in the appropriate local land charges register unless registered in the appropriate part of the register.

(3) For the purposes of this section –

(a)   a person purchases land where, for valuable consideration, he acquires any interest in land or the proceeds of sale of land, and this includes cases where he acquires as lessee or mortgagee and shall be treated as including cases where an interest is conveyed or assigned at his direction to another person;

(b)   the relevant time –

(i) where the acquisition of the interest in question was preceded by a contract for its acquisition, other than a qualified liability contract, is the time when that contract was made;

(ii) in any other case, is the time when the purchaser acquired the interest in question or, if he acquired it under a disposition which took effect only when registered [in the register of title kept under the Land Registration Act 2002], the time when that disposition was made; and for the purposes of sub-paragraph (i) above, a qualified liability contract is a contract containing a term the effect of which is to make the liability of the purchaser dependent upon, or avoidable by reference to, the outcome of a search for local land charges affecting the land to be purchased;

(c) a personal search is material if, but only if –
(i) it is made after the commencement of this Act, and
(ii) it is made by or on behalf of the purchaser or, before the relevant time, the purchaser or his agent has knowledge of the result of it;

(d) an official search is material if, but only if –
(i) it is made after the commencement of this Act, and
(ii) it is requisitioned by or on behalf of the purchaser or, before the relevant time, the purchaser or his agent has knowledge of the contents of the official search certificate.

(4) Any compensation for loss under this section shall be paid by the registering authority in whose area the land affected is situated; and where the purchaser has incurred expenditure for the purpose of obtaining compensation under this section, the amount of the compensation shall include the amount of the expenditure reasonably incurred by him for that purpose (so far as that expenditure would not otherwise fall to be treated as loss for which he is entitled to compensation under this section).

(5) Where any compensation for loss under this section is paid by a registering authority in respect of a local land charge as respects which they are not the originating authority, then, unless an application for registration of the charge was made to the registering authority by the originating authority in time for it to be practicable for the registering authority to avoid incurring liability to pay that compensation, an amount equal thereto shall be recoverable from the originating authority by the registering authority.

(6) Where any compensation for loss under this section is paid by a registering authority, no part of the amount paid, or of any corresponding amount paid to that authority by the originating authority under subsection (5) above, shall be recoverable by the registering authority or the originating authority from any other person except as provided by subsection (5) above or under a policy of insurance or on grounds of fraud.

(7) In the case of an action to recover compensation under this section the cause of action shall be deemed for the purposes of the Limitation Act 1939 to accrue at the time when the local land charge comes to the notice of the purchaser; and for the purposes of this subsection the question when the charge came to his notice shall be determined without regard to the provisions of section 198 of the Law of Property Act 1925 (under which registration under certain enactments is deemed to constitute actual notice).

[(8) Where the amount claimed by way of compensation under this section does not exceed £5,000, proceedings for the recovery of such compensation may be begun in a county court.]

(9) If in any proceedings for the recovery of compensation under this section the court dismisses a claim to compensation, it shall not order the purchaser to pay the registering authority's costs unless it considers that it was unreasonable for the purchaser to commence the proceedings.

Amendments – Local Government (Miscellaneous Provisions) Act 1982, s 34(d), with effect from 13 July 1982; Land Registration Act 2002, s 133, Sch 11, para 13, with effect from 13 October 2003 (SI 2003/1725); SI 1991/724, art 2(2)(a), (8), Schedule, Pt I, with effect from 1 July 1991.

11 Mortgages, trusts for sale and settled land

(1) Where there appear to be grounds for a claim under section 10 above in respect of an interest that is subject to a mortgage –

(a)   the claim may be made by any mortgagee of the interest as if he were the person entitled to that interest but without prejudice to the making of a claim by that person;

(b)   no compensation shall be payable under that section in respect of the interest of the mortgagee (as distinct from the interest which is subject to the mortgage);

(c)   any compensation payable under that section in respect of the interest that is subject to the mortgage shall be paid to the mortgagee or, if there is more than one mortgagee, to the first mortgagee and shall in either case be applied by him as if it were proceeds of sale.

(2) Where an interest is [subject to a trust of land] any compensation payable in respect of it under section 10 above shall be dealt with as if it were proceeds of sale arising under the trust.

(3) Where an interest is settled land for the purposes of the Settled Land Act 1925 any compensation payable in respect of it under section 10 above shall be treated as capital money arising under that Act.

Amendments – Trusts of Land and Appointment of Trustees Act 1996, s 25(1), Sch 3, para 14, with effect from 1 January 1997.

MISCELLANEOUS AND SUPPLEMENTARY

12 Office copies as evidence

An office copy of an entry in any local land charges register shall be admissible in evidence in all proceedings and between all parties to the same extent as the original would be admissible.

13 Protection of solicitors, trustees, etc

A solicitor or trustee, personal representative, agent or other person in a fiduciary position, shall not be answerable in respect of any loss occasioned by reliance on an erroneous official search certificate or an erroneous office copy of an entry in a local land charges register.

14 Rules

(1) The Lord Chancellor may, with the concurrence of the Treasury as to fees, make rules for carrying this Act into effect and, in particular, rules –

(a)   for regulating the practice of registering authorities in connection with the registration of local land charges or matters which, when registered, become local land charges;

(b)   as to forms and contents of applications for registration, and the manner in which such applications are to be made;

(c)   as to the manner in which the land affected or to be affected by a local land charge is, where practicable, to be identified for purposes of registration;

(d)   as to the manner in which and the times at which registrable matters are to be registered;

(e) as to forms and contents of requisitions for official searches and of official search certificates;

(f) for regulating personal searches and related matters;

(g) as to the cancellation without an order of the court of the registration of a local land charge on its cesser, or with the consent of the authority or body by whom it is enforceable;

(h) for prescribing the fees, if any, to be paid for the filing of documents with a registering authority, the making of any entry on a register, the supply of copies of, or the variation or cancellation of, any such entry, and the making of any search of a register.

(2) Without prejudice to the generality of subsection (1) above, the power to make rules under that subsection shall include –

[(a)] power to make rules (with the concurrence of the Treasury as to fees) for carrying into effect the provisions of any statutory provision by virtue of which any matter is registrable in any local land charges register;

[(b) power to make rules providing for the use of electronic means in the making of requisitions for, and in the issue of, official search certificates, notwithstanding subsection (3) of section 231 of the Local Government Act 1972 (service of documents on local authorities) provided that –

(i) such rules shall not provide that a requisition is duly made by electronic means, except where the local authority to whom it is made consents to the use of those means, or that an official search certificate is duly issued by electronic means, except where the person requiring the search consents to the use of those means; and

(ii) such consent may be given either generally or in relation to a specified document or description of documents, and either before or after the making of the requisition or the issue of the certificate; and

(c) power to make rules modifying the application of sections 10 and 11 above in cases where –

(i) the rules provide for the making of a requisition for, or the issuing of, an official search certificate by electronic means, and

(ii) there has been any error or failure in those means.]

(3) The power to make rules under this section shall be exercisable by statutory instrument which shall be subject to annulment in pursuance of a resolution of either House of Parliament.

Amendments – Local Government and Housing Act 1989, s 158, with effect from 16 November 1989.

15 Expenses

There shall be paid out of money provided by Parliament –

(a) any administrative expenses incurred by a Minister of the Crown or government department in consequence of this Act;

(b) any expenditure incurred by a Minister of the Crown or government department in the payment of any amount recoverable from him or them under this Act by a registering authority;

(c) any increase attributable to this Act in the sums so payable under any other Act.

16 Interpretation

(1) In this Act, except where the context otherwise requires –

'the appropriate local land charges register' has the meaning provided by section 4 above;

'the court' means the High Court, or the county court in a case where the county court has jurisdiction;

'land' includes mines and minerals, whether or not severed from the surface, buildings or parts of buildings (whether the division is horizontal, vertical or made in any other way) and other corporeal hereditaments;

'official search certificate' means a certificate issued pursuant to section 9(4) above;

'the originating authority', as respects a local land charge, has the meaning provided by section 5(4) above;

'personal search' means a search pursuant to section 8 above;

'prescribed' means prescribed by rules made under section 14 above;

'the registering authority', in relation to any land or to a local land charge, means the registering authority in whose area the land or, as the case may be, the land affected by the charge is situated, or, if the land in question is situated in the areas of two or more registering authorities each of those authorities respectively;

'statutory provision' means a provision of this Act or of any other Act or Measure, whenever passed, or a provision of any rules, regulations, order or similar instrument made (whether before or after the passing of this Act) under an Act, whenever passed.

[(1A) Any reference in this Act to an office copy of an entry includes a reference to the reproduction of an entry in a register kept otherwise than in documentary form.]

(2) Except in so far as the context otherwise requires, any reference in this Act to an enactment is a reference to that enactment as amended, extended or applied by or under any other enactment, including this Act.

Amendments – Local Government (Miscellaneous Provisions) Act 1982, s 34(e), with effect from 13 July 1982.

17 Amendments of other statutory provisions

(1) […]

(2) Schedule 1 to this Act (which contains consequential amendments of other Acts and of a Measure) shall have effect.

18 Power to amend local Acts

(1) Subject to the provisions of this section, the Lord Chancellor may by order made by statutory instrument repeal or amend any relevant local Act provision that appears to him to be inconsistent with, or to require modification in consequence of, any provision of this Act.

(2) For the purposes of this section, a relevant local Act provision is a provision –

(a) contained in any local Act passed before this Act, and

(b) providing for any matter to be, or to be registered as, a local land charge or otherwise requiring or authorising the registration of any matter in a local land charges register.

(3) An order under this section shall be subject to annulment in pursuance of a resolution of either House of Parliament and may be varied or revoked by a subsequent order under this section.

(4) Before making the order under this section the Lord Chancellor shall consult any local authority appearing to him to be concerned.

19 Repeals and transitional provisions

(1) The enactments specified in Schedule 2 to this Act (which include certain spent provisions) and the instrument there specified are hereby repealed to the extent specified in the third column of that Schedule.

(2) Nothing in this Act shall operate to impose any obligation to register or apply for the registration of any local land charge within the meaning of this Act which immediately before the commencement of this Act was by virtue of subsection (7)(b)(i) of section 15 of the Land Charges Act 1925 not required by that section to be registered as a local land charge, except after the expiration of one year from the commencement of this Act; and a purchaser shall not be entitled to compensation under section 10 above by virtue of section 10(1)(a) or, where the charge was not registered at the time of the search, section 10(1)(b) in respect of a local land charge which at the time of the search was not required to be registered.

(3) [...]

(4) In so far as any entry subsisting in a local land charges register at the commencement of this Act could have been made in that register pursuant to this Act, or to any statutory provision amended by or under this Act, it shall be treated as having been so made, but nothing in this Act shall render enforceable against any purchaser whose purchase was completed before the commencement of this Act any local land charge which immediately before the commencement of this Act was not enforceable against him.

Amendments – Land Registration Act 2002, s 135, Sch 13, with effect from 13 October 2003 (SI 2003/1725, art 2(1)).

20 Short title etc

(1) This Act may be cited as the Local Land Charges Act 1975.

(2) This Act binds the Crown, but nothing in this Act shall be taken to render land owned by or occupied for the purposes of the Crown subject to any charge to which, independently of this Act, it would not be subject.

(3) [...]

(4) This Act extends to England and Wales only.

Amendments – Statute Law (Repeals) Act 2004, with effect from 22 July 2004.

Appendix 4 – Lands Tribunal Rules, Practice Directions and Fees Rules

A4.1   Lands Tribunal Rules 1996 (SI 1996/1022)

1 Citation and commencement

These Rules may be cited as the Lands Tribunal Rules 1996 and shall come into force on May 1, 1996.

2 Interpretation

(1) In these Rules –

'the Act' means the Lands Tribunal Act 1949;

['appeal' means an appeal against a determination of any question by an authority in respect of whose decision an appeal lies to the Lands Tribunal;]

'the office' means the office for the time being of the Lands Tribunal;

'the President' means the President of the Lands Tribunal, or the member appointed under section 2(3) of the Act to act for the time being as deputy for the President;

'proceedings' means proceedings before the Land Tribunal;

'the registrar' means the registrar of the Lands Tribunal or, as respects any powers or functions of the registrar, an officer of the Lands Tribunal authorised by the Lord Chancellor to exercise those powers or functions;

'the Tribunal' means the member or members of the Lands Tribunal selected under section 3(2) of the Act to deal with a case;

Amendments – SI 1997/1965, r 3, with effect from 1 September 1997.

3 Selection and powers of members of the Tribunal

(1) The President may at any time substitute a member of the Lands Tribunal for a member that he has previously selected to sit as the Tribunal or as a member of the Tribunal to hear a case.

(2) Where members of the Lands Tribunal have been selected for a class or group of cases under the provisions of section 3(2) of the Act, the President may from time to time vary the members selected.

(3) Where the President has appointed a member of the Lands Tribunal to be the chairman of any members selected under paragraphs (1) or (2) the chairman shall have the same power as the President to substitute or vary the members selected.

(4) A member of the Tribunal selected to hear a case shall have power to do anything, in relation to that case, which the President has power to do under these Rules.

4 Notice of hearings and sittings of the Tribunal

(1) The registrar shall, as soon as practicable after the commencement of proceedings before the Tribunal, send to each party a notice informing him of the date, time and place of the hearing.

(2) Upon receipt of a notice of intention to respond from a person who is not already a party to the proceedings, the registrar shall send to that person a notice informing him of the date, time and place of the hearing.

5 Hearings to be in public: exceptions

(1) All hearings by the Tribunal shall be in public except where –

  (a)   it is acting as an arbitrator under a reference by consent under section 1(5) of the Act; or
  (b)   it is satisfied that, by reason of disclosure of confidential matters or matters concerning national security, it is just and reasonable for the hearing or any part of the hearing to be in private.

(2) The following persons shall be entitled to attend a hearing whether or not it is in private –

  (a)   the President or any member of the Tribunal notwithstanding that they do not constitute the Tribunal for the purpose of the hearing; and
  (b)   a member of the Council on Tribunals.

(3) The Tribunal, with the consent of the parties, may permit any other person to attend a hearing which is held in private.

PART V
Applications under section 84 of the Law of Property Act 1925(a)
(Relief from restrictive covenants affecting land)

12 Interpretation

In this Part –

  'section 84' means a section 84 of the Law of Property Act 1925; and
  'restriction' means a restriction, arising under a covenant or otherwise, as to the user of or building on any freehold land or any leasehold land held for a term of more than 40 years of which at least 25 years have expired.

13 Method of making application

(1) A person interested in land affected by a registration who wishes to make an application under the section shall send to the registrar in duplicate an application which shall contain –

  (a)   the name and address of the person making the application and, if he is represented, the name, address and profession of the representative;
  (b)   the address or description of the land to which the application relates;
  (c)   the address or description of the land which is subject to the restriction;
  (d)   the address or description of the land which, and the identity of any person (if known) who, has the benefit of the restriction or any person whom the applicant believes may have such benefit and the reasons for that belief;

(e)   the grounds or grounds in section 84 on which the applicant relies and the reason he considers that that ground or those grounds apply;

(f)   a statement as to whether the applicant is applying to discharge the restriction wholly or for its modification, and if the latter the extent of the modification;

(g)   a statement as to whether any planning permission has been applied for, granted or refused within the five years preceding the application in respect of the land the subject of the application;

(h)   the signature of the person making the application or his representative and the date of the signature.

(2) The application referred to in paragraph (1) shall be accompanied by –

(a)   a copy of the instrument imposing the restriction or, if this is not available, documentary evidence of the restriction; and

(b)   a plan identifying the land to which the application relates and, so far as practicable, all the land which is subject to the restriction and the land which has the benefit of the restriction.

(3) An application may be made jointly by two or more persons whether the land in which they are interested is the same land or different parts of the land affected by the restriction.

14 Publication of notices

(1) Upon receipt of an application, the registrar shall determine what notices are to be given, and whether these should be given by advertisement or otherwise, to persons who appear to be entitled to the benefit of the restriction.

(2) For the purpose of paragraph (1), the registrar may require the applicant to provide any documents or information which it is within his power to provide.

(3) The notices shall require persons claiming to be entitled to the benefit of the restriction, who object to the discharge or modification of it proposed by the application, or who claim compensation for such modification or discharge, to send to the registrar and to the applicant notice of any objections they may have and of the amount of compensation they claim (if any).

(4) The notices to be given under paragraph (1) shall be given by the applicant who shall certify in writing to the registrar that directions as to the giving of these notices have been complied with.

15 Notice of objection

(1) A notice of objection to the application and a claim for compensation shall be in writing and shall be sent to the registrar and the applicant within 28 days from the publication of the notices referred to in rule 14.

(2) If the registrar requires, the person objecting shall submit a statement containing –

(a)   his name and address and if he is represented, the name, address and profession of the representative;

(b)   on the basis upon which he claims to be entitled to the benefit of the restriction;

(c)   any ground of objection; and

(d)   his signature or that of his representative and the date the statement was signed.

16 Suspension of proceedings

At any time after the registrar has received a notice of objection to the application the President or the Tribunal –

(a)   of his or its own motion may, or

(b)   on the application of the applicant or of any person who has given a notice of objection, shall,

suspend the proceedings for such time as he or it may consider appropriate to enable an application to be made to the High Court for the determination of a question arising under subsection (2) of section 84.

17 Order without hearing, etc.

(1) If it appears to the President that, having regard to the applicant's interest in the land, the applicant is not a proper person to make the application, he may dismiss it and shall inform the applicant of his reasons for doing so.

(2) Where –

(a)   the registrar receives no notice of objection within the time allowed by rule 15(1), or

(b)   all objectors have withdrawn their objections before a hearing has taken place,

the President may, with the consent of the applicant, determine the application without a hearing.

(3) Where at or after a hearing –

(a)   all objectors withdraw their objections, or

(b)   the Tribunal directs that no objector shall be admitted to oppose the application,

the Tribunal may, with the consent of the applicant, determine the application without any further hearing.

18 Power to direct additional notices

If it appears to the Tribunal at any time before the determination of the application that any person who has not received notice of the application otherwise than by advertisement should have received specific notice, the Tribunal may require the applicant to give notice to that person and may adjourn the hearing to enable that person to make an objection or a claim for compensation.

19 Enquiries of local authorities

If before or at the hearing of an application the President or the Tribunal consider that enquiries should be made of any local authority within whose area the land affected by the restriction is situated, they may direct those enquiries to be made and may adjourn the case until the local authority has replied.

20 Provisions as to orders

(1) Where the Tribunal orders the discharge or modification of a restriction subject to the payment of compensation, the discharge or modification shall not take effect until the registrar has endorsed on the order that the compensation has been paid.

(2) The Tribunal may direct that the compensation be paid within a specified time failing which the order shall cease to have effect.

(3) The Tribunal may determine that any compensation awarded shall be paid into the Court Funds Office of the Supreme Court.

PART VIII
General Procedure

27 Determination of proceedings without a hearing

(1) the Tribunal may, with the consent of the parties to the proceedings, order that the proceedings be determined without an oral hearing.

(2) Where the Tribunal makes an order under paragraph (1), any party to the proceedings may submit written representations to the Tribunal.

(3) On or after making an order under paragraph (1), the Tribunal shall give such direction relating to the lodging of documents and representations as it considers appropriate.

(4) Rule 42 shall apply to proceedings to which this rule applies as if references to the calling of witnesses and the hearing of evidence in that rule were references to representations.

(5) The Tribunal may at any time, on the application of a party to the proceedings or of its own motion, order that the proceedings should be heard and in that event may give directions for the disposal of the proceedings in accordance with these Rules.

28 Simplified procedure

(1) A member or the registrar may, with the consent of the applicant or appellant or, in relation to proceedings under Part IV, the consent of the person who is claiming compensation, direct that proceedings shall be determined in accordance with these Rules.

(2) The registrar shall send a copy of any direction made under paragraph (1) on all the parties to the proceedings and any party who objects to the direction may, within 7 days of service of the copy on him, send written notice of his objection to the registrar.

(3) Rule 38(6) to (9) and (11) shall apply as appropriate where an objection is received by the registrar under paragraph (2).

(4) Paragraphs (5) to (12) shall apply to proceedings in respect of which the registrar has made a direction under paragraph (1).

(5) [...]

(6) The registrar shall –

    (a)   give directions concerning the filing and contents of a statement of claims by the applicant or appellant and a reply by the other parties to the proceedings; and

    (b)   give the parties not less than 21 days notice of the day fixed for the hearing of the proceedings.

(7) The following directions shall take effect –

    (a)   each party shall, not less than 14 days before the date fixed for the hearing, send to every other party copies of all documents in his possession on which he intends to rely at the hearing; and

    (b)   each party shall not less than 7 days before the date fixed for the hearing send to the registrar and to every other party a copy of any expert report on which he intends to rely at the hearing and a list of the witnesses whom he intends to call at the hearing.

(8) The registrar may from time to time, whether on application or of his own motion, amend or add to any direction issued if he thinks it necessary to do so in the circumstances of the case.

(9) The hearing shall be informal and shall take place before a single member of the Lands Tribunal who shall act as if he were an arbitrator and who shall adopt any procedure that he considers to be fair.

(10) Strict rules of evidence shall not apply to the hearing and evidence shall not be taken on oath unless the Tribunal orders otherwise.

(11) No award shall be made in relation to the costs of the proceedings except in cases to which section 4 of the 1961 Act [...] [or subsections (6) and (7) of section 175 of the Commonhold and Leasehold Reform Act 2002 apply], save that the Tribunal may make an award of costs –

    (a)   in case where an offer of settlement has been made by a party and the Tribunal considers it appropriate to have regard to the fact that such an offer has been made; or

    (b)   in cases in which the Tribunal regards the circumstances as exceptional,

and if, exceptionally, an award of costs is made the amount shall not exceed that which would be allowed if the proceedings had been heard in a county court.

(12) The Tribunal may at any time, on the application of a party to the proceedings or of its own motion, order that this rule shall no longer apply to the proceedings and in that event may give directions for the disposal of the proceedings in accordance with these Rules.

Amendments – SI 2003/2945, r 7, with effect from (in relation to England): 7 December 2003: (SI 2003/2945, r 1), (in relation to Wales): 30 March 2004: (SI 2004/669, art 2 (c)(i)), for savings see art 2(c), Sch 2, para 13 thereto.

29 Site inspections

(1) Subject to paragraph (2), the Tribunal may enter and inspect –

    (a)   the land or property which is the subject of proceedings, and

    (b)   as far as is practicable, any comparable land or property to which the attention of the Tribunal is drawn.

(2) When the Tribunal intends to enter any premises in accordance with paragraph (1) it shall give notice to the parties who shall be entitled to be represented at the inspection; where the Tribunal deems it appropriate, such representation shall be limited to one person to represent those parties having the same interest in the proceedings.

[29A Assessors]

[(1) If it appears to the President that any case coming before the Tribunal calls for special knowledge he may direct that the Tribunal shall hear the case with the aid of one or more assessors appointed by him.

(2) The remuneration to be paid to an assessor appointed under this rule shall be determined by the President until the approval of the Treasury.]

Amendments—SI 1998/22, rr 1, 3, 5, with effect from 1 February 1998.

30 Consolidation of proceedings

(1) Where two or more notices of appeal, references or applications have been made which –

(a)   are in respect of the same land or buildings; or
(b)   relate to different interests in the same land or buildings; or
(c)   raise the same issues;

the President or the Tribunal may, on his or its own motion or on the application of a party to the proceedings, order that the appeals, references or applications be consolidated or heard together.

(2) An order may be made with respect to some only of the matters to which the appeals, references or applications relate.

31 Power to select test case in appeals or references

(1) Where the President is of the opinion that two or more appeals or references involve the same issues he may, with the written consent of all the parties to the appeals or references, select one or more appeal or reference to be heard in the first instance as a test case or test cases and the parties to each appeal or reference shall be bound by the decision of the Tribunal on that appeal or reference.

(2) Paragraph (1) is without prejudice to the right of the parties to each appeal or reference to require the Tribunal to state a case for the decision of the Court of Appeal.

[32 Application of Arbitration Act 1996]

[The following provisions of the Arbitration Act 1996 shall apply to all proceedings as they apply to an arbitration –

(a)   section 47 (awards on different issues, etc), as if the words 'unless otherwise agreed by the parties' were omitted from subsection (1) and so that the reference to 'award' shall include a reference to any decision of the Lands Tribunal;
(b)   section 49 (interest) subject to any enactment that prescribes a rate of interest;
(c)   section 57(3) to (7) (correction of award or additional award);]
[(d)   section 66 (enforcement of the award).]

Amendments – SI 1997/1965, r 9, with effect from 1 September 1997; SI 1998/22, rr 1, 4, 5, with effect from February 1998.

33 Evidence

(1) Evidence before the Tribunal may be given orally and may be on oath or affirmation or, if the parties to the proceedings consent or the Tribunal or President so orders, by affidavit.

(2) Notwithstanding paragraph (1), the Tribunal may at any stage of the proceedings require the personal attendance of any deponent for examination or cross-examination.

(3) Paragraphs (2) to (7) of rule 38 shall apply to an application to the President for leave to give evidence by affidavit but as if for 'registrar' in those paragraphs there were substituted 'President'.

(4) Nothing in the Civil Evidence Act 1972, or in rules of court made under it, shall prevent expert evidence from being given before the Tribunal by any party even if no application has been made to the Tribunal for a direction as to the disclosure of that evidence to any other party to the proceedings.

34 Power to order discovery, etc

(1) The Tribunal, or subject to any directions given by the Tribunal, the registrar may, on the application of any party to the proceedings or of its or his own motion, order any party –

(a)   to deliver to the registrar any document or information which the Tribunal may require and which it is in the power of the party to deliver;

(b)   to afford to every other party to the proceedings an opportunity to inspect those documents (or copies of them) and to take copies;

(c)   to deliver to the registrar an affidavit or make a list stating whether any document or class of document specified or described in the order or application is, or has at any time been in his possession, custody or power and stating when he parted with it;

(d)   to deliver to the registrar a statement in the form of a pleading setting out further and better particulars of the grounds on which he intends to rely and any relevant facts or contentions;

(e)   to answer interrogatories on affidavit relating to any matter at issue between the applicant and the other party;

(f)   to deliver to the registrar a statement of agreed facts, facts in dispute and the issue or issues to be tried by the Tribunal; or

(g)   to deliver to the registrar witness statements or proofs of evidence.

(2) Where an order is made under paragraph (1) the Tribunal or registrar may give directions as to the time within which any document is to be sent to the registrar (being at least 14 days from the date of the direction) and the parties to whom copies of the document are to be sent.

(3) Rule 38 shall apply to this rule as appropriate both in relation to applications and where the registrar acts of his own motion.

35 Extension of time

(1) The time appointed by or under these Rules for doing any act or taking any steps in connection with any proceedings may be extended on application to the registrar under rule 38.

(2) The registrar may extend the time limit on such terms as he thinks fit and may order an extension even if the application is not made until after the time limit has expired.

36 Appellant limited to grounds of appeal

(1) On the hearing of an appeal under Part III or of an application under Part V, the appellant or applicant may rely only on the grounds stated in his notice of appeal, statement of case or application unless the Tribunal permits additional grounds to be put forward.

(2) If the Tribunal permits additional grounds to be put forward in accordance with paragraph (1) it may do so on such terms as to costs, adjournment or otherwise as it thinks fit.

37 Right of audience

(1) Subject to paragraph (2), in any proceedings a party may appear in person or be represented by counsel or solicitor or by any other person with the leave of the Tribunal, or, in the case of an interlocutory application, the leave of the President or the registrar.

(2) Where a valuation officer is a party to proceedings, he may not appear in person except with the leave of the Tribunal or, in the case of an interlocutory application, the leave of the President or the registrar.

38 Interlocutory applications

(1) Except where these Rules make other provisions or the President otherwise orders, an application for directions of an interlocutory nature in connection with any proceedings shall be made to the registrar.

(2) The application shall be made in writing and shall state the title of the proceedings, and the grounds upon which the application is made.

(3) If the application is made with the consent of all parties, it shall be accompanied by consents signed by or on behalf of the parties.

(4) If the application is not made with the consent of every party the applicant shall serve a copy of the proposed application on every other party before it is made and the application shall state that this has been done.

(5) A party who objects to an application may, within 7 days of service of a copy on him, send written notice of his objection to the registrar.

(6) Before making an order on an application the registrar shall consider all the objections that he has received and may allow any party who wishes to appear before him the opportunity to do so.

(7) In dealing with an application the registrar shall have regard to the convenience of all the parties and the desirability of limiting so far as practicable the costs of the proceedings and shall inform the parties in writing of his decision.

(8) The registrar may refer the application to the President for a decision and he shall do so if requested by the applicant or a party objecting to the application.

(9) A party may appeal to the President from a decision of the registrar under this rule by giving written notice to the registrar within 7 days of service of the notice of decision or such further time as the registrar may allow.

(10) An appeal under paragraph (9) shall not act as a stay of proceedings unless the President so orders.

(11) Where an application under this rule is made –

(a)   with respect to a case that has been included by the President in a class or group of cases under section 3(2) of the Act, or

(b)   with respect to a case for which a member or members of the Lands Tribunal has or have been selected,

the powers and duties of the President under this rule may be exercised and discharged in relation to the application by any member or members of the Lands Tribunal authorised by the President for that purpose.

39 Pre-trial review

(1) The Tribunal and, subject to any direction given by the Tribunal, the registrar may, on the application of a party to the proceedings or of its or his own motion order a pre-trial review to be held and the registrar shall send to each party to the proceedings a notice informing him of the place and date of the pre-trial review.

(2) Unless the parties agree otherwise, the date of the pre-trial review shall be not less than 14 days from the making of the order that the pre-trial review should be held.

(3) The Tribunal or the registrar –

(a)   shall at the pre-trial review give any direction that appears necessary or desirable for securing the just, expeditious and economical disposal of the proceedings; and

(b)   shall at the pre-trial review endeavour to secure that the parties make all such admissions and agreements as ought reasonably to be made by them in relation to the proceedings;

(c)   may record in the order made on the review any admission or agreement made under sub-paragraph (b) or any refusal to make any admission or agreement.

(4) Where a party seeks a specific direction he shall, so far as is practicable, apply for such direction at the pre-trial review and shall give the registrar and every other party notice of his intention to do so.

(5) If an application which might have been made at the pre-trial review is made subsequently the applicant shall pay the costs of an occasioned by the application unless the Tribunal consider that there was sufficient reason for the application not having been made at the review.

(6) Paragraphs (6) to (11) of rule 38 shall apply to a pre-trial review as if it were an interlocutory application.

(7) If any party does not appear at the pre-trial review the Tribunal or the registrar may, after given the parties the opportunity to be heard, make such order as may be appropriate for the purpose of expediting or disposing of the proceedings.

41 Administration of oaths

The registrar and the Tribunal shall have power to administer oaths and take affirmations for the purpose of affidavits to be used in proceedings or for the purpose of the giving of oral evidence at hearings.

42 Expert witnesses

(1) This rule applies to any proceedings except an application for a certificate under Part VI.

(2) Subject to paragraph (3), only one expert witness on either side shall be heard unless the Tribunal orders otherwise.

(3) Where the proceedings relate to mineral valuations or business disturbance, not more than two expert witnesses on either side shall be heard unless the Tribunal orders otherwise.

(4) An application for leave to call more than the number of expert witnesses permitted by this rule may be made to the registrar in accordance with rule 38, or to the Tribunal at the hearing.

(5) A party shall, within 28 days or receiving a request from the registrar, send to him and to the other parties to the proceedings a copy of each of the following documents relating to the evidence to be given by each expert witness –

(a)   the expert witness's report, including every plan and valuation of the land or property to which the proceedings relate (which shall include full particulars and computations in support of the valuation) which it is proposed to put in evidence; and

(b)   either –
     (i) full particulars of any comparable properties and transactions to which the party intends to refer at the hearing in support of his case and a statement of the purpose for which the comparison is made; or
     (ii) a statement that no comparable properties or transactions will be referred to.

(6) If –

(a)   an application for leave under paragraph (4) is made at the hearing and granted by the Tribunal; or

(b)   at the hearing any party seeks to rely on documents not sent to the registrar or to the other parties in accordance with paragraph (5);

the Tribunal may adjourn the hearing on such terms as to costs or otherwise as he thinks fit.

43 Preliminary issues

(1) The President or the Tribunal may, on the application of any party to proceedings, order any preliminary issue in the proceedings to be disposed of at a preliminary hearing.

(2) If in the opinion of the Tribunal the decision on the preliminary issue disposes of the proceedings, it may order that the preliminary hearing shall be treated as the hearing of the case or may make such other order as it thinks fit.

(3) Paragraphs (2) to (7) of rule 38 shall apply to an application under paragraph (1) above as if for 'registrar' in those paragraphs there were substituted 'President'.

44 Sealed offers

(1) Where any party unconditionally offers or is ready to accept, any sum as compensation or by way of price, or to agree a rent or a rateable value, a copy of the offer or indication of the readiness to accept enclosed in a sealed cover may be sent to the registrar or delivered to the Tribunal at the hearing by the party who made the offer or indicated the readiness to accept and shall be opened by the Tribunal after it has determined the proceedings.

(2) An offer or an indication of readiness to accept which his sent to the registrar or delivered to the Tribunal in accordance with paragraph (1), shall not be disclosed to the Tribunal until it has decided the amount of such sum, rent or rateable value.

45 Withdrawal or dismissal of appeal, etc, before hearing

(1) An appeal, reference or application may be withdrawn by sending to the registrar a written notice of withdrawal signed by all parties to the proceedings or by their representatives.

(2) A party may, at any time before the hearing of the proceedings, apply to the President for an order to dismiss the proceedings and the President may make such order as he thinks fit.

(3) Paragraphs (2) and (4) to (7) of rule 38 shall apply to an application under paragraph (2) as if for 'registrar' there were substituted 'President'.

46 Failure to pursue proceedings or comply with Rules

(1) If it appears to the Tribunal that any party to proceedings has failed to send a copy of any document to any other party or to the registrar as required by these Rules, it may –

(a)   direct that a copy be sent;

(b)   adjourn the further hearing of the proceedings; and

(c)   require the party at fault to pay any additional costs occasioned as a result of the failure.

(2) Where a party has failed to pursue any proceedings with due diligence or has failed to comply with any of the provisions of these Rules, the registrar [or the Tribunal], on the application of any party or of his [or its] own motion, after giving the parties an opportunity to be heard may make –

(a)   an order that the proceedings be heard by the Tribunal; or

(b)   an order that the proceedings be dismissed or that any party be debarred from taking any further part in the proceedings; or

(c)   such other order as may be appropriate for expediting or disposing of the proceedings including an order for costs.

(3) Paragraphs (9) and (10) of rule 38 shall apply to any order made by the registrar under paragraph (2).

Amendments – SI 1997/1965, r 10, with effect from 1 September 1997.

47 Failure to comply with the Rules not to render proceedings invalid

Any failure by any person to comply with these Rules shall not render the proceedings or anything done in pursuance of them invalid unless the President or the Tribunal so directs.

48 Procedure at hearing

Subject to these Rules and to any direction by the President, the procedure at the hearing of any proceedings shall be such as the Tribunal may direct.

49 Default of appearance at hearing

(1) If on an appeal under part III or an application under Part V the appellant or applicant fails to attend or be represented at the hearing the Tribunal may dismiss the appeal or application.

(2) If any party to proceedings referred to in paragraph (1) other than the appellant or applicant, or any party to a reference under Part IV fails to attend or be represented at the hearing, the Tribunal may hear and determine the appeal, application or reference in his absence and may make such order as to costs as it thinks fit.

(3) Where proceedings have been dismissed or determined under this role, the Tribunal may, on the application of the party who has failed to attend within 7 days of the dismissal or termination, if it is satisfied that he had sufficient reason for his absence, set aside the dismissal or determination on such terms as to costs as it thinks fit.

50 Decision of Tribunal

(1) Subject to paragraph (2), the decision of the Tribunal on an appeal, reference or application shall be given in writing, and shall state the reasons for the decision.

(2) The Tribunal may give its decision orally in cases where it is satisfied that this would not result in any injustice or inconvenience to the parties.

(3) The Tribunal may, and on the application of any party to the proceedings shall, issue an order incorporating its decision.

(4) Where an amount awarded or value determined by the Tribunal is dependent upon the decision of the Tribunal on a question of law which is in dispute in the proceedings, the Tribunal shall ascertain, and shall state in its decision, any alternative amount or value which it would have awarded or determined if it had come to a different decision on the point of law.

(5) [The registrar shall serve] a copy of the decision or, where the decision is given orally an order stating its effect, [on every party] who has appeared before the Tribunal in the proceedings, and –

(a)   in the case of an appeal against the decision of a valuation tribunal to the clerk of that tribunal and, if the appeal is a rating appeal, to the valuation officer;

(b)   in the case of any other appeal under Part III< to the authority.

(6) If the Court of Appeal directs that any decision of the Tribunal, on which a case has been stated for the decision of the Court of Appeal, should be amended the registrar shall send copies of the amended decision to every person who was notified of the original decision.

Amendments – SI 1997/1965, r 11, with effect from 1 September 1997.

51 Consent orders

Where the parties to proceedings have agreed the terms of an order to be made by the Tribunal, particulars of those terms signed by all the parties or by their representatives shall be sent to the registrar and an order may be made by the Tribunal in accordance with those terms in the absence of the parties.

52 Costs

(1) Subject to the provisions of section 4 of the 1961 Act [subsections (6) and (7) of section 175 of the Commonhold and Leasehold Reform Act 2002] and of rule 28(11), the costs of an incidental to any proceedings shall be in the discretion of the Tribunal.

(2) The registrar may make an order as to costs in respect of any application or proceedings heard by him.

(3) A person dissatisfied with the order of the registrar under paragraph (2) may, within 10 days of the order, appeal to the President who may make such order as to the payment of costs, including the costs of the appeal, as he thinks fit.

(4) If the Tribunal directs that the costs of a party to the proceedings be paid by another party it may settle the amount of costs by fixing a lump sum or direct that the costs be taxed by the registrar on such basis as the Tribunal thinks fit, being a basis that would be applied on a taxation of the costs of High Court or county court proceedings.

(5) A party dissatisfied with a taxation of costs under paragraph (4) may, within 7 days of the taxation, serve on any other interested party and on the registrar written objection specifying the items objected to and applying for the taxation to be reviewed in respect of those items.

(6) Upon such application the registrar shall review the taxation of the items objected to and shall state in writing the reasons for his decision.

(7) A person dissatisfied with the decision of the registrar under paragraph (6) may, within 10 days of the decision, apply to the President to review the taxation and the President may make such order as he thinks fit including an order as to payment of the costs of the review.

(8) Paragraphs (8) and (10) of rule 38 shall apply to any application under this rule.

Amendments – SI 2003/2945, r 8, with effect from (in relation to England): 7 December 2003: (SI 2003/2945, r 1), (in relation to Wales): 30 March 2004: (SI 2004/669, art 2 (c)(i)), for savings see art 2(c), Sch 2, para 13 thereto.

53 Solicitor to be on the record

(1) Where a solicitor commences or responds to proceedings on behalf of a party to those proceedings he shall be noted on the record of the Tribunal as acting for that party.

(2) A party who has previously carried on proceedings in person may appoint a solicitor at anytime to act on his behalf and if he does so shall notify the Tribunal who shall note on the record that the solicitor is acting for that party.

(3) A party who has previously been represented by a solicitor may charge his solicitor at any time, or may decide to continue the proceedings in person but unless such change or decision is notified to the Tribunal the former solicitor shall be considered the representative of the party until the conclusion of the proceedings.

(4) The notifications referred to in paragraphs (2) and (3) may be given by the party or his solicitor and the person giving the notification shall send a copy to every other party to the proceedings.

(5) A solicitor who is on the record of the Tribunal as acting for a party shall be responsible for the payment of all fees of the Tribunal which are the responsibility of that party whilst he remains on the record.

54 Service of notices

(1) Every party to proceedings shall notify the registrar of an address for service of documents on him.

(2) Where a party to proceedings is represented by a person other than a solicitor he shall –

    (a)   send to the registrar written authority for that representative to act on his behalf; and

    (b)   notify the registrar if the representative ceases to act on his behalf and, if replaced, shall give the registrar details of the new representative together with the written authority for the new representative to act on his behalf.

(3) Any document to be served on any person under these Rules shall be deemed to have been served if sent by pre-paid post to that person at his address for service.

(4) Any document to be sent to the registrar under these Rules shall be sent to him at the office.

(5) Any application or communication to be made to the President or to any member of the Lands Tribunal in respect of any case shall be addressed to the registrar at the office.

55 Change of address

A party to any proceedings may at any time by notice in writing to the registrar and to every other party to the proceedings change his address for service under these Rules.

56 Substituted service

If any person to whom any notice or other document is required to be sent under these Rules –

(a)   cannot be found after all diligent enquiries have been made;
(b)   has died and has no personal representative; or
(c)   is out of the United Kingdom;

or for any other reason service upon him cannot readily be effected in accordance with these Rules, the President or the Tribunal may dispense with service upon that person or make an order for substituted service in such other form (whether by advertisement in a newspaper or otherwise) as the President or Tribunal may think fit.

PART IX
Transitional provisions

57 Transitional provisions, repeals etc

(1) The Rules shall apply to proceedings commenced before the date on which they come into force as well as to proceedings commenced on or after that date.

(2) The Rules set out in Schedule 2 are hereby revoked.

SCHEDULE 1

(Forms relating to Rights of Light Act 1959; not printed)

SCHEDULE 2

REVOCATIONS

(not printed)

A4.2   Arbitration Act 1996

47 Awards on different issues, etc

(1) the tribunal may make more than one award [or decision] at different times on different aspects of the matters to be determined.

(2) The tribunal may, in particular, make an award [or decision] relating –

(a)   to an issue affecting the whole claim, or
(b)   to a part only of the claims or cross-claims submitted to it for decision.

(3) If the tribunal does so, it shall specify in its award [or decision] the issue, or the claim, or part of a claim, which is the subject matter of the award. [See Rule 32 above.]

49 Interest

(1) The parties are free to agree on the powers of the tribunal as regards the award of interest.

(2) Unless otherwise agreed by the parties the following provisions apply.

(3) The tribunal may award simple or compound interest from such dates, at such rates and with such rests as it considers meets the justice of the case –

    (a)   on the whole or part of any amount awarded by tribunal, in respect of any period up to the date of the award;

    (b)   on the whole or part of any amount claimed in the arbitration and outstanding at the commencement of the arbitral proceedings but paid before the award was made, in respect of any period up to the date of payment.

(4) The tribunal may award simple or compound interest from the date of the award (or any later date) until payment, at such rates, and with such rests as it considers meets the justice of the case, on the outstanding amount of any award (including any award of interest under subsection (3) and any award as to costs).

(5) References in this section to an amount awarded by the tribunal include an amount payable in consequences of a declaratory award by the tribunal.

(6) The above provisions do not affect any other power of the tribunal to award interest.

57 Correction of award or additional award

(3) The tribunal may on its own initiative or on the application of a party –

    (a)   correct an award so as to remove any clerical mistake or error arising from an accidental slip or omission or clarify or remove any ambiguity in the award, or

    (b)   make an additional award in respect of any claim (including a claim for interest or costs) which was presented to the tribunal but was not dealt with in the award.

These powers shall not be exercised without first affording the other parties a reasonable opportunity to make representations to the tribunal.

(4) Any application for the exercise of those powers must be made within 28 days of the date of the award or such longer period as the parties may agree.

(5) Any correction of an award shall be made within 28 days of the date the application was received by the tribunal or, where the correction is made by the tribunal on its own initiative, within 28 days of the date of the award or, in either case, such longer period as the parties may agree.

(6) Any additional award shall be made within 56 days of the date of the original award or such longer period as the parties may agree.

(7) Any correction of an award shall form part of the award.

66 Enforcement of the award

(1) An award made by the tribunal pursuant to an arbitration agreement may, by leave of the court, be enforced in the same manner as a judgment or order of the court to the same effect.

(2) Where leave is so given, judgment may be entered in terms of the award.

(3) Leave to enforce an award shall not be given where, or to the extent that, the person against whom it is sought to be enforced shows that the tribunal lacked substantive jurisdiction to make the award.

The right to raise such an objection may have been lost (see section 73).

(4) Nothing in this section affects the recognition or enforcement of an award under any other enactment or rule of law, in particular under Part II of the Arbitration Act 1950 (enforcement of awards under Geneva Convention) or the provisions of Part III of this Act relating to the recognition and enforcement of awards under the New York Convention or by an action on the award.

73 Loss of right to object

(1) If a party to arbitral proceedings takes part, or continues to take part, in the proceedings without making, either forthwith or within such time as is allowed by the arbitration agreement or the tribunal or by any provision of this Part, any objection –

(a)   that the tribunal lacks substantive jurisdiction,
(b)   that the proceedings have been improperly conducted,
(c)   that there has been a failure to comply with the arbitration agreement or with any provision of this Part, or
(d)   that there has been any other irregularity affecting the tribunal or the proceedings,

he may not rise that objection later, before the tribunal or the court, unless he shows that, at the time he took part or continued to take part in the proceedings, he did not know and could not with reasonable diligence have discovered the grounds for the objection.

(2) Where the arbitral tribunal rules that it has substantive jurisdiction and a party to arbitral proceedings who could have questioned that ruling –

(a)   by any available arbitral process of appeal or review, or
(b)   by challenging the award,

does not do so, or does not do so within the time allowed by the arbitration agreement or any provision of this Part, he may not object later to the tribunal's substantive jurisdiction on any ground which was the subject of that ruling.

Lands Tribunal – Practice Directions 2005

Readers should consult the Lands Tribunal website (www.landstribunal.gov.uk) for the most up-to-date version of these directions in view of the changes which can be incorporated from time to time. This printed version is correct as at 15 January 2005.

A4.3   Practice Direction 1/2005

1 Introduction

1.1 Procedure in the Lands Tribunal is governed by the Lands Tribunal Rules 1996 (SI 1996 No 1022), as amended by the Lands Tribunal (Amendment) Rules of 1997, 1998 and 2003 (SI 1997 No 1965, SI 1998 No 22 and SI 2003 No 2945). Practice Directions, issued from time to time by the President, contain information on the way in which the procedure contained in the rules is operated. These Practice Directions supersede all those previously issued. They apply to all proceedings, including references by consent.

A4.4   Practice Direction 2/2005

2 The Overriding Objective

2.1 The Civil Procedure Rules, which apply to the ordinary civil courts of law (the Court of Appeal, the High Court and the county courts), have no application in the Lands Tribunal. Nevertheless in following its procedures the Tribunal does so on the basis of the same overriding objective as that in the CPR. The overriding objective is to follow procedures that enable the Tribunal to deal with cases justly. Dealing with a case justly includes, so far as is practicable:

- (a)   ensuring that the parties are on an equal footing;
- (b)   saving expense;
- (c)   dealing with the case in ways which are proportionate:
  - (i) to the amount of money involved;
  - (ii) to the importance of the case;
  - (iii) to the complexity of the issues; and
  - (iv) to the financial position of each party;
- (d)   ensuring that it is dealt with expeditiously and fairly; and
- (e)   allotting to it an appropriate share of the Tribunal's resources, while taking into account the need to allot resources to other cases.

2.2 The Tribunal expects parties to assist it to further the overriding objective.

A4.5   Practice Direction 3/2005

3 Case management

3.1 Every case will be assigned to one of four procedures, as soon as the Tribunal or the Registrar has sufficient information to enable this to be done:

- (a)   the standard procedure;
- (b)   the special procedure;
- (c)   the simplified procedure;
- (d)   the written representations procedure.

Any views expressed by the parties on the procedure to which a case should be assigned will be taken into account.

3.2 A case will be assigned to the **special procedure** if it requires case management by a Member in view of its complexity, the amount in issue or its wider importance. Once a case has been allocated to a Member (or Members) under the special procedure, the Member(s) will order a pre-trial review to be held under rule 39. The purpose of the pre-trial review is to ensure so far as practicable that all appropriate directions are given for the fair, expeditious and economical conduct of the proceedings. Where appropriate a date for the hearing will be fixed at the pre-trial review and the steps which the parties are required to take, and further pre-trial reviews, will be timetabled by reference to this date. Before the PTR the parties will be asked to the extent that they are able to do so at that stage, to identify the issues in the case, and to state the areas of expertise of each expert witness that they propose to rely on and the general scope of his evidence. Each party should consider whether it is appropriate to make application under rule 43 (determination of a preliminary issue) and rule 42 (leave to call more than the permitted number of expert witnesses) and it should identify, and where necessary make application for, any other order that it wishes the Tribunal to make at the PTR.

3.3 Rule 28 provides for the assignment of a case to the **simplified procedure**. The purpose of this procedure is to provide for the speedy and economical determination of cases in which no substantial issue of law or valuation practice, or substantial conflict of fact, is likely to arise. It is often suitable where the amount at stake is small. The procedure is initiated by a direction of a Member or the Registrar, made with the consent of the claimant, appellant or applicant, that the proceedings should be determined under this rule. There is provision for any other party to object and for determining such objection as an interlocutory matter under rule 38.

3.4 The objective is to move to a hearing as quickly as possible and with the minimum of formality and cost. In most cases a date for the hearing, normally about 3 months ahead, will be fixed immediately, and the parties will be required to file a statement of case and a reply. They must, not later than 28 days before the hearing, exchange copies of all documents on which they intend to rely, and experts' reports must be exchanged not later than 14 days before the hearing. The hearing is informal and strict rules of evidence do not apply. It will almost always be completed in a single day. Except in compensation cases, to which particular statutory provisions on costs apply, an award of costs is made only in exceptional circumstances.

3.5 Under rule 27 the Tribunal may, with the consent of the parties to the proceedings, order that the proceedings be determined without an oral hearing. Such an order for the **written representation procedure** to be followed will only be made if the Tribunal, having regard to the issues in the case and the desirability of minimising costs, is of the view that oral evidence and argument can properly be dispensed with. Directions will be given to the parties relating to the lodging of representations and documents, and the Member allocated to the case will if necessary carry out a site inspection before giving his written decision.

3.6 The **standard procedure** applies in all other cases. Under this procedure case management will be in the hands of the Registrar. He will look to hold a PTR at the earliest time that it appears appropriate to do so, and he will give directions tailored to the requirements of the particular case. These directions may, as appropriate, use elements of the special procedure (for example, timetabling through to the hearing date) or the simplified procedure.

3.7 At any time the Registrar, or the Member to whom the case has been allocated, may direct that it should be assigned to one of the other procedures, provided that any consent from a party that is required under rules 27 or 28 has been given.

3.8 At the time an appellant lodges his notice of appeal or a respondent his notice of intention to respond he will be asked to state to which of the procedures he suggests that the case should be assigned. The same course will be followed in relation to every party to a reference, and to the applicant and objectors in an application under Part V of the Rules.

A4.6   Practice Direction 4/2005

4   Stay of proceedings pending negotiation or ADR

4.1   At the time an appellant lodges his notice of appeal or a respondent his notice of intention to respond he will be asked to state whether he wishes the proceedings to be stayed to allow negotiations for a settlement to take place or an Alternative Dispute Resolution procedure to be followed. Parties to a reference also will be asked whether they wish the proceedings to be stayed for this purpose. Where both parties indicate such a wish, a stay of 4 weeks will normally be granted. If a longer period is asked for, the parties will need to satisfy the Tribunal that in the circumstances of the particular case this would be appropriate.

A4.7   Practice Direction 5/2005

5   Appeals from Leasehold Valuation Tribunals

5.1   In respect of applications to a leasehold valuation tribunal made after 1 September 2003 a party may appeal to the Lands Tribunal under section 175(1) of the Commonhold and Leasehold Reform Act 2002; but by section 175(2) it is provided that an appeal may only be made with the permission of the leasehold valuation tribunal or the Lands Tribunal.

5.2 Procedure in cases where permission required

Where permission is required it must first be sought from the LVT concerned (Lands Tribunal Rules 1996 rule 5C(1)). If the LVT grants permission, notice of appeal must be given to the Registrar of the Lands Tribunal within 28 days of the grant of permission to appeal (Lands Tribunal Rules 1996, rule 6(1) as amended). There is power to extend the time limit (Lands Tribunal Rules 1996, rule 35), but no extension will be granted unless there is justification for it. Forms for the notice of appeal can be obtained from the Lands Tribunal, and a completed form must be sent or delivered to the Lands Tribunal together with a copy of the disputed decision and a copy of the LVT's decision granting permission to appeal.

5.3   If the LVT refuses permission to appeal, application for permission may be made to the Lands Tribunal within 28 days of the decision of the LVT to refuse permission: rule 5C(2). There is power to extend this time limit (rule 35), but no extension will be granted unless there is justification for it. Forms for the application can be obtained from the Lands Tribunal. These provide for the applicant to set out, in addition to his grounds of appeal, the reasons for the application for permission. It is for the applicant to satisfy the Lands Tribunal that permission to appeal should be given and his reasons should therefore be set out fully as provided for on the form. The application must be accompanied by a copy of the decision against which permission to appeal is being sought and a copy of the decision of the LVT refusing permission to appeal.

5.4   On receiving an application for permission to appeal, the Lands Tribunal, unless it decides that permission should be refused without further representations, will serve a copy of the application on each respondent and will inform the applicant of the date when this was done. Respondents will be informed of the time limit specified by the Lands Tribunal within which any written representations must be made. The Lands Tribunal will consider any such representations and the applicant's reasons for his application and will decide whether to grant permission. Only in special circumstances will a hearing be held before a decision to grant or to refuse permission is made. If the Lands Tribunal grants permission, it may do so on such conditions as it thinks fit. In view of the limitation on the Tribunal's power to award costs contained in section 175(6) and (7) of the Commonhold and Leasehold Reform Act 2002, it will not be appropriate to impose conditions relating to costs. It would, however, be open to an appellant to undertake to pay all or part of a respondent's costs.

5.5 Approach of the Lands Tribunal to the grant of permission

On the application form the applicant is asked to specify as his reasons for making the application one or more of the following:

(a)   The decision shows that the LVT wrongly interpreted or wrongly applied the relevant law.

(b)   The decision shows that the LVT wrongly applied or misinterpreted or disregarded a relevant principle of valuation or other professional practice.

(c)   The LVT took account of irrelevant considerations, or failed to take account of relevant consideration or evidence, or there was a substantial procedural defect.

(d)   The point or points at issue is or are of potentially wide implication.

5.6 The application must make clear whether the appellant is seeking:

(i)   an appeal by way of review; or

(ii)   an appeal by way of review, which if successful will involve a consequential re-hearing; or

(iii)   an appeal by way of re-hearing.

Unless the application otherwise specifies, the application will be treated as an application for an appeal by way of review.

5.7 The Lands Tribunal will grant permission to appeal only where it appears that there are reasonable grounds for concluding that the LVT may have been wrong for one or more of the reasons (a)–(c). In considering whether to grant permission on such grounds the importance of the point both to the decision itself and in terms of its wider implications will be a factor to be taken into consideration, in determining the proportionality and expedience of permitting an appeal to proceed. Where a successful appeal by review will necessitate a re-hearing, the Tribunal will have regard to the scope of such re-hearing in considering the proportionality of granting permission.

5.8 Procedure on appeal

The Lands Tribunal Rules Parts III and VIII contain the procedure relating to appeals. Where an application for permission has been made and permission has been granted the application will be treated as the appellant's notice of appeal for the purposes of rule 6. Except in cases where the simplified procedure is followed under rule 28, the appellant will be required to serve a statement of case and each respondent will be required to serve a reply: see rule 8. Where a successful appeal by way of review will involve a consequential re-hearing of all or part of the evidence, unless the review is dealt with as a preliminary issue (see section 7 below), the review and the re-hearing will take place in the same hearing, and appropriate directions will be given for this purpose.

A4.8   Practice Direction 6/2005

6   Statement of case and reply

6.1 Under Part III of the Rules, which relates to appeals, there are requirements that the appellant must serve a statement of case and the respondent must serve a reply. In the case of references there is no such requirement, but a statement of case and a reply will often be the appropriate way of ensuring that the issues are identified as soon as possible. In references, therefore, the Registrar (under the standard procedure) or a Member (under the special procedure) will normally order these at an early stage.

A4.9   Practice Direction 7/2005

7   Preliminary issues

7.1 Rule 43 enables the Tribunal on the application of any party to proceedings to order any preliminary issue in the proceedings to be disposed of at a preliminary hearing. In appropriate circumstances the procedure may enable the proceedings to be concluded more expeditiously and expense to be saved, and parties are therefore encouraged to consider whether there are any issues in a case which can with advantage be dealt with in this way. For its part the Tribunal will draw the parties' attention to issues which in its view might usefully be determined under this procedure.

7.2 Issues which may appropriately be the subject of a preliminary determination may be of law or of fact. Determination of a preliminary issue may effectively dispose of the whole case. Where it would not do so, however, it may nevertheless reduce the issues in the case and thereby avoid the cost and delay associated with the disclosure and inspection of documents, the preparation and exchange of experts' reports and valuations, and the pre-trial preparation on the part of solicitors and counsel, which the issues eliminated would otherwise have involved. On the other hand to attempt to deal as a preliminary issue with a matter which is not in reality severable from other issues in the case can lead to delay and increased cost.

7.3 An application under rule 43 should set out with precision the point of law or other issue or issues to be decided. It should where appropriate be accompanied by a statement of agreed facts, and it should state whether in the view of the party making the application the issue can be decided on the basis of the statement of agreed facts or whether evidence will be required. If evidence is said to be needed the application should state what matters that evidence would cover. The application should state why, in the applicant's view, determination of the issue as a preliminary issue would be likely to enable the proceedings to be disposed of more expeditiously and/or at less expense.

7.4 In order to consider an application that there should be a determination under rule 43 the Tribunal may require that witness statements and documentary evidence should be filed. If it decides to order that the issue should be determined as a preliminary issue it will give directions as to the filing in advance of the hearing of any experts' reports, witness statements, documentary evidence and statement of agreed facts that appear to it to be required.

7.5 An application under rule 43 is not appropriate for the determination of matters of title to the benefit of restrictive covenants for the purpose of applications to the Tribunal to discharge or modify restrictions under section 84 of the Law of Property Act 1925. That section makes specific provision for the giving of directions by the Tribunal as to who may be admitted to oppose such an application to discharge or modify restrictions and for reference to the court of questions relating to the land affected by the restriction, the construction and effect of the restriction, and who, if anyone, can enforce it. The Tribunal has a separate procedure for the exercise of this statutory jurisdiction.

A4.10   Practice Direction 8/2005

8   Extensions of time

8.1 Under rule 38 any time limit within which, either as prescribed by the Rules or as laid down in any order or direction, a party is required to do anything may be extended on application to the Registrar. In general, justification for any such extension will be required, and the Registrar, or the Member to whom the case has been allocated, will consider any such application having regard to the overriding objective. In certain types of case, notably section 84 applications and leasehold enfranchisement appeals, delay may have substantial adverse consequences for one of the parties and the Tribunal will seek to enforce strictly any time limits laid down if such consequences are likely to occur.

A4.11 Practice Direction 9/2005

9 Arranging the hearing

9.1 Where a hearing date has not already been fixed, the parties will be consulted as soon as the case is considered ready (either for a full hearing or for the determination of a preliminary issue). The views of the parties will be sought as to the estimated length of the hearing, the appropriate venue and suitable dates. Whilst every effort will be made to accommodate the parties' choice of counsel, there can be no absolute right to be represented by a particular member of the Bar. If, due to chosen counsel's unavailability, unacceptable listing delays would occur, the appointment of alternative counsel may be necessary. Once the parties have been consulted, and suitable dates determined, the case will be formally set down for the hearing and the parties officially notified. After the hearing has been fixed in this way the Tribunal will not order a postponement, even though the parties are agreed that there should be one, unless very good reasons are made out.

A4.12 Practice Direction 10/2005

10 Venue

10.1 All parties are offered the option of a hearing at the Tribunal's own courts in London, and it is often possible to arrange earlier dates there than in a provincial court and to accommodate larger cases more easily than elsewhere. Where, for reasons of cost, accessibility, or the convenience of the parties and their representatives, it is desirable for a case to be heard outside London, the preferences of the parties will be met as far as it is practicable to do so. However, due to pressure on court accommodation it may be necessary for the parties to travel to the nearest major city, and there may be a smaller choice of dates.

A4.13 Practice Direction 11/2005

11 Negotiations, settlements and withdrawals

11.1 The Tribunal encourages continued negotiations between the parties prior to the hearing with the objective of settling some or all of the issues, but the fact that such negotiations may be in progress will not constitute the sort of exceptional circumstances that would justify a postponement of the hearing. The parties should let the Tribunal know if, as the result of negotiations or other circumstances, time estimates for the hearing change. Where settlement of the case is reached before the hearing, the parties' representatives should advise the Tribunal immediately so that the hearing arrangements may be cancelled. Similarly, where an appeal, reference or application is to be withdrawn (rule 45(1)) or application is made to dismiss the proceedings (rule 45(2)) after the hearing date has been fixed, the Tribunal should be advised at the earliest opportunity.

A4.14 Practice Direction 12/2005

12 Documentation

12.1 In cases assigned to the special or standard procedures, unless the Tribunal directs otherwise, the parties should lodge with the Tribunal not less than 14 days prior to the hearing sufficient copies (for the number of Members sitting) of a fully paginated agreed trial bundle containing the following:

(a) expert witness reports, including all appendices, photographs and plans referred to;
(b) witness statements;
(c) all other documents to be relied upon;
(d) a statement of agreed facts and issues.

The advocates' skeleton arguments should be lodged not less than 7 days before the hearing. Photocopies of any cases relied on should be provided for the Tribunal.

12.2 Plans and photographs should be appropriately annotated and indexed. Plans should be in A4 or A3 format unless there is good reason to use some other size.

A4.15 Practice Direction 13/2005

13 Evidence

13.1 Those giving evidence at a hearing, whether of fact or as expert witnesses, should provide a written statement verified by a statement of truth. The form of the statement of truth is as follows:

> 'I believe that the facts stated in this witness statement are true.'

The form of the statement of truth by an expert witness is as follows:

> 'I believe that the facts stated in this witness statement are true and that the opinions expressed are correct.'

13.2 Evidence is given on oath or affirmation. Expert witnesses should comply with the provisions of the following paragraphs of these Practice Directions. An expert's report will stand as the expert's witness statement unless the Tribunal directs otherwise. A witness statement will stand as the witness's evidence in chief, but a witness giving oral evidence may, with the consent of the Tribunal, (a) amplify his witness statement; and (b) give evidence on new matters which have arisen since the witness statement was served. Notice of any such additional evidence should where possible be given to the other party, and any failure to do so will be taken into account by the Tribunal in deciding whether to give consent to such evidence being given. Paragraph **14.7** refers to supplementary experts' reports.

A4.16 Practice Direction 14/2005

14 Expert evidence

14.1 Introduction

Rule 42 of the Lands Tribunal Rules 1996 applies to expert witnesses and their evidence. The nature of the jurisdictions exercised by the Lands Tribunal means that the Tribunal will be called upon to hear and evaluate the evidence of experts in most cases. Expert witnesses are defined as those qualified by training and experience in a particular subject or subjects to express an opinion. Most frequently the expert witness before the Tribunal will be a surveyor or valuer, but this Part applies equally to any witness whom it is proposed to call to give expert evidence.

14.2 Duty of the expert witness

It is the duty of an expert to help the Tribunal on matters within his expertise. This duty overrides any obligation to the person from whom he has received instructions or by whom he is paid. The evidence should be accurate and complete as to relevant fact, and should represent the honest and objective opinion of the witness. If a professional body has adopted a code of practice and professional conduct dealing with the giving of evidence, then the Tribunal will expect a Member of that body to comply with the provisions of the code in the preparation and presentation of his evidence.

14.3   Where more than one party intends to call expert evidence

Where more than one party is intending to call expert evidence in the same field, the experts should take steps before preparing or exchanging their reports to agree all matters of fact relevant to their reports, including the facts relating to any comparable transaction on which they propose to rely, any differences of fact, and any plans, documents or photographs on which they intend to rely in their reports.

14.4   Form and content of expert's report

An expert's report should be addressed to the Tribunal and not to the party from whom the expert has received his instructions. It should:

(a)   give details of the expert's qualifications;
(b)   give details of any literature or other material on which the expert has relied in making the report;
(c)   say who carried out any inspection or investigations which the expert has used for the report and whether or not the investigations have been carried out under the expert's supervision;
(d)   give the qualifications of the person who carried out any such inspection or investigations; and
(e)   where there is a range of opinion on the matters dealt with in the report:
    (i) summarise the range of opinion, and
    (ii) give reasons for his own opinion;
(f)   contain a summary of the conclusions reached;
(g)   contain a statement that the expert understands his duty to the Tribunal and has complied with that duty; and
(h)   contain a statement setting out the substance of all material instructions (whether written or oral). The statement should summarise the facts and instructions given to the expert which are material to the opinions expressed in the report or upon which those opinions are based.

14.5 The instructions referred to in sub-paragraph (h) above will not be privileged against disclosure but the Tribunal will not, in relation to those instructions:

(i)   order disclosure of any specific document; or
(ii)   permit any questioning in the Tribunal, other than by the party who instructed the expert,

unless it is satisfied that there are reasonable grounds to consider the statement of instructions given under sub-paragraph (h) to be inaccurate or incomplete.

14.6 An expert's report should be verified by a statement of truth as well as the statements required by **14.4(g), (h)**. Members of the Royal Institution of Chartered Surveyors should comply with the form of declaration contained in 'Surveyors Acting as Expert Witnesses – Practice Statement' issued by the RICS. The form of the statement of truth is set out in **13.1** above.

14.7 Lodging reports

The procedures of the Tribunal are designed to ensure that all cases are disposed of speedily, efficiently and fairly. The role of the expert witness in these procedures is of fundamental importance. The directions given by the Tribunal will normally require the lodging and exchange of experts' reports and valuations at an early stage prior to the hearing. It is incumbent on the expert witness to prepare and submit such a report together with any valuation and details of comparable properties or transactions relied upon, fully and promptly for the purpose of lodging and exchange. Subject to **13.2** expert evidence given at the hearing will be confined to those matters disclosed in the expert's report. An expert who wishes to respond to the report of another expert should do so in a supplementary report, which will be treated as notice of additional evidence for the purposes of **13.2**. Experts' reports must not contain any reference to or details of negotiations 'without prejudice' or offers of settlement.

14.8   Written questions to experts

The Tribunal encourages parties to adopt the following procedure. Where he thinks it necessary to do so, a party should put written questions about his report to an expert instructed by another party. Normally such questions should be put once only; should be put within 28 days of service of the expert's report; and should be only for the purposes of clarification of the report. Where a party sends a written question or questions direct to an expert and the other party is represented by solicitors, a copy of the questions should, at the same time, be sent to those solicitors. It is for the party or parties instructing the expert to pay any fees charged by that expert for answering questions put under this procedure. This does not affect any decision of the Tribunal as to which party is ultimately to bear the expert's costs. An expert's answers to questions put in accordance with this paragraph will be treated as part of the expert's report.

14.9 Where a party has put a written question to an expert instructed by another party in accordance with the above paragraph, the Tribunal or the Registrar may order that the question must be answered; and the Tribunal may also make such an order in relation to a question that has not been put in this way. If the question is not answered the Tribunal or the Registrar may make one or both of the following orders in relation to the party who instructed the expert:

(i)   that the party may not rely on the evidence of that expert; or
(ii)   that the party may not recover the fees and expenses of that expert from any other party.

14.10   Where a party has disclosed an expert's report, any party may use that expert's report as evidence at the hearing.

14.11   Discussions between experts

After the exchange of the experts' reports the Tribunal will normally require experts of like discipline to meet in order to reach agreement as to facts, to agree any relevant plans, photographs, etc, to identify the issues in the proceedings and, where possible, to reach agreement on an issue. The Tribunal may specify the issues which the experts must discuss. The Tribunal may also direct that following a discussion between the experts the parties must prepare a statement for the Tribunal showing those facts and issues on which the experts agree and those facts and issues on which they disagree and a summary of their reasons for disagreeing. The Tribunal will usually regard failure to co-operate in reaching agreement as to the facts and issues as incompatible with the expert's duty to the Tribunal and may reflect this in any order on costs that it may make.

14.12 The contents of the discussions between the experts are not to be referred to at the hearing unless the parties agree. Where experts reach agreement on an issue during their discussions, the agreement will not bind the parties unless the parties expressly agree to be bound by the agreement.

14.13 Computer-based valuations

Where valuers propose to rely on computer-based valuations it is of the utmost importance that they should agree to employ a common model which can be made available for use by the Tribunal in the preparation of its decision. Directions should be sought from the Tribunal at an early stage if there is difficulty in reaching agreement.

A4.17 Practice Direction 15/2005

15 Representation

15.1 At the hearing a party may appear and be heard in person (although a valuation officer may only do so with permission of the Tribunal), or may be represented by a barrister or a solicitor or, on obtaining permission from the Tribunal, by any other person (rule 37). A legal executive who is a Fellow of the Institute of Legal Executives and has a certificate covering the Lands Tribunal will be granted permission to represent his or her client, on application made at or prior to the hearing. An application for permission for a friend to represent a party who is an individual, or for one spouse to represent the other, will readily be granted and may be made at the hearing. Otherwise applications for permission to represent a party should be made in good time prior to the hearing, but the Tribunal may grant permission at the hearing as a matter of discretion. In simple cases, permission will usually be granted for a surveyor or valuer to represent a party in order to avoid the additional costs of separate representation. In those cases allocated to the simplified procedure under rule 28, such representation may well be the norm. In general, however, it is difficult and undesirable for the same person to act both as advocate and expert witness. Accordingly, permission will not be granted for a non-lawyer to represent a party in any case where the Tribunal considers that the responsibilities of advocate and of expert witness are likely to conflict.

A4.18 Practice Direction 16/2005

16 Procedure at the hearing

16.1 The procedure at a hearing of the Tribunal is within the discretion of the presiding Member. The Tribunal is a court of law, and the procedure adopted will generally accord with the practice in the High Court and the county courts. In particular, the claimant, applicant or appellant will begin and will have a right of reply; evidence will be taken on oath, and the rules of evidence will be applied. The Tribunal will throughout seek to adopt a procedure that is proportionate, expeditious and fair in accordance with the overriding objective.

16.2 All cases assigned to the simplified procedure list will be heard by a single Member acting as if he were an arbitrator under rule 28. That rule and **3.3** and **3.4** of these Practice Directions should be referred to for further guidance to procedure in these cases.

16.3 The effect of rule 5 is that hearings by the Tribunal take place in public save in certain rare cases, principally where the Tribunal is sitting as an arbitrator under a reference by consent.

A4.19 Practice Direction 17/2005

17 Site inspections

17.1 Where appropriate, the Tribunal may enter and inspect the land or property that is the subject of the proceedings, and, where practicable, any other land or properties referred to by the parties or their experts (rule 29). At such inspection, the Tribunal will (unless otherwise agreed) be accompanied by one representative from each side and will not accept any oral or written evidence tendered in the course of the inspection. The Tribunal may make an unaccompanied inspection without entering on private land.

A4.20 Practice Direction 18/2005

18 Delivery of decisions

18.1 The Tribunal's decision will in most cases be reserved and will be in writing. Rule 50(2) enables the Tribunal to give an oral decision at the end of the hearing, but this course is not normally appropriate.

A4.21   Practice Direction 19/2005

19   Fees

19.1 The fees to be paid in respect of proceedings in the Lands Tribunal are specified in the Lands Tribunal (Fees) Rules 1996. Under the Lands Tribunal (Fees) (Amendment) Rules 2002 the Tribunal has power to reduce or remit fees in the case of hardship. Unless the Tribunal directs otherwise, the appropriate hearing fee is payable by the party initiating proceedings, but without prejudice to any right to recover the fee under an order for costs. A solicitor acting for a party must be on the record, and he will be responsible for the fees payable by that party while he is on the record (rule 53).

A4.22   Practice Direction 20/2005

20   Costs

20.1 Under section 3(5) of the Lands Tribunal Act 1949 the Tribunal has power to order that the costs of any proceedings incurred by one party shall be paid by any other party. This power is limited by section 175(6), (7) of the Commonhold and Leasehold Reform Act 2002 in the case of appeals from leasehold valuation tribunals (see **20.5**). In awarding costs the Tribunal may settle the amount summarily or direct that they be the subject of detailed assessment by the Registrar on a specified basis.

20.2 Costs are in the discretion of the Tribunal, although this discretion is qualified by particular provisions in section 4 of the Land Compensation Act 1961 (see **20.3**) and where the case is heard under the simplified procedure (see **20.9**). Subject to what is said below the discretion will usually be exercised in accordance with the principles applied in the High Court and county courts. Accordingly, the Tribunal will have regard to all the circumstances, including the conduct of the parties; whether a party has succeeded on part of his case, even if he has not been wholly successful; and admissible offers to settle (see **20.3** and **20.6**). The conduct of a party will include conduct during and before the proceedings; whether a party has acted reasonably in pursuing or contesting an issue; the manner in which a party has conducted his case; and whether or not he has exaggerated his claim.

20.3 The general rule is that the successful party ought to receive his costs. On a claim for **compensation for compulsory acquisition of land**, the costs incurred by a claimant in establishing the amount of disputed compensation are properly to be seen as part of the expense that is imposed on him by the acquisition. The Tribunal will, therefore, normally make an order for costs in favour of a claimant who receives an award of compensation unless there are special reasons for not doing so. Particular rules, however, apply by virtue of section 4 of the Land Compensation Act 1961. Under this provision, where an acquiring authority have made an unconditional offer in writing of compensation and the sum awarded does not exceed the sum offered, the Tribunal must, in the absence of special reasons, order the claimant to bear his own costs thereafter and to pay the post-offer costs of the acquiring authority. However, a claimant will not be entitled to his costs if he has failed to deliver to the authority, in time to enable them to make a proper offer, a notice of claim containing the particulars set out in section 4(2). Where a claimant has delivered a claim containing the required details and has made an unconditional offer in writing to accept a particular sum, if the Tribunal's award is equal to or exceeds that sum the Tribunal must, in the absence of special reasons, order the authority to bear their costs and to pay the claimant's post-offer costs.

20.4 On an **application to discharge or modify a restrictive covenant** the general rule as to costs does not apply. The nature of proceedings under section 84 of the Law of Property Act 1925 is that the applicant is seeking to have removed from the objector particular property rights that the objector has. In view of this (and subject to any offer to settle that either party may have made), an unsuccessful objector who had the benefit of the covenant which has been discharged or modified will not normally have to pay any part of the applicant's costs unless he has acted unreasonably, and a successful objector will normally get all his costs unless he has in some respect been unreasonable.

20.5 On an **appeal from a leasehold valuation tribunal** the Lands Tribunal may not order a party to the appeal to pay costs incurred by another party unless he has, in the opinion of the Tribunal, acted frivolously, vexatiously, abusively, disruptively or otherwise unreasonably in connection with the appeal; and where, in view of such conduct, it does order a party to pay costs it may not award more than the LVT could order in such circumstances (currently £500).

20.6 In any proceedings a party may make an offer marked 'without prejudice save as to costs' or similar wording (usually referred to as a Calderbank offer) in respect of the subject-matter of the appeal, application or reference. It may state a period within which it will remain open for acceptance but in order to protect the offeror fully it must be unconditional in point of time. Where an offer is accepted, the Tribunal retains jurisdiction over the costs of the proceedings except to the extent that these are covered by the agreed terms.

20.7 Where an offer has been made, the party making it may send a copy of it in a sealed cover to the Registrar or may deliver it at the hearing (see rule 44). The Tribunal will open the sealed offer after it has given its decision in the proceedings.

20.8 In a simple case or on an interlocutory hearing the Tribunal may make a summary assessment of costs. A party who proposes to apply for a summary assessment should prepare a summary of the costs and should serve it in advance on the other party. Costs which are to be the subject of a detailed assessment are referred to the Registrar under rule 52. The Tribunal will normally award costs on the standard basis. On this basis, costs will only be allowed to the extent that they are reasonable and proportionate to the matters in issue, and any doubt as to whether costs were reasonably incurred or reasonable and proportionate in amount will be resolved in favour of the paying party. Exceptionally the Tribunal may award costs on the indemnity basis. On this basis, the receiving party will receive all his costs except for those which have been unreasonably incurred or which are unreasonable in amount; and any doubt as to whether the costs were reasonably incurred or are reasonable in amount will be resolved in favour of the receiving party. A party who is dissatisfied with the Registrar's assessment of costs may apply to him for a review and, if still dissatisfied, he may apply to the President for a further review.

20.9 Where proceedings are determined in accordance with the **simplified procedure** under rule 28, costs will only be awarded where an offer to settle has been made and the Tribunal considers it appropriate to have regard to this offer, or the circumstances are exceptional. Where a case is determined in accordance with the **written representations procedure** under rule 27 costs are awarded in the usual way and not on the restricted basis of rule 28.

20.10 Where, as is almost invariably the case, the Tribunal issues a written decision determining the substantive issues in the proceedings, this will be sent to the parties with an invitation to make written submissions as to costs. Following consideration of these submissions the Tribunal will issue an addendum to the decision determining the liability for costs. It may be possible, particularly where there are only two possible outcomes of the proceedings, for the Tribunal to invite submissions as to costs at the conclusion of the hearing. This procedure will be followed wherever possible. Where the issue of costs is particularly complicated the Tribunal may hold a costs hearing before making an award.

A4.23 Practice Direction 21/2005

21 Appeals to the Court of Appeal

21.1 Under section 3(4) of the Lands Tribunal Act 1949 appeal lies to the Court of Appeal from a decision of the Tribunal. Appeal may be made on a point of law only. Previously the procedure required the Tribunal to state a case; but now, by virtue of the Civil Procedure

(Modification of Enactment) Order 2000 (SI 2000/941), the procedure is that provided for by the Civil Procedure Rules. Under the CPR there is no longer a requirement for the Tribunal to state a case. Permission to appeal is required from the Court of Appeal. This must be requested in the appellant's notice (CPR rule 52.4(1)), and the appellant must file the appellant's notice at the Court of Appeal within 28 days after the date of the decision of the Tribunal (CPR Practice Direction to Part 52, paragraph 21.9). The decision of the Tribunal takes effect for this purpose on the day on which it is given unless the decision states otherwise; and usually the decision will state that it will take effect when, and not before, the issue of costs has been determined.

A4.24   Lands Tribunal (Fees) Rules 1996
SI 1996/1021

1   These Rules may be cited as the Lands Tribunal (Fees) Rules 1996 and shall come into force on 1st May 1996.

2.1   The '1996 Rules' means the Lands Tribunal Rules 1996(c) and any reference to a rule by number alone shall be construed as a reference to the rule so numbered in the 1996 Rules.

2.2   Any reference to a hearing in the Schedule to these Rules shall include a reference to the procedure under rule 27 (Determination of proceedings without a hearing) and the fee shown as payable for a hearing in the said Schedule shall be payable where the matter is determined in accordance with rule 27.

3   The fees to be taken in respect of proceedings before the Lands Tribunal shall be those specified in the **Schedule** to these Rules.

4   The hearing fee shall, unless the Tribunal otherwise directs, be payable by the party by whom the proceedings were instituted (without prejudice to his right to recover the amount of the fee from any other party by virtue of any order as to costs) on receipt of notification from the registrar.

5   The proceedings referred to in paragraph 1(1), 6(2), 6(3), and 6(5) of the Schedule do not include an appeal against a determination by the Commissioners of Inland Revenue under the Finance (1909-1910) Act 1910(a) or under the Finance Act 1975(b) or a reference under section 47(1) or section 47A of the Taxes Management Act 1970(c).

Schedule

Fees

Item	Fee £
Notices of reference and appeal, and applications	
1(1)　Lodging a Reference or an Appeal (other than a Rating Appeal) On lodging a notice of reference under rule 10 or a notice of appeal (not being a rating appeal) under rule 6	50
1(2)　Lodging an Absent Owner Application On lodging an application for a determination under schedule 2 to the Compulsory Purchase Act 1965 (a) or section 58 of the Land Clauses Consolidation Act 1845(b) (inclusive of the determination)	100
2　Lodging a Rating Appeal On lodging a notice of appeal under rule 6 from the decision of a tribunal empowered to hear rating appeals: 1% of rateable value. subject to: 　　　　　　　minimum fee 　　　　　　　maximum fee	 50 5000
3　Lodging a Restrictive Covenant Application On lodging an application under rule 13 in respect of section 84 of the Law of Property Act 1925(c) (Relief from Restrictive Covenants affecting land)	200
5　Interlocutory or Consent Order Application On an application to the President, Tribunal or registrar: 　　　　(1) Interlocutory application (rule 38) 　　　　(2) Consent order application (which is an application to which all parties consent, disposing of the proceedings) (rule 51)	 40 100
6　Hearing Fees 6(1) Hearing a Rating Appeal On the hearing of an appeal from the decision of a tribunal empowered to hear rating appeals: 5% of rateable value as determined in the final order of the Tribunal, subject to: 　　　　minimum fee 　　　　maximum fee	 100 5000
6(2) Hearing a Reference or other Appeal (excluding one where the hearing fee is calculated on the basis of rental value) On the hearing of a reference or an appeal against a determination or on an application for a certificate of value: 2% of amount awarded or determined by the Tribunal, agreed by the parties following a hearing or determined in accordance with rule 27, subject to: 　　　　minimum fee 　　　　maximum fee	 100 5000
6(3) Hearing a Reference or other Appeal (where the hearing fee is calculated on the basis of rental value) On the hearing of a reference or an appeal against a determination where the award is in terms of rent or other annual payment:	

2% of annual rent or other payment, determined by the Tribunal, agreed by the parties following a hearing or determined in accordance with rule 27, subject to:	
minimum fee	100
maximum fee	5000
6(4) Determining a Restrictive Covenant Application On the hearing of an application or the making of any order under section 84 of the Law of Property Act 1925 ("the 1925 Act") (Relief from Restrictive Covenants affecting land):	
(a) a hearing as to entitlement under section 84(3A) of the 1925 Act	250
(b) order without a hearing (rule 17(2) and 17(3))	250
(c) substantive hearing of an originating application	350
(d) engrossing Minutes of Order	100
6(5) Hearing (No Amount Awarded) On the hearing or preliminary hearing of any other reference or appeal (not being the determination of an application under paragraph 6(4) above) where either the amount determined is nil or the determination is not expressed in terms of an amount	200
Copies of Documents 7 For a photocopy or certified copy of a document, or for examining a plain copy and marking as a certified copy, for each page:	1
8 For supplying published decisions to subscribers, for each page	0.10
Other fees	
9 Case Stated (Order 61 Rules of the Supreme Court 1965 (b)) On applying for a case to be stated for the decision of the Court of Appeal	100
10 Taxation of Costs On a taxation of costs, (rule 52(4)) for every £1 or part thereof allowed	0.05
Directions for payment	
11 A notice. application or other document in respect of which a fee is payable shall, if sent by post, be accompanied by a cheque or postal order drawn in favour of Her Majesty's Paymaster General for the amount of the fee	

A4.25   Lands Tribunal (Fees) (Amendment) Rules 2002
(SI 2002/770)

Citation, commencement and interpretation

1(1)   These Rules may be cited as the Lands Tribunal (Fees) (Amendment) Rules 2002 and shall come into force on 1st May 2002

1(2)   In these Rules, 'the 1996 Fees Rules' mean the Lands Tribunal (Fees) Rules 1996

Amendment to the 1996 Fees Rules

2   After rule 5 of the 1996 **Fees Rules** there shall be inserted the following rules;

6 Where it appears to the Lord Chancellor that the payment of any fee prescribed by these **Rules** would, owing to the exceptional circumstances of the particular case, involve undue financial hardship, he may reduce or remit the fee in that case.

7(1) Subject to paragraph (2), where a fee has been paid on or after 1st May **2002** at a time -

where the Lord Chancellor, if he had been aware of all the circumstances, would have reduced the fee under rule 6, the amount by which the fee would have been reduced shall be refunded; or

(where the Lord Chancellor, if he had been aware of all the circumstances, would have remitted the fee under rule 6, the fee shall be refunded.

7 (2) No refund shall be made under paragraph (1) unless the party who paid the fee applies for it within 6 months of paying the fee.

7(3) The Lord Chancellor may extend the period of 6 months referred to in paragraph (2) if he considers that there is good reason for an application being made after the end of the period of 6 months, and he may do so notwithstanding that the period has expired.

Transitional provision

3(1) In this rule 'applicable fee' means a fee paid under the 1996 **Fees Rules** on or after 1st November 2001 but before 1st May **2002** and 'rule 6' means rule 6 of the 1996 **Fees Rules**.

3(2) Subject to paragraph (3):

an applicable fee shall be refunded where, if rule 6 had been in force when the fee was paid, the Lord Chancellor would have remitted the fee; and

where the Lord Chancellor would have reduced the applicable fee if rule 6 had been in force when the fee was paid, the amount by which the applicable fee would have been reduced shall be refunded.

3(3) No refund shall be made under paragraph (2) unless the party who paid the fee applies for it before 1st November **2002**.

Appendix 5

A5.1   STEWART TITLE LIMITED
INDEMNITY POLICY

STEWART TITLE LIMITED
Stewart House Pynes Hill Exeter Devon EX2 5AZ

RESTRICTIVE COVENANT INDEMNITY POLICY

The Insured has made a Proposal and paid the Premium to the Company for the indemnity set out in this Policy of Insurance. The full particulars of the Proposal form the basis of and are incorporated within the Policy and the Company hereby grants the insurance subject to the terms conditions and exclusions set out in this Policy and any Memoranda endorsed upon it.

Signed for and on behalf of
STEWART TITLE LIMITED

Authorised Signatory

1. DEFINITIONS

In this Policy the words and phrases below shall have the following meanings:

Claim:
A claim against the Insured notified by any third party which seeks to enforce any breach of the Restrictive Covenant which breach results from the Insured Use or Development of the Property.

Company:
Stewart Title Limited whose registered office is at Stewart House Pynes Hill Exeter Devon EX2 5AZ registered in England No. 2770166.

Consent:
Written consent.

Development:
The development as detailed in the Schedule.

Enforcement Action:
Any action(s) or proceeding(s) taken by any third party having the benefit of the Restrictive Covenant to enforce any Breach.

Insured:
The party named as such in the Schedule to the Policy together with:

(i) the Insured's mortgagees

(ii) the Insured's bona fide successors in title and their mortgagees.

(iii) any lessee of the Insured or of the Insured's successors in title and the mortgagees of such lessees.

Providing always that in respect of the parties at (i) (ii) and (iii) above the Maximum Liability is restricted to the extent of their interest in the property

Insured use:
The use as detailed in the Schedule

Market Value: The average of the estimates from two independent valuers of the open market value (as defined from time to time in the guidelines issued by the Royal Institution of Chartered Surveyors).

Maximum Liability: As specified in the Schedule or the extent of the Insured's interest whichever is the lesser.

Policy Date: The date specified in the Schedule.

Property: The property as detailed in the Schedule.

Relevant Date: The date of any final court order by which the Restrictive Covenant is enforced against the Insured.

Restrictive Covenant: The restrictive covenant or covenants which attach to the Property and are detailed in the Schedule.

2. COVER

Where:

(i) the Insured Use or the Development is a breach of the Restrictive Covenant and

(ii) any third party (including any corporation) seeks to prove or proves to have the benefit of the Restrictive Covenant and seeks to enforce the same

the Company will:

(a) indemnify the Insured (subject to the Maximum Liability) against:

(i) any damages or compensation (including costs and expenses) awarded against the Insured in any proceedings brought against him.

(ii) the cost of altering or demolishing the Development to comply with an Injunction or Order of the Court or Enforcement Action.

(iii) where an Injunction, Order of the Court or Enforcement Action prohibits or restricts the Development and/or Insured Use, the diminution in the Market Value of the Property, calculated as the difference between the Market Value on the assumption that the Restrictive Covenant is not enforceable and the Market Value at the Relevant Date where the Property is subject to the Enforcement Action or the Restrictive Covenant to the extent ordered by the Court.

(iv) the costs of the Development (or part thereof) which were commenced or contracted for prior to the notification by the Insured to the Company of a Claim which is rendered abortive by an Injunction or Order of the Court.

(v) all costs charges and expenses incurred by the Insured with the Consent of the Company in connection with any legal action or in any application to the Lands Tribunal, Court or person entitled to the benefit of the Restrictive Covenant for its release or modification or any application or appeal to the Court for the relevant consent for the Insured Use/Development.

(b) assume responsibility for dealing with any Claim made against the Insured.

3.   EXCLUSIONS

The following matters are expressly excluded from the coverage of this Policy and the Company will not pay any loss or damage, costs, fees or expenses that arise by reason of any Claim or Enforcement Action following any communication (written or verbal) made by the Insured or by a party acting on behalf of the Insured to any third party believed by the Insured either to enjoy the benefit of the Restrictive Covenant or to know or act on behalf of such third party without the consent of the Company.

4.   CONDITIONS

1.   The Insured shall not at any time disclose the existence of this Policy of Insurance to any third party other than a prospective successor in title under the Policy.

2.   The Insured shall notify the Company in writing immediately he becomes aware of any circumstances likely to give rise to a claim under the Policy, giving full details of all known facts and shall continue to provide all reasonable assistance to the Company.

3.   The Insured shall make no admission, promise of payment, indemnity or compliance without the Consent of the Company and shall enter into no communications with any third party believed to be entitled to enforce the Restrictive Covenant. Any communications received by the Insured shall be passed to the Company immediately upon receipt.

4.   The Insured shall not make any application to the Lands Tribunal or the Court for the modification or release of the Restrictive Covenant without the Consent of the Company.

5.   The observance of the Conditions of this Policy by the Insured and by those acting on behalf of the Insured and the truth of the information given to the Company in writing shall be a condition precedent to the Company's liability under the Policy.

6. Where the Development/Insured Use becomes the subject of Enforcement Action the Insured will notify the Company immediately. In the event that the Company wishes to challenge the Enforcement Action or apply for necessary consent, the Insured will at the cost of the Company undertake the necessary action and afford to the Company all reasonable assistance.

7. The Company shall be entitled to conduct in the name of the Insured the defence of any action brought against the Insured in respect of the Restrictive Covenant or of any Enforcement Action (including any settlement of such action) and shall be entitled to institute for its own benefit in the name of the Insured proceedings against any third party in respect of any matter arising from the claim. The Insured will afford to the Company every reasonable assistance in the conduct of any proceedings.

8. If, when a claim is made under the Policy, there is in existence any other Insurance under which the Insured is entitled to make a claim in respect of the same risk as covered by this Policy the Company will be liable to pay or contribute towards such claim pro rata with the other insurance.

9. If the Company has admitted liability but the Company and Insured cannot agree the amount to be paid under this Policy the matter shall be referred to an arbitrator to be appointed by the parties (or in default of agreement, in accordance with the law in force at the time). The making of an award by the arbitrator shall be a condition precedent to any right of action against the Company.

10. The parties are free to agree the law applicable to this insurance contract but in the absence of such agreement the contract shall be governed by English Law.

5. <u>COMPLAINTS PROCEDURE</u>

Any enquiry or complaint you may have regarding this insurance may be addressed to:

Stewart Title Limited
Stewart House
Pynes Hill
Exeter EX2 5AZ
Telephone: 01392 680680

If you are still dissatisfied with the way in which a complain has been dealt with, you may contact the Insurance Ombudsman Bureau for assistance whose address is:

Insurance Ombudsman Bureau
City Gate One
135 Park Street
London
SE1 9EA

Appendix 6

A6.1 Plan 1

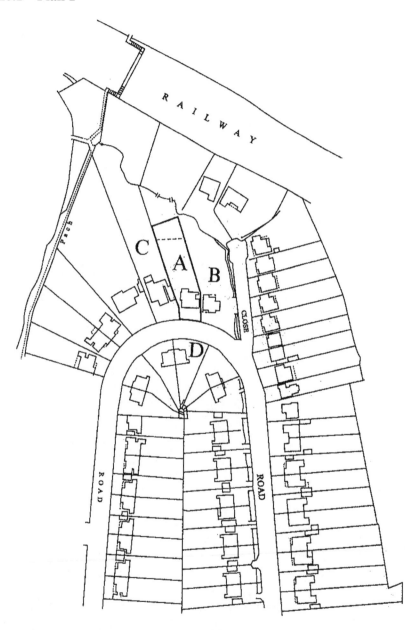

Plot A: sold off by common vendor 1 January 1990
Plot B: sold off by common vendor 1 March 1990
Plot C: sold off by common vendor 1 November 1989
Plot D: sold off by common vendor 1 January 1995. The last plot to be sold by V.

Appendix 7

PRECEDENTS, LANDS TRIBUNAL FORMS
AND CIVIL PROCEDURE RULES
(extracts)

INTRODUCTION

House style: Ancient or modern?

A7.1   In this Appendix an attempt has been made to follow the advice regarding
clarity of language given in Chapter 17 above, and accordingly the style of the
precedents which follow is designed to be more fit for the twenty-first than the
nineteenth century. This may come as a shock to some readers and potential users,
but in view of the need to make forms understood, ultimately, by the parties
themselves, there is no reason why any lawyer should stick to the archaic and
verbose style used by his ancestors. To the extent that these precedents fall short of
complete modernity, this shows how hard it is to produce legal forms which are
easy on the mind and which also work in a technical area of the law.

As modern conveyancing is now dominated by the system of registration of title,
the forms reflect the fact that the instruments in which the covenants invariably
appear will be forms used in that process. To the extent that there are other events
which cause covenants to be imposed, where no transfer of registered land is being
made, it is easy to transpose 'transfer' for 'deed'.

Modern style has also been adopted in certain other specific instances such as the
use of the words 'buyer' and 'seller' rather than the more archaic versions of
'purchaser' and 'vendor'. Where the imposition of the covenants occurs on an
event which is not apt to lead to such a neutral description of the parties, there is no
reason why their names should not be used; eg 'Mr Brown covenants with
Mr Smith'. As with the various types of instrument which may be used to impose
covenants, the transposition from the forms should be straightforward.

One final remark by way of introduction

As the subject of the book is restrictive covenants, the emphasis of the precedents
will be on such covenants. Consequently, there will be little by way of
positive covenant material, save where necessary to make sense of the scheme
of covenants, such as where the provision of services is to be safeguarded. To have
extended the precedent material further into the field of positive covenants would
have required another book dealing with the problems which such covenants pose
as a matter of enforceability and how such problems can so far as possible be

overcome. As a reminder, Chapter 1 above contains a brief summary of the difference between restrictive covenants and positive covenants.

Caveat user

As with any standard form these precedents should be seen as a means to an end and not as an end in themselves. In common with fire, they are good servants and bad masters, so they should be treated carefully. What has been attempted is not an encyclopedia (of which there are already a number published) but a set of forms which can be used as a starting point and around which, using the forms supplied as a framework, there can be built the final structure of the restrictions and obligations to be entered into between the parties.

PART 1

Basic Nuts and Bolts

A7.2   In Part 1 there are set out the basic elements of any covenant over freehold land, of a restrictive nature, designed to bind successors in title of the covenantor and to benefit the land of the covenantee by annexation.

Element 1

The parties between whom the covenants are to be made.

(i)   Where the covenants are being given by *the buyer*
        The buyer covenants with the seller;
(ii)   Where the covenants are being given by *the seller*
        The seller covenants with the buyer.

Commentary

There is no need to introduce words which extend the meaning of the parties to heirs, successors and assigns, etc. Law of Property Act 1925, ss 78 and 79 supply these words.[1]

Element 2

The words which make it clear that the covenants are not personal:[2]

> 'so as to bind the property and each and every part of it whoever may be the owner of it.'

Commentary

As the introduction says, these words remove any doubt as to whether the covenants are intended to be personal. They show that the covenants are to relate to the land defined as the property. The property will either be the land being

---

[1]   See Chapters 5, 7 and 8 above.
[2]   For the distinction see **7.8** above and *Morrells of Oxford v Oxford UFC* [2001], at **7.4** above..

sold (where the covenants are being given by the buyer) or the land being retained (where the covenants are being given by the seller).

Element 3

The words which annex the benefit of the covenant to the land for which the covenant has been taken.

> 'so that the benefit is annexed to each and every part of the land which either
> the seller has retained (ie where the covenants are being imposed on the buyer) [as shaded green on the plan annexed]
> or
> has been conveyed to the buyer (ie where the covenants are being imposed on the seller) [as edged red on the plan annexed].'

Commentary

In view of the decision in *Crest Nicholson v McAllister* [2004] EWCA Civ 410, unless there are words to the contrary, Law of Property Act 1925, s 78 will apply so as to annex the benefit of the covenant to the land intended to be benefited , if that land is clearly identified, see Chapter 8 above. It is, therefore, wise to put the matter of annexation beyond doubt by these words.

The land which is to be benefited must be defined. If this is not done, there may be difficulty with the identity of such land at a later date, in the context of enforcement and title to enforce, or in the context of a release and the right to be joined in any release; see Chapter 8 above.

In practical terms, certainty of definition can be achieved by defining the land to be benefited by reference to:

-   a clear plan;
-   a Land Registry Title No – although there is a danger in this method if the estate on subsequent sales off is given a new Title no.

It is only if there is real difficulty in determining the land to be benefited should that land be defined as land 'adjoining' or 'near' or 'neighbouring' the burdened land and even then some attempt must be made to use a plan to identify it.

See Part 2 below for annexation of the benefit in building schemes.

Element 4

Words defining what is covenanted:

> 'to observe the covenants set out in the schedule below; 'the covenants'.'

Commentary

The effect of these words is obvious in itself; although note the use of the word 'covenants' as opposed to 'stipulations'. Unless you are intending to create stipulations only, which may not have quite the same effect (see **1.2** above) you should avoid the word 'stipulations'.

Element 5

Words limiting liability of the covenantor to the period of his ownership of the property subject of the covenants or any other interest in it.

> 'and it is declared that the [buyer] [seller] will not be liable for any breach of the covenants after he has parted with all interest in or possession of the property.'

Commentary

These words are present to avoid any liability once the covenantor (or his successor) has sold the burdened land, or given up possession of it (or any interest in it); see **14.7** above.

Note: for both registered and unregistered titles: Chapter 4 above deals with the manner of protection of restrictive covenants by registration to ensure that they bind successors in title of the original covenantor.

Putting all Five Elements Together

Specimen Clause in Part 1 set out in its entirety

The buyer covenants with the seller
(reverse order if the covenants are being given by the seller)
so as to bind
the property and each and every part of it whoever may be the owner of it and so that the benefit is annexed to each and every part of the land which the vendor/seller has retained
(*Or* – in the case where the seller is giving the covenants)
'each and every part of the land which has been conveyed to the buyer'
(*and shown on the plan annexed shaded/edged [colour]*)
to observe the covenants set out in the schedule below ('the covenants')
and it is declared that the [buyer] [seller]
(*ie* whoever is giving the covenants)
will not be liable for any breach of the Covenants after he has parted with all interest in or possession of the property.

Element 6 (Optional)

Are there to be covenants given by both parties in favour of each other?

If there are to be such *mutual* covenants use each set of covenants being given by first, the buyer and secondly, the seller and put the covenants themselves in a separate schedule.

For example:

The buyer covenants with the seller
so as to bind the property and each and every part of it whoever may be the owner of it and so that the benefit is annexed to each and every part of the land which the seller has retained (and shown on the plan annexed shaded/edged [colour])

to observe the covenants set out in the First Schedule below ('the buyer's covenants')

and it is declared that the buyer will not be liable for any breach of the buyer's covenants after he has parted with all interest in or possession of the Property And further

The seller covenants with the buyer

so as to bind the property and each and every part of it whoever may be the owner of it and so that the benefit is annexed to each and every part of the land which has been conveyed to the buyer

(and shown on the plan annexed shaded/edged [colour])

to observe the covenants set out in the Second Schedule below ('the seller's covenants')

and it is declared that the seller will not be liable for any breach of the seller's covenants after he has parted with all interest in or possession of the property

PART 2

Additional elements; building schemes

Element 1

A7.3   The Declaration that a scheme exists

The seller declares as follows:

(a)   he has laid out the [ ] Estate {shown on the plan edged blue annexed to this transfer} in plots;

(b)   he intends the [ ] Estate to be developed as a building scheme;

(c)   each transfer of each plot will be substantially the same as this transfer (subject to the rights reserved to the Seller referred to at (e) below);

(d)   the owner of each plot is to have the right to enforce the covenants set out in Schedule [ ] below and imposed on the other plots on the [ ] Estate irrespective of the date of transfer of each plot;

(e)   the Seller may in [his] [its] absolute discretion make alterations in the lotting of those parts of the [ ] Estate which have not been sold at any time and in addition [he] [it] may vary or release or waive any of the covenants set out in Schedule [ ] below whether or not any such variation release or waiver relates (i) to a plot already sold at the date of this transfer; or (ii) to any part of the [ ] Estate which has not been sold; or (iii) to the property.

Commentary

See Chapter 8 for the reasons why it is desirable for a declaration of intention to create a scheme to be expressed. As to the optional power to vary, etc see **8.37** of as to the effect which such a power may have on the scheme. It is important to note that where a new scheme is being set up it is prudent to liaise with the local District Land Registry in advance so that the Registry is satisfied that the proposed form of transfer and plans (which should be lodged) can lead to the Registry treating the area of development as a scheme. See the Land Registry website for practice in such cases.

Note: if a scheme is not wanted you can declare such intention expressly:

For example:

The parties to this transfer declare that the covenants which are contained in it do not create a building scheme and the seller is free to vary or release any of the covenants into which he may enter in respect of his land and to deal with it in any way he thinks fit.

Element 2

The mutual enforcement clause.

The seller and the buyer [vendor and purchaser] (and all other parties to this transfer) declare that the covenants set out in Schedule [ ] below are to be mutually enforceable between each and every Buyer of plots on the [ ] Estate whenever they were transferred

Commentary

This reinforces the declaration of the Scheme under Element 1 above. It is not strictly necessary, but for those who prefer a 'belt-and-braces' approach, it can be added to the form above.

Element 3

The covenant clause

The [buyer] covenants with the [seller] and as a separate covenant with every owner for the time being of any part of the [ ] Estate
so as to bind the property and each and every part of it whoever may be the owner of it
and
so that the benefit is annexed to each and every part of the [ ] Estate
to observe the covenants set out in Schedule [ ] below
and it is declared that the [buyer] will not be liable for any breach of the covenants after he has parted with all interest in or possession of the property

Commentary

This form should be used when the buyer is giving the covenants in the seller's favour and in favour of the owners of the estate within the scheme.

There are variations where:

(a)   the covenant is being taken for the benefit of plots already sold; and
(b)   covenants are also being given by the seller;
(c)   where the buyer covenants to enforce covenants against other buyers, either directly, or in the name of the seller.

Variation (a)

The [buyer] covenants with the [seller] and as a separate covenant with every owner for the time being of any part of the [ ] Estate *and with every owner of any plot sold by the seller before the date of this transfer*
so as to bind the property and each and every part of it whoever may be the owner of it
and
so that the benefit is annexed to each and every part of the [ ] Estate *including the plots sold before the date of this transfer*
to observe the covenants set out in Schedule [ ] below
and it is declared that the [buyer] will not be liable for any breach of the covenants after he has parted with all interest in or possession of the property

Variation (b)
The [*seller*] covenants with the [buyer]
so as to bind {the [ ] Estate or the land retained by the *seller*} and each and every part of it whoever may be the owner of it
and
so that the benefit is annexed to each and every part of the Property and each and every part of it
to observe the covenants set out in Schedule [ ] below
and it is declared that the [seller] will not be liable for any breach of the covenants after he has parted with all interest in or possession of the [ ] Estate

Variation (c)
Add to any of the preceding forms –

Whenever any buyer of any part of the [ ] Estate breaks any of the covenants which he has entered into the buyer may be requested by the seller to enforce any covenant which any such buyer has broken, and the cost of doing this (which may include the cost of court proceedings) will be borne by the seller. If the buyer is requested to take such steps, the buyer must perform the seller's request and if the buyer does not, the seller is entitled to take action to enforce the covenant in the name of the buyer. If the seller takes action in the name of the buyer the buyer is entitled to an indemnity from the seller for the cost and expense of such action.

Commentary

This clause allows the seller to keep control of the scheme even when he has disposed of all the land which otherwise would allow him to enforce. Because this covenant is not truly restrictive, there are problems of enforcement of the obligation to take action when the land (over which the covenant is imposed) is sold. The burden of a positive covenant will not be enforceable against a successor in title; see **1.5** above. There are various means of ensuring that this obligation runs with the land, the chief of which is a covenant that there will be a direct covenant to observe this (and other covenants) with the seller by the new buyer prior to any transfer and a restriction on the register that until there is a certificate of compliance (by entry into the deed) no dealing is to be registered.

PART 3

The covenants

A7.4 In this part the forms of restriction themselves are set out. It is hard to generalise in view of the fact that the ultimate aim of any restriction is to control a particular use of land, and to that extent each situation may require different forms of words to be used. However, there will always be circumstances in which a 'common' form of restriction will be suitable, and the restrictions which follow are designed to cater for the draughtsman who requires such a common form. Beyond these forms lie many situations where only 'tailor made' forms will do, and it will be for the draughtsman to use these forms simply as a framework upon which to clothe the finished article.

In order to assist the user the following broad headings have been used by way of classification so that individual types or classes of restriction can be identified.

Classification
(i)   Covenants which regulate the use of buildings.
(ii)   Covenants which regulate the use of buildings and their surroundings and land use generally.
(iii) Covenants which control changes to buildings.
(iv) Covenants which deal with more specific requirements as to the control of land use including the commercial user.

(i)   Covenants which regulate the use of buildings
(*a*)   *Basic user covenants: residential*

The buyer covenants with the seller not to use the property:

–   other than as a house;

–   other than as a bungalow;

–   other than as a dwelling house;

–   other than as a private dwelling house;

–   other than as a single private dwelling house.[3]

Optional and sensible additions to any of the above:

(1)   and no more than one such house is to be built upon each plot and if one such house is built so that it occupies more than one such plot no additional private dwelling house may be built upon any other part of the plot which is so occupied;
(2)   other than for the occupation of *one* family *or* a *single* household.

Commentary

See **14.14** for the difference between each covenant. The optional words at (1) are designed to avoid the problem referred to at **14.15** where one house is built across

---

[3]   See **14.15** for the recent decision on 'a'. It may, therefore, be better to use the form of words in the text which refer to 'no more than' a given number of houses are to be built.

two plots and where it is desired to build a house on part of one of the plots. The optional words at (2) prevent sub-division of occupation.

(b) Basic user covenants: business and other uses

The buyer covenants with the seller not to use the property:

- for any trade profession or business;
- for any trade profession or business other than as a doctor, dentist or solicitor and if such use is made of the property no business plate is to be placed on the outside of the property.

Commentary

These self-explanatory restrictions are often used to preserve 'high class' estate developments. However, the first form is probably too broad in scope, particularly in an age when many businesses and professions can be run from home. The latter form is more specific and designed to avoid the vice of any activity which might lower the tone of the estate, which preserving a selective measure of control.

(c) Basic user covenants: more specific controls

The buyer covenants with the seller not to:

- divide the property into self-contained flats;
- use any part of the property for holiday lettings (or as an office) (or for accommodating paying guests); or for sharing;
- use any part of the property marked on the plan [and edged green as the case may be] other than as a garage (car space) for the parking of a private motor vehicle;
- park or keep a boat or caravan on the property;
- do anything on the property which is a nuisance or annoyance to the seller or the adjoining or neighbouring property and 'nuisance or annoyance' includes anything which materially affects the use or enjoyment of the property;
- construct more than [ ] (single private dwelling houses) on the property; and
- not to use the land other than for amenity purposes.

Commentary

These specific controls are designed to protect the amenity of residential development and should be used where suitable control is required. Some of the restrictions are specific, eg as to parking of boats or caravans, and reflects concern over the lack of control which the planning system may be able to impose in this instance.

(ii) Covenants which regulate the use of buildings and their surroundings
The buyer covenants with the seller not to:

- keep any animals or birds on the property other than as domestic pets;

- keep any animals or birds on the property which if kept for domestic or commercial purposes cause an nuisance or annoyance to the seller or the adjoining or neighbouring property and 'nuisance or annoyance' includes anything which materially affects the use or enjoyment of the property;
- store vehicles on the property;
- erect any aerial or satellite dish on the external part of any building on the property (which is visible from any road);
- allow any gardens on the property to become overgrown;
- allow drying washing on the property to be visible from any road;
- allow the area shown coloured [ ] on the plan to be used other than as a garden [or] other than as open visibility splay;
- plant any tree, shrub or hedge or erect any fence (beyond the line marked on the plan) *or* (on the area shown coloured [ ] on the plan);
- plant any tree of the variety [*Cupressus Lawsoniae* or *Cupressus Leylandii*] on the property or on any part thereof;
- allow any tree shrub or hedge to exceed [ ] metres in height;[4]
- allow any tree, shrub, hedge, fence structure or erection to be placed on the area [defined by reference to a plan] and not to use that area other than a (grassed lawn) (space kept unbuilt upon and open to the sky);
- obstruct any of the accessways or parking areas [defined by reference to a Plan] or build over or within a lateral distance of [ ] metres from the centre line of any pipes and sewers which may be under the property;
- use any part of the property for access to or from any neighbouring or adjoining land.

Commentary

See the note under the previous set of restrictions. Here even greater specific control is being imposed, and in the context of a well-managed estate most of these controls will be needed.

(iii) Covenants controlling the changes to buildings
The buyer covenants with the seller that he will not:

- change the external appearance of any building erected on the property;
- paint the external parts of any buildings on the property other than in a colour which has previously been approved by the seller in writing (approval not to be unreasonably withheld) *or* as below;
- make any (structural) alteration to the dwelling house and garage erected on the property unless plans and elevations have been submitted for the seller's approval which may be given in writing (such approval not to be unreasonably withheld) *or* (such approval to be determined in the absolute discretion of the seller) on payment of a fee of [£];

---

[4]   See the controls in Part 8 of the Anti-Social Behaviour Act 2004, due to be in force in 2005.

- Erect or make any alterations to any buildings on the property which may interfere with the access of light and air to the windows (and other apertures) of the buildings on the (seller's property).

Provisos to any clause requiring consent
For the purposes of this clause:

(i) the seller in the exercise of his discretion is entitled to have regard to the following matters (but not to the exclusion of anything else which the seller may think material) when granting or refusing his consent;

- the nature of the proposed (alteration) (colour scheme);
- the effect which the proposed alteration may have upon the neighbouring or adjoining land [being the [ ] Estate] and its amenity;
- the effect of the proposed alteration on the [] Estate and its amenity;

(ii) the term 'the seller' includes his successors in title and owners for the time being of the [ ] Estate or any part thereof;

(iii) To the extent that at any time written consent is required under this clause and the seller is the owner of (the [ ] Estate) *or* (the seller's unsold land) the written consent of that person shall be sufficient (provided that if by reason of sales off of the [ ] Estate (or the seller's unsold land) there is more than one owner thereof and it is not reasonably possible for the buyer to identify all the persons whose consent would (but for this proviso) be required under this clause the buyer may obtain written consent from the person or persons who appear to the buyer to be the person or persons whose consent should be obtained);

(iv) if at any time any person whose consent is required cannot be reasonably identified or if the seller (or its successor) is a Limited Company and has been dissolved or struck off the Register of Companies at or prior to the time when consent would (but for this proviso) be required the terms of this clause shall not apply so as to require consent to be obtained and in particular no consent shall be required to have been obtained from the Crown or any other person in whom the rights or assets of the said Company may have become vested).

Commentary

See **14.9** for the problems which consent provisions bring. The optional provisos are attempts to overcome some of the problems which arise, which include potentially numerous persons with the right to grant or withhold consent, and dissolved or struck off companies, where the complexities of requiring consent from the Crown can be avoided by the form given under (iv) above.

(iv) Covenants which deal with specific requirements as to the control of the use of land and buildings

Specific uses
The buyer covenants with the seller that he will not:
Use the Property (previously defined) other than as a [defined purpose]

For example:

- landscaped area for a visibility splay;
- ornamental garden;
- woodland area (with the added obligation not to cut any trees without the consent of the seller) (see (iii) above for consent clauses);
- golf course;
- lake[s] for fish farming.

Commentary

In any individual case it is open to the draughtsman to consider precisely what use is to be permitted and to define the permitted use accordingly. This is particularly important where specific uses are contemplated over parts of land; visibility splay areas being a case in point.

Services

(Where the seller is retaining land through which services run for the benefit of the land being sold off and where the seller may have meters or other installations on his land which control the supply):

The seller covenants with the buyer that he will not:

- interfere with the services (to be defined) which serve the property;
- do anything which would affect the quality of the services (to be defined) which serve the property;
- do anything which would have the effect of preventing the supply of services to the property; which shall include the obligation to pay for the supply of any of the services so far as it may be necessary to do so for the continuation of the supply.

And the buyer covenants with the seller that he will:

- Pay to the seller (or to the provider of any of the services as the seller may direct) for the cost of the supply of the services.

Commentary

Covenants relating to the supply of services raise a number of problems, not all of which can be cured by drafting.

There are two points which arise where services are being provided for the benefit of land being sold off – or retained.

First, there is the (negative) right to non-interference and secondly, there is the (positive) right to the supply.

The first right may be coupled with an easement for the supply and the right to non-interference can be expressed also by means of a restrictive covenant. The second right (namely the positive right to have the supply maintained) is a different matter. The right may be protected, as is suggested in the third obligation, by a restrictive covenant. But the only sure way of doing it is to impose a positive obligation to provide the supply of the service and as a condition therefore, to pay for such supply.

There are two points to be noted as regards such a means of protecting the (positive) right to a supply. First, the nature of a positive covenant is such that it may not be enforceable against successors in title of the covenantor, unless the covenant is protected by an estate rent charge or some right to re-enter – neither of which may be attractive or acceptable other than in certain types of developed estates.[5] Secondly, it is often the case that the service will be provided by a third party, being the water, gas, electricity, or telecommunications providers, and if any positive obligation is to be imposed, such an obligation may not bind such a third party. For example the gas provider may refuse to supply to unsafe appliances.[6]

The covenants above are designed to deal with the two aspects of the problem and in so far as the negative right to non-interference is concerned the restrictive covenants should be adequate. As regards the positive right to supply and the corresponding obligation to pay, only the simplest terms are offered.[7] To offer more would extend the scope of this part of the book too deeply into the field of positive covenants as opposed to restrictive ones.

Commercial purposes

The buyer covenants with the seller that he will not use the property other than for:

- the following classes in the Town & Country Planning Use Classes Order 1987:

    [A1, A2, A3
    B1–8
    C1, C2, C3
    D1, D2][8]

- the retail sale of goods other than hot [or cold] food or intoxicating liquor;
- food retailing.

The buyer covenants with the seller that he will use the property only for:

- a storage facility;
- a wholesale warehouse;
- a restaurant [but with no take-away facility] with a justices' licence permitting the consumption of alcohol with meals;
- the purposes of an open space;

---

5   See Chapter 1 above.

6   For the problems posed by the distinctions between the positive and negative obligations as regards the supply of services see *Rance v Elvin* (1985) 50 P&CR 9, applied in *Duffy v Lamb* (1997) 75 P&CR 364. Consider also the difference between covenants, easements and profits à prendre; as to the latter in the context of the grant of a water supply, see *Mitchell v Potter, The Times,* 24 January 2005 (CA).

7   For more detailed forms of positive obligations as to services see Aldridge, *Practical Conveyancing Precedents* (Longman Professional, looseleaf).

8   The danger with a definition based on a reference to the Order is that it does not allow for any future changes in the Order. It may, therefore, be preferable to define the permitted use specifically by reference to that use, as the alternatives show, and for that purpose the Use Classes Order can be a useful tool in defining such a use.

- an amusement park;
- an hotel;
- a seller of wines beers and spirits for consumption off the premises;
- a public house;
- a private nursing home or hospital;
- a general practitioner's surgery [and pharmacy].

Commentary

Specific commercial uses raise at least two problems for the draughtsman.

First, there is the problem of defining precisely what use is or is not to be permitted. That requires a clear understanding of what the burdened land is to be used for and what the owner of the benefited land is seeking to permit or prevent. That in turn requires care to be taken to ensure that the covenant is not one against competition *per se*, for such covenants may be held to be purely personal; 'tie' covenants not to sell a certain brand of goods may be an example of this.[9]

Provided the definition of the permitted or prohibited is clear the next hurdle to overcome is how far is the defined use to be applied over the whole of the property to be burdened. An example of this problem arises in the modern 'superstore' development which may extend over a number of acres. Part comprises the retail food hall (which itself may need further definition in view of the sale in some supermarkets of clothes, videos, magazines, etc) (currently an A1(a) use within the Use Classes Order) (see above), part comprises a petrol filling-station and the remainder is used for access, parking, bus stops and amenity areas such as a picnic area, children's playground, landscaped areas and facilities for recycling. To define the permitted use over all these areas requires care. One method would be to define the various uses by reference to a detailed plan. What is not recommended is the definition of the permitted use over the whole site by reference to a single use (eg 'food retailing'), for that begs the question as to the other areas within the development which are not being used for that purpose.[10]

A7.5   DRAFT 'CIRCULAR' PRIOR TO PROCEEDINGS FOR A DECLARATION UNDER LAW OF PROPERTY ACT 1925, S 84(2)

See Chapter 15, Pt I for the background).

To the owner of [*address of property*]

We are the solicitors acting for [*owners and address of property; which will be that of the applicant*]. The location of that property is shown on the plan which is enclosed with this letter.

We are writing to you because our client (*Mr [ ] or X Ltd*) has obtained planning consent for [*describe development*].

---

[9] See **8.12** above.
[10] See *Co-operative Retail Stores Services Ltd v Tesco Stores Ltd* (1998) 76 P&CR 328 for a case where the permitted use was for 'food retailing' and it was held that the use of the burdened and as an amenity area and as part and parcel of the superstore site was not a breach of that covenant, but only after an appeal to the Court of Appeal.

You may already be aware of this proposal as you may have been told about it by the [*local planning authority*]. The planning consent reference is [ ] and, if you have not already done so, you may wish to inspect the application and the plans lodged at [Town Hall, etc]. For ease of reference we, enclose the decision letter giving that consent.

Our client's development means that [*houses will be erected on the land shaded green*] [*ie describe the effect of the proposal in clear terms*].

Over the land affected by the proposed development are some covenants imposed in [*date*] by a deed dated [] and made between [ ] and [ ]. We attach a copy of the [*material parts*] of the deed. The covenants which are of particular relevance are [ ] and [ ].

It might be thought that the covenants would prevent our client from proceeding with the development, but we [*have been advised by counsel*] [*have advised our client*] that the covenants are [*no longer enforceable*] [*have a certain meaning*] which leads us to believe that the development would not be a breach of the covenants. [*It may be wise to say briefly why this belief is held, eg no annexation (pre-1925 covenants), or extinguished by past unity of seisin and never revived, nor anyone identifiable who can give consent*].

Because of the nature of the proposed development and the advice which our client has been given, we feel it would be prudent to seek the guidance of the court as to the [*enforceability*] [meaning] of the covenants.

This means that our client will issue proceedings under Law of Property Act 1925, s 84(2) for a declaration that [*the covenants are no longer enforceable*] [*have a certain meaning, etc*]. A draft of the proposed application is attached, and for ease of reference we enclose a copy of that section of the Act.

The request we are making of you is that you consider whether you are able to consent to our client's application in terms of the order sought at the end of it.

It is our belief that you should (on consideration of the matter) consent, in view of the fact that [*you do not have the benefit of the covenant as it was never annexed to your land, etc*] or [*it is clear that your consent is not required to the proposed development*] [*ie explain simply why the consent ought to be forthcoming*]. If you wish to oppose you must be prepared to give legal reasons in due course why you think you are entitled to do so.

If you decide that you are unable to consent you will be able to intervene in the proceedings under s 84(2) once they are started; you will be informed of how to do this in due course. [*If you do so you may be at risk as to costs if the court decides that the advice we have given our client is right.*] [*Note: it is felt that this sentence can be omitted according to taste. Some may feel that it is rather heavy-handed at this stage*].

We have attached a form on which you can express your consent, or objection, with a spare copy for you to retain and a sae for you to return to us.

We appreciate that you will need time to consider our request. We invite you to contact your solicitor if you are in any doubt as to the meaning of this letter and the enclosures. If you are not the owner, or the sole owner of the property at [ ] please would you tell us who is, or forward this letter and enclosures to that person so they may contact us. We would also ask you to tell us on the form enclosed whether there is a tenant at your property and if there is a building society or bank or other lender who has a mortgage over it, and if so give us its identity and if you are able, the branch you deal with for the mortgage. You do not need to tell us anything else.

We would like to hear form you within [ ] days of this letter. If for any reason you think that is going to be difficult please let us know.

We thank you in advance for your assistance.

A7.6   FORM FOR RETURN

Address of property and name of owner (*ie addressee of the letter*)

I have read the letter dated [ ] from A&B solicitors and having duly considered the matter:

* CONSENT to the proposed order sought in the application by [*plaintiff*]

* OBJECT to the proposed order sought in the application by [*plaintiff*] for the following reasons:

[* *delete that which is not applicable*]

The following persons are also owners with me/us of [*the property*]:

The following person(s) own [*the property*] so far as I am aware and I have no interest in it.

The following person(s) has a tenancy of [*the property*]:

The following has a mortgage over [*the property*]:

at [ ] branch.

Signed and dated

LANDS TRIBUNAL FORMS

A7.7   Form LPA – Form of application under section 84 of the Law of Property Act 1925 to discharge or modify a restrictive covenant

- An application to discharge or modify a restrictive covenant must contain the following information, and it will not be registered by the Lands Tribunal if the information is incomplete.
- It should be adapted from the layout below and typed or printed on plain A4 paper.
- The application must be signed at the end and dated.
- The application should be sent to the Tribunal together with the fee payable and such plans and other documents as are relevant.

1   Applicant: Give the name, address, and telephone number of the Applicant or Applicants.

2   Applicant's representative: Give the name, address, telephone number, and status (eg solicitor; surveyor).

Note: All correspondence will be with the representative and not the applicant direct. A DX address is acceptable.

3   Application land: Give the postal address (or OS number) and area.

Note: It should be marked in red on an attached plan. State if it is registered and if so attach a copy of the Land Registry entry.

4   Applicant's interest in the land: State whether freehold or leasehold or contractual.

Note: If leasehold, give the name and address of the landlords and state whether they consent to the application.

5   Land in which the applicant has an interest

Note: Include not only application land but also any adjacent land in respect of which the applicant has an interest. State the nature of the applicant's interest (whether freehold or otherwise) and give details. Outline the land in green on the plan if it consists of more than the application land.

6   Land subject to the burden of the restrictive covenant.

Note: This may be the same as, or a larger area which includes, the application land. If it is a larger area it should be outlined in blue on the plan.

7   Land to which the benefit of the covenant is believed to attach.

Note: This should, if possible, be marked in brown on the plan, and the names and addresses, if known, of all those believed to be entitled to the benefit of the covenant should be listed.

If there is uncertainty the Tribunal will assume, until the matter is clarified, that the benefit attaches to all land in the immediate neighbourhood of the application land.

Any statement made by the applicant under this heading is without prejudice to contentions he may later advance as to the entitlement of particular objectors. If the successors to the original covenantees are not known, give details of the steps taken to identify those entitled to the benefit.

8   The legal instrument under which the restriction was imposed.

Note: Identify, including date and the parties to it. Copies of the instrument (deed, conveyance, transfer, etc.) should be attached or, if no such instrument is available, relevant documentary evidence of the restriction (eg in the case of registered land, an entry in the Register of Title).

9   Whether the applicant is in breach of any of the restrictions imposed by the legal instrument under which the covenant was imposed.

Note: If so, state whether the application is being made following a stay of proceedings under section 84(9) of the Law of Property Act 1925, and give details.

10   The restriction(s) the subject of this application.

Note: The text of each restriction to be discharged or modified must be set out in full word for word. It is for you to specify the relevant restrictions, and the Tribunal cannot pick out the relevant ones from other restrictions. Restrictions means covenants with a negative (restraining) effect; the Tribunal has no powers regarding positive covenants.

11   Whether the application is for

        (i)   discharge, or

        (ii) modification, or

        (iii) discharge or modification in the alternative

Note: One of the three options must be chosen. If option (i), complete 12 below. If option (ii), complete 13 below. If option (iii), complete **both** 12 **and** 13 below).

12   If the application is for discharge of the restriction:

12.1   Specify which of grounds (a), (aa), (b) and (c) of section 84(1) of the Law of Property Act 1925 (as amended) are relied on

Note: Applicants should satisfy themselves that the grounds set out can properly be relied on in the circumstances of the case. It will be rare, for instance, for ground (aa) to be relevant to an application to discharge.

    –   Ground (a)
    –   Ground (aa)
    –   Ground (b)
    –   Ground (c)

12.2   Set out, under each of the grounds relied on, relevant particulars of the grounds.

Note: relevant particulars will include some or all of the following:

(a) changes in the character of the property; changes in the character of the neighbourhood; other circumstances by reason of which the restriction ought to be deemed obsolete.

(aa) the reasonable user that is impeded by the restriction; the relevant provisions of the development plan; planning permissions applied for, granted or refused relating to the application land in the last 5 years or if relevant earlier; planning permissions or refusals of planning permission showing a pattern for the relevant area; the period at which and the context in which the restriction was imposed; other circumstances; if money is said to be adequate compensation.

(b) express agreements to discharge or modification; acts or omissions that imply agreement to discharge or modification.

(c) any matters relied on as showing that there would be no injury.

13 If the application is for modification of the restriction:

13.1 Set out the modification that is sought and specify which of grounds (a), (aa), (b) and (c) of section 84(1) of the Law of Property Act 1925 (as amended) are relied on.

Note: This is not to be combined with 12 above.

Applicants should satisfy themselves that the grounds they set out can properly be relied on in the circumstances of the case. Ground (a), for instance, will not usually be relevant to an application to modify.

> Ground (a)
> Ground (aa)
> Ground (b)
> Ground (c)

13.2 Set out, under each of the grounds relied on, relevant particulars of the grounds *Note:* relevant particulars will include some or all of the following:

(a) changes in the character of the property;
changes in the character of the neighborhood;
other circumstances by reason of which the restriction ought to be deemed obsolete.

(aa) the reasonable user that is impeded by the restriction; the relevant provisions of the development plan;
planning permissions applied for, granted or refused relating to the application land in the last 5 years or if relevant earlier;
planning permissions or refusals of planning permission showing a pattern for the relevant area;
the period at which and the context in which the restriction was imposed;
other circumstances;
if money is said to be adequate compensation.

(b) express agreements to discharge or modification;
acts or omissions that imply agreement to discharge or modification.

(c) any matters relied on as showing that there would be no injury.

14 Signature And Date

- Sign and date the form
- give your name in legibly in capitals
- state whether you are:
  - the applicant

  - the solicitor for the applicant

  - the agent for the applicant (in which case enclose a signed authority to act)

- Write the words:

'I have paid the setting-down fee of **£200** and I accept responsibility for the conduct of the case and the payment of later fees'.

Send the form, the fee and the documents (which may include: site plans, title deeds, Land Registry entries, planning permissions, or plans of proposed development if applicable) to:

The Registrar
Lands Tribunal
Procession House
55 Ludgate Hill
London
EC4M MW
Tel: 020 7029 9780
Fax: 020 7029 9781
DX: 149065 Ludgate Hill 2

The Tribunal office will acknowledge receipt of the Application and the fee, and will inform you of the next steps to take.

A7.8   Form LPB – Restrictive covenant application: publicity notice

1   TAKE NOTICE that an application under section 84 of the Law of Property Act 1925 to [discharge] [modify] [discharge or modify] a restrictive covenant affecting the land referred to below has been made to the Lands Tribunal. If you are legally entitled to the benefit of the covenant and you wish to object to the application, you should object within 28 days of the date of this notice.

2   The application relates to land at _____

_____

3   The applicant is _____

of _____

_____

4   The covenant in respect of which the application is made contains the following restriction: [eg *to use the land as a private dwelling house only.]*

Set out either 5A or 5B or both; do **not** combine the two into one.

5A.   The application seeks the **discharge** of the restriction on the following grounds:

> (a) that the restriction ought to be deemed obsolete;
> (aa)that unless modified the covenant would impede the use of the land as_____; that such use is a reasonable use; that in impeding that use the restriction does not secure to the persons entitled to the benefit of it any practical benefits of substantial
> value or advantage; and that money will be an adequate compensation for the loss or disadvantage (if any) which any such person will suffer from the modification;
> (b) that the persons of full age and capacity entitled to the benefit of the restriction have agreed, expressly or by implication, by their acts or omissions to the discharge of the restriction;
> (c) that the proposed discharge will not injure the persons entitled to the benefit of the restriction.

5B.   The application seeks the modification of the restriction so as to permit [eg *the land to be used for offices]* _____ Modification is sought on the following grounds:

> (a) that the restriction ought to be deemed obsolete;
> (aa)that unless modified the covenant would impede the use of the land as _____; that such use is a reasonable use; that in impeding that use the restriction does not secure to the persons entitled to the benefit of it any practical benefits of substantial
> value or advantage; and that money will be an adequate compensation for the loss or disadvantage (if any) which any such person will suffer from the modification;

(b) that the persons of full age and capacity entitled to the benefit of the restriction have agreed, expressly or by implication, by their acts or omissions to the discharge of the restriction;

(c) that the proposed discharge will not injure the persons entitled to the benefit of the restriction.

6   You may inspect the application, plan and other documents at *[address conveniently near application land]* _____ during office working hours. A copying charge may be payable if copies are required.

7   If you are a person legally entitled to the benefit of the restrictive covenant and you wish to object to the application, contact:

The Registrar
Lands Tribunal
Procession House
55 Ludgate Hill
London EC4M 7JW
DX: 149065 Ludgate Hill 2
Tel: 020 7029 9780 Fax: 020 7029 9781

Ask for a form of objection (Form LPD). The form should then be completed and signed and posted to the Tribunal **within 28 days of the date of this notice.**

8   Persons who lodge objections become parties to the case, and, provided they are entitled to object, they may appear at the hearing of the application, if there is one. The Tribunal may make an award of costs against an unsuccessful party. The applicant may rely on a lack of objections, or a failure on the part of any particular person to object, in support of the application. If you are unsure of your position you should seek legal advice.

9   *[Signed]* _____

Dated _____

Status *[Applicant/Applicant's Solicitor/Agent]* _____

Address _____

Phone no _____

Fax no _____

A7.9 Form LPD – Notice of objection to a restrictive covenant application

Concerning the application to discharge or modify a restrictive covenant:

- made by _____ *(applicant)*

- concerning _____ *(land)*

A THE OBJECTOR

A1   Objector's name _____

A2   Status _____

For example: an individual, partnership, firm, limited company, plc, public authority

A3   Postal address _____

_____

A4   Phone no _____

A5   Representative _____

A6   Status _____

For example: a solicitor, surveyor, agent, director of a company, and officer of an authority

A7   Postal address _____

_____

All correspondence will be sent to this address not to the objector directly. A DX address is acceptable.

A8   Phone no_____ Fax no _____

A9   Reference no _____

B LEGAL ENTITLEMENT

Note: It is not possible to object except by claiming to have a legal entitlement to the benefit of the restriction.

B1   Basis of objector's claim to be legally entitled to the benefit of the restriction

For example: that the objector is the original covenantee; or that the objector owns land of which the title shows that the benefit runs with it; or that there is a building scheme.

_____

_____

_____

B2   Land owned by the objector *(if relevant)* _____

_____

_____ *[see overleaf]*

C   GROUNDS OF OBJECTION

C1   Is this an objection to:

–   the discharge wholly of the restrictive covenant?

Yes   ☐

No   ☐

C2   If YES, give a brief statement of the objector's response to the grounds of the application for discharge [(a)(aa)(b) or (c) as the case may be]

_____

_____

_____ *[Attach an extra sheet if necessary]*

C3   Is this an objection to:

–   the modification of the restrictive covenant?

Yes   ☐

No   ☐

C4   If YES, give a brief statement of the objector's response to the grounds of the application for modification [(a)(aa)(b) or (c) as the case may be]

_____

_____

C5   Any other reasons why the objector opposes the application

_____

_____

[Attach an extra sheet if necessary]

D   CLAIM FOR COMPENSATION

D1   If in the event the application is successful, is this also a claim for compensation from the applicant?

Tick one   Yes   ☐

No   ☐

D2   Approximate amount of compensation claimed:

(This figure is provisional and will not be binding) **£** _____

E   CONSEQUENCES OF OBJECTING OR NOT OBJECTING

- IMPORTANT: An objector becomes a party to the case, with the rights and responsibilities this entails including possibly incurring costs and/or attending the hearing.

- Anyone unsure of their position should take professional legal advice.

- If no objections (or no valid objections) are made, the applicant may rely on the lack of objections in support of the application.

F   SIGNATURE

Signed _____ (on behalf of) the objector

Dated _____

G   WHAT TO DO NEXT

Once completed and signed, copies of the form of objection should be posted to the applicant ['s representative] and to the Lands Tribunal at:

The Registrar
Lands Tribunal
Procession House
55 Ludgate Hill
London
EC4M 7JW
DX 149065 Ludgate Hill 2
Tel: 020 7029 9780
Fax: 020 7029 9781

There is no fee for objecting. The objection should be lodged within 28 days of the date of the Publicity Notice; otherwise contact the Tribunal office about time limits.

A7.10 CIVIL PROCEDURE RULES
PRACTICE DIRECTION – PROTOCOLS

General

1.1 This Practice Direction applies to the pre-action protocols which have been approved by the Head of Civil Justice.

1.2 The pre-action protocols which have been approved are set out in para 5.1. Other pre-action protocols may subsequently be added.

1.3 Pre-action protocols outline the steps parties should take to seek information from and to provide information to each other about a prospective legal claim.

1.4 The objectives of pre-action protocols are:

(1) to encourage the exchange of early and full information about the prospective legal claim,

(2) to enable parties to avoid litigation by agreeing a settlement of the claim before the commencement of proceedings,

(3) to support the efficient management of proceedings where litigation cannot be avoided.

Compliance with protocols

2.1 The Civil Procedure Rules enable the court to take into account compliance or non-compliance with an applicable protocol when giving directions for the management of proceedings (see CPR rules 3.1(4) and (5) and 3.9(e)) and when making orders for costs (see CPR rule 44.3(a)).

2.2 The court will expect all parties to have complied in substance with the terms of an approved protocol.

2.3 If, in the opinion of the court, non-compliance has led to the commencement of proceedings which might otherwise not have needed to be commenced, or has led to costs being incurred in the proceedings that might otherwise not have been incurred, the orders the court may make include:

(1) an order that the party at fault pay the costs of the proceedings, or part of those costs, of the other party or parties;

(2) an order that the party at fault pay those costs on an indemnity basis;

(3) if the party at fault is a claimant in whose favour an order for the payment of damages or some specified sum is subsequently made, an order depriving that party of interest on such sum and in respect of such period as may be specified, and/or awarding interest at a lower rate than that at which interest would otherwise have been awarded;

(4) if the party at fault is a defendant and an order for the payment of damages or some specified sum is subsequently made in favour of the claimant, an order awarding interest on such sum and in respect of such period as may be specified at a higher rate, not exceeding 10% above base rate (cf. CPR rule 36.21(2), than the rate at which interest would otherwise have been awarded.

2.4 The court will exercise its powers under paragraphs 2.1 and 2.3 with the object of placing the innocent party in no worse a position than he would have been in if the protocol had been complied with.

3.1 A claimant may be found to have failed to comply with a protocol by, for example:

(a) not having provided sufficient information to the defendant, or

(b) not having followed the procedure required by the protocol to be followed (e.g. not having followed the medical expert instruction procedure set out in the Personal Injury Protocol).

3.2 A defendant may be found to have failed to comply with a protocol by, for example:

(a) not making a preliminary response to the letter of claim within the time fixed for that purpose by the relevant protocol (21 days under the Personal Injury Protocol, 14 days under the Clinical Negligence Protocol),

(b) not making a full response within the time fixed for that purpose by the relevant protocol (3 months of the letter of claim under the Clinical Negligence Protocol, 3 months from the date of acknowledgement of the letter of claim under the Personal Injury Protocol),

(c) not disclosing documents required to be disclosed by the relevant protocol.

3.3 The court is likely to treat this practice direction as indicating the normal, reasonable way of dealing with disputes. If proceedings are issued and parties have not complied with this practice direction or a specific protocol, it will be for the court to decide whether sanctions should be applied.

3.4 The court is not likely to be concerned with minor infringements of the practice direction or protocols. The court is likely to look at the effect of non-compliance on the other party when deciding whether to impose sanctions.

3.5 This practice direction does not alter the statutory time limits for starting court proceedings. A claimant is required to start proceedings within those time limits and to adhere to subsequent time limits required by the rules or ordered by the court. If proceedings are for any reason started before the parties have followed the procedures in this practice direction, the parties are encouraged to agree to apply to the court for a stay of the proceedings while they follow the practice direction.

Pre-action behaviour in other cases

4.1 In cases not covered by any approved protocol, the court will expect the parties, in accordance with the overriding objective and the matters referred to in CPR 1.1(2)(a), (b) and (c), to act reasonably in exchanging information and documents relevant to the claim and generally in trying to avoid the necessity for the start of proceedings.

4.2 Parties to a potential dispute should follow a reasonable procedure, suitable to their particular circumstances, which is intended to avoid litigation. The procedure should not be regarded as a prelude to inevitable litigation. It should normally include –

(a) the claimant writing to give details of the claim;

(b) the defendant acknowledging the claim letter promptly;

(c)   the defendant giving within a reasonable time a detailed written response; and

(d)   the parties conducting genuine and reasonable negotiations with a view to settling the claim economically and without court proceedings.

4.3   The claimant's letter should –

(a)   give sufficient concise details to enable the recipient to understand and investigate the claim without extensive further information;

(b)   enclose copies of the essential documents which the claimant relies on;

(c)   ask for a prompt acknowledgement of the letter, followed by a full written response within a reasonable stated period;

(For many claims, a normal reasonable period for a full response may be one month.)

(d)   state whether court proceedings will be issued if the full response is not received within the stated period;

(e)   identify and ask for copies of any essential documents, not in his possession, which the claimant wishes to see;

(f)   state (if this is so) that the claimant wishes to enter into mediation or another alternative method of dispute resolution; and

(g)   draw attention to the court's powers to impose sanctions for failure to comply with this practice direction and, if the recipient is likely to be unrepresented, enclose a copy of this practice direction.

4.4   The defendant should acknowledge the claimant's letter in writing within 21 days of receiving it. The acknowledgement should state when the defendant will give a full written response. If the time for this is longer than the period stated by the claimant, the defendant should give reasons why a longer period is needed.

4.5   The defendant's full written response should as appropriate –

(a)   accept the claim in whole or in part and make proposals for settlement; or

(b)   state that the claim is not accepted.

If the claim is accepted in part only, the response should make clear which part is accepted and which part is not accepted.

4.6   If the defendant does not accept the claim or part of it, the response should –

(a)   give detailed reasons why the claim is not accepted, identifying which of the claimant's contentions are accepted and which are in dispute;

(b)   enclose copies of the essential documents which the defendant relies on;

(c)   enclose copies of documents asked for by the claimant, or explain why they are not enclosed;

(d)   identify and ask for copies of any further essential documents, not in his possession, which the defendant wishes to see; and

(The claimant should provide these within a reasonably short time or explain in writing why he is not doing so.)

(e)   state whether the defendant is prepared to enter into mediation or another alternative method of dispute resolution.

4.7 If the claim remains in dispute, the parties should promptly engage in appropriate negotiations with a view to settling the dispute and avoiding litigation.

4.8 Documents disclosed by either party in accordance with this practice direction may not be used for any purpose other than resolving the dispute, unless the other party agrees.

4.9 The resolution of some claims, but by no means all, may need help from an expert. If an expert is needed, the parties should wherever possible and to save expense engage an agreed expert.

4.10 Parties should be aware that, if the matter proceeds to litigation, the court may not allow the use of an expert's report, and that the cost of it is not always recoverable.

Information about funding arrangements

4A.1 Where a person enters into a funding arrangement within the meaning of rule 43.2(1)(k) he should inform other potential parties to the claim that he has done so.

4A.2 Paragraph 4A.1 applies to all proceedings whether proceedings to which a pre-action protocol applies or otherwise.

(Rule 44.3B(1)(c) provides that a party may not recover any additional liability for any period in the proceedings during which he failed to provide information about a funding arrangement in accordance with a rule, practice direction or court order).

A7.11   CIVIL PROCEDURE RULES
PART 44.3

Court's discretion and circumstances to be taken into account when exercising its discretion as to costs

(1)   The court has discretion as to –

    (a)   whether costs are payable by one party to another;

    (b)   the amount of those costs; and

    (c)   when they are to be paid.

(2)   If the court decides to make an order about costs –

    (a)   the general rule is that the unsuccessful party will be ordered to pay the costs of the successful party; but

    (b)   the court may make a different order.

(3)   The general rule does not apply to the following proceedings –

    (a)   proceedings in the Court of Appeal on an application or appeal made in connection with proceedings in the Family Division; or

    (b)   proceedings in the Court of Appeal from a judgment, direction, decision or order given or made in probate proceedings or family proceedings.

(4)   In deciding what order (if any) to make about costs, the court must have regard to all the circumstances, including –

    (a)   the conduct of all the parties;

    (b)   whether a party has succeeded on part of his case, even if he has not been wholly successful; and

    (c)   any payment into court or admissible offer to settle made by a party which is drawn to the court's attention (whether or not made in accordance with Part 36).

(Part 36 contains further provisions about how the court's discretion is to be exercised where a payment into court or an offer to settle is made under that Part)

(5)   The conduct of the parties includes –

    (a)   conduct before, as well as during, the proceedings and in particular the extent to which the parties followed any relevant pre-action protocol;

    (b)   whether it was reasonable for a party to raise, pursue or contest a particular allegation or issue;

    (c)   the manner in which a party has pursued or defended his case or a particular allegation or issue; and

    (d)   whether a claimant who has succeeded in his claim, in whole or in part, exaggerated his claim.

(6)   The orders which the court may make under this rule include an order that a party must pay –

    (a)   a proportion of another party's costs;

    (b)   a stated amount in respect of another party's costs;

    (c)   costs from or until a certain date only;

    (d)   costs incurred before proceedings have begun;

    (e)   costs relating to particular steps taken in the proceedings;

    (f)   costs relating only to a distinct part of the proceedings; and

    (g)   interest on costs from or until a certain date, including a date before judgment.

(7)   Where the court would otherwise consider making an order under paragraph (6)(f), it must instead, if practicable, make an order under paragraph (6)(a) or (c).

(8)   Where the court has ordered a party to pay costs, it may order an amount to be paid on account before the costs are assessed.

(9)   Where a party entitled to costs is also liable to pay costs the court may assess the costs which that party is liable to pay and either –

    (a)   set off the amount assessed against the amount the party is entitled to be paid and direct him to pay any balance; or

    (b)   delay the issue of a certificate for the costs to which the party is entitled until he has paid the amount which he is liable to pay.

INDEX

References are to paragraph numbers